Praise for *Wildlife Wars* and *For Love of Wildness*

"This is a book locked and loaded with larger than life, heroic stories—written by Terry Grosz, a larger than life, heroic man to match. These page-turning morality tales remind us, in harrowing and frightful detail, that often the only thing standing between the public's wildlife heritage and the bad guys who want to despoil it are the brave men and women carrying the game warden's badge. *Wildlife Wars* is the new sportsman's thriller." —Todd Wilkinson, author of *Science Under Siege: The Politicians' War on Nature and Truth*

"From the first chapter till the last, the reader will find no dull moments. This is one of those books that are hard to put down once you start. … After you finish Terry's book, you will be looking forward to the next in the series." —*International Game Warden*

"After reading *Wildlife Wars*, I wondered if Terry Grosz could keep up the pace with a new set of memories and fascinating law enforcement experiences. Not to worry. *For Love of Wildness* takes you into a world almost never visited by even those of us who love the outdoors. Seldom does one who possesses a depth of knowledge in one field of endeavor rise to be able to chronicle that knowledge and experience in an entertaining and compelling manner. Grosz has risen above all but a very few professional authors. Don't miss this one!"
—Larry Jay Martin, author of *The Last Stand*

"His collection of tales needs to be told, for it helps combat an enormous problem concerning our country's natural wildlife. Grosz is obviously a very committed individual—and also a natural storyteller. This collection consists of stories about his early years as a warden in California. They relate many close calls with mother nature: wild creatures and savage lawbreakers. … Those who cherish the outdoors for hunting and fishing as well as those involved in environmental studies will benefit from this work." —*Booklist*

"This collection of experiences as a young warden in his native California paints a stirring picture of the constant struggle to protect our outdoor resource from a constant assault from lawbreakers. The book gives a brisk, sometimes swashbuckling account of Grosz's running duels with a variety of miscreants from market hunters to garden-variety poachers. A wonderful storyteller, Grosz keeps the reader in an almost constant tingle with lively intrigues and chases that include his being deliberately shot in the back. ... A second book ... should be available by autumn. Grosz promises it'll stir plenty of interest and emotion. I can hardly wait."   —Charlie Meyers, *The Denver Post*

"Because wildlife is important, wildlife law enforcement officers are important, and Terry 'Tiny' Grosz was one good one. He recounts his lively and dangerous career as a wildlife cop in the same exuberant, unpretentious style it was lived—something like Louis L'Amour meets Mike Hammer."   —David Petersen, author of
Heartsblood and *Ghost Grizzlies*

"The book is a page-turner, a remarkable if not heroic glimpse inside the cat-and-mouse competition between wildlife enforcement and wildlife poachers."   —*The Reel News*

"We're the top-dog species on this planet. Even the most wily or fear-somely armed critter stands little or no chance against a thoughtful and well-armed human. And when you add malicious amusement and avarice to the mix, entire species quickly find themselves running for their lives—and into the black void of extinction. Or at least that's how it would be if it weren't for a small group of incredibly dedicated wildlife officers who possess the unrelenting spirit (and occasionally, even the mass) of a protective mother grizzly. In Terry Grosz's *Wildlife Wars*, you will meet such an officer—and find out, in very vivid detail, why it's a terribly bad idea to violate the hunting laws regarding one of his treasured creatures."   —Ken Goddard, author of *First Evidence*

"Ultimately, wildlife will be saved by committed individuals—people like ... Terry Grosz. They wake up every day and go off into the trenches, one step at a time, to face up to the many challenges: poachers discharging automatic weapons into innocent creatures; laws that need reforming or implementing; societal trends and ethics that require dis-cussion and reshaping. ... Such individuals fighting to save America's wildlife marshal a special grace, if you will, in the face of terrible crimes and near overwhelming adversity. They are remarkable not because they are necessarily so courageous, but because their common sense is in tune with their conscience."   —Michael Tobias, in *Nature's Keepers*

Defending Our Wildlife Heritage

Defending Our Wildlife Heritage

The Life and Times of a Special Agent

Terry Grosz

Johnson Books
BOULDER

Published by Johnson Books, a division of Johnson Publishing Company, 1880 South 57th Court, Boulder, Colorado 80301.
E-mail: books@jpcolorado.com

9 8 7 6 5 4 3 2 1

Cover design by Debra B. Topping
Cover photograph © Jeffrey Rich Nature Photography. Bald eagle perched in snow blizzard, Homer, Alaska.

Library of Congress Cataloging-in-Publication Data

Grosz, Terry
    Defending our wildlife heritage: the life and times of a special agent / Terry Grosz.
        p.   cm.
    ISBN 1-55566-316-8 (pbk.: alk. paper)
        1. Grosz, Terry. 2. Undercover wildlife agents—United States—Biography. 3. Wildlife crimes—United States. I. Title

    SK354.G76 A3 2001
    363.28—dc21
        [B]   2001038657

Printed in the United States by
Johnson Printing
1880 South 57th Court
Boulder, Colorado 80301

♻ Printed on recycled paper with soy ink.

Contents

THIS BOOK IS DEDICATED to Tom Warren, the quintessential thinking conservationist, visionary, friend, and human being; a man whose soul is in tune with the history of the times, whose handshake will let you know there is a real man on the end of it and that you can take to the bank what that handshake projects, who is a friend to all who truly see, and whose wisdom and gifted counsel is before its time. To the man whom I admire as a wildlife professional possessing a true ethic of the land, respect as a man for all seasons, and love as a brother, I dedicate this book of life stories from one westering man to another.

Preface

IN THE FIRST OF MY SERIES of wildlife law enforcement books, *Wildlife Wars: The Life and Times of a Fish and Game Warden,* the reader met a raw twenty-three-year-old kid fresh out of college and recently hired as a Fish and Game warden in California. His first assignment after graduating from the academy was in Eureka in Humboldt County, enforcing the state's Fish and Game regulations. Humboldt County during the 1960s was still a rough-and-tumble extension of the Old West, and it didn't take that kid long to imbue himself with the same spirit, only as "the long arm of the law." Commercial fishermen taking short salmon, short crabs, or over-limits or fishing in closed waters; deer and elk spotlighters; so-called sportsmen taking too many ducks, snipe, or razor clams; illegal snagging of salmon and sturgeon on the big rivers by out-of-work loggers; Indians gill netting salmon under their treaty rights and then selling them illegally to the fish houses in Eureka; logging operations illegally polluting the waterways and salmon-spawning streams; pulp mills polluting the ocean; brant hunters killing many more birds from stilt blinds and scull boats than allowed; and everything else imaginable went on in this "game warden's stew." These were daunting enforcement prospects, but he was young, full of energy (and sometimes devilment), immortal, and protected by two very busy guardian angels, so it didn't take long for him to bury himself to the hilt and find that life in its many forms ran as far as the eye could see and took on many shades of colors other than the black and white of the laws he enforced. *Wildlife Wars* reflects the essence of that time when a somewhat crazy youngster was trying to be everything possible in the department of survival—his own as well as that of the critters. Alternately funny, serious, deadly, and sad, and sometimes downright pathetic, the book fast-paces through four years in northern California, ending up ultimately in the Sacramento Valley as the wildlife law enforcement profession grows on and changes the author.

My second book, titled *For Love of Wildness: The Journal of a U.S. Game Management Agent*, found the author still in the wild and woolly world of wildlife law enforcement, but now as a maturing young man who is four years older, "ninety years wiser," and carrying the gold of a U.S. game management agent instead of the silver of a California state Fish and Game warden. Although the field work was very similar to that of a Fish and Game warden, the author found himself teaming up with his state and federal counterparts and swinging a bigger bat, and harder, at the big fellows. He had learned a lot in the intervening four years, but the outlaw shooting public hadn't stood still in the learning department either. As a result, the author still occasionally stumbled and went into the soup up to his chin with the best of them, as in the chapter titled "Ain't She a Beaut?" He also discovered that many big-time violators have a bite and more than once found himself walking down the road of life without a hind end in the seat of his pants, if you get my drift. In *For Love of Wildness* the stakes are even higher and the rewards many times greater than in *Wildlife Wars*. Commercial-market hunters night shooting feeding ducks; locals sneaking into the rice fields at night to kill great numbers of ducks for their freezers and those of their friends; massive examples of baiting to attract greater numbers of dove and ducks to the gun; outright conspiracy by landed and wealthy interests to manipulate the land, laws, or state and federal politicians in order to take more than their fair share; interstate commerce by the occasionally misnomered American sportsman guaranteed to turn the toughest stomachs; international intrigue or high jinks on the high seas; the mafia; and still the occasional wreck by an overeager officer of the law all found their way into this work.

Of special note is the quiet maturation slowly taking place in the author as he begins to realize the size of the monster he is facing. For the first time in his career, he has doubts that he will be able to accomplish what needs doing in order to save much of the land's resources for those folks yet to come. The courts are tougher and demand more proof of criminal wrongdoing. Defense attorneys are considerably better and more aggressive when protecting their affluent and politically sensitive clients. Politics from within and without begins to raise its ugly head in earnest, and for the first time the author faces fiscal and equipment limitations in spite of having an excellent supervisor running interference for him. He also begins to realize that many times those carrying the badge have to run the edge in order to apprehend the very worst wildlife criminals. With that approach comes deadly risks, sometimes greater in scope than one imagines. However, being young in spirit (immortal, some say) and cared for by one of the world's greatest wives, he always finds the energy to keep pushing the envelope.

This third and current book, *Defending Our Wildlife Heritage: The Life and Times of a Special Agent,* again continues the wildlife law enforcement progression, only this time the author is working as a special agent for the U.S. Fish and Wildlife Service. Whereas the U.S. game management agent position was split between wildlife management and wildlife law enforcement, the special agent position was that of a wildlife criminal investigator—sort of like the FBI, but of the wildlife world. It represents an even closer look at the soft underbelly of those involved with the smuggling of wildlife, illegal commercialization of wildlife, gross illegal take of wildlife, and the illegal commercialization of the parts and products of wildlife. In *Defending Our Wildlife Heritage,* the author moves up through the ranks of the agency in different parts of the country and, by the varying nature of those positions, takes on different windmills, political situations, special interest groups, outlaws, gutless and thoughtless members of his own agency, and every other kind of standing invertebrate in between. The level of seriousness is even more significant than in the previous books, and the complexity of those actions makes many a mysterious wind before the blow is over. Stories run from the simple, such as "The Parachute Squad," in which a conservation trick is played on the shooters in the Stockton area inclined to take a few ducks and geese too many, to the mystical, as in the story about an old Lakota Indian titled "The Medicine Man." Also, for the first time the author travels abroad to dive into the mazes of international intrigue in the chapter titled "Asia, 1978" and experiences firsthand a sense of just how cheap life—wild or human—*really* can be. Of special note is the chapter dealing with the formation of the world's only forensic laboratory solely dedicated to wildlife forensics and all the associated behind-the-scenes politics and intrigue.

As is evident in the world of wildlife law enforcement, there is enough activity to go around for every law enforcement officer, and all too frequently the author, now a senior-level supervisor, gets called into action at the lower levels because of staffing shortages, sometimes with surprising results. A new arena of law enforcement is showcased in the chapter titled "The Wetland Easement Wars" as the author experiences firsthand those landowners illegally draining the wetlands and witnesses the extremes in the lives of people left out in the prairie winds too long. ... Throughout the rest of the book are stories showing just how small the world is becoming.

In the wildlife war tapestries woven throughout this book, you will see the damaging work done by corrupted politicians; nonexistent federal budgets designed to keep law enforcement under political control year after year; poor senior-level agency leadership, from the director on down; officers limited by their own weaknesses and emotions; death angels in their many forms, regardless of the best efforts of those who serve; and the not uncommon sheer joy of our successes in the face of the tremendous odds faced on a daily basis. You will also experience the lengths to which those of us wearing the federal gold will go to stop the carnage. Bear in mind that these stories are only those from my own experience. There are approximately ten thousand conservation officers in North America at the federal, state, tribal, provincial and county levels who could tell similar tales. Consider that, and the fact that there are about three hundred million people throughout North America, and then consider the odds the "thin green line" faces on a daily basis to protect our fragile environment!

This book is the third in a series of what I hope will be five, each dealing with a part of my life's experiences as a conservation officer. The events on these pages are true, with some alterations so no one will be able to identify many of the real-life characters who have paid their debt to society. I have also incorporated some blind alleys into the text to throw off the really astute students of wildlife law enforcement, be they the pursuers or the pursued. The locations described in the book are real and only occasionally altered to prevent the exposure of the actual characters committing the crimes. You will find these tales sad, disgusting, moralistic, evil, funny, or just plain gross. However, as I said earlier, they are true, and sadly many continue to this day in spite of the best efforts of those holding the "thin green line."

Enjoy the natural resources we have in this great land of ours. Hunting, fishing, hiking, outdoor photography, exploring, and many more activities are all part of our heritage. Do them to your heart's content, but don't become one of those who illegally take until they are slipping in the rivers of blood as the killing gets serious. Leave those fools to the hunters of men—and pray for the latter to be successful in their endeavors. When asking yourself what you as an individual can do, don't do the evil things represented in the stories. Don't mix with those who do, and be sure to teach your children the meaning of conservation. There is a lot one person can do to stop these black-hearted activities so that those yet to come may experience the beauty we see today. I suggest that all Americans get off their dead hind ends and give a hand. If they don't, then they are part of the problem, and just as bad as the poachers.

Acknowledgments

EARLY IN MY RELATIONSHIP with Johnson Books I had occasion to meet that company's marketing director. Being new to the industry, I figured that the chap holding that title would be larger than life and nothing less than a racehorse-shaped bundle of energy showcasing the company's products. Man, did I get a surprise. Marketing Director Richard Croog turned out to be a man of medium proportions who was very professional looking, quiet, and reserved. Little did I see of my perceived industry "race horse" leading the charge to put the author and what he had written before the world for all to enjoy. *Boy, was I wrong!* Richard quickly took my books to all the usual places to acquaint members of the industry with the new offerings. Then he spent time educating himself in wildlife law enforcement, a completely new area for him, and soon discovered many new marketing avenues to pursue. Soon I was doing readings, interviews, book signings, and radio programs by the score.

The "general," as I now call him, was insatiable in his quest for book dissemination avenues, comprehensive in exchanging information with his industry counterparts, supportive with every form of media, and *always* in touch with the author regarding any possible marketing approaches that might help the books reach the public. Ultimately I came to highly respect this quiet man for his exceptional work ethic, talent for human relations, quick appreciation for my message, and love of a challenge. I am forever indebted to Richard "the General" Croog for his tireless support in bringing to the public these books containing a thirty-two-year veteran conservation officer's stories regarding the struggles inherent in protecting this nation's wildlife resources. I didn't get a race horse for my marketing director. I am thankful that instead I got a "grizzly," and a new friend.

1

The Parachute Squad

SOMETIME DURING THE WINTER of 1973, I tiredly pulled into my driveway in Colusa, California, after sneaking into a rice field on a foggy day and apprehending two individuals in the process of killing a large over-limit of ducks. My bride, hearing the commotion of my truck rumbling in, came running out the front door. "Honey," she said, "Buck is on the phone, and he needs to talk to you right now." Buck was none other than Delbert Del Nero, the Stockton, California, state Fish and Game warden, who without a doubt was one of the top ten wildlife "catch dogs" in the state. Kicking my mud-covered hip boots off at the back door, I padded across the kitchen floor in my stocking feet, picked up the phone, and said, "How's it going, Buck?"

Buck's familiar voice said, "Fine, but I have to run in a moment. Judy needs me outside for some damn thing. But first, I need a favor."

Without hesitation because of our longstanding relationship and my immense respect for the man, I said, "Name it."

Buck continued, "I injured my eye chasing a fellow through the willows several nights back, knocking the hell out of my vision, and as of this moment I can't see a thing out of that eye. A friend of mine has a good case going but needs help from someone who is an experienced officer and has worked large duck cases before involving politically fixed people."

After a pause, I said, "Go ahead."

"He wanted me to help him, but I can't. This eye is going to have to be operated on, and fast, and the doctor won't let me go." Buck would eventually lose his retina.

"What's the layout and time frame?"

"This weekend if possible. Terry Hodges, a new man, has good informant-based information on several Delta outlaws who are killing large numbers of pintail on a private hunting club. They kill overages of these, and other species of ducks and geese if they get the opportunity, and from his information it looks like this has the makings of a good case."

Buck's word was always good enough for me. The only thing I didn't like was working with officers I knew little about, especially rookies. In the business of enforcing wildlife laws, politics always played a rather large role, especially when dealing with mean-spirited people on the Republican Party side of things. They just didn't seem to have any sense of humor if apprehended breaking the law. To err in that arena because of the rash decisions of a brash new officer was not making the best use of one's common sense, and it seemed a situation best avoided until the lad in question had proven himself.

I asked Buck, "What's this Terry Hodges like?"

"Terry, this fellow is green, but from what I can see and learn from those around me that I trust, he will be a good one and well worth your investment in time if you have it to give. I've also received rumblings about the shooters he's looking at, and their reputation for big kills is becoming something of a thing here in the Delta."

I too had heard good things about this new man and decided it was worth the time it would take to catch these knotheads killing the ducks. In addition, I was intrigued with the thought of maybe teaching this chap a few tricks of the trade—that is, if he was as good an officer as Buck suggested. Pausing for a moment and then making my decision, I said, "Buck, have him call me here at home."

Buck grunted his thanks, though I was pretty sure he had known I would not refuse his request, and then I heard his wife's voice in the background calling him impatiently. We exchanged a few more pleasantries and then went our separate ways.

Returning to my truck, I started gutting the eighty-eight ducks I had seized earlier from the two wing shooters I had apprehended in the foggy rice fields on Newhall Farms. They had gotten a bit carried away behind some locked gates on a large piece of private land, thinking they were alone. I had had to crawl for at least a quarter of a mile in the mud and dead crawdads to avoid discovery, but the reward of seeing the looks on their faces when I stood up almost at arm's length was priceless. Both had started to run and then, realizing I knew them both, turned and faced the music. This infraction was their second time in the barrel, and suffice it to say, it took a while to pay the piper for this lapse of good judgment.

My bride, sensing I was home only for as long as it took me to gut the ducks so they wouldn't spoil, fixed me a quick meal fit for a king, realizing, like most good officer's spouses, that it might be a long time between chow calls. She knew I would be eager to get back to the business of hunting those humans in the business of extinction who, if local history was correct, would be illegally shooting in the rice fields of the county later that night.

I hadn't gutted more than thirty ducks when Donna opened the door from the house into the garage and said, "Honey, Terry Hodges is on the phone." Putting down my gutting knife and washing my hands in the garage sink, I wondered what type of chap this Hodges would turn out to be and what kind of case he had going. Walking back into the kitchen, I picked up the phone and said, "Evening, Terry. Buck says you have a good one going. What's up?"

The voice on the other end of the line sounded young, but there was also a sureness in his tone that told me we might just have real quality in this officer. I surely hoped so, because I could sense I was about to recklessly jump off into another wild adventure with an unknown entity.

With little more introduction, Terry professionally outlined his problem, stated that he was new to this type of work, and said he wondered whether I might give him a hand in setting the operation up because Buck would be unable to help out. The way this lad matter-of-factly laid out the details and the frankness of his request told me I needed to explore this proposed detail and this new officer in depth.

Quickly running my work schedule through my mind and rapidly shifting some dates for particular activities, I said, "When do you need me there?"

I detected a bit of excitement in Hodges's voice as he said, "Can we get together around Thursday afternoon at my place and put together a plan of attack for this Saturday?"

"Sounds good to me. Give me directions to your house and I will meet you there about one P.M. on Thursday."

We parted ways, he to eat his supper and I to continue cleaning a pickup-load of dead ducks and think of another day in the Delta, matching my wits against a bunch of idiots who couldn't count. Even in the winter night's fog and cold, it was easy to feel a weather-burned smile forming on my face. I wasn't smiling because of the forth-coming death and carnage of wildlife but in anticipation of the looks on the faces of those pulling the triggers when they realized the shadow cast over their shooting pit was caused by something other than incoming clouds of ducks.

THURSDAY AFTERNOON at about twelve-thirty P.M., I pulled down a dirt road that wound through a small grove of walnut trees leading to Terry Hodges's residence. I stepped out of my three-quarter-ton Dodge patrol truck and took a few restful moments to stretch my tired back and legs. I had been up all night chasing outlaws. It never seemed to fail, I thought; every time an illegal opportunity presented itself, a group of knotheads would slip in and help themselves to Mother Nature's pantry. My latest group of outlaws accounting for my tiredness had discovered that large numbers of canvasback ducks, an excellent table-fare bird, would fly into the quiet bays and estu-aries in and around the San Pablo Bay area of San Francisco in the evenings to rest from the rough-water rigors of the day out on the larger bays. As they quietly drifted and slept in these backwaters, the lads were sneaking up on the birds in the dead of night and, using their shotguns where the birds were illuminated by the city's lights, "turning the lights off" on those ducks hapless enough to be caught within range of the deadly pellets. This type of thing was a little tough on my still young but getting-older-by-the-day carcass because I found myself, like most officers, trying to work both days and nights. Many times I remember renting a motel room and never making it back to sleep in it, choosing the front seat of my truck or the ground alongside my critters as a bed instead. Oh well, I thought, that is what you are getting paid for, Terry. Quit grumblin' and earn your keep. Shaking the night's events out of my tired brain and the dust of weariness off my frame, I shut the truck's door and turned toward the house.

The door swung open wide, and out strode a solidly built man who I presumed was Terry Hodges. Not a big lad, I thought, but of course, almost everyone was smaller than I, so I let that pass. He was young but walked with a stride that bespoke more skill and confidence than met the eye at first glance. "Hi, I'm Terry," a strong, confident voice announced, followed by the firm grip of his hand. I just nodded. Exhaustion does that to a man, I've found. Accepting my nod as an introduction, he said, "Let's go into the kitchen; I have some maps to show you." I nodded again and followed him into the house. I liked his style already. All business and no wasted time. I had hoped this lad would be all that Buck had cracked him up to be because after a night in the marshes of San Pablo Bay, I wasn't in a mood to meet a meathead.

Settling down at the kitchen table, Terry spread out several maps of the area in question and commenced to give me an overview of the problem and its geography. He was good—he hardly wasted a word, had carefully scouted the area, and exuded a level of energy that, if sustained, was going to make him one fine officer someday. In fact, he wasn't all that bad at this point in his career from what I had been able to learn prior to our meeting. Almost everyone who knew him had said yes, he was young, but that he had a good commonsense element in his way of doing business and, when he set out to catch someone, did the job in fine style. My kind of guy, I thought.

In this particular case he was watching several men who owned a private duck club on Byron Tract in the Delta. His intelligence was that the shooters, owing to their isolation on a piece of private property, were constantly taking large over-limits of waterfowl in violation of state and federal laws. Apparently it had gotten so bad that someone who had participated in one of these illegal shoots had actually stepped forward and asked Terry to stop the slaughter. You know things are pretty bad when one outlaw's guts are turned by another of his kind. They couldn't have asked a better lad, I thought, because this fellow appeared to have the nose of a mink and the energy of a pair of river otters when it came to leveling the playing field for a bunch of outlaws to go down swinging!

Together we proposed a plan that included using a boat to quietly get to the island's hunting club undetected and a fast chase vehicle to be driven by Warden Dave Nelson in case the shooters got away from us in the killing field proper. I knew Dave from my not-too-distant past as a California state Fish and Game warden. If the lads somehow got away from the two Terrys in the "mud and blood" of the field, they wouldn't suffer that same fate with Dave. He was one of the best wheel men in the state, and once a chase started, Dave would usually finish it! In addition, we would have Jim Dixon, a classmate of mine from State Game Warden Basic School and an officer I trusted, as part of the team. Jim was a skinny (of course, everyone is skinnier than I) officer who would skipper the boat that would carry us two "foot soldiers" to the island. If the shooters tried to rapidly flee the island in a boat after making their illegal kill, they would have him to deal with on the waterways. Jim was a crazy son of a gun but a goddamned good officer. If you broke the law, Jim was going to eventually get ahold of your tail end! With him would be Don McKoskey, another officer, who looked low and slow to the ground but could hang on to the worst of chaps with the best of them until help arrived.

With these two crazies in the boat and Dave on the north end of the island with his hot-rod patrol car, I was comfortable with that part of the game plan. Terry and I would be dropped off by the boat crew and would walk in on the club shooting area in an attempt to apprehend the shooters on the spot if they shot illegally. Jim and Don would cover the waterways, and Dave would cover the north end of the island if the shooters somehow got to their vehicle and fled from us. That left one uncovered road leading off Byron Tract to the north. I suggested that we cover it with two other federal officers, Jerry Smith from the Washington office, who happened to be in the area, and Tim Dennis, my trusted sidekick and deputy. They would take my undercover truck and position themselves on the northwest side of the island. If the shooters got away from Terry and me and ran to the wooded area on the north end of the island, Jerry and Tim would drive in, cutting them off and trapping them between the two teams.

The plan looked good. In fact, you may be wondering why it would take seven officers to capture maybe three or four outlaws. Well, if you are going to set a trap, which always includes many variables, make sure you bring home the bacon at the end of the detail! Neither we nor the critters could suffer an escape once the trap was sprung. If we lost the bad guys and the killing opportunity was still there, they would just be that much harder to catch at a later date. Bottom line: do it right and you only have to do it once.

I asked Terry what time he wanted us to meet at his place prior to jump-off. This was a loaded question. If an officer is worth his salt, he will get at it early rather than waiting until the last possible minute. Terry, thinking aloud, said, "Shooting time is about six A.M., so I suppose we had better be here at my place no later than four A.M. What do you think?" He didn't notice me smiling, but he had passed his first test as "one who speaks for those who cannot."

I suggested, "Three A.M. Arriving at that hour more than gives enough time for the ducks to settle back down from our disturbance before the shooters arrive and allows for members of your team to change tires in case of a flat or any other unplanned eventualities that might arise." I continued, "I always figure out a time I need to be there and then add another hour in front of the operation or at the end, just in case. If you are going to sacrifice your health and family for this job, then be damned successful at it. You do that by planning out the detail to the nth degree and leaving nothing to chance. We don't have the time, and neither do the critters." Terry, seeing the wisdom in planning for possible wrecks, agreed, and with a shake of the hand, the "old and new" parted ways to return to their individual wildlife battlefields.

SATURDAY MORNING the federal officers arrived a few minutes before three A.M. at Terry's house to find the state officers already there and raring to go. A short reunion was held between those of us who knew one another from other times, and then we departed in pursuit of the object of our affection, namely, a muddy harvested corn field on Byron Tract.

The morning was a typical winter day in the Delta, damp, not too cold, and with a moon that eased the boat trip from our launch site miles away to the shooting area on the duck club. Dixon, who was running the boat, idled it down about six hundred yards from the spot where we planned to disembark and finally cut the engine within fifty yards of the island's berm. The boat glided a few more feet and then drifted to a quiet stop. Our ears were instantly greeted with the sounds of several thousand feeding ducks on the island. It wasn't a lot of ducks by Sacramento Valley standards, but enough could be heard happily feeding in the corn field before us to make our day interesting if Terry's shooters showed up with blood in their eyes and pockets full of shells. We heard nothing else, so Dixon restarted the motor and idled the last few yards into the berm, where he again killed the engine while Don anchored the boat fast to the island. Terry and I slipped into our chest-high waders, checked our portable radios and Dixon's to make sure they were working properly, slipped our binocular straps around our necks, and quietly crawled up the island's bank through the dried weeds and stinging nettles until we were level with the top of the levee. When we looked across the levee into the suspected shooting area, we saw no signs of human presence, such as parked vehicles, to foil our plans. Satisfied that the way was clear, we stood up in the soft moonlight to survey our "home" for the next few hours and lay out our line of travel into the shooting area. We gave a few last-minute instructions to Jim and Don, reminding them especially to use the camouflage parachute to cover the boat, and then out into the muddy corn field we went.

I found the wet, muddy field hard going. I am a large man to start with, and I had been working eighteen- to twenty-hour days for the past two months and was close to physical exhaustion. In addition, I had set up a roadblock in the Colusa County foothills weeks earlier for several new Fish and Game officers in an attempt to capture a notorious night-shooting deer poacher. I knew the area well because it was my old state enforcement district, and the operation was

successful. The poacher approached our roadblock about three A.M.
with six illegal deer in the back of his truck. He slowed for a moment
as he came around a turn and saw two warden vehicles partially
blocking his way. I was standing on a rocky overlook above the parked
vehicles so I could look down into the back of the poacher's pickup
to see whether he had any illegal game. If I saw any evidence of
poaching, I would alert the lads at the roadblock. As the poacher
swung around the corner below me, I could plainly see the illegal
deer, plus two little kids sitting on top of the deer. I shouted this
information to the waiting officers below as the poacher was slowing.
Then, without a moment's further hesitation, he floored his acceler-
ator and plowed through the parked patrol vehicles, scattering officers standing in the middle of the road every which way but loose.
One officer dove headfirst into the back of the truck, but he miscal-
culated his dive and hit his head on a large metal toolbox, stunning
himself. The poacher continued speeding down the dirt road, un-
mindful of the stunned warden in the back of his truck, trying all the
while to get his vehicle out of low-range four-wheel drive, as was evidenced by a constant grinding of gears. Taking off from my position
above the "hoorah" and going from zero to sixty in about three steps,
I heard a *pop* and felt a sharp, burning pain above my right ankle.
Ignoring this sensation, I sped alongside the fleeing vehicle and, as it
slowed to make a left turn at a T in the road, dove through the driver's-
side window and wrestled the driver out the other side of the truck
as it slowed and finally ground to a stop. The poacher was arrested,
the children were sent to the county welfare services, and the realization sank into my slow-moving brain that I had torn my right Achilles
tendon *big time!*

That roadblock was taking its toll on me again as I plowed through
the calf-deep mud of the corn field that winter day with Hodges. I told
Terry, "If they run, you are on your own. There's no way I can run
any more than a short distance in this slop on this bum leg."

He said, "No problem; that I can handle." I had no doubt he
could. Terry was in excellent shape, was a skin diver on the side, and
possessed a strong desire to win. This kid really had the "stuffin'" it
would take to be a damn good officer, I thought, and I was glad of

his companionship that winter morning. Win, lose, or draw, we were both going to be better for our joint exposure: he for the field experience and I for the teaching opportunity.

Across the silent corn field we slogged, the mud often reaching the knee-deep mark on our waders. I really hadn't known how exhausted I was until then. I had to stop several times to rest my now throbbing leg, slowing Terry down, but there was no other way because of the damaged tendon. This was a fine example of the reasons I always arrived early for a detail, I thought, but damn, that leg did hurt. After a several-hundred-yard trek across the field, we began to drive up small bunches of feeding mallards and pintail. Pretty soon the air was filled with these super little ducks. Seeing nature like this somewhat atoned for the constant burning pain in my right leg. This was what it was all about, tendon or no tendon, I thought. After all, I still had a good leg on the other side. ...

Eventually we came within forty or so yards of the edge of the duck club hunting area, a shallow-water area built into one end of the several-hundred-acre field. The dike was about three feet high, and the landowner had flooded the area inside the dike, creating a small lake surrounded by the semidry corn field. On the water in the flooded area were several hundred resting ducks, but to the north of Terry and me in the corn field were numerous scattered bands of feeding mallards and pintail that probably numbered ten thousand to fifteen thousand. They were probably the birds we had heard from the drifting boat earlier in the morning.

We picked an area we figured would be central to any illegal activity and lay down in the mud between several harvested corn rows. Gathering up what little cornstalk cover we could, we made like a couple of pintail and waited for the dawn.

Looking back on the moment as I write these words, I think, damn, what a morning. The smell of damp earth and the air filled with thousands of waterfowl whose calls were the very soul of nature, coupled with the anticipation of the hunt. There are few experiences that can rival such moments. Looking over at my stumpy partner, I could see his reactions to the moment were the same as mine as he lay alongside me in our palely moonlit field. There was no better training for the wildlife law enforcement officer's soul than such moments, and I could clearly see that Terry was getting his share. Good, I thought; we lads holding the "thin green line" needed all the help we could get, and I figured this lad was fast becoming one of the force in his own right.

Predawn came and went, but its chill remained with the two sweat-soaked officers lying in the harvested corn field, thinly disguised with a few cornstalks and loaded with high hopes. Dawn was just starting to break, and with it the excited feeding activity of thousands of ducks, some within twenty-five feet of the two large forms lying on the ground.

Our wonder and enjoyment of the display were interrupted by the unmistakable raspy voice of Jim Dixon, notifying us over the radio that a vehicle was approaching on the levee. The vehicle soon moved into our view and stopped at a small parking spot alongside the levee. Three men got out of the truck, hurriedly gathered up their hunting gear, and started at a fast pace down a trace of a muddy farm-equipment road that led to the diked area where the duck blinds were located. I noticed they were carrying gunnysacks and told Terry, "We got these guys. Real sportsmen don't enter the field carrying gunnysacks. These lads are serious about their killing and intend to fill those sacks!" The hunt was on, and both Terrys grinned—Hodges because his information was turning out to be correct and both of us because we loved the thrill of the chase.

The three shooters continued briskly walking toward their blinds near the diked area. When they reached the blinds, they stopped to survey the scene on their duck pond as well as the masses of ducks feeding in the fields just to the north. They kept looking toward the harvested corn field as if they had something on their minds other than a duck shoot over water. I had seen this look before in commercial market hunters and Sacramento Valley duck draggers, and all of a sudden I felt colder than before. Keeping my binoculars trained on the three chaps from my uncomfortable position in the muddy corn furrow, I watched them start to walk around the duck pond toward the thousands of feeding waterfowl north of where we lay. They walked in a stooped-over position for about a hundred yards, then disappeared from view. Now I knew why the cold was beginning to make itself felt. The killing was about to begin! I looked over at Terry and said, "I bet those bastards are going to pull a drag" (a Sacramento Valley term long used to mean shooting the birds tightly packed on the ground as they fed and in the instant they rose into the air to guarantee the greatest kill). Hodges said nothing, but his grim look showed that he concurred.

Nothing happened for about thirty minutes. Then I began to notice that the ducks closest to where our three chaps had disappeared were exhibiting some nervous behavior. A few ducks at a time would get up and fly into bunches of feeding ducks closer to the middle of the field. This "leapfrogging" continued for about ten minutes, and past experience told me that the shooters were close to the birds and the slaughter would soon begin in earnest.

Then all hell broke loose. The entire corn field to the north erupted with a roar of wings as, almost as if on cue, the ducks lifted up like a blanket being raised off the ground and filled the air with the sounds and motion of the typical panic the birds exhibit when surprised by humans at close quarters. At the same time, the roar of three shotguns simultaneously emptying their deadly contents into the frantic waterfowl reached our ears. What bedlam! Because of his newness to this game, Terry started to jump up to run down the shooters responsible for destroying our morning, but I grabbed him and told him to lie still. I said, "There will be lots of crippled ducks when this is done. Let them do our work for us in killing and collecting this still living carnage." His eyes acknowledged my suggestion, and we lay there watching events unfold to the north. The three shooters finally stood up and carefully looked all around to see if anyone had seen their deed or was coming to investigate the recent commotion. Seeing no one, they commenced walking across the muddy corn field, shooting or wringing the necks of dozens of crippled, frightened ducks. The flock that had been happily feeding moments before was rapidly moving out of sight to the northeast. But every few seconds you could see the dead and dying sail out of the flock and head for their last meeting with Mother Earth. I counted 103 ducks dropping from the vanishing flock before they passed out of view.

Damn, I thought, that loss alone was enough to make me grimly continue putting those in the business of extinction *out* of business until I didn't have a breath left. Hodges caught that look in my eyes, and I could see it cross his face as well. Suddenly the pain in my right tendon didn't seem so bad. ...

Soon crippled ducks were walking down the corn rows toward where we lay in an attempt to escape their still shooting pursuers. They came in rapidly increasing numbers, and I started to worry because it was just a matter of time before one of the shooters came along to retrieve this mass of escaping cripples and discovered another adventure lying in wait in the corn field. Sure as hell, a few moments later here came one of our killers, dutifully walking the corn rows, wringing necks and shooting the crippled ducks that had escaped the earlier slaughter. In a few moments, despite our efforts to dissolve into the mud, he spotted us. This customer was cool. He didn't even break stride—just made brief eye contact and, with a gradual turn back toward his buddies, kept killing cripples and collecting their now stilled bodies. Terry looked at me and said, "I think he spotted us."

I said, "I think so too, but let's wait just a moment to make sure." Damn, for a youngster in this game, this kid sure has got good genes, I thought. The lad had just barely given us a look, yet Terry had caught it and had him dead to rights in his next move.

Soon the man who had spotted us lying in the mud trying to make ourselves small reached his buddies. A little powwow quickly took place, and two of them, with a couple of furtive glances sent our way, dropped all their ducks and streaked for the protective cover and potential escape at the north end of the island. The remaining chap started back toward the pickup, but Terry and I happened to be closer to it than he was. I told Terry, "That's it, let's go. They have seen us for sure." Jumping up out of the mud and scattering crippled ducks that had taken refuge right around us, I said, "You grab those two running to the north. I'll grab this one coming back to his vehicle and direct our boat and land officers in to help you." Terry waved in acknowledgment as he churned up out of the mud and began his run after the two fleeing chaps, who by now had a hundred-yard head start. Watching my partner hammer up out of the mud and get going

in pursuit of the two culprits, I thought, You lads better be in great
shape. That little chap coming right up your hind ends, fellows, is
"pure dee" carrying the mail. I felt a familiar grin slowly beginning to
form. It was our time of day now.

Getting Dixon on the portable radio while watching my rapidly
approaching shooter as I quartered across the field to cut him off,
I filled him in on the morning's events. I told Dixon to get the boat
moving fast, head up to the northeast end of the island, disembark,
and cut across the field to intercept the two lads and give Terry a
hand. Dixon answered that he was on the way just as soon as he
started the boat. Good, I thought. Dixon was a runner par excellence,
and any distance under ten miles meant nothing to him physically.
Given that the two lads had done wrong, Dixon could probably run
fifteen miles that day before he was winded. My grin broadened. I was
actually beginning to feel sorry for our two runners. It was obvious
that they were in for a long day with a sad ending.

Still keeping an eye on the approaching third shooter, I called Jerry
and Dave, directing them to break through the locked gates on the
northwest and northeast ends of the island and cut off the chaps that
Terry was chasing. Now our runners really had no damn place to go
except down; they just didn't know it yet. They had trifled with
Mother Nature and lost. Some days you eat the bear, and some days
the bear eats you. ...

About that time the third shooter was upon me, and I made sure
both God and this chap know he was to get his tail end over next to
me, and *now!* The tendon hurt, but he was only ten yards away, and
I was between him and his vehicle. Seeing that flight was not an
option with such a large figure blocking his way, he turned and re-
signedly walked slowly over to me. We met in the muddy field, and
I took out my badge and credentials and identified myself. I informed
him that the chap pursuing his partners was a state Fish and Game
warden and that before it was all over the island would be crawling
with the law. All I got in return was a baleful look.

Wanting to know who Terry was chasing so I could tell the other
officers who our quarry was, I asked my lad to give me the other men's
names. He just looked at me, still in shock at being apprehended.

I repeated my question, and he said, "I can't tell you that. I will have to take the ticket for this mess, but I just can't tell you who they are." Now, that really got my curiosity up—as well as my concern for Terry's safety. I wanted to know who the hell was running in case they turned out to be connected to the Mafia or some such thing, and I wanted to let Terry know before he got close.

I told my fellow, "That's not how we do it. Who are those chaps hot-footing it for the north end of the island?" I got only the same song and dance as before, so I dropped the subject for the time being (I found later that the two runners were local Italian millionaires to whom my chap owed favors). I could see that the two running men had hit hard ground and were starting to distance themselves from Terry's very determined, still-in-the-muddy-field pursuit, so I got on the radio and said, "Dixon, where the hell are you?" Since I didn't hear the boat motor, it didn't take a high IQ to realize something was wrong with my "navy." Sure enough, Dixon's voice came over the radio, and he told me the parachute was caught in the prop but that he would have it freed soon.

Upon hearing the radio conversation, the fellow I had apprehended, who had been quietly standing right next to me, suddenly started to get mouthy with a ton of questions. I just looked at him and didn't say anything. Keep in mind that I was exhausted after many months of long days, I had a damn sore tendon, and now my guts were telling me it was time to get rid of a lot of rich food through the bottom of the "pipe," *fast*. Have you ever tried to do that with a bad tendon, after lowering a set of chest-highs in the middle of ten thousand acres of harvested corn, which doesn't let you get out of sight, with nothing to hang on to? Oh, and in almost knee-deep Delta mud? It is a treat designed to make the sweetest disposition turn to the same stuff that ends up on the ground, if you get my drift! Continuing to look hard at me, my shooter said in a sharp tone, "All right, I own this land, and I have a right to know what the hell is going on. Who is that guy on the radio? What is he doing on my land? How did you get here?"

Well, between no sleep, a sore leg, a bad set of guts getting steadily worse, and a mouthy Italian, I had had about all I wanted to take.

I figured if he wanted to know, I would tell him. I said, "Damn, you weren't supposed to hear that about the parachute."

I could almost see him prick up his ears as he said, "All right, I demand to know what's going on. This is my land, and I want an answer right now or else."

Yeah, sure, this knothead had a right to nothing, I thought—so that was exactly what I gave him. Giving him a long, hard look as if I were trapped in a sensitive situation, I said, "I am part of a very special federal parachute squad that is operating here in the Delta in an attempt to get in on duck clubs without being seen. We come in very early in the morning on clubs like yours and stake them out to ascertain the violation rate, and it's been working very well." From the incredulous look I was getting, this fellow was flat-out stunned! I continued, "You need to keep that to yourself, please; otherwise it really ruins our ability to get the job done."

Still in shock, he asked, "Isn't that dangerous?"

Knowing I had him and not willing to let him go just yet, I said, "Yes; why do you think I am walking around with a damn bad limp? This morning I hit a spud ditch in the dark when I landed and damn near broke my ankle."

Boy, that fish bit hook, line, sinker, and farrow. Common sense might have caused him to ask himself where my parachute was if I had just parachuted in. If I had dropped in on his island from the sky, why would I have carried the 'chute to the boat? Why not just arrive by boat and forget this skydiving thing? Man, this guy was thicker than even a bullheaded German like myself. I could tell that I had this chap sold on my story. Figuring maybe I could use this deception to the ducks' and our advantage, I planned how I would drive the sword in even deeper, if I got the chance, once we were all together.

From the sound of the roar of an outboard, it was apparent that Dixon had finally gotten the boat going and was headed north to assist Terry. Jerry, Dave, and Tim, with the help of my trusty bolt-cutters, cut through a locked gate and came in on the north end of the club. They were in plain sight of the fleeing lads, and this combination of the cavalry and the determined little fellow gaining on them from the rear removed any desire to continue running, so the two remaining culprits just sat down and awaited their fate. Seeing the foot race come to a close, I again had to grin. Now the ducks would get their day in court.

I herded my man north, all the while picking up dead and dying ducks from the mud in the corn field. Terry caught the two fleeing lads and, with the other officers, started back toward me and the "killing fields" where our three lads had had their morning adventure. As the shooters with their law enforcement escort moved south, they picked up the many crippled and dying ducks from the morning's shoot, as the two of us did on our end. After we met on the site where the actual shooting had occurred, the officers continued picking up the ducks we could catch and made a pile of them near a small road. We also picked up the bunches of ducks that had been dropped by our three shooters just before they tried to escape, when they realized Terry and I were lying in the corn field watching them.

As we worked, I noticed our three shooters standing off to one side looking at me. Knowing my bigmouthed Italian had told them my "secret" parachute story, I started Plan B. As I casually approached the other officers as we continued the process of picking up ducks, I quietly told each of them about the lie I had told my Italian prisoner and asked them to play along with it. I didn't have long to wait for my next move.

Pretty soon one of the two lads who had fled to the north approached me, and I saw that he was wearing a 101st Airborne jacket. Oh, damn, I thought. I sure hope he isn't an ex-Airborne paratrooper, because if he is my Plan B might not hold water. Sure as God made little green apples, he marched right up to me and demanded, as any experienced paratrooper would, who was the pilot of the plane from which we had jumped that morning. I looked at him sternly for a moment, then looked past him at Mr. Bigmouth as if I was pissed that someone else now knew our "secret." I also noticed that all the other officers, although still deep in evidence retrieval, were listening carefully. Maybe we still had this in the bag, I thought, and with a "defeated" flourish of the hand, I pointed to Jerry Smith. Now, Jerry just happened to be wearing a surplus air force jacket with a set of wings sewn on the front left side. My 101st Airborne lad walked

smartly over to Jerry and demanded to know at what altitude he had
been flying when the drop was made.

Jerry stopped picking up ducks for a moment and, puffing on his
pipe for effect, said, "You see that big guy with the limp over there?"
The 101st Airborne guy nodded, and Jerry softly continued, "If he
knew how low I dropped him this morning, which was way under
any safe drop altitude, he would kill me!"

I could see the chap eyeballing me out of the corner of my eye, so
I made sure he saw how bad the limp really was as I took a couple of
hobbling steps to pick up more dead ducks. That seemed to satisfy
him, and he walked back to his buddies and commenced to talk rapidly in Italian. I'm sure the conversation was all about how the parachute squad really did exist and the guys now picking up dead and
dying ducks in their field were for real. Amazement, pure and simple,
was written all over their faces. God is good sometimes, and other
times He is truly brilliant!

We finished picking up, if I remember correctly, 198 ducks from
the corn field, and then we all headed for the vehicles parked on the
north end of the island. We issued citations to our chaps for what
they had done that morning and loaded ducks into the trunks of our
vehicles. As Dave opened his trunk, I chanced to spot a cargo 'chute
that he happened to have and said in a loud voice, "Be careful you
don't get ducks or muck on my 'chute." The man in the Airborne
jacket pricked up his ears, then casually moved over to Dave's car and
took a quick side peek into the trunk. He did a quick double-take
when he saw the 'chute, then casually walked back to his two friends.
The Italian language just flew as he described the "evidence" he had
just seen, which demonstrated the absolute truth of the parachute
story. By now all of us good guys were having a hard time keeping
straight faces. Damn, it doesn't get much better than that moment
when the hook has been placed so deeply that you have to be careful
how you use the toilet paper!

Our business done, and done very well, we all went back to Terry's
house in Brentwood to clean our evidence birds, take pictures, and happily swap tales of our actions that morning. Talk about fun—damn,
did we ever laugh about the wool we had pulled over the eyes of the

three Italian shooters. I knew those three lads would be telling our parachute tale all over the county just as fast as they could, but in order for it to really work, Plan B still needed a little more polish. I had to get Jerry back in time to catch a flight to Washington, so we left early, but not before I had asked the state guys to refer all parachute calls to my supervisor. When I dropped Jerry off at the home of Jack Downs, my supervisor, I briefed Jack on what had happened and asked him to keep the parachute-squad tale going, and he agreed with relish.

It didn't take long with our Italian "telegraph," and soon all the major newspapers of the area were calling Jack (and a few me) to ask for information about the heretofore secret "parachute squad." When they called me, I would tell them only that it was an official government secret and that I wasn't allowed to discuss the matter at that time. I would give the reporters Jack's name and address and request that they call him. In their typical eagerness to sniff out a scoop, they would stampede to the phones to call Jack. At that point I wasn't sure who had been "hooked" the deepest: the press or our three Italians. I stayed in the field (on purpose) and had little control over the outcome, but I was later told that the *Sacramento Bee,* the *San Francisco Chronicle,* and the *Los Angeles Times* all carried spreads about the so-called Fish and Wildlife parachute squad. The only information the press ever received came from our Italians, so you can imagine what kind of story that was. God, it was great.

THE MONDAY AFTER our little jaunt in the corn field, Jack got a call from Dante J. Nomelini, owner of a large duck club in the Delta whom I considered to be a bit of an outlaw. Dan wanted Jack to come right down and "have a little duck-a shoot, some good-a wine, a big-a steak, and a little-a more wine." Jack knew exactly why Dante had gotten so friendly all of a sudden and figured he might as well perpetuate our parachute myth, so off he went. Jack told me later that when he drove up to Dante's duck club, there were about fifty cars in the parking lot. When he went into the club, there was a mob of Italians who immediately jumped him to ask for the truth about the story of the parachute squad.

Jack, a master of deceit, feigned surprise and said, *"Who told you that?"* as if he were shocked that our cat was out of the bag. His reaction confirmed the tale in many of their minds. In fact, one fellow came up to Jack and told him, *"We know all about your secret squad—we even have a witness who saw your people jump out of the airplane at three in the morning!"* Well, obviously, with that kind of intelligence Jack could only lamely deny the story. I don't think there was a hook or coffin-lid nail left in town after Jack's visit.

For weeks afterward you couldn't make an over-limit case on ducks in the Delta if you tried. It seemed that every time a small private airplane flew over, all shooting would stop and many duck hunters would simply come out of the field. It was not uncommon to find people quitting with just three or four ducks, even though the limit was eight.

In my business, you do it any way you can, just so long as it is legal. This time the ducks won with the aid of a little ingenuity and a whole lot of luck. Who knows—maybe sometime in the winter you will have the opportunity, under a full moon, to watch ducks trade back and forth across the skies, carrying out their dance with life. Maybe you will also have the opportunity, under that same moon, to watch those ducks fly around several parachutes quietly descending to the ground on some duck club somewhere. If you do, and later on you see a big guy with a limp and a little guy with a determined look, be careful—they might be running with the devil, or maybe just have a little of the devil in them.

2

The War Bonnet

SHAKING DAVE FISCHER'S HAND warmly and patting him on the shoulder, I said, "Damn good job catching those goose-baiting sons of guns, Dave. It'll be a cold day in hell before they try again to illegally manipulate those corn fields with their combines in order to kill a few more Canada geese."

Dave grinned, more than pleased, and said, "I'll keep in touch with you if they decide to go to trial. But I'll bet you a homemade snapping-turtle stew they just pay up and hope none of their goose-shooting buddies or fellow farmers find out they were caught red-handed by a couple of beat-up old feds."

With a broad grin and a wave of the hand, I got into my patrol car and began my trip north back to my duty station in Bismarck, North Dakota. There is a certain kind of happiness that comes from a difficult job well done, and this was one of those times. I was tired from the long, sleepless hours of surveillance and the bone-chilling cold that comes from lying in a corn field most of the night, but as I sped down the road I could feel a large, satisfied smile slowly cracking my windburned face.

Dave Fischer was one of my special agents, stationed in Pierre, South Dakota. I was the senior resident agent, or first line supervisor, for the U.S. Fish and Wildlife Service's Division of Law Enforcement, for North and South Dakota. Dave and I had just spent the better part of a week, in the bitter cold of a South Dakota winter, staking out a large corn farming operation in the Oahe River bottoms south of Pierre. Days before I had arrived, several standing corn fields in the area had been swarmed by hungry Canada geese, and goose-hunting "sportsmen" in their sunken pit blinds had shot the hell out of the birds. Realizing something was wrong when the geese worked these few corn fields more heavily than any others in the area, even though they were under heavy fire, Dave began to check those fields at night for signs of bait.

After two nights' work, Dave discovered that the farmer was harvesting six to ten rows of standing corn per night, which was OK because that activity was within the definition of what was then known in our hunting regulations as a "normal agricultural practice." However, Dave also learned that the farmer had set the combine to pump all the seed, chaff, and stalks right out the harvester and onto the ground instead of separating and keeping the corn. This practice made the corn readily available to the geese and fell outside what was then considered a normal agricultural practice because it created a potentially baited area. As cold as it was, the energy-deficient geese eagerly descended on this new, easily accessible food supply and quickly disposed of the whole-kernel corn. Adding the goose shooters the next day closed the legal ring on what was considered taking migratory game birds over a baited area, a violation of state and federal laws.

As if that were not problem enough, Dave was the *only* special agent in the entire state of South Dakota owing to the Service's black history of insufficient funding for its Division of Law Enforcement. As the only man enforcing numerous federal laws, Dave always had his hands full of violators in wildlife-resource-rich South Dakota. He was an older man, a former B-24 bomber pilot who had served in World War II and walked with a limp. It seemed that after helping one of his crewmen out the door of his fatally flack-stricken aircraft over Ploieşti, he had been left with the option of crashing with the burning aircraft or jumping even though he was too low to land safely. He had hit the ground just as his parachute opened, jamming his hips back into the pelvis, an injury that would affect his walk for the rest of his life. But that disability and a dying wife did not stop Dave from performing his duties, and he was a legend in South Dakota for his work ethic, his strong friendships, and always having enough on the table for anyone who showed up with an empty gut. Hence my trip south from similar duties in North Dakota to give him a hand and an extra heartbeat.

He may have been a "beat-up" old man, but he always managed to work the hell out of me or any state Fish and Game officers who worked with him. During Dave's tenure, the critters of South Dakota were lucky to have him as an enforcing angel.

After several nights' work documenting the harvesting method designed to illegally attract geese and watching the shooting activity during the day, we sprang our two-man trap. When the dust, feathers, and corncobs had settled, we had ten very long-faced local goose shooters for taking over-limits of geese, use of unplugged shotguns (capable of holding more than three shells), and taking migratory game birds over a baited area. The farmer operating the combine was later cited for aiding and abetting in the above violations. None of the men wanted to carry this embarrassing affair any further, so they each forfeited $500 bail per offense in federal court two weeks later and were not heard from again when it came to violating fish and game laws.

Because I had plenty of my own law enforcement problems in North Dakota, I couldn't spare Dave much time for other activities; hence my hasty departure soon after helping him wrap up the baiting case. I left Pierre and drove north on state Highway 83 until I came to the junction with state Highway 212. Turning west on 212, I crossed over Lake Oahe into the Cheyenne River Indian Reservation. It was my usual habit to take different roads going to and from places within my enforcement district so that I could improve my knowledge of the geography of the two states to which I was assigned. I had never been this way before and looked forward to what the trip would offer in the way of new country and experiences. I planned to travel right through the Cheyenne River Indian Reservation, then north through the adjacent Standing Rock Indian Reservation, then home to Bismarck. Like Custer, I ran into a little more trouble than I had planned for.

I had just crossed Lake Oahe into Dewey County on the Cheyenne River Indian Reservation side when I noticed a small curio shop on the north side of the highway. On the side of the building hung several homemade signs indicating that the shop carried authentic Indian artifacts, jewelry, blankets, and the like. I always liked to inspect such places because I would often find items for sale—articles of clothing with feather decorations, for example—that violated the provisions of the Bald and Golden Eagle Protection Act or the Migratory Bird Treaty Act.

Though federally recognized Indian tribes, of which there are more than five hundred, are considered by the U.S. government to be a type of sovereign nation, citizens within those nations are held to most of the same laws as other citizens of the United States. For example, for members of almost every tribe, as for all other U.S. citizens, the taking (killing), selling, import, or export of bald eagles or golden eagles or their parts is illegal under federal law. At the time of writing, the Service was investigating the possibility of allowing the import or export of eagles and their parts and products between the United States and Canada in order to allow Native Americans the right to legally practice their cultural and religious customs. But until such changes are made, a Native American who violates the Bald and Golden Eagle Protection Act can expect to be tried and prosecuted in federal court. Laws such as the Bald and Golden Eagle Protection Act and the Migratory Bird Treaty Act were created to protect and preserve those species of birds identified under those laws as needing conservation measures. Even though many Native American tribes use feathers and other parts from these species, preservation of the birds was and is an overriding conservation concern. Today many Native Americans by treaty right may pick up dead birds of prey on their reservations or may lawfully obtain hundreds of dead eagles (birds that have been electrocuted by power lines, been illegally trapped, been taken as evidence, or died natural deaths) from the Fish and Wildlife Service's National Eagle Repository. However, regardless of the powerful protections provided by these federal laws, many Southwestern Indians and those from the Central Plains still illegally trap or shoot these species in large numbers for their personal use as well as for illegal commercial markets in Canada, Europe, Japan, and the United States. It was the possibility of this type of poaching that made me interested in checking out the small Indian curio shop that day so long ago.

Pulling into the small parking lot by the building, I went through the front door and was greeted by a diminutive old Native American man.

"Good morning," he said. "Can I help you?"

"No; I'm just looking for some ideas for presents for my children after a long business trip," I responded.

"Well, help yourself, and if you find something or need some assistance, call me," he said and then returned to his morning newspaper, which was spread out over the counter.

The shop contained the usual tourist curios: a mixture of newly made arrowheads, commercial-grade pottery from the Southwest, T-shirts with Indian designs, and the like. Not finding anything out of the ordinary, I started to leave. As I paused to thank the proprietor, I noticed several artifacts hanging on the wall behind him. Walking over to the counter and looking more closely at the wall, I saw a coup stick alongside a bow with a quiver of arrows that appeared to be very old and a short, double-train war bonnet, which was also old but looked newer than the other two items. Each item carried a price tag announcing its cost in bold black numbers to any interested buyer. The coup stick had no feathers, so there was no violation of federal laws there. The same went for the bow and quiver of arrows because the feathers on the arrow shafts appeared to be turkey, a species not protected by federal law. However, the war bonnet was a horse of a different color. It comprised an old high-crowned felt hat with the brim removed. Sewn all around the base of the crown on red cloth were what appeared to be old eagle feathers. Hanging down the back side, also on red cloth backings, hung two strands of seven eagle feathers each. Because both "trains" appeared to be made from eagle feathers and had a price tag affixed, I was pretty sure I was looking at a violation of the sale provisions of the Eagle Act.

"May I see that war bonnet?" I casually asked. Without a word, the shopkeeper turned, removed it carefully from the wall, and laid it on the counter in front of me. "Is this a *real* war bonnet?" I asked like Joe Dingbat.

"Yes, it is," responded the shopkeeper. "It belonged to an Indian called Crooked Foot, who is now dead, and his kids sold it to me."

Well, I thought, there is another violation of the Eagle Act because no one is allowed to sell eagle feathers or their parts or products. Looking closely at the feathers on the war bonnet, I counted thirteen tail feathers on the crown of the hat. Ten of those feathers were from a golden eagle, and the remaining three were from an immature bald eagle. The two trains hanging down in back contained fourteen tail feathers in all, twelve from a golden eagle and two from a juvenile bald eagle. This certainly was an authentic Indian war bonnet, I thought, made with real eagle feathers. I examined the price tag and saw that $450 would buy the item. "Is this what you want for this item?" I asked, pointing to the clearly affixed price tag.

"Sure is, and that is firm. I paid that same amount to Crooked Foot's boys, and that's what I have to have in order to break even."

I continued to look at the war bonnet as if sizing up the purchase. Actually, I was double-checking my initial identification of the eagle feathers. I was right the first time, I thought; a total of twenty-two golden eagle and five bald eagle tail feathers.

The old man, realizing he might have one on the hook, took more interest in my presence and the possible sale that might be in the offing. "That war bonnet is made from real eagle feathers and is at least sixty years old," he said.

That is a good statement to make, old man, I thought. The seller's showing knowledge of the exact species for the feathers certainly wouldn't hurt this case in a court of law, if it went to trial (as most cases involving Native Americans did). Still carefully examining the item as an interested buyer would, checking out the stitching, wear and tear, and the like, I said, "I thought it was illegal to have something like this in your possession."

"Oh no," he said. "Indians can have them and even sell them if they like."

Wrong, I thought. Still looking at the war bonnet I said, "Is it legal for a person like me to have something like this?" I was trying to elicit not only the old man's knowledge but his illegal intent as well. Keep in mind that in federal court the investigating officer has to show the culprit's knowledge of the illegality of his actions beyond a reasonable doubt if he is going to file criminal charges.

"Well, white men are not supposed to have things like this according to the Eagle Protection Act, only Indians. But once you get it home and in your house, the authorities can't touch it without getting a warrant first," he said. "And that's pretty hard to do."

It was obvious that the man was making every effort to sell me the war bonnet, violation of federal law or not. Making every effort to get more information out of the old man regarding his knowledge of the wrong he was committing, I continued, "What if I buy this—can I drive down the highway with it if I have a bill of sale from you, a Native American?"

"Well, I would suggest that if you buy this, you put it in the trunk of your car until you get home. That way no one will see it, and you shouldn't have any problems with the law."

I said, "Look, I am a reputable collector of pieces of history such as this for several museums as well as myself, and if I am not mistaken, it is *really* illegal for anyone to sell items like this with the eagle feathers and all. There have to be several federal laws that prohibit the selling of these items by anyone." I held my breath. It was a very strong cautionary statement for me to make, but one I felt was needed to prove or disprove his underlying knowledge and intent in this transaction. I had never brought a case like this before my attorneys in South Dakota, and I wanted to make sure I covered all my bases.

"I will tell you what, mister," he replied. "You're right, it is illegal to sell these under the Eagle Act, but if you are a bona fide collector and appreciate authentic things like this, I will sell it to you for only $400. No one will know except you and me."

I thought, OK, you just went over the top; let's get it on. "Will you take less than $400 for the headdress?" I asked.

"No, I have to sell it for no less than $400," he said.

"OK, I'll take it for the $400 you just quoted, but I'll need it wrapped so no one knows I have it."

"That is a sale, mister, and probably a good idea to wrap it up. I don't want some of my Indian friends to see it in your possession and get upset. I'll get a box and some paper and wrap it up for you," he said.

While the shopkeeper busied himself with wrapping up the war bonnet, tag and all, I got out my personal checkbook. "Will you take a personal check?" I asked.

"Where you from?" he asked.

"North Dakota," I responded.

"Yes, that will be all right," he replied.

Filling out the check to the man I now knew as Frank Duschenaux, Sr., from a card he gave me with the name of the shop and his name, I footnoted the check, "for purchase of an eagle-feather war bonnet." I handed him the check, and he handed me the boxed war bonnet along with a handwritten receipt denoting "one headdress with eagle feathers from Crooked Foot"(I had asked him for some kind of authentication and history of the item). Thanking him, I started out the door, then hesitated. "Excuse me," I said, turning back toward the counter. "I forget to note in my checkbook the information from that check. May I have it back for a moment so I might note the purchase in my checkbook?" Frank handed me the check, and with that final bit of evidence safely in my hands, I took out my badge and credentials and identified myself as a special agent with the Fish and Wildlife Service. The look on his face was pure shock, to say the least. "Mr. Duschenaux," I said, "as you seem to be well aware, it is illegal under the Eagle Act to sell eagles, their feathers, or their parts and products."

"Well, I knew I couldn't sell to white men, but I needed the money and just took a chance," he lamely replied.

"Not a good gamble, Mr. Duschenaux, to sell items like this at any time," I said.

"What are you going to do now?" he asked.

"Well, I am going to fill out this pink slip, getting some personal information from you. Then I'll seize the war bonnet and file charges against you in federal court in Rapid City."

"You're going to take my war bonnet too?" he asked.

"Yes, I am," I replied. "It was advertised for sale, and you did in fact sell it to me, all in violation of the Eagle Protection Act. It is a key piece of evidence and as such will be seized."

He looked at me, and I could see the anger slowly rising in him. "How can you do that here on the reservation? You have no authority here in this place. This is Indian country!" he shouted.

"Well, Mr. Duschenaux, I identified myself to you as a federal officer, and since I am in the United States, and you are too, I do have the authority to enforce the federal laws on all U.S. soils. The Eagle Act is a federal law and strictly prohibits anyone from doing what you did here this morning, even as a Native American. In addition, Mr. Duschenaux, I am familiar with the Cheyenne River Indian Treaty, and nowhere does that treaty give any Native Americans of the tribe the express right to sell eagles or their feathers."

"I don't care who you are; you are on my reservation, you have no authority here, and now you are going to steal my war bonnet," he yelled.

"Mr. Duschenaux," I calmly replied, "what you did here this morning was illegal under the Eagle Act. You yourself have even admitted to me that you know that fact. In addition, just having the eagle-feather items marked for sale is illegal. And selling those items is also illegal and makes them subject to seizure as evidence and possible forfeiture if the court finds you guilty of the above offenses.

"I don't care about your damn white man's law; I just know you cannot do what you are doing," he shouted. "My son is the chairman of the tribe and a personal friend of the Secretary of the Interior. I am going to call him and have you arrested. What is your name again, and who do you work for?"

I handed him my card and, seeing I was going nowhere with the conversation, left his copy of the evidence tag describing the seized item and left the building as Frank began yelling over the phone to someone about the federal agent in his store. Keeping a sharp eye on the front door in case Frank came out with a Winchester, I locked the box containing the war bonnet in the trunk of my sedan after taping an evidence tag to the outside of the box. About that time Frank came bursting out the door and told me the Indian police were coming and I had better wait for them.

"How long before they get here?" I asked, figuring I would explain to them what had transpired if they were not too long in coming.

"I don't know," he said, "but it shouldn't take more than an hour or two because this is a big reservation."

Well, I thought, I have more important things to do than to wait around for the police to get here! I decided I would head on down the road. "Are there any other questions you might have relative to this matter, Frank?" I asked.

"No," he replied, "but you better wait for the police."

"Just have them call me at my office later on today and I will explain the issue to them, Frank," I responded. "Or, I am heading to Eagle Butte. If they get here shortly after I leave, please advise them which way I am going, and maybe they can catch me on the road and I will explain to them at that time what happened here today."

Ignoring my suggestions, he stormed off the steps of his house and walked over to me. "You white bastard, you will be back," he yelled. "There is no way you'll be able to keep my headdress. You'll be forced to bring it back; you just wait and see. My son the tribal chairman is very powerful with you damn white people; you'll see. You will find out Indians can do anything they want to do on the reservation. You'll see!"

Thanking him in a calm manner, I got in my car and headed on down Highway 212 toward the town of Eagle Butte, figuring I could gas up there, since I was low on fuel, and then keep working my way north on the back roads toward Bismarck. Boy, did I soon get a lesson in the crooked tribal politics common to many of the Plains tribes!

Eagle Butte was thirty or so miles to the west, and as I continued down the highway I drank in my surroundings, letting my mind wander back into the history of the land. I was brought up short from that bit of mental diversion by a set of flashing red lights coming up fast in my rearview mirror. They matched the ones flying down the road toward me from Eagle Butte as well! Soon my unmarked patrol car was surrounded by a swarm of tribal police, all waving guns and ordering me out of the car with my hands up! Getting out of the car, I reached slowly into my shirt pocket with my left hand and took out my badge and credentials, holding them up high for all to see. One of the lads closest to me holstered his sidearm and walked over to where I stood motionless for fear of starting a shoot-out by some ill-trained (if trained at all in those days) tribal police officers. Taking my badge out of my hand and carefully examining it, he said, "Damn, you really are a federal agent. Put the guns away, guys; he is a special agent with the federal government." Turning to me and returning my badge and credentials, he said, "You will have to follow me, Special Agent Grosz."

"What for?" I asked.

"Because the tribal chairman wants to see you," he replied.

"Am I under arrest?" I asked.

The officer looked at me for a moment and said, "You are coming with us, Mr. Grosz, or *else!*"

Realizing the odds were four to one, I said, "Lead the way." With that, I started off behind a tribal police car, with all its lights flashing and siren blaring, followed by another tribal police car doing the same. If one of them didn't wake the dead for miles around, the two together certainly did.

I followed the patrol car into the town of Eagle Butte and to the main office building for the Tribal Council. Getting out of my patrol car and locking it, I followed two burly tribal officers, with another two trailing me, into what appeared to be the Tribal Council chambers. Seated around a table were eight Indians in civilian dress, one pot-gutted tribal officer who appeared to be the chief of the tribal police, and one white wanna-be trying to look like an Indian with braids clear down to his hind end. You can probably guess that I was starting to get just a little steamed over the treatment being given one federal officer by four others.

One civilian-dressed Indian stood, introduced himself as Tribal Chairman Duschenaux, and asked, "Who might you be?"

I told him I was Special Agent Terry Grosz with the Fish and Wildlife Service.

"Do you have any credentials proving who you might be? If you do, give them to me," he said, holding out his hand as if he were talking to a small child and was used to being obeyed.

I took out my credentials, held them up for all to see, and then returned them to my shirt pocket.

"I said I want to see them," barked the tribal chairman, this time with an edge to his voice.

"I don't hand my badge or credentials over to anyone but a proper representative of the Service," I coldly replied. By now my eyes were speaking volumes, and in a language that should have been clear for all to understand.

There was a long silence in the room as all of us just stared at each other, and then the wanna-be with braids stood up and told me that he was the attorney for the Tribal Council, and I had better do what the chairman said or else. With that threat and everything else that had happened up to this point, I was really getting annoyed! I had identified myself to everyone but God and was still being treated like a three-legged coyote in a coop full of Farmer John's prize chickens. This kind of treatment did not make me happy, and I was willing to show it.

"Or else what?" I fired back to the attorney, looking him right in the eyes. "Braids" just sat back down as if he had been hit with a stick. I could tell he was happy he had survived that exchange, let alone having to come up with a definition of the "or else" verdict.

"Well, Mr. Grosz, if you aren't about to cooperate in that area, I would at least like an explanation as to what went on between you and my dad at his store," spoke the chairman.

"Mr. Chairman, I am an authorized special agent for the U.S. Fish and Wildlife Service, empowered to enforce the provisions of the Bald and Golden Eagle Protection Act. As such, I identified myself properly to all assembled here in this room. Acting in that capacity earlier today, I had the opportunity to enter your dad's public place of business, where I observed an eagle headpiece hanging on the wall clearly advertised for sale. I asked to see that item and in so doing positively identified the feathers on that item listed for sale as being from two species of eagles. I was quoted a price of sale for that item by your dad. Those acts of advertising for sale and selling said item are in violation of the Bald and Golden Eagle Protection Act, and your dad was so advised. I seized the illegal eagle-feather item listed for sale and will present this case to the U.S. attorney's office in Rapid City for consideration in the criminal prosecution of the gentlemen who sold it to me."

"Braids," finally getting some air back in his bladder after our last exchange, popped up and said, "Mr. Grosz, you have no authority here on the reservation, and I suggest you return the item before you are arrested for grand theft and prosecuted in tribal court."

By now I was *really* steamed and had no use for this idiot-stick attorney representing a profession that I consider the weakest link in the chain of democracy! "In what school did you study law?" I icily asked. Before the chap could say anything else, I said, "The last time I looked, this was still part of the United States, and my credentials say my enforcement authority extends clear across the land! In addition, for your information, the tribal court has no criminal jurisdiction over a white man, period! I suggest you go back and review your basic law and case laws." With that, the attorney clammed up and had nothing more to say for the next few moments.

"Where is the headdress now?" asked the chairman in a rather pointed tone of voice.

"In the trunk of my government vehicle, identified as evidence," I responded.

The tribal chairman turned to the pot-gut (whose belly was even larger than mine) wearing the chief's uniform and said something in his native tongue. "Pot-Gut" stood and said, "Give me the keys to the trunk of your car."

"And what authority might I ask do you have, sir, to enter an automobile belonging to the federal government to retrieve a federal evidentiary item?" I pointedly asked.

Bristling up to show all assembled what a tough guy he was, he pointed toward his tribal police badge and hollered, "That is all the authority I need, asshole. Now, hand me your keys or I will come and get them!"

Boy, I would have relished that. … I would have knocked him flat on his hind end with one punch once he had laid his hands on me and then sued him civilly for his share of the reservation. Trying to maintain some kind of professional decorum in light of my not-so-slow-burning rage, I said, "Again, Chief, that is federal property, and no one gets in it but me or an authorized Service representative."

I could tell that my continuing to question his tribal authority set the hair on his ass, and he was now about to bust a gut! "Are you armed?" he yelled. The other members of the Tribal Council started to look a bit alarmed by the direction this inquisition was rapidly heading.

"Yes I am, sir," I flatly stated so he wouldn't misunderstand what was being said between the lines now.

"Give me your gun, and *right now!*" he shouted.

"Again, sir, no disrespect, but no one takes that piece of federal property unless they are authorized to do so," I calmly replied. I casually slipped my left hand into my vest pocket in such a way as not to arouse suspicion and, grasping my spare magazine to the loaded Colt .45 hanging on my hip, turned it so it could be inserted into the pistol rapidly once I shot it dry—if it came to that!

"Take it away from him," he yelled to the two tribal police officers standing right alongside me. I quickly took a step back to place them in front of me and fixed a stare on those two officers that told them they'd better not obey that order unless they wanted to "dance"!

Seeing that the situation had escalated beyond the value of a head-dress, the tribal chairman quickly held up his hand and called a halt to the events. It didn't take a college professor to ascertain that I wasn't going to back down and let them have their way, and that point wasn't lost on anyone except the chief and the wanna-be attorney. I think the chairman may have also figured that I was likely better trained and a lot better shot than his five officers.

"You can take the headdress for now, Officer Grosz, but before the week is out, you will be bringing it back; you will see. It is coming back. There is no way a white man can take something such as a headdress away from an Indian for any reason on *my* reservation and get away with it. You will see."

"Is there anything else, sir?" I asked, still feeling the heat of the moment.

"No; be on your way, and don't give me any reason to have you arrested, because if you do you can count on spending a few nights in our jail."

The cold way he said that, I figured he meant it, so I locked that bit of wisdom in the back of my mind. Walking out the door, I got into my vehicle and drove across the street to a gas station to fill up my car for the trip home. I had no more than put the nozzle into my gas tank when a tribal police officer came screaming into the gas station in his patrol car and, jumping out, jerked the hose from my hand.

"You get no gas here, you stinking white man," he uttered.

Fine, I thought. Getting back into my car, I headed down the road and pulled into the next gas station in town, only to have the same theme presented there. Realizing I had a problem as long as I was on the Cheyenne River reservation, I took a long, hard look at my gas gauge. It was not good. Getting out my map of South Dakota, I tried to figure a way out of this mess that wouldn't violate any tribal provisions. I couldn't backtrack because of distance and lack of facilities, so I figured I would take Highway 63 north off the Cheyenne River reservation and then transfer onto Highway 65, which would take me through the Standing Rock Indian Reservation to a little town called McIntosh. That would be a backcountry distance of eighty miles. There was no other way out of this mess; I would just have to get as far as I could and then walk if I had to.

With a friendly wave to the tribal police, I headed north, only to have two patrol cars fasten themselves to my tail and stay there. Damn, I thought; I will keep my car moving at thirty miles per hour in an attempt to save as much gas as I can. Besides, maybe those lads will get tired of me going so slowly and get bored. Fat chance—they stayed with me the full distance until I reached the boundary of their reservation. That wasn't so bad, but having to go to the bathroom and not being able to stop along the almost deserted highway and take care of that problem was a larger-than-life issue. I knew that to do so would invite arrest for some sort of indecent exposure, so I just kept everything capped and toughed it out. Fortunately, my slow-driving gas-saving idea worked, and when I got to McIntosh I put twenty gallons of gasoline in a tank meant to hold twenty gallons.

Arriving back at my office in Bismarck, I promptly got on the phone to my supervisor, Duane Luchtel, in Kansas City, Kansas, to tell him about the morning's events. Briefing Duane, who was the assistant special agent in charge, as I would an attorney, I spent about thirty minutes giving him every detail of my time on the reservation. After listening and asking a few questions, he concurred that it was an excellent case and one the Service ought to run with in order to settle the issue once and for all of whether Native Americans could legally sell eagles or their parts or products. Duane said he would get Chuck Hayes, the special agent in charge, involved, and we parted ways. Then I went upstairs in the federal building and, sitting down with Dave Peterson, assistant U.S. attorney, briefed him regarding the day's events on the reservation. I had a copy of the Cheyenne River Treaty, which he reviewed as well. Dave got on the phone and discussed the issue with Lynn Crooks, an assistant U.S. attorney in Fargo, and they agreed that I had an excellent case. Both said they would try the case if it were in their jurisdiction and if it were presented to them for prosecution.

Returning to my office, I saw that I had a telephone message from Chuck Hayes, the special agent in charge in Kansas City. When I called him back, he asked me to brief him in detail, which I did, including the results of my recent discussion with the two assistant U.S. attorneys in North Dakota. Hayes had a few questions for me and then said, "Terry, this is one heck of a good case, and we are going to run with this one all the way. The way I see it, we finally have an eagle sale case that is strong enough to go all the way to the Supreme Court if we have to in order to settle the 'sale' issue among the Indians. Get your case report in to me just as soon as you can so we can review it, and get it in to the chief of Law Enforcement as well. He can get it to the Department of Justice and the U.S. solicitor's office and get the necessary clearances to move forward with this as a criminal investigation." The Secretary of the Interior is the nation's caretaker of the tribes, and it was necessary in those days, if an Interior Department agency was going to investigate a case involving an Indian, that a clearance be first obtained through the Department of Justice and the U.S. solicitor's office in order to ensure that the investigation and subsequent prosecution did not violate an existing treaty right. That policy has since been changed to require clearance only to prosecute, not to investigate.

Next I telephoned the assistant U.S. attorney in Rapid City, South Dakota, and discussed the case with him. He strongly concurred with his two counterparts in North Dakota that I had a very strong case, one that he felt would stand on its own merits all the way to the Supreme Court if necessary. He agreed to prosecute it vigorously when it got to his doorstep and congratulated me on a job well done. Hanging up the phone, I had a grin from ear to ear. Both of the Dakotas were full of Native Americans, and there were invariably lots of tangled legal issues regarding what they could and could not do with migratory birds and eagles. As with most of the issues, there was clear case law to back the stand the Service took on what the Indians could or could not do. However, in 1976 in the case of sale of eagle parts there was still a real question regarding what, if any, latitude the

Indians lawfully had. The Service was always looking for a solid case in which this issue could be legally addressed through the court system so that both sides would ultimately have a legal and understandable path to walk. Sitting back in my chair, I could see nothing but an airtight case against Mr. Duschenaux, and I looked forward to processing it through the federal court system. With clear case law on the issue of Native American sale of eagle feathers, the problems of definition and understanding by the tribes should fade away, I happily thought. Well, the legal and political weather soon took a turn for the worse, as is characteristic of issues like this when dealing with Native American tribes.

I had a detailed case report in to the office in Kansas City within a week. After review, my superiors called and expressed their pleasure in the completeness of the case file. They submitted it to the chief of Law Enforcement, Clark Bavin, who was located in Washington, D.C. I waited for about two weeks and heard nothing.

Finally, in week three, Duane called to tell me that the people in Washington did not feel the case was one in which they wanted to move forward, but they would review it one more time! I couldn't believe what I was hearing. The case was a good one in the eyes of three of the best assistant U.S. attorneys in the country! What the hell was Washington's problem? I thought. Duane said that Chuck felt so strongly about moving forward with the case, he was flying to Washington to see what the problem was. Satisfied that my boss was taking Washington to task, I relaxed and got back to my other work.

Some time later, I got a call from an individual in the regional solicitor's office from another region. Solicitors are the government's attorneys and advisers. I am sorry to say that I had little respect for many of the solicitors I met over my years in the Service. Even though they were supposed to be our legal advisers, I found most of them to be without a bucket of guts and lacking the brain or will to really get in there and fight for the Service on its many issues. It was as if many of them (not all, but most I met) couldn't get a job or compete in the legal field anywhere else, so they came to work as a solicitor for the government as a last resort. In turn, the government got what it paid for. It seemed that one of the solicitors in the regional office that was calling me had married Frank Duschenaux's daughter and was questioning the investigation and the legality of seizing the eagle-feather headdress from a Native American! The lad who called said he wasn't attempting to skew the investigation but was just *interested* in the investigation in general. I explained the case and, when he hung up, figured it was a dead issue.

A few weeks later the word came down from the Washington Law Enforcement office that the Justice Department and the solicitor's office wanted a stronger case before they initiated prosecution. They indicated that they just wanted the strongest case possible in the event that the matter ended up in front of the Supreme Court, as they suspected this one might. Before you could shake a stick, I had just about everyone on high pissing backward and not wanting to go forward with the investigation or prosecution. I could not believe what I was hearing. I knew enough about the law to realize I had a very good case. The U.S. attorney's offices in two states were strongly supportive because they saw a good chance for a win that would provide good subsequent case law that could do nothing but improve their legal hand in any further such matters. My immediate superiors held the line and told Washington that the case was sound. They steadfastly refused Washington's rejection and continued requesting the clearance so we could proceed with the investigation—and so it went.

The required clearance to investigate further and prosecute was not forthcoming, and pretty soon the chief of Law Enforcement was putting the pressure on my superiors to drop the investigation and *return* the seized headdress! For over a month Chief Bavin, on behalf of the standing invertebrates in the Department of Justice in Washington and the regional solicitor's office, kept up the pressure on my superiors to fold their tents and go home. Finally the special agent in charge bowed to the pressure and called me regarding the matter. I was mad and frustrated but listened to my superior's recommendation that I call it quits and back down from a perfectly good case just because the Department of Justice and regional solicitor's office didn't think this was a good case for the Supreme Court. I argued with my boss about the merits of the investigation and requested that he show me one weak point in the case. He could not do it, and neither could the Department of Justice or the solicitor's office, for that matter; they just didn't want to take on the issue at that time for whatever the real reason—a political one, I suspected.

I convinced my boss again that the case was sound, especially after I had him talk to the assistant U.S. attorney in South Dakota, and he went back to the drawing board. He called the chief of Law Enforcement and again requested that the investigation be allowed to go forward, based on the strength of the case and the assistant U.S. attorney's recommendation to prosecute. Again he was refused, and that time the chief called me directly and told me that he wanted the case dropped and the property returned. Needless to say, I went into orbit. I sat on the case for the next two weeks, hoping my German stubbornness and common sense in the higher ranks would break down the current thinking. The next thing I discovered was that the U.S. attorney's office in South Dakota was under pressure from the Department of Justice in Washington to back off from supporting the prosecution. Man, I couldn't believe all the pressure that was being put on the Service and the U.S. attorney's office in the field to abandon this investigation! As I look back on it now, I realize that this case was the only time in my career that I experienced that level of pressure to let go of an investigation. However, knowing that I had a good, airtight case, I continued to hang tough.

Finally Chief Bavin called me again and ordered me to drop the investigation and return the war bonnet to its owner posthaste. I reminded the chief that he was only a staff officer and adviser to the director of the agency. He had no authority to give a line officer a direct order, and he knew it. Only the special agent in charge or my regional director could do that, and until they did I was holding firm! Clark hung up, and ten minutes later I received a call from my special agent in charge ordering me to drop the investigation and return the seized property.

"Chuck," I said, "where is this coming from? Who and what the hell did I grab that they can fly in the face of the law of the land with impunity?"

"Terry, don't ask and I won't have to lie to you," he replied. "Get it done and drop the case."

"Yes, sir," I replied and slowly hung up the phone.

Again, it didn't take a rocket scientist to see that I had an excellent case. It was airtight! I had confirmed that assessment by talking with two of the best attorneys in North Dakota, Dave Peterson and Lynn Crooks, not to mention a close friend high up in the Justice Department in Washington. They were always right on when it came to the laws, and they strongly supported the investigation. In fact, one of them had told me, "Terry, if I couldn't win this one hands down, then I'd better get out of the business." Shaking my head at this latest turn of events, I loaded up the headdress and headed for Frank Duschenaux's place of business in South Dakota. I was not a happy camper, but I did know how to obey a direct order.

When I reached Frank's shop later that afternoon, I picked up the headdress and walked into the store with it. As soon as he spotted me, Frank began to rag my ass about being wrong: "I told you you'd have to bring it back; I told you you had no authority here on the reservation."

I didn't say anything, just handed him the war bonnet and had him sign the evidence release form. I don't think I'd ever been so pissed, except maybe the time I was shot in the back by a commercial-market hunter in California. It didn't help to have this little half-pint of piss in my face like a wanna-be dog yapping at my heels all the way. "I told you my son would get the bonnet back, didn't I, didn't I?" he kept squalling. I walked out, with him yapping at me all the way to the parking lot, got into my vehicle, and headed home.

For the next couple of hours while driving, I stewed about the affair, and by the time I got to my office I was flaming! Politics had somehow gotten involved in a great eagle-sale investigation and had forced everything off the deep end. I had no idea whose chain I had pulled, but it had to be a ship anchor's chain if the degree of reaction I had gotten was any indicator. I sat in my chair in the quiet of the office to unwind before I went home so I wouldn't bring this nasty piece of business into my family life. Then the phone rang. Not wanting to answer it in my current frame of mind, I let it ring three times. Then I thought, Damn, Terry, the people of this land are paying you to work, so grab the phone. "Good afternoon, Fish and Wildlife Service, may I help you?"

The unmistakable voice of Chief Bavin came through loud and clear: "Terry, you haven't taken that war bonnet back yet, have you?"

"Yes, sir, I did," I replied somewhat coolly.

"Get back in your car, go back down there, and seize it again," he said.

"What?" I said, not believing what I was hearing.

"You heard me; go back to Frank's and seize that war bonnet again, and that is an order. After further review in Washington we have decided to go through with the prosecution in this matter because the powers that be now feel it is one hell of a case after all. Terry, with this case we can settle the legal question of sale and forever put the issue to rest with the Indians. You need to get rolling and go back there and get our evidence. Then be sure and let my office know when we are going to court."

I couldn't believe what I was hearing. I just sat there for a moment in shock. Finally the bile rose up in my miserable carcass, and I gave the chief an earful he would never forget! "What the hell is the matter with you bastards? I hand you the case of the century to settle a legal issue that has haunted the Service for years, and you turn me down based on some lame damn excuse. You had the investigative report in your hands for the better part of several months, and you just now realized it was a good case? Did anyone even bother to read it before this horse-crap decision to return the bonnet was made? Then, to top it off, I get ordered to return the bonnet, and in the process get my ass eaten clear off by the subject of the investigation, and now you want me to go back on a hostile Indian reservation and seize the war bonnet once more? You can go to hell and take the horse you rode in on with you! If you want another Custer massacre, you lead the charge because you have less hair to lose than me!"

With that, let's just say my conversation with the chief (who was almost bald) was abruptly terminated.

I never did find out why the Service pissed backward on that investigation and then recanted almost immediately after I had been ordered to return the war bonnet. The issue of sale of eagle parts was not really settled until seven years later with another case called the Dion investigation, when a group of our undercover officers investigated a similar case in South Dakota. That case went to the Supreme Court, and the Service prevailed after years of legal battling and bad blood all around over Native Americans' right to sell eagle feathers (a very lucrative illegal market, I might add). With its finding in the Dion case, the Supreme Court once and for all made it plain that Native Americans did not have the right under their treaties to sell eagles or their parts and products.

I have often wondered how many more eagles we allowed to be killed and sold between my investigation and that one many years later. It probably would not have made any difference if we had prosecuted Frank Duschenaux, but I like to think it would have. The desire to take eagles is very strong among Native Americans today, especially among the more shortsighted and less law-abiding of the lot. There is so much money in the illegal eagle feather trade, nationally and internationally, that I doubt my case would have made much difference anyway. But you never know.

Looking back after all these years, I would say I got politically ambushed by someone with a large stake in the matter. As it turned out, no one was the winner—not even the Indians. However, there was so much manure scattered around Washington as a result of that investigation, I can't help but think there had to be a "pony" somewhere.

As a postscript to show how crazy things can get in the eagle feather trade and in Native American politics, I recently learned from an article in *PEER Periodical* (published by Public Employees for Environmental Responsibility [PEER]) that the Hopi Indian Nation in 1999 presented a federal permit to the National Park Service (NPS) to take forty golden eagles and an unlimited number of red-tailed hawks on the Wupatki National Monument in Arizona. The monument's superintendent denied the Hopis access to the park for such taking, citing supporting federal law, a decision that was upheld by the NPS regional office and the director of the NPS. A bit later Don Barry, then assistant secretary of the Interior for Fish, Wildlife, and Parks, allegedly overruled that decision and allowed the take to proceed. Word got out to the public and the press, and the Hopis, not surprisingly, withdrew their request (for now). The issue had become controversial, and, in my opinion, the American people would have brought this outrageous practice to a screaming halt and would have lynched those political folks for allowing such a dubious action in the first place. In addition, if the Hopis had been allowed to go into a national park and harvest eagles and other birds of prey, it would have been a matter of about two heartbeats before all five hundred other federally recognized tribes wanted authorization to do the same. I could foresee that permitted collection activity for religious and cultural purposes eventually being extended to not only all the national parks but the five hundred–plus National Wildlife Refuges and covering every other kind of plant (yes, plants) and animal of value until wholesale slaughter or commercial-market hunting would again be on the rise, this time in our most sacred sanctuaries.

Bear in mind that a really good double-train war bonnet, with well-matched feathers, done by a well-known Native American artisan, can command a price of up to $25,000! In Europe or Asia, ten times that amount may be paid for the same illegal item! If collection were allowed in parks and monuments, the problem would continue to increase. Then the Natives in Alaska would want the same privileges on the parks and national wildlife refuges in their back yard, and would get them because of the precedent set in the lower forty-eight states and the powerful but not environmentally friendly congressional delegation from Alaska. As if that were not enough damage, every other person in the nation is entitled under the Constitution to practice his or her religion. And if that religion happens to involve the great out-of-doors and feathers from the eagle, we will probably find white people requesting the same consideration as the Native Americans and possibly being granted the same opportunities. If such a situation were to occur, the natural resources, which belong to all of us, would be severely diminished or totally destroyed.

If Secretary of the Interior Norton allows the beginning of such a chain of events, then she will be as bad as the robber barons of the nineteenth century for dealing away another element of the few remaining precious natural resources of the land belonging to the American people. And all for a few people wishing to exploit wildlife under the often dubious excuse of a religious practice ...

Only time will tell, but if anyone cared to look around at the world of wildlife, they would discover that nature hasn't fared well at the hands of humankind. Let us hope that these destructive acts will not be further sanctioned by political forces lest we soon find many species facing the black hole of extinction—a result that may easily be accomplished for an animal at the top of the food chain such as an eagle.

3

The Wetland Easement Wars

WHEN THE VARIOUS ICE AGES in North America receded, they left thousands of footprints behind in the forms of shallow depressions gouged in the land by the weight and movement of their tremendous glaciers. Over time these depressions filled with water and in modern jargon became known as wetlands. Wetlands come in all shapes and sizes, from those that go dry by May to those that remain deep-water basins throughout the year, even during the driest of years. Many such wetlands are found in central Canada, northwestern Minnesota, southeastern Montana, and central to eastern North and South Dakota.

The wetlands area within these four north-central states creates a unique macroenvironment affecting just about every kind of life known to this sometimes harsh region of the United States. With the water of the wetlands, held by water-impervious soils within the basins, come the collateral plant communities. Then comes every kind of water-loving life form, from the smallest single-celled creatures to the complex warm-water fish communities in the larger, deeper basins. Following quickly in those footsteps come a myriad of avian creatures, from shorebirds dependent on the wetlands' biological communities to all the others that love water. With that living rush of aerial biomass also come the terrestrial animals to drink from the wetlands' life-giving glory. Historically these have been represented at or near the top of the food chain by the great herds of bison, elk, antelope, and deer. Working those living edges, the great carnivores followed the herds of ungulates, profiting indirectly but handsomely from the wetlands in the warm flesh taken from these grazing animals by the grizzly bear, wolves, and coyotes. Today, for the most part, those great herds are gone, with just remnants of their greatness left as records between the musty pages of books. The dainty deer and antelope still enjoy the wetlands' bounty, along with many other smaller species of wildlife, from mice to the clever coyote, but the great days of the larger animals are gone forever.

Early humans, once introduced to the horse, soon realized that these watered areas contained many birds and animals necessary for their survival, and today many of the more permanent wetlands still bear mute testimony of ancient humans' lifestyle and culture in the forms of tepee rings, burial mounds, vision quest sites, the occasional artifact, and numerous arrowhead-flaking sites. Then came modern humankind from Germany, Russia, Bohemia, Norway, Denmark, Finland, Sweden, and Ukraine, in their great wagon trains and later on in even greater numbers on the Iron Horse, with their dreams of equality, new homes, raising families, and other life adventures as they plowed their way across the waving seas of prairie grasses. They too realized the value of nearby water sources and settled throughout this vast watered region to raise crops, hay the abundant native prairies, freely graze their livestock, and raise their families. For years this balanced use of the land was in harmony with human aims. Then, with the Industrial Revolution that introduced new farm machinery in the 1800s, came changes that altered human life and the land forever. More land was put to the plow, much of which should never have been turned. The previously balanced use of the land through haying, raising varieties of crops, and raising livestock changed to a single-crop approach. Be it corn, wheat, barley, or flax, the plows broke major portions of the soil that had lain protectively over land untouched for eons. With that change, many farming the land now found the wetlands in the way of progress because they wanted the land under the water to increase their "production." Not realizing the value of the wetlands in everything from weather modification to providing subterranean percolation of water to their crops, especially during the dry years, humans rushed to drain the wetlands and put more land under the plow. At first, because of equipment limitations, drainage was limited. Then, as technological advances were made, drainage increased more and more until the new land rush was on.

This mad push to drain and put more land into single-crop production without any compensating conservation measures culminated in part in the great dust storms and land ruination of the 1930s.

After this disastrous time, many of the surviving landowners began to practice soil and water conservation in an attempt to restore the land to a modicum of its former fertility and production. However, depressed crop prices still kept many farmers in the business of wetland drainage in order to perpetuate their farms by increasing the number of acres producing crops. After all, it seemed that wetlands produced nothing but ducks, which often depredated the farmers' hard-fought-for crops. So in many cases efforts were made, especially as new drainage technology became available, to drain the remaining wetlands on farms. At about the same time, through the advancing science of wildlife biology and wildlife management, resource managers began to realize the value of the nation's wetlands and the part they played in the overall ecosystem. In the '30s, '40s and '50s, waterfowl populations in the lower forty-eight states fluctuated wildly based on the cycles of drought and recovery of the wetlands in the upper Midwest, or "duck factories," as they were called. Aerial and ground surveys soon showed that North Dakota alone produced almost 65 percent of the total duck population of the lower forty-eight states!

The wetlands' value to the land and associated plant and animal communities now unquestioned, the federal government began its wetland preservation programs. Early on the government, understanding the value of procuring land bases for waterfowl production, began to purchase large tracts of lands rich in wetlands and marshes for membership in the National Wildlife Refuge system. Realizing that many smaller (too small for national wildlife refuge status) valuable marsh lands remained, the government soon began buying such properties through another preservation program as Waterfowl Production Areas. Drainage still outpaced the rush to preserve some of the valuable marshes and wetlands, so the government instituted another wetland protection program in which wetland managers surveyed many parcels of private land and then offered the landowners written contracts to refrain from draining, burning, leveling, or filling any delineated wetlands. During dry cycles the lands could be farmed, but during wet years they had to be left intact in the form of the natural wetlands. In exchange the government gave the land-owners a one-time payment based on the landowner's wetland acreage under the new wetland easement contract. In time lands protected in fee title (National Wildlife Refuges, Waterfowl Production Areas) and lands under wetland easement contracts (no draining, burning, or fill-ing during wet years) numbered in the millions of acres in Montana, Minnesota, North Dakota, and South Dakota. However, with the advent of newer and better farm machinery, increased fuel and equip-ment prices, and reduced crop prices, the urge to put more lands, including wetlands, under the plow, superseded common sense and threatened the understanding of the lessons of history learned in the dust bowl era.

This point is about the time that I came into the picture. As a newly promoted senior resident agent, I was transferred to Bismarck, North Dakota, and placed in charge of both Dakotas for enforcement of federal wildlife laws. I remember walking into the Service's area office in Bismarck shortly after I arrived to meet some of my man-agement counterparts. One of the first I met was Area Manager Jim Gritman. Jim was an ex-marine, still wore a crew cut, and ran his state of North Dakota (all Service functions except law enforcement and research) like the U.S. Marine Corps. His men loved him, and he got the job done in short order owing to his no-nonsense approach. He had a powerful work ethic and feared absolutely no one, including the Service high brass all the way up to and including the director! He was a tough, commonsense wildlife manager with a mission and a time frame, and to his way of thinking, time was running out.

Striding up to me, he stuck out his hand and said, "Good morn-ing; my name is Jim Gritman, and I am the area manager for North Dakota. You're the new senior resident agent, I take it. What are your policies on wetland easement enforcement?"

I said, "Yes, I am the new senior resident agent, my name is Terry Grosz, and what the hell is a wetland easement?" To this day, I wish I had never asked that question. Having just arrived from my previ-ous duty station in California, where there were no wetland ease-ments at that time, I had no idea what they were, how valuable they were, or how damn controversial they would quickly become. I was soon to learn. Over the next two years of my enforcement service in the Dakotas, I was sworn at, had bawling women spit on me, had little kids hit me, had farmers threaten to kill me, had dogs sent after me, was chased with tractors, had crazies (who'd been in the prairie wind too long) threaten to kill me, saw old people break down and cry over being caught breaking the law, and had to deal with some officers of the Service looking the other way in an attempt to avoid the unpleasant rigors of wetland easement enforcement. All in all, I soon came to call the situation "the wetland easement wars."

The bottom line of the problem ran in many directions. Many of the farmers who had signed the original wetland easement contracts were getting older and passing on their farms and their contracts to their children. The children, ignoring the contracts because their folks had signed them, not they, were illegally draining the wetlands protected under the contracts, a criminal offense. Or there was such a push to put more lands into production that the contracts were just being stubbornly ignored by those now leasing the lands for farming. Or public agencies such as the township boards of small towns across the Dakotas chose to drain wetlands protected by contract because they felt that they were above the law. Or certain other federal agencies were paying the farmers to drain the very wetlands the Service was trying to protect. Or the very agency I worked for didn't really understand what a wetland easement was, didn't realize the value of those contracts, didn't care about the problems, or all of the above. Or the U.S. attorney's office was in constant battle with the Department of Justice, especially the solicitor's office, for assisting my tiny enforcement corps as we tried to enforce the contracts. In fact, the regional solicitor for Region 6 (prairie-mountain states) once had his higher-ups give the U.S. attorney's office in North Dakota a warning not to cooperate with my enforcement wing because he felt civil penalty litigation, not criminal prosecution, was the way to handle violations of wetland easement contracts. And as if that were not enough, he thought such cases should be processed only through his solicitor's office! I fought that notion tooth and nail because the solicitors (government civil attorneys) were so inept that a routine drainage violation was taking three to five years to adjudicate (a prosecution that normally took only fourteen to thirty days if handled criminally through the U.S. attorney's office), and in the meantime the farmer had often essentially erased the wetland basin from the face of the earth. Or the general political attitude, including that of a few federal judges (not Judge Benson of North Dakota, though, who was superb), was for setting a course of moderation and taking one's time before doing anything to rock the boat. Or narrow-minded North and South Dakota politicians without any sense of land history fought our enforcement efforts every inch of the way and made life unbearable for the Service directorate because of our unpopular enforcement efforts. Or our realty division (those setting up the wetland easement contracts with the landowners) felt that if I did anything to prosecute the folks illegally draining the current wetland easements, the willing seller market would dry up and they wouldn't be able to sell the wetland easement program in the future. Or I didn't have enough people or money to do the job right. I think you will get the picture of just how difficult the whole bloody mess of wetland easement enforcement was! It was some of the worst work I had to do during my entire career, and yet some of the best because when we were successful we could quickly restore the habitat for wildlife production.

After reviewing the laws protecting the wetland easement contracts and assuring myself of my right to criminally prosecute those violating the contracts, I set out a plan to get the illegal drainage of these wetlands under control. I met with Hal Bullis, U.S. attorney for North Dakota, and Assistant U.S. Attorney Lynn Crooks (two of only six attorneys I met in my thirty-two-year career whom I considered honorable and ethical beyond any doubt), and we instituted a fair and objective battle plan. My three agents in the two states and I would personally contact every easement contract holder and remind them of the history and legal terms of the contracts. We would also inform them that any further illegal drainage, burning, or filling of the wetland basins would result in criminal prosecution. That contact would then be followed up with a certified letter containing the same information. I would also go to every newspaper and radio station in the state with the message for the farming community that to violate the wetland easement contract provisions would result in criminal prosecution in the federal court system. During the informational process, we would also tell the landowners that *any* previous easement contract violation had to be rectified. After this meeting, I contacted every federal judge who would be involved in hearing such matters in North Dakota to inform them of my future plans. Following the chain of command, I notified my supervisors and theirs of our forthcoming actions to curtail illegal drainage in the Dakotas. Finally, anyone in the entire Service leadership who had anything to do with wetlands and their administration or management was also advised of the upcoming program.

Talk about a firestorm—it came from every point on the compass! It seemed that no one in the world of higher-ups had anything but negative reactions to heap on my head regarding the proposed program, with the exception of those land managers closest to the program that was being slowly drained to death in the Dakotas. The refuge, wetland, realty, and law enforcement teams held their collective breaths in the hope that I would succeed and not bend under the mounting storm of Service and political pressure. It seemed that everyone had an opinion or a criticism, but all were short on solutions. Even Clark Bavin, the chief of Law Enforcement, had no real understanding of the value of wetlands or the reason for the fuss I was kicking up. He told me several times that it would be better to keep the historical course and refrain from new wetland easement enforcement programs. Being the stubborn sort of lad I can be and not hearing any valid reasons to stray from my course, I kept the faith and continued on.

From the late summer of 1974 to the late summer of 1975, four Dakota-based agents trudged through years of neglect and basically nonenforcement of the easement contracts, contacting thousands of soon-to-be-unhappy landowners and farmers—more than ten thousand, to be precise! Because we never seemed to have adequate funding in the Division of Law Enforcement, Jim Gritman saw to it that we could use $50,000 of his money for travel and per diem compensation to get the job done. In addition, the entire refuge and wetlands contingent in North Dakota (where the illegal drainage problem was the worst and first to be addressed) was always there to support law

enforcement in our soon to be monumental efforts. In fact, out of
the hundreds of folks in North Dakota, I had only one field person
who refused to jump into the fray—so I just did his easement enforcement work for him.

When the enforcement program started in South Dakota a year
later (I had to do the states one at a time because I just didn't have
enough resources to do the work otherwise), the land managers were
somewhat reluctant to initiate such a controversial enforcement program. Their area manager, Rolf Walestrom, was just the opposite of
Jim Gritman, the area manager in North Dakota. Simply speaking, he
wanted no part of the wetland easement wars, or any rocking of the
boat. He seemed, in my opinion, content to let the farmers have their
own way with the wetlands and hoped the problem would go the way
of the prairie winds. If it hadn't been for one man at the law enforcement start-up meeting for all the South Dakota Service land managers,
I feel it would have gone that way. I met early one morning with all
my management counterparts in South Dakota and laid out the plan
to be spearheaded by my enforcement lads. I already had the U.S.
attorney's office on board—not as gung ho as the one in North
Dakota, but on board—and now I needed help from my own people,
whose own program was being gutted by the farmers through their
many styles of illegal drainage. When I finished my presentation with
a request for a teamwork approach, I was met with icy silence. There
didn't appear to be a bucket of guts in the entire room! I just stood
there in front of them for several awkward moments until Rolf finally
looked around and said, "Well there you have it, Terry. We don't want
your law enforcement program instituted here in South Dakota."

I couldn't believe what I was seeing or hearing. This was the Service's
own wetland management program, and they wouldn't stand up for
it! I just stood there looking at a bunch of hanging heads that didn't
want to look back at me. Then a lad in the back of the room stood
up, looking as if he had had a bad night, and said, "What the hell is
the matter with all of you? For years we have been getting the snot
kicked out of us under the wetland easement program, and all of us
have complained that the Division of Law Enforcement needed to
step forward and give us a hand. Now that we have a new man and

he is willing to do so, all I see in the room is a bunch of blobs of Jell-O sitting around hoping no one notices them. Well, I for one would love to have you come to my area of responsibility and help me get my illegal wetland drainage issues under control. My name is Steve Berlinger, and we can get together after this meeting is over and work out the particulars." He sat down and then jumped right back up. "You damn guys, including you, Rolf, ought to be ashamed of yourselves. I know I am personally ashamed of *all* of you. What the hell is the matter with all of you?" After this remark—a dangerous one for his career, since he had singled out his area manager!—he sat down again, and again I waited through a few moments of silence. Then one, and then another, and finally everyone in the room told me that they needed help and would support the program. Rolf, seeing that his management team was supportive of the new enforcement program, to his credit finally gave his blessing. I always made it a point after that meeting to see that when Steve needed assistance or support from law enforcement, or me personally, he got it, and *now!*

After that it was like a big family in both Dakotas trying to right a gigantic wrong. Knowing just how close the wolf was to law enforcement's door, everyone pitched in to assist their "hired guns." They fed us at their families' tables, gave us places to stay to keep the costs of motels down during the intensive individual landowner contact portion of the operation, fueled our vehicles from their refuge fuel stocks, lent us their mechanics to repair our vehicles, replaced our worn-out tires, and provided a ton of emotional as well as physical support. Keep in mind that while all of this was going on, we still had to do all of our other enforcement work as well as patrol the international border with all its illegal wildlife importation problems! And somewhere in there, we still had our families, or what was left of them, to consider. During this two-year period one of my agent's wives had a nervous breakdown, and another lost his wife of many years after a long illness. All of us were so busy, mostly testifying in court, that no one could even attend that officer's wife's funeral. ... The Dakotas can be harsh, in more ways than one.

Finally the day came on which, after following the federal judges' and U.S. attorneys' guidance, we were free in North Dakota to criminally enforce the terms and conditions of the wetland easement contracts, which had been in effect since the early 1960s but never systematically enforced! It was late summer of 1975, and many of the farmers were in the fields readying the land for the winter and next spring's planting. It was also the time of year in which the land was at its driest, so they could hook a plow into their small wetlands under easement contract and drain them without getting their tractors stuck. The plowing process not only drained the wetland but wrecked that basin for the future year's wildlife production because the plow would break the clay seal in the bottom of the basin, allowing the water to escape by percolation, or the farmer would place a deep furrow, which was actually a drain, in the lip of the basin and create a ditch so that any existing or future runoffs would find their way to that drain and out of the wetland basin. Others would bring in their own or contract ditching equipment and dig a drainage ditch, some of which were fifteen to thirty feet deep, through adjacent terrain, thereby destroying the wetland forever just so they could increase the harvest acreage of their land by bits and pieces and make another $1.58 on a bushel of wheat at the expense of the nation's wetland heritage.

For that period and during the next year, until I was transferred to Washington, D.C., as a senior special agent, my small cadre of officers and I, along with the ever-helpful refuge and wetland folks, went after those who chose to disregard our personal and written warnings and continued to illegally drain those wetlands under the protection of government contracts. Now that we had the official go-ahead to directly take on those violators, I took it upon myself to always travel the backcountry roads when I was going from point to point in the state so that I might catch someone in the act of illegal drainage. The Refuge Administration Act basically stated that it was illegal to injure any lands under easement contract. That meant that we government officers had to demonstrate injury to the land in order to meet that criterion. Having a drained wetland basin or one filled in with dirt, rocks, old car bodies, or manure met that element of the law. In addition, we had to show that the person who was the object of our legal attention had directly caused the injury to the wetland under contract or had performed the injury himself. In short, it was always best to apprehend the lad in the act of drainage. This wasn't totally necessary because of the other means of discovery, such as through the interview and affidavit process and the like, but it was the easiest to prove.

On a beautiful fall day in North Dakota, I was running the dirt roads to Valley City to meet a wetland manager regarding another drainage issue. Whipping over those roads as I usually did, I came over a hill to see a farmer out in an already plowed field with a large plow, hooking it into the lip of a large but shallow wetland, and pulling out about a one-hundred-yard drain into a barrow ditch along the very road on which I was traveling. Stopping, I got out my plat books and files on lands in that area under wetland easement contracts and had soon figured out what piece of land I was overlooking. The whole damned piece of land was under wetland easement contract! Hot damn, I thought; you finally have one in which you have the lad in the action of illegally draining a protected wetland! With that, I headed my patrol car down off the road, through the barrow ditch and right out into the field with my drainer. Pulling up alongside his tractor as he continued to deepen the ditch, I cruised slowly along beside the farmer until he became aware of my car. Stopping, he reduced the throttle on his tractor and, as I got out of my car, climbed down from his seat. I walked over to him, shook his hand, and then identified myself to him and asked who he was.

"Mr. Gromme, are you aware that this land is under wetland easement contract and can't be drained, burned, or filled without a permit?" I asked.

He looked at me for a second while we both heard the gurgling of water flowing from the wetland down his new ditch as it headed for the ditch alongside the county road. "Yes," he said, "but no one has said anything to us for years if we drained, and so I thought I'd take advantage of the fine afternoon now that my other farming is done and get rid of some of these wet spots."

"Well, that is not the thing to do, Mr. Gromme, considering you signed the contract years ago not to drain this wetland."

"Yes, but the Wildlife [as many of the farmers called the Fish and Wildlife Service] has never enforced the contracts. I watched my neighbors who are also under contract do the same thing to increase their production, and so I did it too."

"Were you not personally contacted this spring by one of my agents and advised not to drain any of your wetlands under contract?" I asked.

"Yes, I was, but I just figured you was bluffing once again and ignored what was said. I also ignored the letter I got from you folks because I felt it was like all the other hollow threats you folks have made over the years." I could see him getting all red in the face and neck, and finally he just blew up. "By the way, how the hell do you expect us farmers to feed the world if you government bastards continue to harass us? First we lose our markets, and then the price of our equipment and diesel fuel goes out of sight and our land taxes keep going up, and then you bastards come along and tell me I can't farm. I am just getting damn sick and tired of it." With that, he turned to go back to his tractor.

"Mr. Gromme," I said, realizing he was starting to really get hot under the collar, "I have some further business with you."

"I don't think so," he replied as he started to board his tractor. "I have some work to do before supper and need to get it done."

Walking over to his tractor, I said, "Mr. Gromme, I still have some business with you regarding this illegal ditch, if you don't mind."

"You and all the rest of you government parasites can go and piss up a rope as far as I am concerned," he said as he reached for the throttle. "I am *never* filling up that ditch, so stick that where the sun don't shine!"

"Mr. Gromme, if you don't let me finish my legal work with you, I will have no alternative but to arrest you for a violation of your easement contract and seize your tractor as evidence."

I could tell the words *arrest* and *seize your tractor* hit the nerve that needed hitting. Bailing off the tractor, he said, "What the hell do you mean, arrest me for digging a ditch on my own land? And, what do you mean by seizing my tractor. For what?"

"Mr. Gromme, you are aware of the presence of an easement contract covering certain activities on this land, drainage of covered wetlands in particular. Second, despite that knowledge and the presence of an easement contract on this land, you chose to illegally drain it anyway, a federal criminal violation—and in front of an officer of the law, I might add. You have also made it plain that I can go where the sun doesn't shine and you are 'never filling up that ditch.' How am I doing so far?" I asked.

Gromme cooled down a little as he began to see that there was a rather large fly in the ointment (me) and that I hadn't cracked a single smile during the conversation so far. I think he figured out that the rough-and-tough attitude he had exuded earlier was taking him nowhere and that he had better back off a trifle. "Well, what now?" he asked in a slightly more conciliatory tone.

"You will receive a federal citation with a mandatory appearance in court for the violation witnessed by me today. It is just as simple as that." When I uttered that statement, I quickly thought back on the year's hard labor it had taken to get to this stage. Yeah, *just as simple as that!* I thought. Taking out my citation book, I laid it on the hood of my car and, looking over at my farmer, who was now in total shock at what I was doing, asked for his driver's license.

"Can't I just fill up the ditch and we call it even?" he asked.

"No, not after your statement regarding filling the ditch," I replied. "You and others like you clear across the state were given clear verbal and written warning that this kind of activity on lands covered by wetland easement contracts would no longer be tolerated, and you chose to ignore it. Now you must pay the penalty, whatever that might be."

He handed me his driver's license, and as I started to write the very first ticket in this wetland protection program, he asked, "What is the fine for this?"

"I don't have the foggiest idea because you are receiving the very first ticket issued for this type of violation in the history of the program. There isn't any precedent for me to follow, so I can't tell you what will happen other than to tell you that you must appear in federal court on the date on this citation or be found in contempt of court. If that happens, a warrant will be issued by the court for your arrest, and that you will be."

Gromme just looked at me like a man in total shock at what was happening. He had been right when he pointed out that over the many years before my arrival in 1974, the Service, for whatever reason, had basically failed to enforce the terms and conditions of the wetland easement contracts. By the time I arrived in the state, there were almost 400 serious violations on the books in North Dakota and more than 150 in South Dakota because the message that had been sent to the contract holders was pretty weak-kneed! Well, with what was at stake, times were changing. ... They had to!

Gromme appeared in federal magistrate's court several weeks later and pled guilty. He was fined $500 and given thirty days in jail. The thirty days were suspended providing he never again appeared in that magistrate's court with a like violation. Gromme was also told by the judge that if the ditch were not completely filled up, with a 10 percent overfill (to allow for settling), within thirty days, he would find himself back in court posthaste for contempt of court. Man, the magistrate really read Gromme the riot act, and, as I later found out, for good reason. The judge, who was also into farming, wanted the word to get out, hoping the news would prevent a lot of other drainage problems from landing on his docket.

It was barely three days after Gromme's court appearance when Dave Goeke, the wetland manager from the Valley City District, was on the phone. "Terry," he said, "my phone has been ringing off the hook. Every farmer in my district is calling wanting to know what is going on. I have been telling them that the agents in the Service are now cracking down on the drainers and to avoid going to court, they had better fill up any ditches they have illegally dug over the years. I have also been telling them that we will be flying over all our easements shortly and that if we find any ditches, that information will be turned over to the agents for prosecution as well. Man, you can't believe what an impact that is having in my district. Ditches that were illegally dug years ago are being filled right and left." I could tell from Dave's tone that he was happy with the work to date, and *real* glad the agents were doing the dirty work, not him! I just grinned. I guess that was why we got paid the big bucks, and if that effort on our part took a little strain off our management counterparts, so be it. That little action with Gromme did have a great impact on the local farmers, and many got off the fence and left the illegal draining to their neighbors. Still, there were a lot of neighbors. …

DAVE GOEKE CALLED me one day as I was doing some administrative work in the Bismarck office. "Terry, that bit about us managers calling you guys when we had a tough nut to crack, is that still the process?"

I had told all the managers in the Dakotas during the many meetings we had held before dropping the hammer on the violators to give us a call if they had a bad one, and we would handle it or go along with them to provide protection. Though this suggestion might seem a bit overblown, it wasn't. The farmers in both of those states when I was there (including some farming kinfolk of my own), probably like those all over the country, were an independent lot. They had been fighting the elements; poor prices; disappearing markets; increased tariffs, taxes, machinery costs, and fuel costs; and government red tape all their lives. True, no one asked them to take up that profession, but many do it because it is the love of their lives, and because of that feeling, they are often intolerant of what they consider ignorant outside interference! Throw in the heat, constant wind, dirt, machinery breakdowns requiring $400 parts, missed meals, and threatening notes from their bankers, and some have a tendency to slide over the edge toward outright hostility. Such was the situation Dave was calling about.

"What do you have for me?" I asked.

"Well, I have two old bachelor brothers who are a little weird. They farm just north of Valley City and have a long, deep drainage ditch that cuts across two wetlands under easement contract. They had it put in this spring by a contractor and now tell me they will not remove it. To tell you the truth, they are kind of scary, and I would prefer it if you went with me on this one. Maybe if you lay the law down, they will comply and fill up the ditch."

"When do you want to go?" I asked.

"How about right away? The weather is such that if they get on it right away, they can have the ditch filled in about a week or so."

"I'll meet you tomorrow at your office at eight A.M., and you be ready to go. Also, if you have any other tough nuts on hold, let's do them at the same time. Last but not least, we are low on money, as always, and if you could provide me a tank of gas I would appreciate that very much."

"That is the least I can do, Terry. You bet. You help me with the Glopec brothers, and I'll gladly fill up your tank—two or three of them, for that matter."

The next morning I met Dave at his office, and with an armful of plat books and easement files, off we went to the little burg of Luverne, North Dakota. Dave directed me into a little farm that looked like all the other typical farms of North Dakota: a small house with a detached garage, both badly in need of paint. Clustered around the house were several shabby outbuildings that had seen better days, also in need of a coat of paint. The whole assemblage of buildings, land included, was probably worth about $50,000. Around the farmhouse, on its lawn and scattered about the outbuildings, was about $400,000 worth of farm machinery. As I said, it was a typical North Dakota farmstead in those days. The house was just able to keep the wolf away from the door, and a zillion dollars' worth of equipment was scattered about. ... Go figure. Getting out of the car, I took a quick look around that might give me a clue about the two bachelor brothers living there because all Dave would say was that they were "different." Yeah, they were different, as I was soon to find out!

Walking up to the front door, Dave knocked while I stood behind him and to one side. In those days I wore a Colt Commander .45 ACP with two extra magazines and figured that was enough firepower if things got hot. I was a good shot, and if I couldn't do it with that gun, then I didn't belong there anyway. Many of you readers, and probably my copy editor, may be thinking about now that I'm getting a little too "cowboy" about all this. Not really! Over the years I found that refuge and wetland managers tend to be fairly gently folks with a tendency to be a bit underdescriptive when explaining a tough issue. I was soon to wish I was carrying my .44 magnum!

A tall, thin man about sixty years old answered the door and politely asked, "Yes, what can I do for you?"

"John, it's Dave. Remember me, the man from the Wildlife?"

The man stared at Dave for a moment as if trying to assemble some knowledge from far back in the recesses of his memory. Then it registered. "Yeah, now I remember; the man from the Wildlife. Come on in." He turned and walked back into the darkened house as Dave and I followed. The second I stepped into the man's living room—at least I thought it was a living room—I was hit with a heavy, sharp, acrid smell that was so strong it almost made me sneeze! As my watering eyes adjusted to the dim light in the room, I became aware of the situation causing the intense smell. Aside from a narrow trail through the room, there was raw garbage covered with mold, the odd maggot, a world of flies, and fungus from the floor clear to the ceiling! I couldn't see anything in the way of furniture or windows, just garbage of every kind from floor to ceiling! In fact, if my shoulders had been any wider, I would have had to plow the garbage aside to get to where we were going.

Leaving that room before I could recover from my amazement, we walked into what must have been a functional kitchen at one time. To my left were a counter, cupboards, and a sink. Along that same wall, only farther to the right, was a range. To my right was a kitchen table with two chairs. The rest of the room was full of garbage clear to the ceiling! The cupboards were jammed full of garbage; the oven door was open and full of garbage; and in the sink was something that appeared to be liquid in nature but wearing a "coat of many colors." Never in my life had I seen such a mess! Everything not covered with garbage was indescribably filthy. The smell in this room was even more pungent than that in the first room because the garbage in the kitchen was composed more of food leavings—coffee grounds, eggshells, rotten vegetables, bread wrappers, moldy bread, meat bones, and everything else imaginable that comes from living in a place forever and never discarding any trash!

Trying not to touch anything and watching where I put my feet, I was introduced by Dave to John. John stuck out his hand, and I swear, for once I was not in the mood to show any friendship with the shake of a hand. I did it anyway and was careful what I used that hand for later on, especially when it came to touching any body parts.

Dave, as if it were old hat, sat down on a once-white kitchen chair, and John took the other after he had offered us some coffee. For once, I was sure glad I didn't drink coffee. The air was full of thousands of huge blowflies, so big they were hardly able to fly, and just about every pile of kitchen garbage was moving with maggots! There were so many, in fact, that they would roll off the steep sides of the garbage to the small trail on the floor and then scuttle back to their home of happy dreams just inches away to climb to the top once again! I just shook my head in disbelief and tried to limit my breathing to shallow puffs, not wanting to poison my lungs and die before I got out of this manmade hellhole.

Dave began to talk to John about the long and deep drainage ditch on his land, and once again (at my instruction) went over the facts of the preexisting easement contract on the land, John's knowledge of that contract, and the fact that John had ordered the contractor to ditch out the wetlands covered by the easement contract. John clearly admitted to everything, and I quietly said to myself, Good. Now that we have established all the elements of the crime, let's get this meeting over and be on our way! However, Dave kept trying to persuade John to fill up the ditch, and John flatly and stubbornly refused. He told Dave the ditch had cost too much; he was not going to fill it up, and that was final. I could tell by the way John spoke that that was his bottom line, no matter what. Dave looked at me as if seeking assistance, and as he turned I noticed he had a greasy three-inch-wide splotch clear across his uniform shirt where his shoulder blades had rubbed against the back of the chair. Ugh, I thought; he is taking that off before he gets into my patrol car, plastic seats or not!

"Terry," Dave said, "do you want to talk to John about this ditch?"

Realizing it would be up to me to try to get this hardheaded farmer to comply, I gave it a go. "John," I said, "we have a new enforcement program in the Dakotas regarding drainage of those wetlands protected under the easement contracts, and it doesn't leave any latitude for you to drain, burn, or fill those basins without being permitted to do so. In fact, after determining who did what to the wetlands, it is now standard procedure to issue citations to individuals if they fail to comply with our requests to restore the basins as they were before any ditching was done. Bottom line is, if you will not comply with Dave's request, I won't have any choice but to issue you a citation with a mandatory appearance in court and have you meet with the federal magistrate."

I saw his eyes dart to the sidearm on my hip, and then he said, "Why are you wearing that gun?"

Without batting an eye, I said, "Because it is part of the uniform, and I am required to wear a sidearm on duty as a law enforcement officer."

John just grunted, walked past me toward a garbage-filled staircase leading to a basement, and went down the stairs. Dave got all his papers back into his now-grease-covered folder and looked at me as if he were ready to leave, not to mention getting nervous. Watching John in case he was planning to come back armed, I saw him go to a closed door at the bottom of the stairs and take a key out of his soiled pants pocket. Inserting the key into the lock, he opened the door and called out, "Seth." I could hear something scrambling around in that trash-filled room and thought maybe he was calling his dog to turn him loose on us. But instead another filthy individual came to the basement door. John turned and walked back up the stairs, and this other man, maybe sixty-five or seventy years old, dressed in overalls and no shoes or shirt, followed. The entire front of his pants had been soiled by what appeared to be body fluids, and when he got closer the smell confirmed the thought. When they reached the top of the stairs, John introduced Seth, his brother, who had the wildest set of eyes I'd ever seen. A bony hand was thrust into mine before I could move away, and then Seth wouldn't let go. Finally I put my other hand on his filthy, blackened hand and pulled it away.

Seth said to John, "Shall I get the gun?"

"No, not yet," said John. "This man needs to talk to you, and then you can get the gun."

I looked over at John as if to ask what the hell he was saying, and he said, "As I been meaning to tell you, this is my brother, and he is in charge of the work on the ditch. You need to talk to him about getting it filled up. Convince him and we will get it filled up."

Realizing that I was talking to one madman, with another standing alongside me, I gave it a go anyway. By now Seth was starting to drool through the worst set of teeth I had ever seen, and his breath, even at a distance, was overpowering! I explained to the man behind those wild-looking eyes what I had told John, especially the part about getting the ditch filled up. Seth just looked at me for a moment and then turned to John and said, "Do I get the gun now?"

John said, "Yes, you can go and get the gun now."

With that and a whirl of surprising speed for a man of his vintage, Seth was down the stairs before I could even move. Damn, I thought, what the hell? Am I going to have to shoot a filthy, ancient, crazy man over an unfilled ditch? Dropping my right hand slowly to my pistol and without taking my eyes off the basement door, I told Dave to head for the car. But before he could move, up the stairs came Seth with a Civil War–vintage cap-and-ball rifled musket. My eyes darted to the nipple, and I could see that there was a cap on it! (This type of gun has a hammer that strikes the cap, which is filled with fulminate of mercury and crushed glass, on the nipple of the rifle. The cap ignites, firing a flame down the nipple, which has a hole in it, into the black powder in the barrel. When the powder ignites, it forces a lead ball or conical bullet resting on a wad over the powder out the barrel.) I wasn't sure whether it had been previously fired and not replaced with a new one, but I wasn't going to take any chances and find out the hard way.

"Do I use it now, John?" Seth asked.

"No, not yet," John replied.

"When do I get to use it?" he whined.

"Pretty soon," John replied, and at that point I noticed that his eyes were beginning to match his brother's! Realizing that I was dealing with a pair of certifiably crazy people and not wanting to shoot either of them, I made a bold move. Seeing that Seth did not have his finger on the trigger of the ready-to-fire weapon, I quickly reached out and removed it from his bony hands. The move surprised him, and he took a step backward without saying a thing. With that, Dave was by me in a flash, and when he passed me, creating a diversionary opportunity, I flicked the cap off the nipple of the rifle with my thumbnail. The cap spun off into the garbage on the floor, and neither of the men noticed what I had done. I quickly followed that move with a quick look at the gun and told John what a wonderful old antique it was. Having gotten his attention with my praise for the rifle, I hoped to defuse the situation a tad.

John said, "Yes, it is. It was my grandfather's, and he brought it home when he returned at the end of the war."

Realizing I at least had his attention, I said, "Well, you and Seth think about the ditch. It must be filled or you folks will have to come to court and settle up with the judge."

About then Seth wanted the gun back, and I handed it to him as if nothing out of the ordinary had occurred, minus the cap so he would not go wild on me. He didn't seem to notice the absence of the cap and persisted with the "Is it time to shoot?" routine. I headed out the path through what had been the living room, across the porch, and toward my vehicle. Dave was already in it, and I made for the car rather briskly because I wanted to reach safety before Seth discovered that he was lacking the cap on the nipple of his rifle. Getting into the car, I looked back to see the brothers talking on the porch as they continued to watch us. Starting up the car, I backed out of the driveway as Seth pointed the rifle toward us several times, then drove down their lane and out onto the county road, keeping an eye on my two crazies the whole time so I could return fire if necessary.

"Damn, Dave, next time the farmer you want me to meet is that bad, let me know in advance."

Dave just grinned and said, "We got out alive, didn't we?"

Before I could answer, I was distracted by a terrible odor. I said, "What is that awful smell?"

Taking a whiff of himself, Dave said, "It's us. Isn't that the pits? We picked up the smell of that garbage pit of a house on our clothes, and now we smell just as bad as it does."

With that, we headed for home so we could clean up. For him it was only a few minutes' drive. For me it took several hours, and even with the windows open it was bad. When I got home, my wife made me undress in the garage before she would let me into the house, and even after a shower a faint remainder of the smell was still there.

To avoid having to kill someone, I told Dave to let the ditch ride, and when they died and the farm was sold, we would square the situation away with the new owners. The ditch was filled in September 1977 after the saner of the two brothers died, leaving the one who was crazy as a loon to fend for himself. The county removed him once his condition became clear, and I heard from Dave that the county declared the house a health hazard and burned it to the ground. The farm was sold, and the new owners complied with the easement contract (which was transferred to the new owners). I ran into a lot of crazy dirt farmers in North and South Dakota, but none were as bad as these two gentlemen. I guess they had been out in the prairie winds a little too long. ...

LATER THAT YEAR, with the help of Jim Gritman's money, I was able to put together a team of six agents from adjoining states to help get the existing violations in the Dakotas prosecuted. Not being able to get the job done with just my three officers, in addition to all our other work, I figured the more heat I could put on the dirt farmers, the more they would police themselves and clean up their violations—and it worked! As I usually did in such matters, I held a briefing for all the officers working this detail and spent several hours going over the problem, its history, legal angles, and the type of people we were dealing with. This time we were working in the Devils Lake region of the state, and the farmers there were known for their across-the-board hatred of the easement contracts and those who attempted to enforce the contracts under the law. I was especially pointed in instructing the officers that they were to wear sidearms all the time, and I went over the federal firearms policy regarding when a weapon could be used. I could tell that the officers new to this kind of work and this part of the country passed that warning off as just hot air. Oh well, I thought; they will learn in one meeting with a farmer, or two at the outside. I told the lads that because of recent rains making the ground difficult to work, we were giving the farmers in this area forty-eight hours to fill up their ditches before we returned and cited them. In extreme cases, we could give the farmers more time to fill in the ditches if it appeared to be needed. With that, off the teams went to their various assigned areas.

That evening when they returned, I could tell that the farmers had stuck it right up their tail ends! Every one of them had been in several shouting matches; several had had farmers threaten to whip them right on the spot; and worst of all, those working near the Fargo and Grand Forks areas in the Red River Valley had found zero wetlands! The farmers in those areas had completely erased any and all traces of any wetlands covered under the existing easement contracts from the face of the earth. By not enforcing the prohibitions over the years, the Service had allowed them to get a head start on the process of destruction, and the farmers had taken that advantage and run with it! Man, were my guys mad. They had tried to be nice guys and had been mauled by the farmers. They certainly learned a lesson that day, and a damned good one.

Come the second day, they all went out with the bit in their teeth and, come nightfall, had fared a little better. However, they had yet to discover their first wetland in the Red River Valley (eastern North Dakota)! All that was left was flat-as-a-plate-of-puke farmland. They could see the wetlands on the old aerial photos, but when they conducted ground inspections, it was plain to see that the farmers had erased those areas for all time. In fact, though hardly anyone in North Dakota will come out and say it because of the power of the farmers in that state, the Red River Valley floods that buried the city of Fargo in flood waters a few years back more than likely occurred because of the farmers draining every wetland to the north. When the heavy snows that year melted, instead of draining into the wetland basins and slowly percolating out, the waters rushed into the Red River Valley drainage because they had nowhere else to go, and down the flood plain they came with a vengeance. As the good people of Fargo found out, it isn't nice to mess with Mother Nature. ... The good people of the Devils Lake area are now finding out the same with their flood plain problems, high water tables, and the historically high waters of the lake. What *good stewards of the land* (a favorite political term of former Secretary of the Interior Babbitt) the farmers have been to the north of the Red River Valley when it came to draining every wetland in sight, thereby reducing that land's ability to retain water as well.

By day three my lads had begun to work their way west from the Red River Valley area and ran into an even meaner group of farmers. This time they reached a draw, and many farmers found themselves out until midnight filling up their illegal ditches to avoid working their way through the federal court system in Devils Lake. That magistrate was a good one. He was honest, ethical, and a damn good judge for the times and the problems at hand. In his court everyone got an opportunity to address the issues, and then he made his rulings. I always found his decisions to be fair, and the farmer never left his court without understanding what his marching orders were. I never had a repeat offender go through that system in Devils Lake either!

By day four my lads were settling into their traces, and we were getting a lot of work done. My law enforcement partner and I picked up a wetland manager as a ride-along and headed out. I had the usual number of minor ditches that needed filling, and my first three contacts were friendly enough. Of course, maybe having another lawman alongside and a wetland manager providing technical assistance had something to do with it. The farmers admitted they had put in the illegal ditches and that they had been wrong in doing so. They agreed to fill in the ditches with a 10 percent overfill. I had no reason to disbelieve the lads, so we moved on. The day was getting warm, so I took off the light vest I had been wearing to conceal the sidearm on my right hip. Because the last three contacts in this neck of the woods had been with reasonable folks and I didn't want to piss anyone off unnecessarily, I took off my sidearm too and shoved it under the seat. Remember, now, I had directed all my guys to wear their sidearms at all times. Oh well, being the boss, I guess I could break the rules if I wanted. ...

Farmer number four that day was a chap who had steadfastly refused to fill in his ditches and had basically told our wetland manager to take a hike. Heading for his house in the Starkweather area north of Devils Lake, I pulled into his yard amidst a bunch of barking dogs. The man's wife came to the door, and when I told her I was looking for Robert Grimn, she said he was out in the fields. She gave me directions, and we headed for the field she had indicated. It just happened to be the one in which we had located the illegal ditch coming from a large wetland covered under an easement contract. Driving to the edge of the field, I could see Grimn working in the middle of the freshly plowed field, working a forty-foot harrow to break up the clay-heavy clods of dirt. We parked the car, walked out to the area where he was working, and waited in a spot he would pass once he returned from the far edge of the field. As he approached the spot where we were standing, I moved away from the other two lads to where he would make his next pass and stood there. Pulling up alongside me in his huge eight-wheeled tractor, he stopped in a huge cloud of dust, completely hiding me from view for a few seconds. I ignored this "friendly" gesture. When the dust had subsided enough that I could see him, I moved over to the rear tire of his rig and, taking out my badge, tried to identify myself over the still roaring, high-revving engine. He had not backed off on the throttle one bit, making it extremely difficult for me to be heard even when I shouted.

"Mr. Grimn?" I shouted.

"Yeah," was his response. He was obvious unhappy at being stopped.

"My name is Terry Grosz, and I am a special agent for the Fish and Wildlife Service. I wonder if you might reduce the throttle a bit so we could talk about that three-hundred-yard-long ditch over there in the southwest corner of your field?"

"What about it?" he responded.

Seeing that I was getting nowhere over the noise of the roaring engine but realizing that that was the way he wanted it, I continued shouting. "Mr. Grimn, that ditch is in violation of your easement contract, and I need to talk to you about getting it filled."

"I am not filling that ditch, and you can stick it in your ass," he growled. With that, he slid the tractor into gear, and it lurched forward at a high rate of speed! I was in imminent danger of being crushed by the large set of dual wheels just inches from my left shoulder. Knocked sideways, I somehow managed to get away from the spinning dual wheels, only to find myself facing another danger. Immediately at my heels was the hurtling leading edge of the forty-foot harrow Grimn was towing! A harrow is a flat-on-the-ground, rectangular, steel-framed piece of equipment with many crossbars, which are dotted at regular intervals on the bottom side with six- to eight-inch spiked teeth. The harrow is dragged over the plowed field at a pretty good clip, breaking up the clods of earth in preparation for the planting that is to follow. If I fell under this piece of rapidly moving equipment, I would immediately be torn to pieces by the hundreds of harrow teeth weighted down by the many hundreds of pounds of steel framing! I am not sure how I got clear, but I am sure that my two guardian angels had something to do with it. The short of it was that I had to sprint off to the side ahead of that harrow, now flying down the field at my heels. Because it was forty feet wide, I had to run to get outside the twenty feet that hung out on my side of the tractor. Somehow I got outside that instrument of death in the split second after almost being tripped by it, and then, mad beyond belief, I ran alongside the tractor yelling for Grimn to shut it down or else! I was so mad, I'm sure he heard me, even sitting inside that cab and over the engine noise! In fact, thank God for the hot day and my having left my sidearm in the car. If I had been wearing it, I would have shot Grimn clear out of that cab for felony assault and battery on a federal officer! The fact that he had nearly hit me with his tires, which had almost dragged me under their rubber lugs, and then nearly clipped me with the harrow, which would have killed me if I had stumbled and fallen under it, certainly would have qualified Grimn for the plowing of other, more ethereal fields than that one in North Dakota that fine fall day, if you catch my drift.

Stopping his tractor, a contrite Grimn got out of the cab and, walking around the front of the tractor, said, "I guess I shouldn't have done that." Those were the only words he got out of his mouth before ten minutes of one of the world's finest ass chewings! I made it very clear to everyone within a country mile what he had done wrong. I told him that if I had not been fast on my feet, he would have been facing murder charges. Then I discussed how lucky he was that I was not armed and that, if I had been, his lifeblood would be oozing out of him onto the floor of the tractor at that very moment. Then I launched into why I was there in the first place, namely, that goddamned ditch illegally draining one of *my* wetlands! I was so mad that I don't remember all I said, but the bottom line was that he had only six hours (remember the forty-eight hours I had directed my men to give all the other farmers) to fill his ditch with an overfill, and if it weren't done in that time frame, I was coming back to throw his ass and that of the tractor he rode in on into the nearest federally approved jail, and when he hit the floor, he would find himself so far back in the bush the chickens there would have square faces!

At that point I realized that I was yelling at about the same decibel level where his tractor had been when we first met. Yeah, it was certainly obvious that I was *furious!* The whole time, the man just hung his head and said nothing. He could tell I was pissed at almost having been killed by a damn pissed-off farmer over a three-hundred-yard-long ditch that was there illegally in the first place! I finally ran out of things to say, so I said again, "Don't forget. That ditch filled in six hours or you are going to jail, and what happens after that won't be pretty." With that, I turned and stomped off only to remember that I had two other chaps with me. Turning, I located them about twenty yards away, standing silently and wisely avoiding involvement. They could tell I was madder than a wet hen and chose to keep their distance until I cooled down. I normally don't get that riled up unless someone is trying to shoot me. I guess getting crushed by a huge tractor and a forty-foot harrow would qualify in that department!

Walking back to my car with my lads silently walking at my side, I jerked open the door and, reaching under the seat, retrieved my pistol and strapped it on. To hell with what these folks think about my wearing a weapon in plain view, I thought. From now on I would give myself a fighting chance and not end up being ground up like a damn old dirt clod. Looking back over my sedan at the farmer, I could see him unhooking the harrow and heading for the barn.

"Let's go," I said to my two still silent officers, "we are burning daylight." We loaded up and, knowing where we were going next, I headed on down the road.

I had driven about four miles in total silence when Marty, an agent on loan from Missouri, said, "Lose your cool much, boss?"

With that, I got to laughing, as did my two partners. In fact, we all began laughing so hard at the picture of me standing there in the field yelling at the poor damn dirt farmer that I had to pull over until the tears left my eyes so I could safely drive once more. After our great laugh at my perilous escape we managed to meet with two more farmers, who agreed to comply with the terms of their easement contracts, before Grimn's six-hour stay was up. We returned to the field where I had run for my life and drove across it to check the illegal drain. What we saw made all three of us just roar again. I actually had come back hoping that Grimn would not have achieved the impossible in his six hours. In fact, there was no way he could have filled that three-hundred-yard-long ditch, as deep as it was, on his own. But there it was—totally filled from end to end with about a *four-foot* overfill instead of the normally required 10 percent! He would need a tank to get over the huge overfill he had laid in that ditch if he wanted to farm the area on the other side in the future! It was apparent that Grimn had gotten several of his neighbors together and used at least three crawler tractors with large blades in order to fill that ditch in such a humongous style. The three of us laughed until our sides hurt. It was apparent from the thousands of cubic yards of earth moved that my message had more than gotten through to Grimn and would be reinforced every time he went into that field and looked at his eighth wonder of the world blocking any future farming operations.

Neither of us had truly realized the danger of that moment hours before, but today, so many years later, I bet both of us sure do. Come to think of it, maybe my guardian angels were working overtime for Grimn as well as for me. Rarely did I go into the field unarmed after that.

DURING THE LATE SPRING of 1976, Ralph Fries, refuge manager in the Devils Lake Wetland Management District, called me with a problem. It seemed that a subordinate manager, in his backcountry travels in the Cando area of North Dakota, had discovered a farmer on a twenty-year easement (good for only twenty years, unlike most of the others, which were perpetual) who had been pumping out a large wetland basin. Every time Ralph's people on the ground went by the wetland, they noticed that its water level was getting lower and lower. There were no ditches around it, and after a thorough ground inspection the lads discovered tractor tire tracks next to the basin, and another set of tracks as well. Then the lads found that the prairie grasses had been smashed down as if a pipe had laid on them, and walking up to the dirt road adjacent to the wetland, they discovered those pipe tracks going across the road and down the bank on the other side. At the end of the tracks' they found a spot where a tremendous amount of water had emerged, smashing down the grasses and spilling into the barrow ditch. From there the water, which had been illegally pumped out of the protected wetland, had moved down on that farmer's neighbor to the south.

Telling Ralph I would be in that area no later than the next week, I got the coordinates for the place where this operation was going on and hung up. Sitting there trying to get a bunch of case reports typed for the U.S. attorney's office, I thought, What next? I never should have asked. Pumping a wetland dry was a violation of the statute protecting the wetland easements, and yet these farmers just kept trying every way possible to get out from under the contracts they had happily signed earlier for the money. I made up my mind that if I caught that chap, I was going to seize not only his pump but his tractor as well. If those folks wanted to play hardball, I knew just the catcher for their team.

For the next month, every time Ralph and I were in the area being pumped, we drove by. We were never able to find the tractor and pump in operation so they could be seized. It was almost as if the man knew we were coming. Then one Sunday afternoon, when I should have been home with my wife and kids having a nice chicken dinner with all the trimmings, I happened to be in that neck of the woods. Swinging down by the wetland without any hope of catching my lad, and still thinking of that chicken dinner, I rounded a turn in the road and by damn, there it was! So the crafty old farmer was pumping on Sunday afternoons when all those in the immediate area were home where they belonged, after church, having their chicken dinners. Pulling alongside the running tractor, I parked my car, took my camera, and got out. Alongside the running tractor, hooked up to a power take-off unit, was a portable pump. The pump was pumping water for all it was worth up out of the protected wetland, across the road in an eight-inch pipe, and over the side into the barrow ditch. As nice a case as anyone ever wanted to make, I thought as I got out my notebook and diagrammed the area and then took pictures to back up my notes. Then I took close-ups of the serial numbers of the tractor and the pump in preparation for seizure. I had no sooner finished than I saw a red-and-white Ford pickup come hurtling down a road from a farm about half a mile away. It went out of sight behind a small hill, and pretty soon I could hear it coming down the road over which the pipe pumping water was laid. It sounded like it was flying. Slamming up over the hill, the Ford roared down to where I was standing by the tractor with my camera in hand and skidded to a stop amidst flying rock and dirt. Out stepped a mountain of a man, at least six foot eight in height, and it was apparent from the get-go that he was more than pissed!

"What the hell are you doing by my tractor?" he bellowed.

Hoping to defuse a situation that might be uncomplimentary to my body, I said, "My name is Terry Grosz, and I am a special agent for the Fish and Wildlife Service. I am here investigating what appears to be a violation of the Refuge Administration Act, namely, the illegal drainage of a covered wetland."

"I don't care what the hell you're doing, just get the hell off my land," he continued to shout as he strode toward me at a rather brisk pace.

Taking out my badge and credentials, I held them up for him to see and said, "The authority I carry as a federal officer allows me to enter private land if I feel a violation of law that I am empowered to enforce is ongoing. Besides, I am standing on the county road right-of-way, the same as where your tractor is sitting."

Those words had little effect on the giant as he continued toward me as if to throw me off his land, and a few miles farther for the general good of things! Striding right up to me and then thinking better of his plan because I wasn't a little guy either, he stopped and said, "Let me see that badge again."

Digging it out of my shirt pocket, I held it up for him to see as he quickly reached for it. Just as quickly pulling it back, I said, "You will just have to look at the badge from there. I don't surrender it to anyone other than someone who is entitled to possess it."

He looked as if I had stung him and then said, "What's wrong with what I'm doing? I'm just taking a little water off the top that was left here last winter by the snows so I can get my tractors closer to the edge of the wetland when I'm plowing."

"No," I said, "that is not how it is done. During dry years you are legally entitled to farm as much of the wetland as you can. But during wet years you must leave all the water alone in the basin. That is the core premise of the contract. The wetland is like a living organ. Sometimes you win and get to plant more ground, and sometimes the ducks win and they get more of a pond to paddle around in."

"Screw the ducks," this pleasant person bellowed out. "All them bastards do is eat up and trample my windrowed crops." In the far reaches of the north country, sometimes the growing season is so short that the crops won't ripen on the stalk. So the farmers mow and windrow their crops, leaving them on the ground. If the weather cooperates, this system allows the crops to ripen more quickly. However, when a farmer lays wheat or barley on the ground, it becomes accessible to the ducks trying to put on a layer of fat before migration. In no time, they can make a mess of one's hard work and grain crop.

Changing the subject, I said, "Is this your tractor and pump?"

"Who the hell wants to know?" he curtly responded.

Man, by now I was really getting tired of his mouth and belligerent attitude. "As an officer of the Service investigating a criminal violation, I am. Is this your tractor and pump?" I asked once more.

"You're damn right it is, and so what?"

"Did you place it here and start the pumping of the water out of this basin and over into the barrow ditch?" I asked.

"Who the hell else would?" came the answer in the arrogant tone I was becoming used to.

"Well, did you place the tractor and pump here and start the pumping of the wetland over the road?" I asked once more.

"You're damn right I did. I already told you I was trying to just top off this wetland so I could get my tractor in closer to the basin. I am here to tell you that you guys can take back this goddamned wetland easement contract any time you want to. In fact, just as soon as it expires in a few years, I am going to drain this wetland and every other one on the property and pull up every tree around them as well. Then I will get you bastards off my back once and for all," he huffed.

Damn, a typical farmer. Stand in line with their hands out for the money the government is willing to pay for what the farmer considers a worthless piece of real estate, namely, a "can't do anything with it anyway" wetland. Then, when he has the means to drain it, he is pissed at the government for the contract that the farmer often initiated! It just doesn't figure, I thought. The dirt farmer stands around with his hand out all the time, yet if the government wants some control or compliance on the part of the farmer for its largesse, he acts as if he has been deflowered! Without another word, since I had all the evidence of the crime that I needed, I walked over to my patrol car and retrieved some evidence tags. Walking back to the tractor, I shut off its engine and placed one tag on the steering wheel.

"What the hell are you doing?" he shouted, walking forward as if he were going to remove the evidence tag.

"Mister, I don't know what your problem is, but if you touch that tag, which is now tied to a piece of government property, in addition to the refuge violation you will have another hanging around your neck for destruction of government property and interfering with a government investigation." The tone of my voice finally got through to my rather mouthy chap, and he froze in his tracks with his hand outstretched toward the tag. "Think it over because once you cross over that line, there is no coming back," I added quietly.

The man held his hand out for a few more seconds, all the while staring at me intently, and then went verbally berserk! I quietly and without a lot of fanfare lowered my hand to the butt of my pistol. He was a huge man, and even though I was no slouch in size, I knew that given his explosive temper and matching size, I would have my hands more than full. Throwing his hat down on the road, he stomped it flat, all the while cussing up a blue streak. I don't think he missed anyone in his rantings and ravings, which included every kind of government scum that left a trail of slime. I just stood off to one side and let him go on with his tantrum, hoping he would confine the stomping to his hat. About that time I noticed movement in the pickup and, quickly glancing that way, saw a boy about thirteen or fourteen getting out of the truck on the passenger side. It quickly became apparent that the lad was paralyzed from the waist down and was awkwardly trying to stand and close the door. He had on the type of crutches that attached to his forearms. When he finally completed the process of getting out of the pickup, he began to relieve himself at the side of the road. Nothing wrong with that, I said to myself, but this kid must be this man's son.

Getting a thought that might take a little steam out of the still raging-like-a-bull old man, I said, "Say, is that your son?"

Pausing just long enough in his stomping about to take a quick glance toward the pickup, he said, "Yeah, so what?"

"What kind of legacy are you going to leave him if you end up draining the wetlands on your farm and level it flat?" I asked. I figured a question like that might calm him down and make him think about what he had said earlier about draining the land dry. Man, did I ever get a surprise.

"Screw him!" he shouted. "No one left me anything, and I will be damned if I will leave anything to that sorry piece of crippled crap! He is on his own. If he can't make it, then he deserves to die!"

I was floored! I had never heard a parent speak about one of his offspring like that! Here was a father with a handicapped son who apparently didn't care if the boy lived or died. The boy could probably make it as a farmer if his dad helped him, especially if he left his son the farm, but no. He apparently hated the boy for what he represented, and that bile was right on the surface. Feeling hurt clear to my soul for that kid, I walked to my patrol car and called Bismarck via the radio towers. Soon, at my request, the sheriff's office had called the lads at J. Clark Salyer National Wildlife Refuge to the northwest, and they had agreed to send a truck and trailer to fetch my seized tractor and pump. Returning to the farmer and expecting the very worst, I said, "Sir, I will need your driver's license, please."

"What the hell for?" he said, continuing to speak well above a normal tone.

"You are going to get a citation for violating the terms of the wetland easement contract you signed some years back, and I need that information so I can fill out my seizure tags."

That sent him into orbit once more, and I had to wait a few minutes while he verbally covered what he thought of me and my lineage as well as my employer, the U.S. government. Finally he cooled down a bit and then tried to bargain with me. "I'll tell you what, officer. I will remove my tractor and pump and swear to you on my mother's grave that you will have no trouble from me ever again. Is that a deal?"

"You are a little late for that, my friend," I said. "The wetland has been reduced by at least a third of its surface area, and you have plowed all the way to the current water level, effectively destroying any and all vegetation around the wetland. No, you are a little late to be interested in obeying the law at this stage. Also, as you probably heard, there are some folks on the way to seize your tractor and pump, and before I leave you will receive a citation with a mandatory appearance in federal magistrate's court in Devils Lake."

With a long, hard look, he finally reached into his rear pocket, withdrew his wallet, and handed me his driver's license. I breathed a little easier because he would have been a tough one if he had chosen to have a go at me. Turning and seeing his son still standing by the side of the truck, he yelled, "Get your worthless ass back inside the truck before I come over and lay a club on the side of your goddamn head!"

I almost said something, and I am sure that if I had it would have led to fist city. At that moment, I couldn't think of anything I would rather have done than beat that man to a bloody mess with my fists, and not for the easement violation either. ... He went on to pay a $500 fine and thirty days in jail (suspended), and I never saw him again. Rudy Dahlstrum, as I came to know him, went to J. Clark Salyer National Wildlife Refuge after the court proceedings and retrieved his court-ordered-returned tractor and pump, but not without cussing out the refuge staff and discussing their lineage as well. He had a twenty-year easement on his property, and when I revisited that area eighteen years later, I could hardly recognize it. His entire farm was minus every single wetland, and the soil throughout was ashy gray in color (almost devoid of humus). It looked as if he had accomplished what he wanted to do, but it appeared that the prairie winds had blown all his topsoil to Kansas in the process. Driving by, I noticed a large crowd of people gathered around an auctioneer in the farmyard. It seemed that Rudy had gone belly-up and the farm had been sold. All that remained was the farm equipment, which was being auctioned. Driving into the yard, knowing that Rudy would probably not recognize me after all those years, I arrived just in time to see the tractor and pump from that day eighteen years earlier being auctioned off. What irony, I thought as I turned to leave, passing the handicapped boy, now a man, and his mom standing off to one side sadly watching the proceedings. Their innocence wasn't the only thing that was lost, I thought as I sadly drove by a once rich farm, now worn out from abuse.

JOHN "COOP" COOPER, my agent from Minot, and I headed north on state Highway 83 toward the town of Bottineau. John had a few wetland easement cases he wanted to work, and since I was his supervisor, I thought it a good time to work together and observe how my man operated in the field. It was late spring, and North Dakota had just finished having one of its surprise blizzards. It wasn't bad as far as blizzards went, but it did leave about two feet of snow on the ground and killed a lot of cattle. As the two of us headed north and then east on state Highway 5, I got a warm feeling. All that snow meant the farmers would not be able to get out early to drain, and with this wet snow, a lot of wetlands would be jug-full of water, much to the happiness of the world of birds utilizing such habitats. John had four easement violators we planned to visit that day, and then we were going to meet with a bunch of refuge folks and revisit our wetland easement enforcement policy to see what was working and what wasn't.

Our first contact would be the John Schramn farm just south of Bottineau. Working off our plat book and maps, we soon located the entrance to the property. According to our files, it was a small farmstead, only 640 acres. John Schramn had been the original signer of his easement contract, and according to Cooper, this was his first violation in over twenty years. The violation was a ditch that went to three wetlands under contract, draining all three into one long ditch, which emptied into a barrow ditch, partially flooding his neighbor to the south. His neighbor had complained, and as a result we were there that fateful day.

Driving into the muddy, wet farmyard, we saw the layout of a typical poor dirt farmer: buildings run down and in need of paint. Fences all askew, and a few motley chickens trying to find something to eat in the snow and mud. The house was poorer than usual, being at most a one-level, three-room home. From the outside it was nothing more than a tarpaper shack, and in need of paint and repair at that. Pulling up out front, John and I were met by a new combine parked in the front yard that had probably cost four times what the house was worth. In front of the door to the house was a ten-foot-high drift of snow from the recent blizzard. John and I crawled up one side of the hardened snow and slid down the other to the front door, and then Cooper knocked. At first there wasn't any sign of life, but finally we could hear some rustling inside. Coop and I had decided before we got there that John would handle John Schramn and I would act as observer and backup if any were needed.

Soon the door was opened, and there stood a very old man. "Mr. John Schramn?" Coop asked.

"Yes, it is; what can I do for you?" he responded.

"Mr. Schramn, I am John Cooper, special agent for the Fish and Wildlife Service. I am here today to talk to you about several ditches on Section 18 of your land. May we come in?"

"Yes, come on in." With that he walked back into the house, and we followed. As I said, it was a tiny home. Once inside we found ourselves in a kitchen without running water and with an old-fashioned wood stove merrily heating away in the corner. "Can I get you fellas a cup of coffee?" Mr. Schramn asked.

Coop accepted (standard fare in a farmer's home in the Dakotas), and I declined because I never learned to drink the stuff. Coop and Schramn sat down at a small kitchen table with only two chairs to examine the aerial maps Coop had brought along with the easement files so he could show the violation in graphic form. I just stood there and looked around. Through a doorway from the kitchen was a living room, and almost behind me was what I figured was a bedroom with a blanket draped from the top of the doorjamb to the floor instead of a door. That was it! Damn, I thought, even on my government salary I lived better than this. No two ways about it, this man was nothing but a hardscrabble farmer holding on for dear life by his toenails!

As Coop laid out the maps and other documents on the table, Schramn hunkered over them, trying to figure out where his farm was. Once he got oriented, Coop said, "Mr. Schramn, there is a deep ditch leading to these three small wetlands and then out to the barrow ditch along the road. That ditch is draining those wetlands in violation of the easement contract. Now, looking at the original easement contract, I see you were the one who signed the contract, so I know you were aware of the restrictions against any drainage. Did you put that ditch in draining those wetlands, or did you have it contracted?"

Until then Schramn had just listened and said nothing. Now, in a heavy German accent, he said, "I haff done it myself. I needed more land to farm, and I drained dose vetlands mit my tractor und plow. They drain goot now."

Coop took a quick look at me like, oh man, here we go. And go we did. ... For the next twenty or so minutes, Coop would go over the contract and the presence of the illegal drain in very simple terms. Then Schramn would admit to doing the drainage, and then Coop would tell him that it was illegal. Then Schramn would tell Coop, "Yes, butt dat ist my land," and the conversation would start all over again. In this situation, all we wanted was for the man to fill in the ditch, and we would call it even and be glad to leave this poor soul alone.

Then, without warning, out from behind the blanket to the bedroom came this little old gnome of a woman. She had to be at least ninety years old, wrinkled as a prune, and covered with an old print chicken-feed sack for a dress from head to toe. It appeared that all she had done was cut a hole in the top of the sack for her head and neck, plus two arm holes in the sides. She was very short, and I could see her feet sticking out the bottom of the sack without any socks or shoes. Her hair was dirty and hung in a bowl haircut down to her shoulders, and she was wringing her hands. I could tell in a heartbeat that she was upset, and our being government men carrying badges and weapons didn't help any. Not wanting to be surprised by her coming out of the bedroom with a weapon of any kind in her current state of mind, I kept an eye on this increasingly distraught person. She would run over with her little quick steps to the two men huddled over the aerial photos and easement contract, and then she would scoot back into the bedroom behind the blanket door. In a few moments, out she would come as if she had been shot from a cannon. She'd go to the table again and then zip back into the bedroom. This was repeated several times, and then she began to utter words. Most of what she said was in German, and because of the softness of her speech and my fragmentary knowledge of German, I caught little of what she was trying to say. However, she did telegraph her distress, outright worry, and sometimes terror by the looks she gave me as she whizzed by.

Looking over at Coop, I said, "Coop, pick up the pace will you?" and then nodded toward the bedroom, into which the lady had just disappeared once again. He acknowledged my concern and gave it a renewed try with the old man, trying to get the ditch filled. Damn, I thought. My agent from Minot is sure long-winded! Out she came once more, and this time her voice was getting louder as she went by me. As near as I could tell, she was saying, "Oh, mein Gott, they are here, vee vill be kilt, oh, mein Gott." Then she shuffled back into her bedroom, still mumbling in German. I looked over at Coop, my eyes telling him to get this squared away, and *now!* Catching my look, he made another push to explain the requirements under the easement contract and the need to fill the ditches. Out came the old lady from behind the curtain, and she was *really* agitated now. "Oh, mein Gott, the Gestapo, they are here. Vee vill all be kilt, oh, mein Gott, help us," and on it went with the word *Gestapo* being mentioned several more times! As she passed by me en route to her bedroom sanctuary, *I saw it!* On her left inner forearm, I saw a stenciled number! God-damn, I thought, these folks have been in a German concentration camp, or at least she has! Why else the numbers on her arm?

"Coop, wrap it up. We are out of here, and I do mean *now!*" Catching the urgency in my voice, Coop told the farmer to be sure to get those ditches closed, grabbed his maps and files, and went out the door. I thanked the man for the offer of coffee and started to leave as well, but not before the little old lady, with terror written all over her face, started to confront me. Looking down at that poor damn woman, I thought, Brother, what have we done to her day and world? Using my best German (hardly used since I was a boy), I leaned over, smiling, and said, hoping I used the right words, "Ist nicht Gestapo; Amerikaner." With that I turned and went outside. I climbed over the snowdrift and got into the car, and neither of us spoke until after we left their driveway.

"What the hell was going on in there?" asked Coop as he steered around a muddy place on the farm road.

"John," I said, "those poor folks were from a Nazi concentration camp. She had numbers stenciled on her arm, and as we left I looked over at the old man, and even though it was hard to see, it appeared he had one on his arm as well! There is no way I am going to push those folks to fill a ditch after what they have been through. They don't have anything to their names but each other, and I will be damned if we are going to bring them more grief. You get hold of the wetland manager for this district and advise him to just write off this violation and *never* bother these two old folks again!"

Coop, a two-tour veteran of Vietnam, silently drove down the road for a bit and then said, "You got it, Chief. No one will ever bother those folks again." And they didn't.

THESE STORIES ARE only a few of the many I experienced in North and South Dakota while stationed there. Already I can see my copy editor telling me this story is too long and needs to be shortened, so I had better quit. But the story about an almost unknown but hugely important part of the conservation picture needed to be told. It is so important that over forty million ducks will use those wetlands in *just* North Dakota each year, either as breeders or during their spring or fall migrations! That number doesn't take into consideration all the other wildlife directly affected by having some kind of cover and wetlands to call home. …

Don't get me wrong; I met a lot of great farming people in those states while trying to reduce the illegal drainage. And I met a lot who were downright ugly. But the wetlands were worth fighting for, and as a result of the enforcement efforts by the refuge, wetlands, and law enforcement folks, we stopped much of the ongoing drainage, reducing it to a manageable affair. But I am here to tell you, those were two of the toughest years in my career. Yet they were two of the most rewarding years in my career as well. There is something to be said for getting a farmer to realize the error of his ways and for getting the wetlands restored. There is even more to say when you drive by that same wetland a year later and see numerous pairs of coots, ducks, or geese making it their home as they swim by with that year's brood. That sight gives one in the business that much more "go" to carry on for the critters.

It is ironic that Special Agent Richard Grosz (my oldest son) is, at the time this story is being written, the resident agent in western North Dakota. He too is imbued with the soul needed to continue the wetland easement wars, and yes, they are still ongoing. Anytime one balances greed or ego on one side of the scales of justice and the critters on the other, there is going to be a dangerous tip. ... That is why as long as there are critters, there will hopefully be officers of the Service with the soul needed to take up the challenge and leave a piece of themselves behind. I hope that someday God will recognize that sacrifice and do what needs doing. But I hope he hurries.

4

The Moon of the Duck

THE COLD WATER LAPPED GENTLY against my hip boots with quiet splashing sounds as the rain pelted off my waterproof camouflage hunting coat, sounding as if it were striking a canvas tent. The wind was still blustering out of the northwest, but not as strongly as before, making it easier for me to see through the sometimes stinging sheets of falling water sweeping across the prairie. The smell of the marsh methane gases was pungently refreshing, as were the sounds of the coots (a small ducklike waterbird found in most marshes) bobbing in the water, making their familiar croaking sounds as they fed among the reeds surrounding me. From my side of the three-acre marsh I could just see through my binoculars the figures of two men moving around the wetland at the edge of the reeds in the predawn dark as they put out several dozen duck decoys. Every now and then I could see a beam from a small flashlight reflecting off the water as the duck hunters untangled the weight lines on their decoys. I could hear the soft *kaploosh* of the decoys hitting the water in front of an old duck blind along with the muted voices of the two hunters. I strained to hear what was being said, but to no avail because of the occasional gusts of wind and the waves lapping noisily against the dense stand of reeds in which I stood.

Watching the two hunters to be sure they didn't discover me, I began moving slowly toward their blind, seeking a position where I could see and hear better. In addition, being closer to my shooters would allow me to better identify the ducks they killed by species and sex as the birds made their final trip over the decoys. Identifying the ducks killed was important because the state of North Dakota had a species and sex limit that year on some ducks such as the mallard. Also, I needed to get close enough to be able to prove who shot what beyond a reasonable doubt in any subsequent proceedings in federal court.

Finally reaching a position not more than thirty-five yards from their blind, behind it and off to one side so as to be out of their antici-pated line of fire, I stopped, hidden by my protective cover of reeds, waiting to see what the morning shoot would bring. Standing there, I could feel the bubbles of methane gases bumping up along the sides of my hip boots, disturbed by my travels from their years of lying in the mud. Within seconds the rotten-egg smell of those gases made itself known. Upon seeing my arrival, coots that had earlier sought refuge from the gusting winds in the belt of reeds at the edge of the marsh moved out into the deeper water of the basin for a better look at what had disturbed them. Seeing no further movement on my part, a dozen or so cautiously moved back into their hiding places among the reeds. With the marsh smells and the life going on around me, and being on the hunt once again for my fellow human, it felt great to be alive.

It was November 1975 in North Dakota, just days before Thanks-giving, with the duck and goose hunting season in full swing. Migrat-ing birds of every species, including millions of waterfowl, were flooding out of Canada and Alaska in ever growing numbers as the weather grew worse in those northern reaches. Before that day in the marsh I had been working every day for three months on illegal drainage problems involving wetland easements, and I was mentally and physically exhausted from that work. I had had dogs set on me by farmers angry at being caught violating their wetland easement contracts, farm women bawling as I hauled their men off to jail, farm-ers chasing me with tractors, farmers threatening to get their guns and shoot me on the spot, constant lying by the drainers trying to justify their illegal actions, and the like. Suffice it to say that a few days of working long hours during the moon of the duck, chasing the duck hunters was going to be pure relaxation by comparison.

In those days duck season really didn't get going in the killing de-partment until those few weeks before Thanksgiving. Oh, sure, quite a few ducks were killed on the opening weekend of duck season weeks earlier, but the serious duck and goose killing took place during the height of migration, just before freeze-up. It was as if everyone who liked to eat duck and goose tried to kill every one of those species they could before the birds migrated to Mexico and the Mexicans got to eat them instead. Hence the phrase *moon of the duck* because the great numbers of waterfowl usually lasted less than one cycle of the moon on the prairies. I had heard the phrase used by the very old hunters, and some of them gave credit for the term to the Lakota Indians who had inhabited the prairie in the days of their youth. Several old-timers told me that the Indians called that short period between the serious start of migration and freeze-up *the moon of the duck* because the hunting was so good and the birds were so fat. Hundreds could be killed by the Indians (and later by the commercial-market hunters and local farmers) in a very short time, and then the birds were gone. Then came the intense cold, snow, and ice. The combination made for a passel of good tales to be told around the fire at night when the cold northern winds howled around the corners of the house.

Finished with the placement of their decoys, one of my two hunters retired to the blind, and soon I could see the flame from a match as he lit up a smoke. The other lad got into their vehicle, which was parked nearby, and drove it over the hill and out of sight so as not to scare the incoming ducks. Soon he returned, joined his partner, and lit up a smoke as well. Within moments I could smell their cigarettes and marveled at just how good a dog's nose must be if even I could smell the offending cigarette smoke downwind from thirty-five to forty yards away. With life in the marsh continuing around me, I let my mind wander as I waited for legal shooting hours to commence. I had been working the last of my wetland easement drainage violations a quarter-section away the day before and had heard intense shooting coming from the area I now patiently occupied. By the time I had finished with the drainage problem and located this wetland, the hunters were long gone and the shooting over. Walking over to the duck blind I had just discovered on a small spit of land jutting out into the wetland, I was amazed at the number of spent shotgun shells scattered around in the mud. There had to be at least two hundred casings in and at the edge of the blind and twenty or thirty more floating in the water and reeds surrounding the blind in silent testimony to the good shooting. Realizing I might have a problem with over-limits here because of the remoteness of the wetland and good duck numbers in the immediate area, I decided to start my duck hunting enforcement over the next few days on this marsh, and maybe through those efforts send a few more birds winging their way south. My decision was based not only on the inordinate number of empty shotgun shells but on the fact that during my time there the ducks poured into the secluded little wetland by the hundreds, making me suspect it had been baited. I looked quickly around the area, seeking spilled bait or empty grain bags on the spit of land on which the blind sat, but found nothing. I knew that lingering in the area in the light of day might invite discovery by my shooters, so I got the hell out with a plan rattling around in my head as I bounced over the rough prairie trail in my sedan.

Returning that evening after dark to execute Plan B, I got my bait scoop (a screened device used by dragging it along the bottom of a watered area in search of illegal bait) from the trunk of my patrol car, which I had hidden earlier behind a large rock pile in a fallow field. With one last look around for any human activity that might lead to my discovery, I walked over several rolling hills to the duck blind. When I reached the edge of the wetland, I surprised at least a thousand ducks feeding hungrily in and around the area where the decoys would likely have been placed during previous hunts. Strongly suspecting the placement of grain in those areas because of this unusual concentration of ducks, I rolled up my hip boots and slowly walked out into the water, shuffling my feet along the bottom of the unknown marsh to avoid going in over my head. This disturbance was too much for the remaining feeding waterfowl, and they hurriedly departed with the roar of hundreds of beating wings. Finding the spot I suspected of being baited was easy. When ducks feed on grain on the bottom of a marsh or pond in great numbers even over a short period, the constant pounding of their bills in the mud eventually packs the bottom, so it is not unusual to find yourself squishing through the muddy bottom and then all at once on a semihard surface. If that occurs, you should take your sample right there because that is where the bait has been or is.

When I reached the packed area where the ducks had been feeding, I dragged my bait scoop about twenty feet over the hardened bottom. Lifting it for examination, I found it to be loaded with a little mud, a few marsh plants, and lots of fresh grains of barley. I took my sample back to shore to photograph it, then made two more drags with the bait scoop to confirm (based on my past experience working this kind of case) that there had to be at least two hundred to three hundred pounds of barley around the blind and on the edge of what appeared to be the area of the decoy set. I gathered up my gear and, still dripping evidence, walked back to my vehicle and headed for the little town of Medina, a motel, and a good night's rest. Happy thoughts swirled around in my head as I anticipated having Christmas come early for some fine so-called sportsmen shooting over an illegally baited area.

Now, from my hiding place in the dense stand of reeds, I watched flight after flight of ducks moving into the wetland. As was typical in a baited area, there was none of the usual cautious circling before landing. The ducks dropped straight into the decoys, tipped, and immediately began to feed in the shallow waters. To the practiced eye, those actions portended something rotten in the henhouse. In normal circumstances, after waterfowl had just landed there would be a lot of craning of necks as they looked around for any sign of danger. These birds exhibited none of that usual alertness, just the hunger and greed that comes from being habituated to a rich food source that is easy pickings, and they wasted no time in going after it. Looking to the east, I could see that dawn was still some time off, so I snuggled further down into my hunting coat as I became aware of the cold seeping into my feet and legs through my uninsulated hip boots (in those days the Division of Law Enforcement couldn't afford insulated waders or hip boots!). To my young legs, the cold didn't matter much. I was going to live forever anyway. ... Today, at sixty years of age, I often wish I had taken better care of my body during times like that. Arthritis is now a constant reminder of all the long, cold, wet days I spent outdoors protecting those critters who didn't have a voice in what happened to them. You know, now that I think about it, it is a small price to pay.

Coots continued to feed contentedly around my silent form, and a muskrat came over to my knees to investigate. The air had a chill in it, and I knew the final migration of birds from the arctic was not far off, nor were the hard, cold Dakota winter winds that followed. The intense cold that comes just before the dawn was now upon me, as was an eagerness for the show to get on the road. I was shivering from stem to stern as a result of standing silently in the cold water for almost two hours, so I took out a stick of greasy Italian salami from my game bag, bit off several chunks of the fatty meat, and let the juice from chewing flow around in my mouth before I swallowed. Hoping the fat would provide the fuel I needed to keep me from getting any colder, I took a few more bites, then returned the unwrapped remaining portion of the salami to my pocket, which also contained duck calls, a small bottle of water, some plastic bags, the lint that comes from years of use, and a few old duck feathers from last season. I grinned as I imagined what might be stuck on the end of the salami when I retrieved it later.

Forty minutes before legal shooting time (which was one-half hour before sunrise), my two lads stood up and loosed a barrage from their shotguns into the mass of madly feeding ducks on the water. Damn, what an uproar! I thought as I pulled my head back up from where it had instinctively retreated at the surprising and unexpected sounds of the shooting. Ducks were going every which way, floppers with broken wings were moving away from the blind on the water, low-flying cripples were sailing across the wetland and, unable to fly farther, crashing into the reeds looking for the protection of cover, while those that escaped were heading for the heavens as if there was no tomorrow! For those ducks lying still on the water, with only an occasional leg kicking in the air as they lay on their backs, summer was over. ... The two lads sat back down in their blind and did not move again until thirty minutes later. Damn smart move, I thought. Shooting a quick barrage and then staying quiet for another half hour would make it almost impossible for a game warden to catch them unless he was right there in their back pockets ... *as he was!* And for lads that intelligent in their art of killing, it was a good thing he was.

Once it got light enough to see, the two middle-aged lads, whom I could now clearly see through my binoculars, stood up slowly and looked all around the hills surrounding the wetland basin. If they had carefully looked at the reeds some thirty-five or so yards away and slightly behind them, they might have seen what they were looking for! However, seeing nothing but more small groups of waterfowl trying to land in their decoys for what still lay beneath the water in six-inch-deep swaths, the hunters got out of their blind and walked into the water. Picking up the dead and badly crippled ducks, they tossed the mallards, after wringing their necks, toward the blind and stomped any duck of lesser species into the soft, muddy bottom. You bastards! I thought. Stomping ducks and wasting game will cost you, not only the penalty in federal court but some real embarrassment when digging them out of the mud at a later time so they can be added to your total illegal kill. What a waste, I thought. As near as I could tell, they stomped two pintail hens, three redheads (a totally protected species), one green-winged teal (the smallest duck in North America), and three gadwalls (usually strong tasting) into the muddy bottom of the basin. They also tossed seventeen mallards (large in size, excellent eating) into the blind, and four of those appeared to be females (only one hen per shooter per day was allowed). As far as Uncle Sam was concerned, that count put the lads in plenty of trouble for shooting over a baited area, early shooting, wanton waste, taking restricted species (redheads), and an over-limit of mallards—two hens over the prescribed daily bag limit as well as a general over-limit! Not bad for a cold country boy standing in the reeds, I thought. That seeping cold in the lower limbs was no longer noticeable.

About that time the lads scurried back into their blind as if they had seen a ghost. Then I saw it. Out of the west came a flock of ducks heading their way, numbering at least a hundred! Having nothing better to do, I just stood there in the concealment of the reeds and water, waiting for the next big show. That flock circled only once after seeing a pair of mallards skidding in low from the east and landing among the decoys. Figuring it was safe, they followed suit. The newcomers had obviously having been on the baited area before because they immediately dove and started feeding. There was no movement from the blind; not even a wiggle. More birds poured into the feeding frenzy among the decoys until there were about two hundred feeding birds, oblivious to the possible danger of the duck blind just thirty yards away. In the blink of an eye, my lads were up once more and shooting into the mass of frenzied ducks on the water. I counted ten shots that time, which told me that the men had pulled the plugs from their shotguns in order to maximize their kill by increasing the shell capacity of the magazines from two to four. There were dead and dying birds everywhere, with more falling out of the air as they tried to fly away! Again the shooters disappeared back into their blind, and neither man came out or even poked his head up for at least another thirty minutes. Then they stood up and repeated their earlier procedure of examining the skyline as if expecting a game warden to show his hand. Seeing none, they hurriedly left their blind and began picking up the dead and chasing down the cripples that were too badly injured to escape. In the thirty-minute period after the shoot, I had counted thirteen ducks swimming off into the protective collar of vegetation surrounding the wetland basin. Some did not stop there. I had seen several, with their low-to-the-ground waddle, walk through the prairie grasses away from the pond and out of the area. I thought sadly that they were just walking into the waiting mouths of the ever present fox and coyote. Again I watched as the two shooters stomped into the mud four more gadwalls, a hen pintail, three spoonbills, and two more redheads! Again they tossed the larger, better-tasting mallards toward the blind, and the bodies were sailing through the air in such numbers that I could not count the number of hens, or the total number, for that matter.

Figuring I would take the men before they shot any more ducks, I waited to see what they were going to do next. Pretty soon the one who appeared older left the blind and strode by my hiding place without so much as a look-see, disappearing over the hill. I presumed he was going after their vehicle and, seeing my chance, took it. Out of the reeds and water I scrambled and without delay trotted over to the duck blind on stone-cold, stiff, and almost wooden legs, arriving just in time to catch the chap inside tying the heads of the ducks together into bunches with butcher twine for easier transport. Man, you talk about surprised when I peered over the wall of the blind unannounced!

"*Whoa-ho-ho!*" he yelled as he started to stand up and then fell over backward through the rear reed wall of the blind. "Who the hell are you?" he yelled from his position flat on his back. "Where the hell did you come from?"

"Federal agent," I quietly stated as I held out my badge and credentials for him to see, then offered my hand to help him up.

"Goddamn, you like to scared the shit right out of me!" he continued to yell as I helped him up.

"Sorry," I said, "just thought I would check in on you fellows and see how you were doing." Now that the greetings and salutations were over, he realized the crap he was in as he looked down at his feet at the huge pile of mallards. "How many you got?" I asked innocently.

There was a pregnant pause, and then he said, "Don't rightly know, but a few."

I reached over and, taking his shotgun, which was leaning against the side of the blind, unloaded it. Using my old rubber-plug checker (now carried by my son, Special Agent Rich Grosz) from my California days as a game warden, I checked to see if his shotgun was plugged. It was, and I grinned. After shooting their big barrage at the ducks without any plugs in their Browning semiauto AL-5s, they more than likely had squatted back down in their blind and put the plugs back in, thinking they would fool the game warden if he happened to be in country. He was, and he wasn't fooled! I imagined the other lad had done the same, but there was no way to check at the moment because he had taken his shotgun with him.

"I would like to see your hunting license, duck stamp, and driver's license, please," I said. He dug the items out of his wallet and handed them to me. I could sense the dread in this fellow even though he was pretty quiet. Standing in a large over-limit of ducks will do that to a person, especially if the law is standing in them as well! Well, well, well, I mused. I had thought that I recognized the man, and sure enough, according to the name on the driver's license, he was an easement violator I had caught late in 1974. "Let's count the ducks, Archie," I said, looking hard at him. Sixty-two mallards later, eleven of them females, I said, "Damn, you guys had a hell of a good shoot." Archie just looked at me like a mongoose studying a small bird. The only problem was that he was looking at a rather large federal "eagle!" His body language told me he was pissed that I had caught him. If looks could have killed, I would have been a dead man, and he was now physically shaking out that anger like a dog crapping peach pits. Taking a casual half step to the side in case he tried something foolish, I said, "Who is your pal, Archie?"

"Screw you," was his immediate reply.

"OK," I said. "We will just wait right here until he returns with the vehicle." Archie just looked at the ground as he dejectedly sat back down on his shooting stool in the blind. About fifteen minutes later I heard a pickup grinding its gears as it drove into sight, maneuvering carefully around the boulders in the prairie, and came down the spit of land to the blind. When the lad stopped and stepped out of the truck, I could tell from his clothing and his face, which I had seen through the binoculars, that he was Archie's partner. Stepping out of the blind with Archie's shotgun and keeping an eye on Archie, who remained in the blind, I said, "Good morning; federal agent."

"Who the hell are you?" he bellowed in surprise.

Damn, I thought, these North Dakota dirt farmers sure have a lot in common in the language department. "Federal agent, sir; my badge and credentials," I said as I held them out for him to examine. He reached for them, and I pulled them back.

"What the hell? I want to see those credentials!" he yelled.

"Sir, you will have to examine them from a distance. I never surrender my badge, credentials, or sidearm to anyone unless it is another officer."

"Well, let me see them again then," he said, whereupon I again held them out. After a long look, he said in a loud, angry tone, "What the hell are you doing on my land?"

"Sir, I have excellent hearing, and it is not necessary for you to shout."

"I am not shouting," he bellowed once more. "I just want to know what the hell you are doing on my land!"

"Sir," I responded calmly, "I have been standing in those reeds over there since about four o'clock this morning. My reason for being there was to observe you and Archie during your hunting activities to see if both of you stayed within the confines of the law. What I saw here this morning was not what I expected, and that is why we are visiting here and now."

"And just what did you see?" he said, his tone now more normal.

"Well, in addition to the taking of an over-limit of ducks, the illegal take of the restricted species of redheads, stomping of the unwanted ducks in the mud (wanton waste), early shooting, and the use of unplugged shotguns will do for starters. In addition, you and your partner shot over a baited area."

"The hell you say," he said, his voice again getting strident and defensive.

"That is the way I see it, and that is what I am prepared to testify to in federal court if necessary," I replied in an equally strident tone. I figured that of the two fellows, this was the one who would want a physical go-around with me, if it came to that. He looked long and hard at me, and I at him.

"Well, what are you going to do?" he finally asked in a softer, measured voice.

"Well, first of all, I am going to seize all the birds as evidence supporting the charges to be lodged against you and your friend, and then your shotguns as well since they were the instruments of the crime. Then I am going to take the personal information off your driver's licenses and issue the both of you federal citations at a later date for what occurred here today."

"Why are you taking my shotgun?" he asked through tight lips.

"Because, as I said, it was used as an instrument in this crime and will be used as evidence in court if necessary."

In fact, both of these men were well over six feet tall and closer to 250 than 200 pounds in weight. I did not feel it wise to leave the shotguns in their hands in their excited states of mind, especially in light of the gravity of the violation and the remoteness of the area. Turning abruptly, my chap walked the few steps back to his truck and pulled his shotgun from the front seat. As he turned around, he could plainly see me standing with my hand on the cold steel butt of my .45 Colt semiautomatic pistol. I had already cocked back the hammer and, after unsnapping the holster retainer, stood there to see what he was going to do. He had moved so quickly and unexpectedly to his truck and brought forth his shotgun in such short order that I hadn't had time to control the situation. So I felt that being prepared, and letting him see me so, was the second-best thing to do.

When he saw me standing in the ready position, he slowly lowered the shotgun barrel away from me and methodically jacked the three shells out onto the ground. Then he laid the shotgun carefully down on the hood of his truck and stepped to one side. Boy, his body language, like Archie's, showed that he was pissed!

"Now, if I might have your hunting license, duck stamp, and driver's license, sir," I said. Without a word, he gave me the items. Again I kept a defensive stance and some distance between us in case he tried something stupid. Sensing that things were under control, I stepped over to the hood of his truck and, still keeping my eyes on the lad, scooped up the shotgun and racked the bolt back to make sure it was empty. Then I instructed the lads to go out into the decoy area and start digging up the nineteen ducks they had stomped into the bottom of the marsh. While they were doing that and not looking at me too closely, I unscrewed the magazine caps on their shotguns about three turns so they wouldn't fire, pulled the barrels forward, and laid the guns back down out of the way of my two chaps. They were still very angry as they dug up the stomped ducks, several times sinking over their shoulders in the water as they pulled out the birds and tossed them to shore, aiming a bit close to my feet in an act of defiance.

Once they were done I told them to pick up their decoys if they wanted to, and in the meantime I would record all the information I needed from their driver's licenses. They whispered together as they picked up their decoys and piled them near the blind. I took that time to stack the eighty-one ducks they had killed alongside their shotguns and then just stood there until they were through. Then Dwight, the second fellow, asked, "Now what?"

"Well, gentlemen, you are free to go, but just be advised, I will be mailing both of you citations for taking an over-limit of ducks, taking an over-limit of female mallards, shooting over a baited area, taking protected species in the redheads, wanton waste, early shooting, and using unplugged shotguns to take migratory waterfowl. So don't be surprised when a fistful of them show up at your door in the local mail." I was surprised that they did not contest the unplugged shotguns charge because both had been plugged when I checked them. I guess they figured I had the goods on them, including seeing them shoot with unplugged shotguns, and just let it ride.

There was a long silence, and then Dwight said, "How much is that going to cost us?"

"I don't know, gentlemen; that is up to the federal magistrate. But I can tell you this: what you did here today is pretty serious in the eyes of the court, so the fine won't be like a traffic ticket. There is one other thing," I said. "You will not be allowed to hunt ducks in this area for the rest of this duck season." They looked long and hard at me. I could tell they didn't like what they had just heard. "Federal law is that the lure and attractant in a baited area must be gone and then a ten-day waiting period must elapse after that before it can legally hunted once again. I figure by then all will be frozen over. So no hunting over this area for the rest of the season. If anyone does, and I catch them, they can expect the same medicine you fellows got here today for shooting over a baited area."

I gave them evidence receipts for the ducks and guns and told them how to get their guns back when the case was closed. Without so much as a backward glance, they drove out of the area. After they were gone, I circled the wetland and picked up six more ducks that had crawled to the edge of the grassy basin and died before making their escape. That brought their total kill to eighty-seven ducks, not counting the cripples that had escaped out of the wetland to die a lonely death on the prairie at a later time. Going back into the baited area, I took two more samples with me and bagged them in two plastic bags in case evidence was needed later in court to show that the baiting was contemporaneous with today's shooting. I photographed the eighty-seven ducks, laid out so they could easily be counted in case they disappeared in my absence, then stashed them in a corner of the marsh because there were too many to carry. Then I gathered up the shotguns and walked out of the wetland to my car. I drove around the section-line prairie trail surrounding the wetland, located my culprits' recent tire tracks, and followed them back to the shooting area, where I loaded my evidence ducks into the trunk for safekeeping. Still watching for the angry lads, I drove out of the area and headed for home so I could clean and preserve the evidence. It had been a great day, I thought, except for the ducks. The intense dark-blue North Dakota sky portended another fine day on the morrow, and I looked forward to it as I headed down the dusty prairie road toward home.

Three weeks later the two lads, still pissed but with bowed necks, came into my Bismarck office and reclaimed their shotguns. They grumbled about the $1,150 fine each had had to pay and then left in a huff. I was to catch Archie in 1976 for another wetland easement violation, but that time he was more composed—just as hardheaded, but more composed. That violation cost him $100, plus he had to fill up his ditch, which pissed him off even more than the fine, especially because he had to plow up his standing wheat in order to get enough dirt to meet the court-ordered compliance requirements. I wondered just how many years those two dirt farmers had been shooting that way during the moon of the duck. You can bet that the duck kill had numbered in the thousands over those years, however many there were! Today, if those two were still alive, I could picture them stopping a local conservation officer and asking him, "what has Fish and Game done with all the ducks? We just don't see them like we used to. ..."

FOR THE NEXT COUPLE of days I patrolled the northeastern part of the state with Tom Sechrist, my agent in Devils Lake. We ran the back roads in areas that historically saw high waterfowl hunting pressure but didn't find many hunters. That wasn't unusual in North Dakota, partly because of the land's remoteness and partly because of its small resident waterfowl hunting population. Before we went our separate ways we caught four individuals late-shooting waterfowl in the Devils Lake area and several others with no duck stamps (anyone over the age of sixteen must have a federal waterfowl stamp in their possession while taking migratory waterfowl), but all in all it was pretty quiet. The weather was beautiful as only a North Dakota prairie can be just before the winter storms arrive to cover the land in cold. The temperature was in the high sixties, and the sky was an intense, smog-free dark blue. The prairie grasses were such gorgeous golden-brown, yellow, and tan colors that it almost hurt my eyes to look at them, and the wetlands took on the look and color of the sky. It just made me thank the good Lord above for such visual blessings. When driving across those gold-colored prairies, with the deep blue of the wetlands contrasted with the golden brown of the prairie and the stark blue of the sky, I formed an image in my mind of just how beautiful the prairie can be that will remain there until I die. The other thing I remember about those days was the unusual lack of wind. It was nonexistent or appeared only in the form of mellow little breezes carrying the smell of the curing prairie grasses. It was great, but anytime the Dakotas are that beautiful and calm, hell is a-comin', and in the not-too-distant future.

Leaving Tom to continue checking the northeast for waterfowl hunters, I headed south down the back roads toward the waterfowl areas in and around Valley City. Cruising down one of those innumerable north-south gravel roads in farm country, coming from nowhere and going to the same place, I drove through several large wetland basins whose waters abutted the road's berm. I always liked to do that because it gave me the opportunity to practice my identification skills on the resting waterfowl as I passed by. Emerging from the first wetland, the road cut through another smaller one, and this time I got to practice my waterfowl identification up close. Lying not forty yards off the road in the marsh was a large bundle of brilliant white floating gently on the deep-blue waters. Locking the brakes, I skidded to a stop amidst a cloud of the billowing dust ever present on North Dakota's gravel roads. I knew what it was even before I put my binoculars on that pile of white. It was an adult swan that appeared to have been killed by someone driving down the road that intersected the wetland.

I parked on one side of the road, then jumped up on the front bumper of the car and, taking my binoculars, did a quick 360-degree sweep over the countryside just in case the swan killer was still around. Seeing nothing out of the ordinary, I got down and put on a pair of hip boots. Walking out into the wetland, I retrieved the arctic or tundra swan and brought its lifeless body back to the patrol car. It had been shot once in the body and once in the neck, as I could see from the bright red blotches against the brilliant white of its feathers. Because the damage was minimal, I surmised that the swan had been killed by a light-caliber rifle, probably a .22. Damn, I thought; this is an adult bird, and swans mate for life. Somewhere a swan was heading south with a heavy heart, and without its mate.

Walking back out on the road, I could see in the dirt where a vehicle had pulled over to the edge of the road bisecting the wetland. It was almost exactly directly across from where I had picked up the swan. I didn't find any .22 brass along the road, so I figured that the person who had shot the bird had done so from inside a vehicle. There were no footprints either, but I did get a good look at the tire tread and took a picture of it as well, burning its image into my mind. Needless to say, this random shooting of a totally protected bird as graceful as the swan ruined my joy at being in the out-of-doors during this beautiful time in the late fall. Then the agent in me kicked in. The brilliant red blood on the pure-white body of the swan had not yet congealed. Rigor mortis had not set in, and the bird's body temperature was still warm. That told me my killer had to still be in the area. Quickly throwing the bird on the passenger-side floorboard of my car, at my dog's feet, I took off down the road leading to the next town in the hope of catching someone driving slowly down the road, illegally shooting other birds from the vehicle. However, I arrived at the edge of the small town of Hannaford without seeing anyone on the road. I returned to the scene of the crime and then visited every house along the gravel road within a mile of the wetland where the shooting had occurred. No one was home at the first house where I stopped, so on I went to the next farmhouse. A housewife who was hanging clothes on an outdoor clothesline remembered a red pickup driving slowly down the road with only one occupant at about the time I figured the shooting had occurred. She was unable to give me any more information, and the only reason she even remembered the vehicle was because it was going so slowly that it didn't raise a lot of dust, which would have settled on her fresh wash on the clothesline, and she appreciated that. Next I spoke to a farmer tilling his land alongside the gravel road, and he also remembered the red pickup and told me it was a late-model Ford, but he could not tell me any more than that except that it had been heading toward Hannaford and had a North Dakota license plate. I checked at the last two farmhouses in the immediate area but drew blanks.

Hotfooting it into Hannaford, I stopped several people on the street to ask about the red Ford pickup. No luck. Stopping at a CO-OP gas station, I asked the gas monkeys if anyone had seen a red Ford pickup recently getting gasoline, but no one had. As I started to leave, an old farm couple who had apparently overheard me speaking to the lads at the gas pumps walked over and asked if I was interested in a red Ford pickup.

"I sure am," I replied.

The old man told me he had seen a "hippielike" fellow driving a red Ford about the time I was inquiring about. The old fellow had been getting his tires balanced at the CO-OP and had seen the "hippie" drive up, park his truck, and go inside to get a soft drink. The old man described him as tall, thin as a reed, in need of a bath, and with long black hair done up in a ponytail. Damn, I thought; that isn't much to go on even if the lad in the red Ford is my shooter, but it's better than nothing. The old guy wanted to know why I was looking for this red truck. Taking him and his wife over to my car, I opened the door and showed him the broken body of the swan.

"Why, that poop," he exclaimed. "He needs a bullet in the head if he did that to that magnificent bird." I grunted my approval of his sentiments. "Say," he said, "I don't know if this will help you much, but I do remember three numbers of the plate on that truck." I looked at that old codger in disbelief. Who the hell would remember three numbers on a license plate from nowhere? Seeing my doubtful look, he explained, "The only reason I remember it, son, is because that is how many stitches I required in my back and legs after getting blown up on a ship during the war."

I couldn't believe my luck. Recording the numbers in my notebook along with his name and address, I thanked him, promptly got on the car radio, and called Bismarck state radio dispatch. I gave the partial license plate number, the color of the pickup, and its late-model status and asked if there was any way to run that information and give me a list of possible hits in the state. The dispatcher said it was possible but would take some time. I said that would be fine and then headed for the office of Dr. Gary Pearson, a veterinarian I had met earlier in the year who was a friend of wildlife and often would do wildlife rehabilitation work for free. When I arriving at his clinic in Jamestown, I asked him to x-ray the swan for any bullets in its carcass. Even though he was busy with another person, he promptly did what I asked. The bullet striking the neck had shattered and was useless, but there was a bullet in the body that he thought he could retrieve. He had to take care of his patient but said if I wanted it, he would dig out the bullet later that night and would have it for me in the morning. Wanting to continue with my patrol efforts in the area anyway, I agreed, and out the door I went to check on the local duck hunters.

The next morning saw me back at Gary's clinic to see what he had found. He said the bullet had indeed been from a .22-caliber rifle, probably a Marlin.

I said, "What?"

"Yeah," he said. "I dabble a little in the forensics of things, and this bullet more than likely came from a Marlin rifle because it shows microgroove rifling with a left-hand twist, which is characteristic of Marlin rifles."

Damn, I thought; if I can just find that "rifle in a haystack," I might just have something here! Of course, I had to find the "license plate in a haystack" first. ... Taking the bullet and a set of x-rays, I thanked Gary for his time and information. Then out the door I went to contact Bismarck on the radio and see what they had found regarding the possible license plate. Bismarck reported that there were seventeen possible license plates in the state that belonged to late-model red Ford pickups. Oh, great, I thought; not much help there. Then, gambling on a long shot, I asked if any were from around the Valley City, Jamestown, or Hannaford areas. I picked those three because Hannaford was in the immediate vicinity of the kill and the other two, Jamestown and Valley City, were the largest towns in the immediate area. There was a long pause as the dispatcher examined the records, and then she told me that four of the vehicles were in the Valley City area, none in the Hannaford area, and none in Jamestown. Hot dog, I thought. At least I had a starting point, and if my shooter just happened to be driving that red Ford and was living in the area, I might have a chance, with the aid of a damn good interview, to catch him. Quickly writing down the names and addresses of my four "possibles," I headed for the sheriff's office in downtown Valley City.

When I introduced myself to the sheriff of Barnes County (for the life of me, I cannot remember his name), he got excited at the prospect of looking for a "hippie in a haystack" and asked if he could join me in the search. He said he knew the town and its people like the back of his hand and could be of assistance if I needed any. Happy to have such a good resource, I quickly agreed, and the two of us set off on our quest. That turned out to be a damn good move on my part because the sheriff was top drawer and a good partner. The first owner of a red Ford truck we visited turned out to be a bust. The truck was owned by a young female college student. She had not lent her truck to anyone in the past two weeks, nor would she have let anyone else drive it. It was her first car, and she was so damn proud of it, I doubt she would have allowed even her mom or dad to drive it. We looked at the second name and address, and the sheriff zeroed us right in on the residence. There in the driveway sat a red Ford, and my hopes went up again. This time the truck turned out to belong to a very old woman, and after a few pleasant words and two pieces of homemade apple pie, we discovered that she had not lent the truck to anyone. With thanks for the company and pie, we left.

"Damn, boy, we only have two more chances left," said my partner.

"Well," I told him, "I am not even sure the shooter was in the red Ford, but it was the only lead I had, so I had to chance it."

The next address was an apartment complex, and our suspect was not home. According to his neighbor, he was at work in a local lumberyard but should be back around five in the afternoon. We thanked that gentlemen, and as we walked away I told the sheriff that this was such a fishing expedition, I didn't want to go to the man's place of work and possibly screw him up with his boss. He agreed.

Our last address turned out to be the home of an African American man, and after a few pleasant words, we left. Since the old couple in Hannaford had identified a white male with a ponytail, I figured this too was a dead lead. I took the sheriff out for an early dinner, and we talked about my profession at length. I could tell that if he had half a chance, he would become an agent in a heartbeat. Come five, we were back at the house of our last suspect, but no one was home. The two of us waited in my car, and about thirty minutes later, in drove a red Ford pickup. A tall man got out of the truck, and when he turned to lock the door, there was the long black hair in a ponytail. My heart skipped a beat as the two of us walked across the street and introduced ourselves to a very surprised young man. I asked if we could go inside and talk, and he said, "Sure." Following him past the pickup to his apartment, I had a chance to look into the cab. There on the floorboards and seat were about twenty spent .22-caliber casings! I looked at the sheriff and nodded at the items scattered around in the pickup, and he grimly noted the possible evidence. The spent casings in the cab confirmed in my mind that someone had been shooting from the vehicle; every time they jacked an empty casing out of their firearm, it would fly into the cab instead of falling outside on the ground. In most states, including North Dakota, it was unlawful to shoot from a motor vehicle. I looked down at the treads on the Ford's tires, and it appeared to be the same pattern I had seen on the road where the swan had been killed. I also stored that information in the back of my mind in the hope that it wasn't for naught.

We went into the suspect's house, and he asked, "What is this all about, officers?"

Figuring I had a long shot at this one, I decided to try a ruse to see if I could capture my swan shooter that way—*if* this was the shooter. "I am here investigating the illegal killing of several deer on the Hobart Lake National Wildlife Refuge just south and west of us," I said (away from the actual kill area so as to throw the swan killer off his feed, so to speak). "That is why I am here, it being a federal violation on federal lands and all." My sheriff partner looked at me as if to ask what the hell I was doing, but he was cop enough to keep his mouth shut until he saw where I was going. "During this shooting yesterday, several farmers remembered a red Ford truck like yours in the area and reported it to my office. So the sheriff and I are trying to run down any red Ford trucks in the city to see what their owners were doing around four o'clock yesterday afternoon in the Hobart Lake area."

The relieved lad, who obviously had not been in the Hobart Lake area, said, "It sure wasn't me. I was in the Hannaford area about that time yesterday, just driving around."

I said, "Do you have any heavy-caliber hunting rifles?" (Again, the question was designed to throw the lad off the trail.)

"Yes; I have a .270 Winchester and a .308 Remington," he responded, "but I sure as hell didn't kill any deer on the refuge."

"May I see them?" I asked.

Knowing he had not been involved with any deer killing (since I had made the story up!), he headed into the back room of his apartment to retrieve his rifles. The sheriff again looked at me questioningly, knowing I was looking for a .22-caliber rifle, but I just gave him a silent high sign to hold his horses. In a moment the lad came out with his two rifles and handed them to me. Both of the rifles had scopes, and I quickly said, "These aren't the rifles, Sheriff; they both have scopes, and the outlaw was using a rifle without a scope." If they hadn't had scopes, I would have been looking for rifles *with* scopes— it is a tactic to relax the chap being interviewed. The lad looked very relieved. and as he started to put his rifles away, I asked, "Do you have any other rifles?"

He said, "The only other guns I have are a shotgun and a .22-caliber rifle."

Bingo! I was now where I wanted to be in my interview. "What kind of .22 do you have, sir?" I asked.

"Oh, it's only a Marlin lever-action," he responded.

Now that he was thinking he was past the hard part regarding the deer rifles, I shot the first round across his bow. "May I see it?" I innocently asked.

"What for?" he asked.

"I am thinking about buying a .22, and the Marlin is high on my list," I responded.

"Sure," came his "I am innocent of killing deer" reply. He went into the back room again, came back with the Marlin, handed it to me. I quickly checked to see if the chamber was empty of any live ammunition (the *very* first thing anyone should do when handed any kind of firearm), and except for live shells in the tubular magazine, which were legal, none were in the barrel. Good, I thought. Live ammunition in the rifle would make an easy match for the boys in forensics if I had the right chap. My guess was that the bullet in the swan and the bullets in the tubular magazine of the Marlin would be manufacture-lot matches chemically. If they were, I had one more nail in the lid of the coffin for the one who had pulled the trigger.

Now I tried my second shot across his bow, or perhaps more into the midsection. Come to think of it, I may have shot even lower. ... "Sir, I am going to be very frank with you." Looking him right in the eyes, I saw a glimpse of fear run across them. "Yesterday, on a small wetland just east of Hannaford, someone shot a swan resting on the water." There was that look of concern flashing across his eyes again, plus he now crossed his arms (a stance that indicates a closed person) as he stood looking at me. "The shooter was driving a red Ford pickup just like yours. In addition, the shooter was identified by two farmers in the area as a man matching your physical description, and one of the farmers' wives even took down all but two of the letters on your license plate before you drove off; that is how we located you [not true but another interviewing tactic]. The swan was shot with a .22-caliber rifle, and the bullet retrieved from the body of the swan showed that it was a Marlin because of the microgroove rifling found on the bullet."

Now, most of you readers are thinking, Where the hell did he get all that information? Well, I made it up. ... In interviewing a suspect with just bits and pieces of information, one can often try a "Hail Mary" question, like the desperation pass in football, and that was what I was doing. It is OK to try such a ruse, but you'd better have a lot of bits and pieces leading the way you want to go or you will find yourself out in left field, and your subject will know it. I knew a .22-caliber firearm had killed the swan. The bullet retrieved from the swan had microgroove rifling and was more than likely from a Marlin rifle, which has microgroove rifling as a trademark. A red Ford pickup had been seen in the area, and the old couple had described someone very like this thin person with a ponytail standing in front of me. The fact that his tire-tread design appeared to match the one at the scene of the shooting and the spent .22 casings littering his cab strengthened my suspicion that he was the shooter. Last but not least, the lad had said he had been in the Hannaford area the day before, where, unbeknownst to him, he had been seen by the old war veteran.

With all those bits and pieces and my gut instincts derived from years of chasing and interviewing poachers, plus the body language this lad was now displaying, I fired my final gut shot. "Your tire tracks match those found alongside the road where the swan was killed, and I would bet a month's pay that when we run the ballistics on this rifle, which we are going to do, it will come back confirming that the killing bullet came from this gun." With that said, I looked hard at the lad, waiting for his response.

"I didn't kill no swan," came a rather mousy and hard-to-believe response.

"Then you won't have any problem if we run the ballistics on this rifle through the FBI lab, correct?" The lad just looked at me like a field mouse just before getting hit by a great horned owl. ... Digging out my pencil and notebook and taking my final gamble, I said, "I will need your driver's license, please."

Without a whimper the lad dug out his driver's license and handed it to me. "How much is this going to cost?" he quietly whispered.

"Nothing if you didn't pull the trigger," I said. Looking at the name on his driver's license, I said, "Mr. Laban, did you kill the swan yesterday up by Hannaford?"

"Yes," came the reply, with downcast eyes. "I was trying out my new rifle and just wanted to see how it shot."

"Why don't you just sit down, Mr. Laban; I need to get something out of my car."

He walked into the kitchen and sat down. I asked the sheriff to watch him while I went out to the car and got some affidavits. When I returned, I swore Mr. Laban in and instructed him to write, in his own words, a description of the previous day's events leading up to and including the killing of the swan. As a kicker, I removed the x-rays Gary Pearson had taken from their envelope and showed Laban the bullet clearly lodged in the visceral cavity of the swan. After seeing that last piece of evidence, he took the affidavit from my hands and commenced to write. The sheriff and I waited until he was through. I had him sign and date the document and had the sheriff sign it as a witness. In the affidavit, Jim Laban clearly spelled out how he had shot the swan from the road with his new Marlin .22-caliber rifle and let it lie where it fell. No further questions were necessary.

Seizing the Marlin rifle as evidence, I left Laban an evidence tag for the seizure and told him he could have the rifle back once the FBI forensics people were through with it. The Migratory Bird Treaty Act does not allow for forfeiture of a firearm used in the commission of a routine violation. Seizure of equipment used in the commission of a felony under that law, however, is allowed. His rifle would be returned in this matter because killing a swan in those days was only a petty offense. His eyes never left his shoes after he realized I was going to have the FBI run a ballistics check on the bullet removed from the body of the swan and on his rifle for a match. You readers are probably wondering why I would run a check on his rifle after receiving a full confession on the affidavit. A smart officer should never go on *just* what the subject of an investigation confesses to. The culprit could change his story on the stand, and then what do you have? It is always better to have corroborating evidence; hence my ballistic checks on the bullet and rifle. The FBI did corroborate that the bullet taken from the body of the swan had been fired from the Marlin .22-caliber rifle seized that day in Laban's apartment. Tests also corroborated that the photograph I took of Laban's tires when the sheriff and I left the apartment very closely matched the picture I had taken of the tracks at the scene of the shooting. Laban went on to pay a $500 fine in federal court for his day of target practice (that was the maximum fine in those days for a violation of the Migratory Bird Treaty Act). His rifle was returned, as promised.

Thanking the sheriff for his excellent assistance, I beat it back to Gary Pearson's in Jamestown and gave him a run-down on the results of the investigation. He was very pleased to have been of help as I thanked him for the valuable information about the Marlin. I told Gary that without that bit of information, I doubted I would have been able to make the case. Shaking hands, I left his clinic and headed for the Harvey area of north-central North Dakota to see if I could catch some lads who were not too good in duck identification, namely, killing protected redheads in some of the passes between local wetlands.

As a postscript to this story, my son Richard is a special agent for the Service in Bismarck as this tale is being written. He too was involved in a waterfowl investigation and had occasion to drop in on Dr. Gary Pearson to make use of his x-ray equipment. When Gary asked Rich if he was related to Terry Grosz, suffice it to say Rich was very surprised and amused that he was using the same fellow to help him with an investigation some twenty-four years after I had done the same thing! This apparent coincidence speaks worlds for Gary, not only as a professional but as a public-spirited citizen helping in any way possible to do his part to ensure that some of the world of wildlife remains for those yet to come. The American people need to doff their hats to such folks because the services that they render often help the critters win. That won't mean much to a lot of people until their grandson or granddaughter asks, "Grandma or Grandpa, what kind of animal is that?" The fact that children are still able to ask that question means that God and some human beings such as Dr. Gary Pearson cared enough to give a hand.

CAMPING OUT on a pair of wetlands just north of Harvey to save what little money the Division had, I rolled out my sleeping bag and then sat on an ice chest next to it to watch the sun set among some ominous gray clouds. It won't be long now, I thought, until the icy winds come howling down from the north and everything freezes up. Already it was cold enough that I put on a coat as I sat there having a rather meager dinner. I was trying to lose weight again and was on one of my innumerable diets. Tonight dinner consisted of a can of cold green beans. Man, how I longed for some of my bride's home-fried chicken, mashed potatoes, gravy, fresh peas with butter, and a slice of pie. Damn, let me tell you, a can of cold green beans is a long way from "home"! Opening a can of dog food for my retriever Shadow, I listened to her noisily eat as I watched the ducks trading back and forth between the wetlands. Both wetlands were jug-full of winter migrants, and I thought, If any hunters show up tomorrow, I may be able to write enough citations to pay for the gas and oil (an old saying of mine as a matter of measure because all fine monies went into the government's general fund and not into my pocket or the gas tank of my patrol car). Finally crawling into the sleeping bag, I listened to the birds overhead and my dog's snoring until sleep overtook me as well.

A hour before daylight the next day I was again quietly sitting on the ice chest, watching and listening to the day awakening around me. Breakfast was a couple of bites off the end of the stick of salami from a pocket in my hunting coat, feathers, lint, and all. The air was full of birds looking for that special spot for breakfast; the coyotes off to the west were singing in joy for the blessing of another day; and a red fox trotted out from a coulee below me, not noticing my presence, and commenced some serious mousing along a fence row. Shadow spotted the fox and looked up at me as if to say, Do you want me to chase 'im, boss? Reaching over, I gave her big, shaggy head and neck a long hug and was rewarded with the happy thump of her rudderlike tail. That little bit of movement caught the fox's eye, and it was gone as silently and quickly as a gust of wind over the drying prairie grasses. For the next two hours I sat in solitude with my dog, as is often typical in the North Dakota prairie, because not one hunter showed up for the party I had planned. The land was just so big, raw, and covered with waterfowl at that time of the year that there were a million places for hunters to enjoy their sport without anyone at their elbows. That was all right with me, though. I hadn't realized how tired I was until this morning. Hell, I could have slept another hour or two if my biological clock had not awakened me around four in the morning. However, it felt good just to sit there and watch the world of wildlife waking up around me and, not being disturbed, doing what came naturally with only my eyes to intrude. Grebes, coots, ruddy ducks, and loons had flown over my head all night as I tossed and turned in my unfamiliar prairie-grass bed. Their distinctive calls and the sounds of their wings had told me who they were. Being poor flyers, those species found it safer to migrate at night than during the light of day. Right at dawn the Canada geese had noisily lifted off the lake and flown right over where I sat in silence. Several times I had heard their droppings landing around me and felt the drops of water from their feathers on my face and hands as they passed overhead. Once daylight overtook us, the ducks were up and zooming overhead as they passed from one wetland feeding place to another. At first Shadow closely watched the birds flying over, expecting me to shoot. Once she found that she was not going to get to retrieve any ducks that day, she went back to sleep and retrieved them in her dreams, as evidenced by her foot movements and snorting sounds.

Boom-boom-boom-boom went the quick, soft thump of what sounded like two shotguns far off to the west. Hearing them with only a passing interest, I continued to watch the birds in the wetlands below. By now it seemed that the entire world of waterfowl was in the air, some just because they were alive, some because they were looking for breakfast, and many for the sheer joy of flying prior to their big migration south. I thought of my oft-repeated dream of wishing I could fly like them. *Then* think how many bad guys I could catch in a day. Damn, I would have been a holy terror! Yeah, right, I thought; and some damn fool, thinking you were the world's biggest goose, would give you a load of number 4 shot right up the tailpipe! Oh well, a "catch dog" could dream, couldn't he? *Boom-boom-boom-boom-boom* went the guns to the west again, but this time something was wrong. I replayed the shots in my "in-head tape recorder," carefully listening for the exact timing of the shooting sequence. Then I played it again. That was not two guns; it was one gun! It was illegal for one gun to be able to shoot more than three times at migratory waterfowl—*if* that was what the shooter was doing.

I no longer focused on the life around me but zeroed in on the sound from the west, hoping it would come again. I cursed myself for not paying better attention to the first set of shots, but you can't cry over sloppy field work. You just can't repeat it, and I was not about to. Just to find a certain shooter in this vast prairie would take some doing because of all the wetland shooting opportunities, prairie trails, gravel roads, and the like. Damn, I thought; an opportunity may be lost. A hunter does not hunt with an unplugged shotgun unless he intends to do some real wildlife damage, and this was certainly the time and country in which to do it. *Boom-boom*—there it was again! But only two shots, which wouldn't help me reconstruct whether the shooter was using an unplugged shotgun. *Boom-boom—boom-boom.* There! That was the same gun, with a delay in the shooting sequence. It had just shot four times, which meant it was unplugged. Time to swing into action, I thought as I got up off my dead hind end and in one fluid movement swung the ice chest into the back seat of the car. The instant I stood up, Shadow was up and on her feet. She was still about half asleep but, realizing something was up, didn't want to be left behind by not being ready. I opened the passenger-side door, and she sprang into the front seat. Quickly rolling up my sleeping bag, I tossed it into the trunk, checked the area one more time to make sure I hadn't left anything, including trash, loaded up, and headed in the general direction of my shooter with the unplugged shotgun.

Working my way west and then south on gravel roads, I ended up just south of Martin around a small string of wetlands. Getting out of the car, I lit a cigar, hoping to quiet the rumblings of hunger in my stomach, and silently stood drinking in the events swirling around me. The prairie grasses were rustling in the light northwest winds, and a hawk soared far off to the north, too distant to identify. A mouse ran across the road not five feet in front of me as if the devil were after him and hid in the grasses alongside the road. A minute or two later a long-tailed weasel, still wearing his summer coat, crossed on the same route, obviously with breakfast in mind. I heard a rustling in the grass, a small squeak, and then nothing. Just another day in the life of a weasel, I thought. Nothing else happened for about ten minutes; then, *boom-boom,* the soft sound of a shotgun, still several miles away. It sounded like the same shotgun, so I piled into the car and began working my way even farther west as my dog hung her head out the window in the joy of a new day and adventure. Several miles later I stopped in the middle of an overgrown grassy prairie trail (making sure my catalytic converter was over a bald spot to avoid the

specter of igniting a raging prairie fire), got out, and listened again.
I had no sooner paused in the middle of the trail when just to the
north I heard the familiar *boom-boom-boom-boom!* That is my man, I
exulted as I sprang for the patrol car.

Roaring down the overgrown prairie trail, I moved another three
hundred yards and then plowed to a panic stop! There, partly hidden
at the edge of the grassy prairie trail, lay a dirt bike. Damn, I thought,
another ten miles per hour and I would have driven right over it before I could stop! Quietly stepping out and avoiding slamming the
front door, I walked over to the dirt bike and touched its motor. It
was still warm. *Boom-boom—boom* went my suspected shotgun to the
west and behind some rolling hills. Near where I stood a wetland
ended right at the berm of the road, then meandered out and around
the hills to the west and out of sight. *Boom—boom-boom* went my
friend again, and in less than a couple of minutes four redhead ducks
swung down the wetland, over the road where I was standing, and
down the coulee to another wetland some one hundred yards away.
As they went by I noticed that a nice male redhead had one leg hanging down, typical of a bird that has just been wounded by a shotgun!
Quickly pulling on my hip boots and letting Shadow out of the car,
I removed the keys and locked the car where it sat. Then, by removing one little wire, I made sure that the dirt bike would not run until
I got back to replace it. With that, the dog and I headed out into the
wetlands and sloughs on another adventure.

Taking our time because I didn't want to break a sweat in the cool
of the morning, and I didn't have a whole lot of energy because of the
diet I was on, we moved slowly along at the edge of the wetland, hidden by the rolling hills. We had walked about one hundred yards
when again, *boom—boom-boom-boom—boom* went the shotgun.
Moments later a pair of redhead ducks and one gadwall swung below
us just feet above the marsh and continued on down the meandering
shallow wetland. Taking more time now and doing a lot of scanning
with my binoculars before I moved any distance, I finally located the
lone hunter in a large patch of reeds right at the end of a pass over
which ducks and coots were streaming from one wetland over the
narrow land isthmus to the next wetland. He was in a perfect place

to ambush his prey, and the birds wouldn't know he was there until they passed over his hiding place at a height of no more than thirty yards. About that time four redheads tumbled over the pass heading my way. My lad stood up from his hiding place in the tall reeds, the ducks flared, and then two dropped dead away as I heard the familiar *boom-boom-boom-boom!* Perfect, I thought. He had just fired four shots at migratory waterfowl right in front of me, a violation of state and federal wildlife laws. In addition, he had fired at and killed several redhead ducks, a totally protected species in North Dakota that year. Either way he was mine legally, and I was between him and his means of land transportation. And he didn't have a clue that the "sword of Mother Nature" was watching his every move!

My lad walked out into the shallow marsh waters and retrieved his two ducks. Then he stood for a long moment, looking all around to see if anyone else was in the vicinity. Satisfied that he was alone, he returned to his hiding place and disappeared. More birds continued to fly overhead, but he rose to shoot no more. Shadow and I waited in our hiding place in a nice stand of buffalo berry. There was no more shooting, even though ducks were swarming all over his hiding place as they moved from one wetland basin to another. An hour went by with no sign of my lad. I knew he had not escaped us because I held the high ground and could see all around his place of concealment. Then I saw him standing up, still well hidden, looking all around as if expecting someone or something to appear. Satisfied, out he came from his hiding place and started walking toward me as if leaving the shooting area en route to his dirt bike. In one hand he carried what appeared to be a limit of gadwall and in the other his shotgun. I noticed that he had a small backpack strapped to his back. I let him get within fifty or so yards and then emerged from my hiding place and started walking down the hill to cut him off. When he saw that he had company in his little hidden-away duck hunting spot, he stopped, casually worked his shoulders out of his backpack, and let it slide into the tall marsh grasses where he stood. Then, without so much as a backward look, he recommenced walking.

Intercepting the lad at the base of my hill, I hailed him: "Good morning, sir; federal agent. How was the hunting?"

"It was all right," he said as he stopped, laid down his ducks for inspection, and unloaded his shotgun. I showed him my badge and credentials, and he looked and acknowledged them as if nothing were out of the ordinary. I took his shotgun and checked it for a plug with my plug checker (a foot-long piece of soft rubber hose that would fit inside the magazine of a shotgun and carried markings cut on the outside to show when the magazine was of sufficient inside length to hold more than two shells), only to discover that it was now plugged. He must have replugged the shotgun during his long period of inactivity when he was still hidden deep inside his reed patch, I thought. It made no difference, though, because I had seen him shooting at ducks more than the three times legally allowed. Stepping over to the pile of ducks on the ground, I found him to be within the legal limit and carrying no restricted species such as the redhead. I found that very interesting because I had seen him killing and retrieving at least two redheads.

"Do you have any more ducks, sir?" I innocently asked.

"No, what you see is what you get," he matter-of-factly answered.

Turning to Shadow, I said, "Get the ducks," and used a hand signal to show her which way I wanted to her to start. I signaled toward the dropped backpack, and she went off like a shot. She sailed right over the top of the backpack before she realized what she had done. I saw her putting on the brakes and returning, then sniffing the backpack. Then she looked up at me as if to say, "Here they are, boss!"

"Bring the ducks," I shouted. Shadow instantly lowered her head, grabbed the backpack, and with difficulty staggered toward me, walking in a swinging gait as the backpack swung back and forth in front of her and between her legs. Looking at my lad, I said, "Looks like you might have dropped something."

"That ain't mine," he retorted.

"I think it is, since I saw you walk out of that patch of reeds at tenfifty-one with it on and then drop it off your shoulders at ten-fiftyfive when you saw me rise up out of the bushes I was hiding in," I said. He just looked at me and said nothing. Soon Shadow came huffing and puffing up to me, dropped the obviously heavy backpack at my feet, and then returned to a sitting position at my side. "You care to open it, or do you want me to?" I asked. The man, who was about thirty years old, just shrugged, so I opened the backpack. Inside I saw what appeared to be plastic bags filled with fillets from the breasts of ducks. "Looks like you had an exceptional shoot after all," I said. He still said nothing. "May I see your hunting license, duck stamp, and driver's license, please?" I asked as I stood up to face my shooter, who now had several legal problems staring him in the face. He obviously had a large over-limit of ducks and was also in possession of ducks in such a condition that sex or species could not be determined. State and federal hunting laws require hunters to leave a fully feathered wing or head attached to their birds so officers can determine the sex and species of the birds taken in order to check on whether hunters have observed legal limits.

The man's hunting license and federal duck stamp checked out, and I handed them back to the lad, now known to me as Thomas Schmidt. Emptying his backpack, I counted the duck breasts in the plastic bags and discovered that he had twenty-three more ducks than those he had carried in his hands, as represented by just the fillets of breast meat. That explains why he disappeared for so long in the reeds, I thought. He was busy taking the breast fillets from his ducks and putting them in plastic bags. Less chance of discovery and less to carry. It was a good move for a poacher; just the wrong time and place! Taking the information down on one of my field identification reports, I let him head on down the road because he said he had a lot of farm chores to do, including getting forty-five cows milked, fed, and watered. I told him I would be sending him a batch of citations in the mail for the use of an unplugged shotgun, over-limit, possessing birds in such a manner that sex or species could not be determined, wanton waste for the eatable parts (legs and thighs) he left behind on the breasted-out ducks. I told him I was going back to his reed blind to pick up the duck carcasses, and if I found any redhead carcasses in that bunch, he would be charged accordingly for taking protected redheads as well. I don't think I ever saw a man take a good dressing-down as he did that morning. It was almost as if he didn't care or had been there before and it was no big deal. I gave him an evidence receipt for the ducks seized (all of them, to show an over-limit) and for his backpack. Because I needed something to carry all the ducks, I seized that as well (it was later returned). I sat on the little hillside and watched him walk back toward his dirt bike; then the dog and I headed into the reed patch to see what awaited us.

Inside the patch of reeds we discovered the carcasses of twenty-four ducks, or one more than he had breast fillets in the plastic bags. Apparently, in his haste to breast out all the ducks he had overlooked one, which I added to the tally. As I dug through the carcasses, I found that the pile contained thirteen redheads, and I duly noted that in my notebook. Putting on the backpack, now loaded with everything I could put in it, I grabbed the remaining duck carcasses by their necks and started to return to my patrol car. Then it dawned on me! I still had the chap's dirt bike ignition wire in my shirt pocket. Remembering that he had forty-five cows that were probably very anxious by now to be fed and milked, I picked up the pace. When I reached the car, my shooter was nowhere to be found, and his bike still lay in the grass at the edge of the road. Opening my trunk, I tossed in all the evidence and then, pulling the ignition wire from my pocket, reattached it so the bike would run. Then I loaded the bike into the trunk and, after tying down the trunk lid, bounced down the prairie trail until I found the first improved county road. Swinging to the east, I headed for Schmidt's farm and hadn't gone a mile when I spotted my lad running at a dog trot toward his farm. I guess his thoughts were on his cows. Pulling up alongside him I said, "Hey, you forgot your dirt bike."

Stopping, he said, "Yeah, the damn thing won't run. Can you give me a lift to my farm? I need to get there and start my feeding and milking."

"Sure, hop in," I told him, which he did. I drove the last few miles to his farm and pulled into the driveway and around back to the milking barn. On the way, I spotted a large bunch of ducks hanging in plain view from a beam in one of his equipment sheds! Schmidt got out and ran to the milking barn while I unloaded his dirt bike. Standing it over by the bunch of ducks hanging from the beam, I walked over and began counting. There were twenty-two mallards in that stringer, all of which had been gutted or drawn for cooling, though none had been picked. Writing down what I saw on the stringer just in case someone moved it before I was through, I went into the milking barn to talk to Schmidt once more. Finding him frantically trying to get his overburdened cows attended to, and having worked in a dairy as a very young lad, I pitched in and gave him a hand. In about an hour we had things more or less under control, with a lot of cows showing a lot less of the worried big eye and a whole lot less udder.

"Tom, who do all those ducks hanging in that shed out there by my car belong to?" I asked.

"Me," came the reply.

"When were they taken?" I asked.

"Yesterday," replied my fast-sinking man of few words.

"Tom, when you get a minute, we need to meet outside and discuss those birds as well because I fear you might have some more trouble with the government on limits and such," I flatly stated. Going back outside to the hanging ducks and rechecking them, I discovered that all of them were drakes. That would make it a little better I thought. Not having any hens would certainly produce less complexity in Tom's life because of their bag restriction of one per day. Pretty soon Tom came out of the milking barn and walked over to me. I asked him, "Did you shoot all of these?"

He said, "Yes; I got those yesterday on a pond below the barn."

"Well, Tom, you already have twenty-four ducks over the limit, and now, with this group of twenty-two more mallards, you have a problem." He just looked at me as a man would if you had him down and were standing on his throat. "Tom," I said, "how many people in your family?"

"Just me, my wife, and the baby," he answered.

"Good," I said. "I will consider that you gifted one limit of ducks to your wife and another to the baby. I will ignore the fact you took all of these yesterday because you are in enough trouble with the law after today's shoot. Now, however, that still leaves you ten over the limit for yesterday, and I will have to seize those and issue another citation accordingly. I notice there is a freezer here in the shed. Is that full of ducks as well?"

Schmidt looked at me like a trapped rat. Before he could respond, I said, "I would like to look in that freezer if I may, Tom." Without a word he walked over to the freezer, opened the lid, and stood off to one side. Walking over to the open freezer, I peered in. Inside were several packages of frozen chicken, some pork, hot dogs, and twenty-one more mallard ducks, drawn but not picked and frozen as hard as a bullet! Turning, I said, "Damn, Tom. Do you have any plans to leave a few ducks for that kid of yours when he grows up?"

There was not much he could say of any redeeming value, so he just looked at me and I at him. Finishing my case work shortly thereafter, I drove out of the life of Mr. Schmidt with fifty-five illegal ducks, all the while shaking my head. Here was a guy who had the best duck hunting in the country and yet had gotten carried away three days in a row (counting the ducks in the freezer). Before it was all over Tom was cited for taking an over-limit of ducks, taking protected species of ducks, having several over-limits of ducks in his possession, taking migratory waterfowl with the use and aid of an unplugged shotgun, and possessing migratory waterfowl with no means of identification as to species or sex. I didn't charge him for the wanton waste of the bird carcasses left in the reeds where I had first found him in light of all the other charges. Suffice it to say, Tom had to sell a lot of milk in order to settle up with the federal court for $1,450 worth of errant behavior! I was finally beginning to sense the happiness over the moon of the duck for the Indians, commercial-market hunters, old-timers, and all the others with itchy trigger fingers or empty larders. There were so many birds in the area that killing was a cinch. And the real numbers had yet to arrive!

THE DOG AND I spent the rest of the day in the Woodworth area, checking what few duck hunters we could, and then at dark started for home, heading west on state Highway 36. It was dark, so I turned on my headlights with dreams of a great home-cooked meal and to hell with the diet. Suddenly I noticed that my headlights were not as bright as they should have been. Looking down at my gauges, I saw that my amp gauge was zeroed out, probably meaning a dead alternator. Stopping and opening the hood, I saw that the belt had come off the alternator; unless it was fixed, I would have only the time left in the battery and then I would be walking. Not having any tools in the vehicle other than a few of my own (the Division would not purchase any for us), I headed for the nearest help. Pulling into the small burg of Wing, I found a farmer who would lend me the right tools, and together we put the belt back on the alternator. When I offered to pay him, he just turned me down and drove off with a wave of the hand. Typical good North Dakotan, I thought.

I was starting to get back into my vehicle when I noticed a Chrysler station wagon going east on Highway 36 with three ice chests tied on top of the luggage rack. The vehicle had four hunter types inside, and as it went by I saw that it had Minnesota license plates. Now, in the Dakotas in those days, anyone from Minnesota was always a good bet for wildlife violations. I don't know why, but it just seemed that if you found such a group, you'd best shake them down because they were bound to be "wrong." I suppose part of it was that they were away from home and felt safer violating the wildlife laws in another state, and I am sure part of it was the high cost of nonresident hunting license fees. Many who strayed across the line probably figured that since they had spent $500 on this hunting trip, they wanted to take $500 worth of meat home. I don't know for sure, but I did know they were good bets for violations, and my gut instincts told me to follow this particular group. Incidentally, this attitude did not apply only to those good folks from Minnesota. Working big-game problems in the West, I found that anyone from California, Texas, or Louisiana was an equally good bet for wildlife violations—and *big* ones! When I worked on the East Coast with dove or duck hunters, it was anyone from Maryland, Illinois, or New York. And if the hunters were sons of Old Italy, well, what can I say? … Texans seemed to be the most arrogant when it came to major violations and Louisianans the most common and determined. The Texans' attitude seemed to be that they could just take what they wanted, and hell be damned. Not all Texans, mind you, but a damn high percentage of those I worked in my later years in the West in the major hunting areas seemed to be hell bent on election, if you get my drift.

Spinning my car around, I took off after the vehicle from Minnesota. In a short time I overtook their car and passed it. As I drove by, I looked inside. In the back of the station wagon was a dog carrier and all kinds of camouflage hunting gear, with shotguns in carrying cases lying on top. Pulling far ahead, I stopped in the middle of a long straight section of road and got out. When the Chrysler approached, I flagged it down and walked over to the driver's side. When he rolled down the window, I identified myself and asked the four men, still dressed in hunting gear, if they had been hunting. The heavy smell of whiskey rolled out the window, and I could see the chaps in the back seat trying to hide their open containers.

"Yeah, we have," the driver said, "over near Audubon National Wildlife Refuge."

"You boys do any good?" I asked.

There was lots of looking back and forth at each other for a few long moments, and then the driver said, "Well, we got a few."

"Ducks or geese?" was my next rapid-fire question.

"Mostly ducks," he replied.

"Are you lads carrying your birds on top in the ice chests to keep them cool?"

"Yes, sir," came the reply.

"May I have a look inside the ice chests and inspect your ducks?"

There was a long pause, and finally the driver said, "We are heading home and in kind of a hurry. How long will this take?"

"Five minutes at the most," I replied.

"Well, I guess it's OK," said the driver, and he got out of the car. The other three remained in the car and didn't move. That was strange, I thought. I would at least have gotten out to stretch my legs or let the dog out if I were stopped on a deserted road like this. The driver reached up and untied the ice chest nearest the rear of the vehicle. Lifting it down and opening it, I could see that we had a problem. Inside were thirty to forty completely dressed ducks. In other words, there was no means of identification as to species or sex.

"These are you folks' ducks?" I asked.

"Yes, sir," came a rather halting reply.

"Where are the fully feathered wings or heads for identification?" I asked.

"I guess we didn't leave any, mister," he responded weakly.

"Did you know that was a state and federal transportation re-quirement?" I asked.

"Well, yes, but we were going home and just figured that by cleaning them now we wouldn't have to do it late at night when we got back."

"Well, we have a legal problem here in that you can't transport waterfowl in such a condition that sex or species can't be told," I said.

"Yes, sir," he said lamely.

"What is in the other ice chests?" I asked.

The man hesitated and then said, "Oh, just some dirty clothes and food we didn't eat."

"May I look at those as well, please?"

He looked at me and then slowly got the ice chest down from the middle of the carrying rack, opened the lid, and stepped back. My flashlight beam illuminated another thirty to forty completely picked and cleaned ducks! Ignoring his lie about dirty clothes and uneaten food, I said, "Whose birds are these?"

"Oh, they belong to the rest of our hunting party."

"Where are those folks?"

"They left earlier today, and we told them we would bring their ducks back for them," came the even lamer reply.

Looking the lad right in the eyes, I said, "Look, don't let yourself get any further into this mess by lying to me. I suspect you folks had a really good shoot, and now that is coming home to roost. Do you want to share the truth, or do you want me to work hard and get it anyway?"

"Mister, I am sorry; these are our birds. We killed them yesterday and today, and they belong to all of us."

I looked at him for a moment, then thanked him for acting like an honorable man and telling the truth. Then I said, "What is in the last ice chest?"

"More of the same."

I looked at the lad. ...

"Do you want to see those birds as well?"

"Yes, I do, please," I responded. He got down the last ice chest and opened the lid, and there lay another thirty to forty picked and cleaned birds. Walking to the driver's-side window and leaning in,

I said, "The rest of you lads might want to get out of the car; it seems we have a problem here." Without a peep they all tumbled out of the car, their whiskey toddies forgotten. "Gentlemen," I said, "we seem to have a real problem here. We not only have a slew of picked and cleaned ducks, contrary to law, but a mighty possession over-limit as well. Does anyone have anything to say?"

The lads just looked at each other, and then a big fellow with a pot-gut that matched mine said, "Mister, what can we say? We had a good shoot, and now we are going to pay for it."

Looking at the lad, I asked, "Do any of you know how many ducks each of you individually took?"

They all looked at each other, and then the lad built like me said, "No. We just shot until we had as many as you see and then figured we had better go home before we got caught."

"Well, while I am counting out the number of ducks you have here, why don't you folks dig out your hunting licenses, duck stamps, and driver's licenses." With that I emptied one ice chest onto a small tarp I always carried and began counting. When I finished counting the ducks in all three ice chests, the figure stood at 105 over their collective limits! Shaking my head, I collected their driver's licenses but returned their hunting licenses and duck stamps, which were in order. Returning to my vehicle with their driver's licenses, I started recording the driver's data on my field identification report. I filled out a report for each man, then wrote out an evidence receipt for all the ducks and the largest of the ice chests (to carry my evidence). Returning to the hunters' car, I explained the federal court process and the citations that were to follow. All of the men were very quiet as I delivered the instructions.

Suddenly I noticed a Ducks Unlimited sticker on the side window of their car and asked if anyone was a DU member. After a moment of silence they all admitted to being charter members in the DU chapter in Moorhead! I said, "Does that stand for unlimited numbers of ducks in your ice chests or unlimited numbers of ducks for those yet to come?"

There was abject silence in the car and a lot of looking in other directions instead of at me. I let my question sink in for a moment, then

thanked them for their cooperation and walked back to my car. It took
a bit of doing, but I finally got the ice chest laden with all the evidence
birds onto the back seat. Turning my vehicle around, I headed for
Bismarck and that long-awaited homemade meal and some time with
my little family. As the miles ground on, I hoped my children would
have the opportunity to hunt ducks when they got older. ...

My four chaps from Minnesota never showed up in federal court
in North Dakota, preferring to settle the issue out of court through
the bail system. After paying $1,000 each for the error of their ways,
I wonder if they ever thought of going out and putting the same
amount into beef. I think it would have been a better deal!

Arriving home and stepping out of the car, I realized for the first
time that day how warm it was. My dad had taught me how to read
the weather as the Indians had taught him, and it was easy to see that
we were in for a *real* change. Any day now the arctic should empty
out in preparation for winter, I thought. Hearing the front door
opening behind me, I turned and was rewarded with the sight of
Donna carrying Kimberlee, our adopted Vietnamese baby, and saying, "Dinner in twenty minutes." Then out tumbled my two sons,
who were quickly impressed into helping their dad put away his law
enforcement gear, draw those birds not gutted, put the evidence birds
in the freezer, and feed Shadow. Finished and with both boys in tow,
full of questions about the day's events, which they thought had to be
considerable based on the number of "bodies" we had unloaded from
the trunk and back seat of the car, I went up the steps and into a
house filled with great sounds and smells. It was good to be home, if
only for a few hours, and you could bet damn the diet this evening!

DAYLIGHT FOUND ME sitting on the fender of my patrol rig just
south of Rugby. There was a warm air gently flowing from the northwest, and the air was full of migratory birds of every kind. From the
time I had arrived in the predawn dark until first light, I had been
overwhelmed in my senses by the huge numbers of birds in the air,
all heading south. Even during the drive up to my stakeout spot just
south of some great grain fields and wetlands that were commonly

hunted, I had noticed that the light from my headlights had been filled with little birds of every type known to God. As the sun rose even higher, I could see that we had the makings of a clear, dark-blue sky without a single cloud as far as I could see. Taking off my heavy-duty hunting coat, I opted for a much lighter one such as I would normally wear during dove season in September! All around me I could hear the soft *boom-boom* of shotguns going off, and I sat there trying to pick out the ones that sounded the most interesting for my line of trade. But I was in such awe, I just couldn't leave where I was sitting. The sky was literally filled, horizon to horizon, with skeins of birds by the tens of thousands, if not hundreds of thousands! You couldn't look at any piece of the dark-blue sky of North Dakota that day without seeing some kind of flying critter occupying that square foot of air! There were the stately white swans silhouetted against the dark-blue sky as they plowed their way south; there were ragged flocks of snow geese, some in the thousands, squalling as they went; and ducks, well, they were the filler in between everything else that flew. Soon the shooting around me slowed and then stopped as if everyone had paused to stand and witness the mass of migration leaving the arctic. The azure color of the sky seemed to get even more intense, and then, as if there weren't enough critters already in the air, even more birds crowded the already crowded skies from their homes to the north! Loons, with their odd silhouettes, came pouring by in the thousands, and birds of prey, out of place in the world of water birds, hustled their way south as if privy to what was coming next. Smaller insectivorous birds of every color and size flitted by like flocks of bees, hardly stopping for even that odd piece of grain left alongside the road. They were *really* on a mission to go south, and *fast*. Then the long, lazy skeins of sandhill cranes overflew everything below them by the tens of thousands with their melodious croaking calls. White-fronted geese by the tens of thousands came winging by, also going south with no stops, intermixing with the cranes. Canada geese by the thousands, intermixed with all their different species of kin, plowed southward not one hundred yards off the ground as if to avoid the traffic in the high airways. This experience was so grand, I just sat there in amazement!

I began to notice thousands of ducks spiraling like tornadoes out of the sky and stopping in the many wetlands surrounding the spot where I sat to rest and get a drink. Soon every available inch of water had a duck bobbing on it. It was not uncommon to see one- to three-acre wetlands holding five thousand ducks each! As this aerial circus continued, I noticed that the wind was beginning to flow a little more steadily, and now the prairie grasses around me were rustling and talking to each other. I was so awestruck by the magnificence around me that I didn't even notice the passage of time. It was now around two in the afternoon, and the only reason I even noticed was the drop in temperature. Instead of the balmy 65 to 70 degrees we had experienced at daylight, it was now only in the high 50s. The aerial display of every type of flying machine known to God and humankind seemed to peak during that hour, and I could see that the air was less and less filled with flying creatures. Don't get me wrong; there were still hundreds of thousands of birds in the air, but not the millions I had seen earlier. Those still there were flying with a sense of purpose noticeable even from the ground. I had never witnessed a mass migration out of the arctic and Canada such as this, and I didn't want to miss a moment of it—it was probably a once-in-a-lifetime opportunity for me.

The air flow turned from a series of gentle breezes to the start of a strong blow, and now I returned to my heavier hunting coat as the temperature continued to drop, now maybe in the high 40s. Birds continued to fill the skies, and I noticed that the ducks that had been happily bobbing in the wetlands were now lifting off in great black, noisy clouds and continuing their trip southward. Hunters who came by stopped to visit and trade amazement at what they had been witnessing throughout the morning. The temperature continued to drop, and now the stronger wind out of the north had a raw edge to it. For the first time I noticed a long gray line of clouds marching out of the Canadian Shield toward us to the south. Against that line of gray still came thousands of birds, almost as if fleeing something sinister, and those birds were not staggered all over the sky but determinedly staying on a course that allowed them to get from Point A to Point B in the fastest possible time. I became aware of at least a twenty-knot cold wind whipping around me, with the air temperature now in the upper 30s. The sky was not a beautiful dark blue, as before, but had become a lighter blue, signifying dust and other particulates in the air.

The skies were almost empty now as my watch told me along with my stomach that it was late afternoon. I changed into an even heavier coat and then realized that my face and bare hands were beginning to really chill as the wind picked up to about a steady thirty knots and the temperature dropped even further. I realized there was danger at hand and turned on my car radio for a weather report. North Dakota weather stations were predicting a blizzard with wind-chill temperatures in the *high minus seventies* by nightfall! Damn, I thought. Now I knew the reason for the mass exodus of birds from the north. This was the storm and the start of winter as the northern states knew it, as did the birds. With the low behind them, the birds had sensed the change and ridden the high pressure south. Realizing I had some distance to travel to get home, I started my patrol car and headed south. I was not alone, as all the duck hunters, realizing something was amiss, were heading home as well. Soon I drove into a huge dust cloud and snowstorm coming from the northwest and couldn't see more than twenty yards in any direction. Because all roads in North Dakota either run north-south or east-west, I just continued heading south on dirt roads, knowing I would eventually hit a main highway and could continue home on that. Now I really noticed the cold. The engine temperature never got off the cold mark on the temperature gauge, and that was using the hottest thermostat I could buy along with pure antifreeze in the radiator! Soon I was constantly wiping ice off the inside of my front window in order to see where I was going because the heater was producing only cold air! By the time I reached Bismarck many hours later, there was a wind chill of minus sixty, and the emergency authorities were advising everyone to stay off the highways. Nineteen people were to perish in that storm before it was over.

I had to marvel at my day. First the mass migration of millions of birds just ahead of this storm, and now a temperature swing of at least one hundred degrees in a period of about twelve hours! I also had to marvel at my brief period of waterfowl enforcement efforts over the several preceding days. I had spent several days away from wetland easement work and worked just the duck hunters. In that short time I had turned some damn fine cases, some of which I never duplicated in North Dakota! I had been in the right place at the right time and had been quick enough with my senses that I was able to educate some very serious shooters about the importance of conservation. I don't know how many converts I made, but you can bet some of them looked over their shoulders before they ever pulled the trigger again in similar circumstances.

What had started out as the moon of the duck in all its splendor in the fall in North Dakota had ended in the first blizzard of the season and the end of the moon. I would go on to work many more moons, but never again one that started with so many of the deaths for which the moon was named and ended with a flow of new life from the arctic that was nothing short of ethereal in its magnificence!

5

The Medicine Man

LIKE MOST KIDS GROWING UP in the West, I played cowboys and
Indians. For some reason, even as a little guy, I understood that the
cowboys always shot up the Indians because the Indians were the bad
guys. I remember how hard it was to get some of my classmates to
play the parts of the Indians. Plain and simply, they didn't want to be
Indians because, as I said, they were the villains and always got killed.
When I was in seventh grade my teacher, Miss Billy Jean McElroy,
got me interested in reading books, and man, what a great new world
they opened up for me. Pretty soon I was reading everything in sight,
especially books based on the true-life adventures of miners, outlaws,
explorers, fur trappers, cattlemen, homesteaders, and the like. Because
I was being raised in the Sierra Nevada mountains in the California
gold country, it didn't take long, with the world of books as a corner-
stone, to turn my heart and soul to the history of the land around me
and her peoples, both living and dead. That meant reading books
about the California Indians and, even more importantly, being privi-
leged to grow up among a few of them. Plumas County was home to
the Maidu Indians of California, and some of my best friends in the
little mountain towns of Quincy and Taylorsville were among those
people. I didn't look at them as Indians in those days, just friends, but
I knew they were a living part of the history of my county and often
wished I could have been part of *their* history. Through my newly discovered world of books I was also exposed to the history of the Plains
and the Indians who lived there. Man, did my mind race as I gobbled
up everything I could find on the history and lifestyles of those tribes
and their wonderful, in the eyes of an adventuresome boy, nomadic

ways of life. Soon I was fairly knowledgeable about the different tribes—where each one lived, how they lived, how well they fitted in with the land and its resources—and even learned some of the language of the fierce Lakota.

As I continued to read and mature, I became dismayed by how the Indians had been treated by the early white settlers. And, though of course I could not judge completely accurately because I had not lived during that dynamic time, in my young mind I condemned outright the people responsible for the Native Americans' misery and the destruction of what appeared to have been a rich and colorful way of life. That period in the development and settlement of our country carries one of the dark stains that runs through our heritage to this day. This destruction of aboriginal peoples and their many ways of life, many times intentionally, is not a piece of history to be proud of. One could almost equate it with what the United States did not do for Europe's Jews as they were forced into Hitler's programs before and during World War II, or the forced movement of Japanese Americans into detention camps at the start of World War II. However, human beings are prone to mistakes, in this country as in others, and I guess that is one of the prices we pay for living in a democracy. ... Of course, to a growing boy such issues often appear to be black or white, and my vision was no exception.

Then my mother remarried a unique and wonderful man with pioneer roots. He turned out to be such a good man that I started calling him my dad, and the name stuck. Dad had been raised in North Arm near the small mountain town of Taylorsville and went to school with numerous Indian boys from the Maidu Tribe who were living in the same area. Before long several young Indians had all but adopted Dad, and they spent countless hours after the chores were done teaching him Indian ways—respect for other people, respect for all living things, independence, tracking animals—as well as some of the language and all the natural pursuits of boys growing up together. Dad in turn, being an excellent brawler with a high threshold of pain, defended his Indian friends among the other white boys when racist remarks were made or insinuated. Even today, when I am visiting the Taylorsville area, I hear stories about my dad and his ability with his fists when he was riled up.

It wasn't long before Dad began to teach me some of the ways of his Indian friends, and he couldn't have found a more willing pupil. Dad taught me a lot about how to read the weather; to track an animal, especially a wounded one; to walk quietly; to be sensitive to the ever-changing country around me; and most of all to respect my fellow humans and Mother Earth. That guidance, along with my book world, cemented my ideas of the beautiful nature of the American Indian and all those peoples stood for. It wasn't long however before those idyllic notions were shattered.

In college I majored in wildlife management and finished my master's degree in 1966. Donna, my bride of but a few years, was pregnant at that time with our first child, and I needed a job. The good Lord took a liking to me, and soon I was employed by the California Department of Fish and Game as a game warden and stationed within ten miles of my old college. Working the mountains, ocean, and numerous salmon streams in the Eureka area, I soon ran into—or crossed swords with is more like it—members of the Yurok, Klamath, and Hupa (called Hoopa today) tribes living in that area. I discovered for the first time in my narrow view that traits such as drunkenness, child abuse, rape, incest, murder, arson, a tendency toward violence, and criminal abuse of the resources of the land were no less frequent among Native peoples than they were among any race. Theses people's misuse of the natural resources was especially noticeable when dealing with the salmon and sturgeon in the mighty north-coast river systems of California. Illegal spearing, dip netting, gill netting, use of dynamite, snagging, and use of rifles to take the migrating fish in the shallow riffles were all commonplace practices, especially on the great rivers that ran through the reservations. Coupled with these excesses was the tendency to illegally sell these fish to the white sport fishers along the rivers or to the big commercial fish houses in Eureka. In short, I began to realize, through my everyday contacts and experiences, that the Native Americans were really no better than anyone else as caretakers of the land. In fact, only the lack of resources, population numbers, or technology kept them from being just as efficient a destroyer of wild things as any white person going!

Despite my dad's teachings about treating every human being as you would want yourself or your family to be treated, I found my heart starting to harden in regard to American Indians. Everywhere I looked as a young game warden in northern California in those days, I saw the heartless destruction of a tremendously valuable land resource, with the Indians often leading the charge. Be it logging, commercial fishing, tribal fishing, mining, or anything else they touched, the illegal way seemed to be a routine thread in their everyday fabric of living. Soon the ideas I had learned from books and television about Indians living in harmony with the land, respecting the land, and taking only what they needed were falling on hard times within my soul. However, because of the gentleness of my dad's teachings, I kept trying to be as objective and humanistic as possible in my dealings with those inclined to destroy the land and its resources. It was not easy given the destruction I saw on a daily basis, but that objectivity had to be adhered to, and I am proud to say it was. However, it was at great cost to the idealistic notions about the "noble red man" that I had garnered from my world of books and my dad's teachings.

In 1967 I transferred from the Eureka Fish and Game office to the Yuba City office in the heart of the Sacramento Valley and was again faced with many resource challenges. There were some California Indians living in the area, but only rancherialike reservations (small pieces of ground with only remnant tribal populations) remained, and if one didn't personally know those natives were around, one would never see them. So for the next seven years I principally chased white offenders and thought no more about American Indians. I had seen how destructive they were to the deer, elk, and fish populations on the north coast of California, and that was enough for me. I had developed what was probably the same kind of closed mind-set that the peace commissioners, Indian agents, and land grabbers of old had when they dealt with the Indians during the 1800s. ...

In 1974 I was transferred to Bismarck, North Dakota, as senior resident agent for the U.S. Fish and Wildlife Service and, faced with a whirlwind of new types of law enforcement activities and their associated challenges, fell to with a youthful vengeance. One of those challenges was trying to keep bald and golden eagles alive and well in the face of a goodly number of Native Americans from the vaunted Plains tribes who were illegally shooting, trapping, and poisoning them. Once an eagle was in their hands, they would dismember the bird and use the feathers and other parts in handcrafted articles and in religious or ceremonial activities. In addition, the sale of items such as dance bustles, coup sticks, eagle wing-bone whistles, dance fans, and double- and single-train war bonnets to unscrupulous foreign and American collectors was big business, and I soon found this market to be monstrous in scope and out of control. How some of those Native Americans who professed that the eagle was sacred could kill them in large numbers, mostly for commercial gain, was beyond me. Entire reservations became killing grounds for the eagle, and when those supplies ran low, the killers would move off the reservations and take eagles wherever they could, including national wildlife refuges, national monuments, national parks, and state parks. The killing got so bad that the Service finally had to initiate a covert operation to investigate the illegal take and sale of eagles and their parts and products in the Western and Midwestern states. Bear in mind that the secretary of the Interior is the legal caretaker of the nation's Native American tribes through one of his or her agencies, the Bureau of Indian Affairs. The Fish and Wildlife Service is also under the secretary of the Interior. In essence, that meant that the secretary was turning loose the "law dogs" from one agency against his charges under another. Politically, such an act takes some doing and is usually simply *not* done unless the crimes being committed override the political considerations and the associated fallout.

Faced with the illegal killing, sale, and the recent addition of exportation to Canada of eagles and their parts and products for commercial dance activities, I couldn't help but revisit my romantic assessment of the American Indian. Confronted by the abject poverty and rampant abuse of alcohol and drugs on the reservations, I was hearing not only of the criminal abuse of wildlife resources but also the same old songs of rape, child abuse, murder, theft, and corruption, not to mention the uprising in the mid-1970s that led to the killing of two FBI agents on the Pine Ridge Reservation. I began to drift away from my longstanding respect back into an attitude of disrespect and prejudice against Native Americans in general. Those feelings made it difficult for me to reach out to people who seemed hell-bent on self-destruction and the destruction of a very beautiful part of the ecosystem that belonged to all of the American people. As more and more abuses filtered into my law enforcement intelligence system and I began to apprehend more and more Native Americans involved in the taking and sale of eagles, I hardened even further. I was no longer interested in Native cultures but in who was moving eagle contraband in commerce, when and where. Being in charge of North and South Dakota, I had my hands more than full of reservations, Native Americans, the illegal take and sale of eagles, and smuggling of artifacts and handicrafts, and no end was in sight.

One day I was working in my Bismarck office, preparing to present a case to the U.S. attorney's office for prosecution of a Native American for the killing of a golden eagle, when the phone rang. I was pleased to hear the voice of Refuge Manager Steve Berlinger from the Lake Andes National Wildlife Refuge, just northwest of Yankton, South Dakota. After calling each other a few good-natured names, we got down to the business at hand, which that day centered around some drainage violations in his area. After squaring those matters away so he could address the legal issues with the local landowners, Steve surprised me with his next concern. For years the Service had had an eagle repository in Pocatello, Idaho. The policy was that anyone in the Service who ran across a dead and salvageable eagle was supposed to box up the carcass if it still had any value and send it to Pocatello. American Indians from federally recognized tribes (of which there are over five hundred) could apply for those eagles and their feathers or other parts for cultural or religious purposes. It seemed that Steve knew an old Lakota medicine man who had applied for some feathers for a very special religious ceremony, but when he received the feathers from the repository, they were totally unfit for use. According to Steve, this was after the old man had waited over two years to receive the feathers! Steve, trying to be an understanding federal servant, was contacting me to see if the wrong could be righted. Now, in those days, as today, eagles were in very short supply, and their distribution was very tightly controlled. Even certified tribal members had to stand in a long line to receive an eagle just because there were more hands out than eagles to place in them.

"Well," I rather coldly said, "there isn't much I can do, Steve. You know the policy, and to be frank, there aren't enough eagles to go around with all the damn illegal selling and trading going on by all the tribal members across the land. They have created many of their own problems."

"Yeah, I know, but Terry, this guy is special—*really* special," Steve argued. "He is a medicine man, and it is very apparent that he is on a life mission. You need to meet him and see if that is not true in your eyes as well, and then maybe you can do something to help him out. I saw the feathers that were sent by Pocatello, and they are really bad. So bad in fact that he really can't use them for this ceremony, or anything else for that matter. You guys in Law Enforcement have the horsepower to release eagles and feathers outside the system, and I guess I'm asking you to come take a look and then decide for yourself."

Yeah, I thought, everybody is either a preacher or a medicine man these days when they want something. Not wanting to get involved, much less travel clear across the states of North and South Dakota to check out this Indian and his problem, I told Steve flat-out that I had more than enough to do with illegal drainage problems in Devils Lake and couldn't see coming clear down there just for that issue.

"Terry, I know the Indians have been giving you guys in Law Enforcement fits lately, but I wish you would reconsider. I have six good eagles in my freezers on the refuge and could give him one of those if you would approve it, and that would save you a trip," he said in a hopeful tone.

"No, I won't release any eagles to circumvent the system," I brusquely told him. "He will just have to reapply and wait for another shipment." Throughout the conversation I had been thinking that this Indian would probably just make something with the eagle feathers and sell it the same day to some white trader or collector. Then, without warning, something of the kid inside me rose up, along with a whisper of my dad's teachings. It was not a powerful sensation like the gut feeling I normally get in times of extreme danger but a feeling like a soft breeze moving inside me. Having experienced many similar subtle instances during my career and been rewarded for paying attention to those forces, I calmed the negative juices flowing around inside me regarding Native Americans in general and focused on this particular issue. Steve was a good man and a damned good professional. He was not prone to stretching the truth or pulling my leg. When he spoke it usually paid to listen, and listen I did—not only to him but even more importantly to those forces now whirling around inside my rather large carcass.

Sighing and without explanation, I did an about-face. I told Steve I would try to make it down to his neck of the woods within the next day or so, but it was going to cost him an oil change and lube, not to mention a tank of gasoline (it is hell to have to beg all the time for the basics that your enforcement division is unable to provide because the agency doesn't really give a damn whether the job gets done or not).

"Great," came his obviously happy reply. "And plan on a great home-cooked dinner as well."

I laughed and said, "Steve, not only had this detail better be as you said it is, but you'd better plan on showing me around the refuge as well as some of your problem easements to make the trip pay in effort expended."

"You got it," he said, and with that we hung up. For the life of me, I still don't know why I changed my mind in that instant—but I did.

Two days later I was en route to the Lake Andes National Wildlife Refuge, stopping at all the other refuges on the way to visit with their staffs and see if they had any problems and dropping in on all the local game wardens as well. More than likely, I was stalling because my negative feelings had returned and I just was not in the mood to give an Indian special resources only to have him turn around and illegally dump them into the black market. Yeah, special ceremony, I thought. …

Finally I met Steve. We had dinner, and afterward the talk drifted to the subject of the medicine man. Steve contended that the man was different than all the other Indians he had ever met. "Terry," he said, "I really think this man is the real thing. I really think he *is* a medicine man of the highest quality, and I hope you think so as well."

Looking hard at Steve and remembering my last nine years of dealing with American Indians tearing the hell out of the environment, I said I would reserve judgment until I met the man. Don't get me wrong; I am very much aware of spirituality and the role it plays in human life, especially in the world of the Native American. But I was skeptical of the need to kill eagles and sell their body parts to practice that spirituality.

The next day was warm and pleasant, almost as if it had been planned that way for a reason. I was in Steve's office awaiting the arrival of his friend, and to pass the time, knowing that Native Americans ran on "Indian time," that is, whenever they decided to get there, began to pore over some maps related to one of Steve's problem wetland drainers. All of a sudden there came a soft knock on Steve's office door, right on time, I might add. "Come on in," Steve called. Turning, I saw an old Indian man, tall and thin, dressed in a very clean pair of pressed jeans and a faded but clean denim shirt. His hair was mostly gray, with a few strands of black, clean and shiny, and combed back into two braids. He carried himself ramrod straight without appearing to try to do so, and his coal-black eyes were intense but calm. His angular, darkly tanned face was a dead ringer for the old photographs of the great chief Red Cloud. He wore handmade moccasins with beautiful red-white-and-blue beading, and he walked with a quiet grace and presence I had not seen in a human being in a long time. The passage of time had lined his face in such a manner that it could have been read like a history of his people. I watched him closely as he strode over to Steve and greeted him warmly. Then Steve turned to introduce him to me. I took his hand and was pleased at the firm and meaningful shake on his end of it. Clutched in his other hand was a medium-sized box, which he gently laid on Steve's desk as if it held a bomb or some other thing that needed to be handled delicately. Steve introduced me as the senior resident agent, the man in charge of the area, and asked the fellow to tell me in his own words what the problem was.

The old man acknowledged Steve's words, turned to me, and in firm yet moving tones described his problem. "Mr. Grosz, I am an old man and will die very soon. It is because of that little time I have left on Mother Earth that I must appeal to you, a white man, for your help. I was the keeper of a very sacred medicine bonnet for my people until it was lost in a fire several months ago. It had been in my care since 1920 and was passed on to me by my father, who was the keeper before me. My father had been the keeper for many years and had received the bonnet from his father. My father's father had received a vision from the Great Spirit when he was a young man about the bonnet and its sacredness to our people. The Great Spirit told my father's father there was a great and powerful medicine bonnet made by the Great Spirit's own hands in a cave along the Choteau River. My father's father was told to go and get the bonnet, and as long as the bonnet was in the hands of the keepers of the tribe, it would bring them through much sadness and keep them together and strong as a tribe. My father's father did as he was told and found the medicine bonnet in a small cave in the rocks, and for years this prophecy was true. As the moons passed my tribe suffered many things but always was able to survive to greet the sun from another day. But now, with the medicine bonnet gone, there is beginning a great uneasiness among my people, and bad things are being spoken about. That was until several months ago. During that time, I had a vision from the Great Spirit to go to the white man and get some eagle feathers from him but expect trouble in so doing. Then I was told, after the trouble to make a new bonnet and after a purification ceremony, to pass the bonnet and all its powers to my son. He will be the new keeper of the bonnet, and his son after him. Once that is done, I will die within three days and be united with my ancestors." After he finished speaking he closed his eyes and stood as if the two of us were not even there.

Steve and I were transfixed by the old man's story, not so much by what he said as by the manner and tone in which he delivered the story. There was a deep reverence in his voice that was not of this world! Though the atmosphere is hard to describe, it was a beautiful and moving moment that I will remember forever.

The old man again began to speak, almost as if he had needed the pause to gather his energy once more. Reaching for the box he had brought with him, he slowly removed the lid and stood back. I noticed genuine tears of great sorrow rolling down his cheeks and darkly staining the front of his shirt, but he showed no sign of shame. Reaching into the box, the old man removed several golden eagle tail feathers. His bronzed hand visibly shaking, he held out the feathers for me to examine. Instead of being removed by pulling them from the base of the tail, thereby preserving the entire feather, shaft and all, they had been carelessly cut away from the rump of the eagle with a knife or pair of scissors! Even my untrained eye could see that they had been ruined and essentially wasted. "No man should ever treat the sacred feathers from an eagle like this. They are ruined and I cannot use them in the making of the medicine bonnet," he stated. "I waited for over two years for these and know I will have to wait again for some more time if I want any others. I have no time, Mr. Grosz. *I have no time.*" His voice trailed off as he gently put the ruined eagle feathers back in the box and replaced the lid as if not wanting to see them anymore. He stood quietly for a moment with his hand on the box, then turned back to me and in a soft voice repeated, *"I have no time."* There were still tears in his eyes, and I could tell he was speaking from the heart and soul.

Without a moment's hesitation I turned to Steve and said, "Where is the freezer with your eagles?" Steve, too moved to speak, just nodded toward the next room. Walking into that room, I went to the freezer and opened the lid. I gently removed six eagle carcasses and laid them side by side on a nearby table. The old man's eyes never left those eagles as I laid them out. Turning to him, I said, "Take what you need to make the sacred medicine bonnet."

He looked at me with the most unusual look I have ever seen in a man's eyes, then or since. To me, it had represented 150 years of history, many years of wrongs and now a right. After that long, feeling look he walked over to the row of eagles and slowly moved his hand over them, almost as if trying to bring them back to life. He quietly chanted something in his own language as he picked up each eagle and examined it. Steve and I stood quietly by, spellbound by the intense and deeply moving moment. The old man carefully separated four eagles from the six and laid them off to one side. Then he repeated the examination process over the four, this time taking longer, until only two eagles remained on the table. Then the old man turned to face me and said, "I would like those two." He had a look on his face that I cannot describe here in terms that would do it justice, so I will say only that it was from another world and time. … Suffice it to say that I judged it as a look of great hope, almost suggesting eternal happiness.

The old medicine man left with his two eagles, but not before he gave Steve and me specific instructions on how the ruined eagle feathers should be destroyed—by fire from a sage bush and after a blessing by another Lakota. Then he left as he had come, quietly and with dignity. Neither Steve nor I talked much about what had happened that morning as we spent the rest of the day reviewing wetland easement drainage and stock-watering pond issues. It was almost as if we had had the opportunity to look into a sacred moment, and we did not want to break the spell.

I left that night for Bismarck and, in order to save per diem expenses, drove straight through, arriving in time for breakfast the next morning. I was happy to see my wife and couldn't wait to tell her of my latest adventure with the medicine man. She listened quietly, as she always did, and then said, "Learned something yesterday, didn't you?" Then she turned away and continued to cook breakfast for me and our children. Thinking over her question, I marveled at her always wise words, especially on matters as significant as the one I had just shared with her.

Three weeks later, as I was working up a case report on a complex wetland easement violation for the U.S. attorney, the phone rang. Picking it up, I said, "Good morning, Fish and Wildlife Service; may I help you?"

There was a long pause, and I almost hung up, thinking someone was playing a prank on me. Then someone spoke, and I recognized Steve's voice. "Terry, he got the medicine bonnet put together, and I was asked to watch the ceremony, from a discreet distance, of course. I saw the process of presentation from our medicine man to his son and new tribal medicine man. The ceremony was beautiful." There was a pause as I waited for him to continue, and when he did, I was shocked. "Our medicine man is dead! He died just as he said he would, three days after transferring the bonnet to his son. He just died quietly in his sleep, according to his family around him. *Terry, can you believe that?*" His voice choked with emotion, and I felt my eyes filling with tears as well, as they still do at the time I'm writing this story, twenty-three years later. ... We had shared a very special moment with a man who had the gift of being able to look into time. I have never had such an experience since. Even today Steve and I have a hard time talking without our eyes welling up with tears about that day with the medicine man as he picked out his eagles— and his time to die.

I am thankful that that moment brought me back to the basic lessons of life and the realization that other cultures have a lot to offer and a lot to wonder about as well as reminding me of the essential humanity of all people. Partly because of that lesson in life and my opportunity to participate in that sacred moment, there is a Lakota special agent in the Service, the first to my knowledge. Like the medicine man, he came to me in a time of need, and I did not turn my back or seal my heart because of that lesson the medicine man had quietly taught me so many years earlier. The Service is now blessed with an officer who, like the medicine man, is serving not only his own culture but all the American people. Somehow I think there was big medicine in that move to acquire him, first as a wildlife inspector and then as a special agent.

I have often thought about that medicine man over the years. I don't know why ... but I have. May all of you reading these lines walk the Red Road throughout your lives, and the lives you touch as well. To understand what I just said, you may have to read a good book on the Plains Indians. To do so would be to start to walk the Red Road.

6

The Border Wars

THE BORDER BETWEEN Canada and the United States is the longest undefended international border in the world. Spaced along that border at strategic crossings on the U.S. side in North Dakota are numerous U.S. Customs Ports of Entry. Many of the major Ports of Entry are staffed twenty-four hours a day by officers of the U.S. Customs Service and Immigration and Naturalization Service. There are also minor Ports of Entry scattered across this same area in remote locations along the border that are open and staffed only some of the time. Between those Ports of Entry are thousands of dirt or gravel farm, logging, hunting, and mining roads, most not appearing on any map. These roads are traversed on a daily basis by citizens of both countries who have legitimate business such as farming on either side of the border. These rural roads are also known and used by numerous illegal aliens, gun runners, drug runners, smugglers of human slaves, smugglers of wildlife, merchants of death dealing in explosives, and felons one step ahead of the law, be it U.S. officers or the Royal Canadian Mounted Police.

According to Central Intelligence Agency documents in 1997, the number one leader of commerce in the world is the sale of drugs. Number two in importance in world trade is the trade of wildlife and their parts and products. And number three in world trade, just recently replaced as number two by the trade in wildlife, is the sale of weapons and explosives. Just think about that for a moment. One would think that feeding the world's populations would be number one. ... Hell, it didn't even make the top three! The countries or areas of the world that most often deal legally or, more often than not, illegally in wildlife trade are Japan, Europe, and the United States. In fact, it is estimated that 45 percent of the world's wildlife and its parts or products is imported into and consumed in the United States alone! It stands to reason. "Advanced" countries whose populations have money and leisure time are going to import more of those things considered exotic than a developing country just trying to survive and feed its masses.

In writing this story, I was able to reflect back over a thirty-two-year career in wildlife law enforcement. At no time in that career was the smuggling of wildlife, the gross illegal take of wildlife, and the illegal trade in wildlife parts and products greater than on the day I retired and walked out the door in 1998! In addition, as I look back over that long career, I realize that the poacher's dedication to the moment, the increase in sophistication of his illegal trade, the scope and degree of his tendrils reaching into every part of government seeking information or political power, the ever-expanding black market, and the lust to fulfill the demands of this enormous greed and ego have never been greater then they are today. Many of the plant and animal communities reduced through illegal collection and trade have increased in value to the point that this trade will be lead to the endangerment or extinction of many of these species.

Everyone, from police officers to priests, the very rich to the very poor, those politically connected to those without any political power, has a dark side and is in some way responsible for the death and destruction of many of these plant and animal communities. Even seemingly responsible repositories such as colleges, zoos, zoological and botanical institutions, circuses, research facilities, and national showcase institutions are responsible—in part—for the continuing losses in the illegal trade occurring throughout the world today. One classic example of this apparently legitimate sleight-of-hand trade among responsible parties, in my humble opinion, is the giant pandas being sent from China to zoos throughout the world. These animals are highly endangered and are protected by some of the toughest environmental laws in the world. Yet, *for a price and because of politics*, they are allowed to enter countries such as the United States under the guise of scientific research or species propagation when in reality they are nothing more than a unique exhibit for the public to view in a cage on the zoo grounds. Sure, the recipient of these magnificent animals pays a high premium for the privilege of possession, and those monies allegedly go to scientific research in the donating country, but in the end viable genetics are removed from the wild populations to feed this type of craving with who knows what ultimate results. And for those zoos possessing such animals, an extra feather is placed in their cap in the world of zoo competition as they try to be the biggest, best, or most unique in what they have to offer. They have precious little to offer in the way of really lasting scientific research or propagation of this rare species, the main reasons given to justify bringing pandas into the country. And so it goes. ...

History is replete with examples of man's inhumanity to man. Yet modern-day scholars still fail to *really* understand our history and the history of the planet as it relates to our lives and survival today. God may have given humankind dominance over the plants and animals, but I doubt he meant for us to destroy them as we have done and are doing. I suspect that someday those who are destroying the world of wildlife for their personal gain may find themselves in a fiery resting place as an eternal reward for their destructive greed and egos.

While stationed in Bismarck, in addition to protecting the wetlands and national wildlife refuges; protecting waterfowl during the hunting seasons; protecting eagles from illegal aerial gunning by Service Animal Damage Control employees, along with shooting and trapping by Native Americans; protecting fur bearers from illegal aerial gunning, again by Service Animal Damage Control employees and the airborne shooting public; assisting the state Fish and Game agencies in their enforcement endeavors; providing training at the National Academy; attending state and federal courts; protecting the national fish hatcheries; and much more, I was also responsible for monitoring the international border and enforcing federal laws against the illegal flow of wildlife to and from the United States. As such, I was responsible for the seventeen Customs Ports of Entry along the North Dakota border, with only three agents in that state to address all the above issues and those of the border. After taking a hard look at the border problems and the magnitude of their geography, not to mention

all the other enforcement problems facing me, I personally knew how
Custer and Fetterman felt in their last moments! My trips and those
of my men were infrequent at best, but every official visit showed that
the quantity of wildlife flowing into the outback of North Dakota
through just two of the main Ports of Entry was tremendous. A number of ingenious methods were used to smuggle wildlife primarily into
the United States. With the import problem looming large, we made
an attempt just to address some of these issues, as opposed to taking
on the entire ebb and flow of wildlife commerce. Unfortunately, I had
other more pressing and serious issues facing me, and as a result we
fought the border wars with one hand usually tied behind our backs.

THE CUSTOMS PORT OF ENTRY at Portal, North Dakota, is in the
far northwestern portion of the state on state Highway 52. I first became aware of the import problems associated with this port through
conversations with Special Agent John Cooper, who was stationed in
Minot. Because I was his supervisor, it was not unusual for John to
grouse at me about all the illegal wildlife flowing through Portal in
violation of the Black Bass Act, Lacey Act, Migratory Bird Treaty Act,
and Bald and Golden Eagle Protection Act in the hope that he would
get some extra help along the border. Throw in the marine mammal
products sifting through the porous border in violation of the Marine
Mammal Protection Act, and you had potential work for a dozen officers in addition to the three of us stationed in North Dakota. In 1973
and 1975 came the Endangered Species Act and the Convention on
International Trade in Endangered Species of Wild Fauna and Flora,
respectively, and for all intents and purposes regarding import enforcement, we went under.

As if that weren't enough, the Service, through its usual processes
of brilliant reasoning, saw to it that the enforcement arm, mandated
by Congress to enforce federal wildlife laws, was perennially underfunded. Do you know what it is like to be an enforcement officer, one
of four for the states of North and South Dakota, with a mountain
of responsibility, and have to call the special agent in charge in Kansas
City to get permission *every time* you purchased a tank of gasoline

because money was so tight? Or to sleep on the ground when on the road, even in the dead of Dakota winters, because per diem expenses were lower that way? Or to take refuge cars after their mileage had been maxed out by refuge staffs and use them as law enforcement vehicles because your own assigned vehicle had over 200,000 miles on it and was flat worn out? Well, figuratively speaking, those were the times when we had only one Winchester between the four of us, and a handful of cartridges at best, if you get my meaning. ... But we made do, and made many of those crossing the conservation line drawn in the sand pay, and pay dearly. I can't help but think back on those times of fiscal and political limitations and what we were *not* able to accomplish for the American people and those critters without a voice because of those thoughtless limitations. What a waste!

In the fall of 1975, during the waterfowl and big-game hunting seasons, Cooper, several refuge officers, and I ventured north to Portal to conduct inspections on Americans returning from their hunting trips throughout Canada. When taking on the border and all its problems, it would have been nice to go prepared with the number of officers needed to *really* do the job. However, in light of the Service's policy of constant underfunding, that approach was not possible. Oh well, as they said in Texas for years, "one ranger, one riot"! As we were soon to find out, working our side of the border meant inspecting a flood of hunters coming home from Saskatchewan, Alberta, British Columbia, the Northwest Territories, and sometimes even Alaska. Boy, did we ever get our eyes opened to the magnitude of the wildlife importation problems—and got our hind ends worked off in the process.

Cooper had made advance contact with the Customs supervisors and received permission to work at the Port of Entry facility as long as we didn't get in the Customs officials' way or cause safety problems. When we arrived, the Customs supervisor showed us a little side area in which we were to work and basically turned us loose. The plan was that the Customs officials, once they finished with their own business, would question entering citizens to see whether they had been hunting or fishing. If they had, their vehicle would be directed to either Cooper's team or my team in our little corner. Boy, that sounded great. All two teams of us, four dingbats in total, as we were later to find out ...

I remember to this day the very first group of hunters I checked. They were returning from a duck hunt in Saskatchewan and drove over to my point of inspection in a bus customized into a huge motor home. Out tumbled eleven drunk, dirty, foul-smelling lads, with a two-week growth of beard per man and attitudes to match their appearance. I was instantly greeted with, "What the hell do you guys think you are doing? This is still not America, and only Customs has any authority up here." More of the same followed, which I just tuned out. When you can't legally break a loudmouth's jaw with a right cross to get everyone's attention, you just have to learn to adapt. I politely informed the gentlemen that they were incorrect; this was American soil, and the Fish and Wildlife Service was there to inspect any game they had taken in Alaska or Canada for compliance with U.S. laws. Well, I got a runaround as they claimed that they had to be in compliance only with Canadian law; to hell with U.S. laws because their game had been taken in Canada, and yes, they were in compliance. "Now can we go?" the vehicle's driver asked in a booze-laden voice.

"No, sir," I replied. "My partner and I still have an inspection to make, and if everything is legal, then you will be free to go."

"Well, hurry up, then," he replied as he turned and shouted at the other ten members of the party to get out their hunting licenses and ice chests so "these cretins can check our birds and be done with it."

I didn't appreciate being called a cretin but held my tongue and walked to the compartment side of their bus, where other members of the party were dragging out large ice chests—heavily laden ones, given the way they were handling them. My partner and I spent the next fifteen minutes or so checking eleven possession limits of waterfowl and upland game birds, accompanied by constant grumbling and bad-mouthing of the Service and its officers for creating such problems for decent, law-abiding American citizens. Again Jim, my refuge partner, and I held our tongues and, after counting all the birds in the myriad ice chests, asked whether they had any other birds or game on board. The driver of the bus, with a fresh drink in hand, began to insult me and my lineage. He let me know in no uncertain terms that all the game they had was in those ice chests, and since I had already looked there, my question was pretty damn stupid.

Having had a gutful of my loudmouthed chap, I moved off to one side of the bus and quietly told Jim to go into the Customs office and call the North Dakota Highway Patrol. I wanted a Highway Patrol officer to run a sobriety check on the bus driver before he drove anywhere, and I would hold them by conducting further wildlife inspections until that officer arrived. Jim grinned knowingly and headed for the Customs office while I turned to the driver and said that I wanted to check the inside of the motor home for any other game before he left. That brought a fresh firestorm of abusive language from not only the driver but several others in his party as well. They made it clear that I should be looking for some other kind of work because just as soon as these lads got somewhere civilized, they were calling Washington, D.C., and complaining to their congressmen.

Holding my hand up to silence the chatter, I said, "Gentlemen, the quicker I get to conduct an inspection of your vehicle, the quicker you can be on your way."

There was a long pause and some more angry muttering, with a few more "we need to call this guy's boss" remarks thrown in, before the driver consented to let me search the vehicle.

Entering the motor home, I was greeted with the sweet, heavy smell of stale cigars, booze, and dirty bodies. It was so bad I almost had to brace myself against gagging before I could continue. Starting in the messy bedrooms at the rear of the vehicle, I worked my way forward, carefully checking any area in which someone might have hidden extra birds if he had such a hankering. Arriving at the bathroom door, I found it locked and was greeted with a voice from inside letting me know he was taking a "Fish and Wildlife Service officer." Ignoring those remarks, I moved through the rest of the bus to the kitchen without finding anything of interest. Checking the refrigerator and its freezer compartment, I discovered a plastic sack of frozen breasts of what appeared to be duck or goose by the color and texture of the dark meat. Turning, I asked the driver what was in the sack. He weakly said, "I don't know, some hamburger I suppose." By that time Jim had come back, and I handed him the sack of frozen breasts and asked him to thaw them under some warm water in the Customs building and count out the pieces.

"You aren't going to thaw and ruin that meat, are you?" asked the driver.

"Yes," I replied. "That is the only way I can ascertain how many birds are represented in the sack. That is important to know since you folks are already limited out." Returning to the fridge I noticed four half-gallon milk cartons sitting in the back of the refrigerator compartment behind a bunch of plastic food containers. A closer look revealed that all had been opened. I thought that strange because usually one finishes one carton of milk before opening another. Digging through the other food, I picked up one of the milk cartons and pulled it out for a closer look. Suddenly I noticed that no one was on my backside with biting remarks as they had been earlier. Maybe a little more worried now, I thought, over my latest discovery. All was quiet on the western front, so to speak, but every eye was on me. Opening the first milk carton, I was greeted with a gob of duck breasts sitting in salted water! Removing the remaining three milk cartons, I discovered more of the same. I took all four cartons out to a table in our work area, dumped them out into a big pan, and began counting. Seventy-two half breasts representing thirty-six large ducks, probably mallard or pintail, was the result of my count. At about that time Jim returned and told me that the bag of frozen duck breasts contained twelve and a half ducks (apparently half of one duck breast had been eaten or discarded).

Looking over at the "mouth," I was pleasantly surprised to find that his motor was no longer running. In fact, he and his now quiet buddies were looking a little sick, and it wasn't from the booze and cigars. Returning to the motor home, I walked back to the bathroom door to find it still locked. I knocked, and a voice from behind the door told me that the occupant was still in the middle of a "government agent" and didn't want to be disturbed. He was unaware of the extra duck fillets I had just discovered, which had put his hind end in a lot more trouble than it was hanging out over the toilet seat. I told him that until he left the bathroom and I inspected it, his whole crew wasn't leaving the Customs checkpoint. With that I heard a little movement, and the door opened. I noticed he had opened the door awfully fast after I told him I was waiting until hell froze over—far too quickly to have taken care of the "paperwork" and gotten his pants hiked up and fastened. Also, I noticed that he hadn't flushed the toilet, and the characteristic "perfume" of a just-used bathroom was noticeably absent. As the man came out, I took a quick look at "bigmouth," and all I could see was a man with two feet in his mouth and a worried look on his face. Taking a quick look around without finding anything out of the ordinary, I threw back the shower curtain. There on the floor of the shower was a zinc washtub full of picked and cleaned, iced-down ducks!

I called Jim to come give me a hand, and the two of us carried the tubful of ducks out of the motor home. I asked Jim to fetch a Customs officer. While he did that, I started counting out the ducks. Fifty-two ducks later, which now put the lads 101 over the limit (the half breast counted as one), I finished my count. Walking back to my duck hunters, now quiet as a bunch of mice pissing on cotton, I asked for all their hunting licenses and driver's licenses. About that time Roger from the Customs Service approached me and asked what was the trouble.

"Roger," I said, "did these guys declare an extra 101 ducks over their limits on their Declarations of Entry?"

"No way, Terry. If they had, you know I would have sent them right over to be cited by you guys."

"Well, in light of that, along with their over-limits of waterfowl, they are also in trouble for smuggling, and your chaps might want to give them a toss to see what else they are hiding," I said with a grin.

Roger walked over to the group of hunters and asked who was the owner and driver of the motor home. The one with the big mouth, which had shrunken considerably by that time, stepped forward, and Roger asked if he had smuggled the ducks in without declaring them on the entry documents. The driver tried to hem and haw over the word *smuggling*, but Roger cut him short. "Did you or did you not declare the overage of ducks when you came through?"

Realizing Roger was getting a little hot under the collar and really not sure how to deal with a Customs officer, the driver gulped, "No, sir."

"Wait here," Roger said as he whirled and headed back toward the Customs office. Within moments Roger and two other officers briskly walked back to the motor home as Jim and I watched, feeling vindicated. Roger said, "All you men gather around me." When they had done as he asked, Roger informed them that if they had anything in the motor home that they had purchased in Canada and not declared, they had five minutes to get it out and hand it over. When they finished that little task, the Customs officers would go through the motor home with a fine-toothed comb, and if they found any more contraband, "You can kiss this motor home good-bye under our seizure laws."

Man, you talk about a scramble! Those guys streamed back into the motor home, and everything from Cuban cigars, condoms, booze, and new socks to a rifle purchased from the farmer on whose land they had hunted came flying out! About that time, as if things had not gone badly enough, the North Dakota Highway Patrol officer arrived and met with Jim and me. We informed him about the heavy drinking by all concerned, especially the driver, and he said, "Well, even with Customs rattling their collective cages, let me see what I can do." As it turned out, the driver was marginal for driving under the influence, as were three others who could drive the motor home. As a result of those field sobriety tests, the Highway Patrol officer made them sit there for two hours until the alcohol had metabolized enough that they could safely drive. That worked out pretty well for us, though. By the time we were finished writing up all the lads for their over-limits and seized all their ducks, Customs had about finished up with the paperwork relative to the items smuggled into the country. Suffice it to say, by the time all of us were done with the lads, and they had been standing outside in the cold North Dakota wind for the hours they were detained, they ended up a pretty tame bunch. When they were finally allowed to leave, as the driver passed Jim and me in his big motor home, he gave us a dirty look and flipped us the bird. As he drove out of the detention area and onto the highway, I heard a loud *bang!* Looking at the motor home, I noticed it pulling off to the side of the highway with a left front tire flatter than a pancake! Jim and I got to laughing and then roared. The man had no more given us the bird than he blew a front tire. Who says there isn't a God? Especially one who loves game wardens ...

By now hunting traffic was flowing into our areas at such a volume that the four of us were unable to check every vehicle coming through and ended up checking every third to fifth one, depending on the volume at the moment, and letting the others just pass through. Jim and I spent most of the day writing citations for minor violations such as over-limits of ducks, geese, cranes, and several species of fish. Soon the freezer that Customs had lent us was full, as were all our ice chests, and the evidence flowed out onto the cement walkway next to the Customs office. It seemed as if every other car had a wildlife problem, and we just couldn't keep up with the illegal flow. I was disappointed that day in the American hunters and their lack of sportsmanship when it came to recreation in another country. We saw a lot of slobs that day!

About four in the afternoon, a truck with a utility bed and its dozens of locked side compartments swung into my side of the inspection area. Greeting the driver, I asked how he had done, and he replied, "Very well, thank you. I got limits of ducks, geese and grouse."

"May I check your birds and licenses please?" I asked, and he agreed.

Getting out, he walked to the back of the truck, and there, among suitcases of clothing and the like, sat three taped-shut ice chests. "The birds are in there," he said, pointing to the ice chests as he dug through his wallet for his licenses. While he did that, I cut open the ice chests and took a look at his birds. He had complete possession limits of ducks, geese, cranes, two species of grouse, walleye, and northern pike, all of which were well taken care of. Anytime I find someone with complete limits of everything possible, I get a little suspicious. True, they are legally entitled to them, but something inside me always says to check further to see if they are greedy and have any more hidden away. Turning, I found that the lad had all his hunting licenses out and in order for me to examine. Still a bit uneasy, with my cautionary instinct on a roll, I asked if he had any other game to declare, and with just a moment's hesitation he said no. Something was just not right, and several times I caught Jim looking at me like a robin at a worm, as he suspected something out of the ordinary as well.

Finally realizing I had to make a move or let my happy hunter go, I said, "I would like to look in the locked boxes and compartments alongside the bed of your truck if you don't mind."

"Sure," he said quickly and, digging out a set of keys, began unlocking the compartments. As he unlocked each compartment, he stepped back so I could look inside. Being a plumber, he had a ton of tools and plumbing supplies in every box that he opened for inspection. Each time I stepped forward and looked in at all the boxes of gear; then he closed and locked the door. Then he would open another locked door and we would repeat the process. Something was still wrong, my instinct kept telling me, and when he opened the next compartment, instead of just looking in, I unloaded a few things and shoved my hand down into the black of the compartment to feel around in the bottom. My hand hit a gunnysack, and *it moved!* Jerking my hand out in surprise, I looked at my chap, and he just looked back with a sick expression. Shoving my hand back down into the very bottom of the compartment, I grabbed the gunnysack and lifted it out. Whatever was inside, it was still moving, so I untied the top of the sack and looked in. There in the bottom were two live and crippled spoonbills (ducks), looking woefully up at me. Both had been shot in the wings and, although the wings were not broken, could not fly. It appeared that my happy hunter had retrieved them and was bringing them home alive for some reason. The only problem was that it was illegal to have live sport-shot waterfowl in one's possession. In addition, he already had full limits of everything imaginable, and these live birds would now put him over in that department.

Jim just looked at me with a case of the big eye, not believing what he was seeing. Turning to my lad, I asked him to reopen the earlier boxes, and when he did I unloaded the gear on top and reached down into the bottom of those compartments as well. Each time I felt a moving gunnysack! Bringing the next bag out into the light of day, I discovered a crippled wing-shot Canada goose with his bill taped shut so he could not call out. Again and again and again and again, I repeated this exercise until I had retrieved a total of thirty-seven live, crippled ducks, geese, and one arctic swan! My now not-so-happy hunter just stood there as I retrieved bird after bird, saying nothing. Finally finished with the search, I turned and asked the lad, "Why?"

"I was just taking them home for my little girls as pets," he sickly replied.

"Well, these thirty-seven birds put you over the limits for ducks and geese, so you will be receiving citations accordingly, and there is no open season on the swan. In that case, there will be a citation for the illegal possession of a protected game bird, to wit, one swan as well. Plus you are going to lose all of your waterfowl because of your over-limit status." He just continued looking at me as if someone had just taken a rather large chomp out of his hind end. "Additionally, it is illegal to possess live crippled sport-shot waterfowl, and another citation will be issued for that," I told him.

My man just looked at his feet as Jim and I seized all the birds, filled out the evidence tags, and issued the citations. By the time we finished, our chap was almost physically sick and had to excuse himself several times when he felt like he was going to upchuck. I felt sorry for the lad, but I felt a whole lot sorrier for the crippled birds riding in those cramped and dark compartments for hours on end without any water and with taped bills. The Customs lads chewed off the remainder of his tail end for not declaring the wildlife and let him go on down the road with a warning for smuggling. That he did, and man, did he ever have a hitch in his giddy-up as he drove out of sight.

Finally we got so backed up that all four of us had to take vehicles and conduct inspections on our own in order to keep things moving. As the day slowly turned into night, we continued checking literally hundreds of white-tailed deer, bear, moose, elk, ducks, geese, fish, grouse, live circus animals, zoo animals being imported for various zoos throughout the Midwest, live birds of prey imported by falconers, scientific specimens going to college collections, sperm from rare birds of prey, Native Americans trying to import or export eagle feathers (prohibited at that time), live tropical fish, wildlife parts and products, research primates, and everything else imaginable under the sun. We made so many seizures for the illegal importation of sport-shot wildlife that the items just stacked higher and higher on the sidewalk next to the Customs building, which drew crowds looking on in amazement and disgust.

About ten in the evening, I got a break in the traffic and took the time to watch my refuge partner checking out six goose hunters. They had arrived with full possession limits, or sixteen geese per man. In those days you could take only three white-fronted geese per day and could have only three in possession no matter how long you hunted. The other five geese in your daily bag limit could be any species. Those of you who have never eaten a white-fronted goose, or "spec" as they are sometimes called because of the speckled black breast feathers (which are an indicator of the bird's age), have not lived. White-fronts are almost exclusively seed eaters and as a result are a culinary delight! Because they are such excellent table fare, it is not uncommon for hunters to kill more of that species than the other lesser-tasting goose species and to smuggle their picked and cleaned bodies across the border as one of the lesser ones more liberally allowed in the bag. U.S. law requires a fully feathered wing or fully feathered head to be left on the bird during transport for identification purposes. That privilege is granted to the hunting public so they can pretty well clean up the birds before transporting them and not have to bother with a wholly feathered bird and all the associated mess. But, as we found out, many hunters picked the wing almost clean, and then it was up to the officer to try to determine the species so he could ascertain whether the hunters had stayed within the prescribed bag and possession limits for the province in which they had hunted.

Well, that particular evening I was standing off to one side watching Jim check out his hunters and noticed that the entire group had picked their birds almost clean out to the last wing joint, leaving just the primary flight feathers. In addition, the birds were wet, having been frozen, and were a mess to identify. Jim was trying to spread out the partially frozen wet wings in the dark and identify the species from what little had been left on the wings. His task was made even more difficult by the men, who were squalling about being in a hurry to get home to Rapid City, South Dakota, and were ragging on Jim to hurry up. I stepped in to give him a hand. I could tell Jim was relieved because his duck and goose identification skills were limited to those species most often checked in North Dakota, and usually in full feather in the field.

"Evening, gentlemen. My name is Terry Grosz, and I am a special agent with the Fish and Wildlife Service. Since you are apparently in a hurry, why don't I have Jim check your licenses and I will check your birds. That way we can speed up this process and get you on your way." They all nodded in agreement, and as Jim began checking their licenses, I checked the birds. "You boys hunting in Saskatchewan?" I asked as I checked out the wings.

"Yes, sir," came several replies. I needed to know so I could determine how many birds they could kill as well as numbers allowed of each species. By count, they appeared to be numerically correct, and then I noticed something ...

Standing up, I asked, "Who shot the over-limits?"

Man, you could have heard a pin drop. Even Jim, who had made a cursory check of the birds, had a questioning look on his face. "What are you talking about?" one lad said cautiously. "I didn't shoot any over-limit."

"Well," I said, "let me ask all of you several questions. Did all of you shoot these geese?"

"Yes," came the collective reply.

"Did all of you kill a limit of Canada geese and white-fronts each day you hunted?"

"Yes, sir," came the collective reply once again.

"Then why did all of you bring just the white-fronts across the border, in violation of U.S. and Canadian laws?"

There was instant denial and such a roar of disapproval regarding my identification of the birds as you never did see. Getting them shut down for a moment, I said, "Lads, every bird in that bunch in front of us is a white-front! Even without most of the wing, as is required by Canadian and U.S. laws, I can still tell they are all white-fronts." Man, more howling followed that statement, and I could tell from the questioning look on Jim's face that he was in the dark regarding my discovery as well. "Gentlemen," I said, "let me explain."

"Yes, please do," said a heavyset lad, "because I would like to know how in the hell you know those are white-fronts and not Canada geese."

The way he said it told me this chap was in a challenging mood, and if I didn't want a "hoorah" right then and there, I had better have a damn good response. "Gentlemen, I have a college degree in wildlife management and a master's in waterfowl management as well. I have taught waterfowl identification for the past ten years not only at the National Academy but at various state Fish and Game schools and academies. Now, let me show you why I say these geese are all white-fronts and not a mix of white-fronts and Canadas, as they are supposed to be." Taking a wing from one of the frozen geese lying on the tarp on the ground, I spread out the remaining primary feathers and pointed to the shafts on the feathers. "As you can see, gentlemen, the shafts on the primaries are dark brown or even tan. The shafts on the primaries of Canada geese are coal black."

The lads just looked at me, and not one of them seemed to even blink at that revelation. I walked over to the huge pile of ducks and geese seized earlier from other hunters, picked out a Canada and a white-front, and walked back to my lads as they silently stared at me and what I was carrying. Boy, if they only realized that most people, if they are innocent, will keep squawking about their innocence the whole time, not just stand there and remain silent like these lads! Just another tip of the trade I thought I would share with Jim when we finished. Taking a Canada goose wing, I spread out the primaries and showed the lads the coal-black shafts. Not a word was said. Then I grabbed my white-front and, spreading out the wing, showed them the brown shafts on the primaries. Looking up at all the faces, I saw only resignation and wonder. The whole bunch thought they could cut a fat hog in the ass by picking the wings almost clean and then running them across the border in the dark. Little did they know they just picked the wrong chap to look them over.

"Well, gentlemen, what about my identification? Am I right on or all wet?" The lads just looked at each other, all waiting for someone else to speak up with a story, but none came. With that kind of body language, I knew it was all over, and it was. Without waiting for a response, I said, "Jim would you please write up all these chaps for possessing an over-limit of white-fronts, to wit, ten over the limit, seize the birds, and give each man an evidence tag for what is seized." With that, I turned and walked back to my own spot as another carload of hunters drove up for inspection. Turning, I said, "Oh, Jim, be sure to write the lads up for not having fully feathered wings for identification on the geese, as is required by law, as well."

My goose shooters just looked at me and said nothing. Game, set, match, I thought. ...

The hordes of hunters and a few commercial shipments of wildlife continued to flow, and all of us, skipping dinner, kept up the pace. By now our feet felt like plates after walking on concrete and asphalt for the last fourteen hours, and no let-up was in sight. Around midnight a new Blazer drove up, pulling a homemade wooden trailer that was at least twelve feet long. Right behind it pulled in two more new Blazers, a Suburban, and a Plymouth Ram Charger (not a Dodge). All the rigs prominently sported decals of conservation organizations: "Ducks Unlimited," "Trout Unlimited," "Pheasants Forever," "Safari Club International," and the like. As the group of twenty well-dressed men got out and stretched, I could tell by the cut of their clothes that they were moneyed folks. They were in Cooper's inspection line, and, realizing he would need some help to process that many chaps, I headed over to give him a hand. I wish I hadn't!

I heard Cooper's tired but cheerful voice saying, "How did you guys do?"

"We all got limits," answered the driver of the Blazer pulling the trailer.

"Do you folks mind if we check your birds?" asked Cooper.

"No, go right ahead, we need some time to stretch anyway," responded the driver as he headed back and unlocked the rear door to the trailer. Coop and I each took a side of the bottom-hinged heavy door and lowered it to the ground so we could walk up it and into the trailer to check the birds. There greeting our senses was *not* a sight for sore eyes. Taking up the front third of the trailer was a mound of ducks, geese, cranes and grouse *fully five feet high!* And that wasn't all. As Coop and I started up into the trailer to check the birds, the warm, sickly-sweet odor of rotting flesh slammed into our nostrils. It was so bad I quickly stepped out of the trailer to avoid puking as Coop started dry-heaving right in their trailer! It turned out that not a bird had been gutted, and as they had shot, the hunters, thinking it was cold enough for the carcasses to be preserved, had tossed them into a warm pile in their trailer to slowly decompose. God, what a horrible mess! Other hunters began to gather around to look at the "great kill" by all these members of the elite from the various conservation organizations, and the crap hit the fan when these other members of the hunting fraternity got a whiff of how these lads had taken care of over four hundred ducks, geese, cranes, and grouse! That wasn't the worst part. As Cooper and I began dragging out the various piles of ducks and geese, many still in their duck straps, to count and identify them, *their heads pulled off their necks* owing to the state of decomposition they were in! As Coop and I worked through that bunch of birds, we could not believe what poor care these "sportsman" had taken of their bounty. Nor could all the other less fortunate hunters with just a few birds in their limits who were standing around looking on. Pretty soon insults began flying back and forth between the members of the party with the rotten birds and the general hunting public observing in disgust: "That is a typical Ducks Unlimited member all right. Too damn lazy to clean his birds." "They ought to be shot for putting such little care into those birds." "I ought to whip your ass right here and now for what you guys did to those birds," and on it went. Eventually Coop and I had to climb out of the trailer and break up the angry crowd.

It turned out that the lads were in full compliance with their bag and possession limits, and all their licenses were in order. Since our federal regulations did not address wanton waste in such situations, there was nothing Coop and I could do but let them head on down the road for home. It took about twenty minutes to get everybody else who had seen this example of disrespect for the sport calmed down and off their high horses.

By the way, our "sports" with the warm pile of ungutted birds *lived in Ohio.* They figured they still had a two-day trip ahead of them before they got home.

THE CUSTOMS PORT OF ENTRY at Pembina, North Dakota, is about as far east in the state as one can go without crossing into Minnesota. It is located on the north end of Interstate 29 where it intersects with the Canadian border. Frankly, it is so far in the outback of the state that all the chickens running around up there have square faces. In the late fall of 1975 Tom Sechrist, my special agent in Devils Lake, was unable to provide much enforcement coverage in the way of monitoring the American hunting, fishing, and commercial wildlife importing and exporting public through the Pembina Customs Port of Entry because his wife had been taken sick. After receiving a call from Tom about his temporary inability to provide assistance to the Customs officers and not having visited that port myself yet, I agreed to slide over to the port for a few days. I figured since I was going to be in the general area anyway doing some wetland easement enforcement work, I might as well as fill in for Tom and get an idea of the wildlife traffic at Pembina in the same breath. Again, it was one of those situations such as one finds himself in when eating raw tripe. The assignment, once undertaken, just got bigger and bigger and bigger.

Not having been at Pembina before and not really knowing what its border war workload would be like, I went it alone. I introduced myself to the Customs lads on shift and asked the supervisor if he would have a problem if I checked a few returning sportsmen or commercial importers of wildlife as they entered the United States. He had no problem just as long as it didn't interfere with his officers' work, so we were set. In fact, we were more than set. It seemed that one of his officers had always wanted to be a special agent for the Service, and once off duty with Customs, he offered to give me a hand to see what Service fellows did for a living. Happy to have the company, I accepted. For about the next three hours, I checked the run-of-the-mill sportsman coming home with a few ducks too many, ducks with no evidence of species or sex (no fully feathered head or wing attached, as required by law), too many grouse, and so forth—and so it went into the evening. The Customs lad was having the time of his life and was now sure this was the kind of career he wanted. Every time another car pulled up for inspection, he just couldn't contain himself, hoping for another violation. He sure was eager; I had to give him that. He left for about an hour to eat dinner, then back he came to help me some more as the evening turned late. He should have stayed home. ...

In came a Ford 350 with a cab-over camper, pulling a large homemade trailer. From the looks of the trailer's flattened-out springs,

I could see that the hunter had a load. Once Customs had finished with him, he drove over to where the Customs lad and I were standing to conduct his wildlife inspection. The door to his pickup flew open, out came the driver, just a-flying, and he puked right there in front of us! We jumped back so the slop bouncing off the pavement wouldn't land on our boots or pants, and I asked, "Are you all right?"(A real bright question!) After a few more heaves of what had obviously been a rather nice Chinese dinner, he quieted down and without any explanation shook his head and started digging out his hunting licenses while the snot from heavy puking started running out of his nostrils, only to hang up on his bearded chin. I noticed that his hands were shaking as if he were about to crap a bunch of razor blades, and eye contact was nil as the line of snot broke off and dropped into his open wallet! Sensing this lad was in the toilet with some kind of serious wildlife violation, I said, "Why don't you just tell me where the illegal game is located and get it off your chest?"

His eyes whipped up to look at mine, and he said in a very loud and pissed (not to mention pukey-smelling voice), "Who told you about that?"

Calmly looking at my battle-rattled chap, I said, "You did. It isn't often a man pukes because he is so scared about being checked and then is so shaky that you would not want him to be the man alongside you pouring liquid nitroglycerin into a vial. Now, where is the illegal moose?" I was taking a guess on the moose, but he had what appeared to be a Weatherby .340 (a very large-bore hunting rifle, good for large, thin-skinned game animals) hanging in his cab gun rack, he was driving a pickup meant for tough loads, and his trailer was sprung heavy and, at the moment, sagging on those springs.

The lad just looked at me for a moment and then in a sharp tone said, "Since when do you guys run game checks at the border like this?"

"Since now," I replied.

He just looked at me for another long second and then said, "All right, we might as well get this over." He headed for his trailer. The Customs chap and I followed, and once the trailer tailgate was down, our chap backed off and we looked in. Not seeing much in the dark of the trailer, even with my flashlight, but a mound of canvas, tents, and other outdoor gear, I crawled in. That was the last thing I should have done! The floor of the trailer was covered with rancid-smelling grease, and soon it was all over my hands, knees, feet, and pant legs. Digging under the canvas, I was greeted with an aroma that spelled only one thing: meat starting to rot! Pulling back the tarp, I was greeted with the view of the cut-up bodies of two *huge* bull moose that smelled as bad as a set of aroused mink! Talk about stink now that the tarp was off the meat! As I started to pull the mass of moose chunks apart so I could count how many moose were in that fetid pile, slimy green decomposing meat, like snot, came off in my hands! When my Customs helper who wanted to become a special agent in the worst way got a whiff of that aroma and saw the green slime dripping from my hands, he headed for the bathroom inside the Customs building, and that was the last I saw of him for the duration of my stay. Dragging out enough chunks of partially rotting meat for two moose and the hindquarters from another, I turned to face my chap. I was one slimy, stinking green mess, but the lad who had caused this bit of unpleasantness was now the property of the U.S. government. It seemed he had a buddy in Manitoba who owned a large ranch and who had invited my lad up for the hunt of a lifetime. Three moose later and way over the Canadian limit, my lad figured he'd better quit. However, he got greedy and brought the parts from two and a half moose, with the limit being one, across the border, figuring no one would be checking hunters there.

Seizing the moose meat and stacking it up outside the Customs house, hoping it would freeze and thereby reduce the smell, I set out to do the paperwork on my lad. Damn, it seemed everything I touched smelled of rancid moose-in-rut grease, and I hurried to be done with my chap. The Customs guys just stood off at a distance and watched me do my thing with all kinds of little self-satisfied grins that they didn't work for the Fish and Wildlife Service at that moment. Recording the information, I sent my chap on his way minus about 1,800 pounds of rotten moose meat. I had asked him what he was going to do with the meat and he said he had planned to make everything into salami. Man, it would take more than a herd of hungry Italians to eat that stuff the way it smelled and all, I thought. He boarded his big Ford and whirled out of the parking lot as a man pissed off at himself will do. I wasn't sure why he was so mad, though. Through my efforts to relieve him of all that moose meat, he would now get better gas mileage on his way home … and avoid some serious food poisoning later on! The rest of the evening was uneventful except that every time I checked another group of hunters, they all had to comment on how bad I smelled or just roll their eyes when they thought I was not looking. Compared to some of their unshaven and unwashed bodies, I took those reactions as a shot!

The next day I arrived early at the port, and it wasn't until about ten o'clock that morning that things really got to hopping. I had written several over-limit tickets on two groups of hunters when a Customs officer hailed me over to a panel truck. "Are you interested in checking any live fish?" the on-duty Customs inspector asked.

"Sure," I said and walked over to the truck to meet a very nervous chap with a handful of Canadian export documents. Introducing myself, I asked what he was transporting, and he told me a shipment of live tropical fish. "Can't bring them in at this Port of Entry unless you have a very special import permit," I advised, knowing he didn't have one. It was up to the local agent to approve the issuance of a nondesignated Port of Entry permit because it required an on-site inspection by an agent, and the main office had not called me for that approval.

"OK, can I just go back to Canada and wait until I get that permit?" he asked.

I just grinned. "Mister, you are talking a government permit here, and you will be lucky to get one, if you do, in less than thirty days. By that time all your fish will be in the form of soup."

"OK, can I just leave and return to my home in Canada? Maybe I can sell them there before they all die."

Not having worked any of the ports much and wanting to be a good guy and not seize his illegal entry over such a minor import violation, I said, "Sure, head on back. Hopefully the Canadians will let you back into their country with all these live fish before you lose them." Besides, if I did seize his illegal shipment, what the hell would I do with five thousand live tropical fish in the dead of winter in North Dakota?

He quickly closed the doors to the back of his panel truck and briskly walked back to the cab when my curiosity overcame my reluctance to conduct a thorough inspection. "Say, what kind of fish are you carrying anyway?" I asked.

"Oh, just a bunch of common tropical fish," he said as he entered the cab and started up the engine.

"Whoa!" I said. "Let me take a quick look at those fish before you leave."

The chap turned off his engine, boiled out of the cab of the truck like a mad hornet, and said, "I thought you said I was free to go!"

"I did, but now I think I need to look at your fish a little more closely. You seem in one hell of a hurry to leave, and maybe there is a reason for that kind of behavior."

"There sure is, and it is called five thousand dead fish. If I don't get them out of this cold and on their way, they will run out of oxygen and I will lose my entire shipment."

"Understandable, but I will make it fast," I said. The chap opened the doors again, and I took several looks at the plastic bags of live fish, not noticing anything out of the ordinary. Just a bunch of common species of tropical fish, including those Asian bony tongues in that bag over there. *Asian bony tongues!* Terry, I thought, those are protected under the Endangered Species Act! "Wait a minute, whoa. Those fish there," I said, pointing to the bag, " are all Asian bony tongues and are endangered if I am correct." A quick look at the lad's face told me I was on to something. Turning to my Customs counterpart, I asked if they had a warm garage I could pull this truck into to do a more complete inspection. They did, and off we went. After twenty more bags of protected Asian bony tongues, the reason for the lad's insistence on moving quickly back into Canada was partially evident. Seizing the rare Asian species, I discovered a live box under the mass of bags of fish toward the front of the panel truck. I asked what was inside and was told "Turtles."

"What kind of turtles?" I asked.

"Just box turtles," came the not-so-satisfactory response.

Looking at my lad for a moment and not believing him for a second, I dug out the live box and opened the lid. Inside, looking lost and definitely out of place, were fourteen green sea turtles not much past hatchling size and very well protected against importation by a law called the Endangered Species Act. Digging deeper into the mess of bags of fish and boxes of turtles produced many more of the same of both species. By the time Customs got through with him for smuggling and the Service took a whack at him as well, he was one sick fellow. The last time I saw our chap, he was walking down the highway looking for a motel and I had an off-duty Customs lad driving the panel truck, critters and all, to a fish dealer in Fargo who I knew could be trusted to take care of the live seizure until I could get the appropriate disposal from the federal courts. The Customs lad was to bring the truck back to Pembina in order to maintain the needed chain of custody for the smuggling charges Customs planned to lay on the outlaw importer (they eventually gave the truck back to the owner, but not before collecting a hefty fine).

The next six vehicle loads of American hunters returning from their duck hunts in Canada all ran "afowl" of the law. Every one of the lads in those vehicles had over-limits of ducks or geese or both! For the next two hours I processed paperwork, seized birds, and stored them in the only available Customs freezer until it was jug-full! These weren't large over-limits, mind you, twelve over being the largest, but just the same they were good cases, bringing each of the violators a $500 fine for the error of his ways. In fact, as a result of my work at Portal and Pembina, I later called my boss in Kansas City and had him order two very large freezers for shipment to each Port of Entry so we might have our own freezers in which to store evidence on future details. Because the money for the freezers came from a fund in Washington and not from our small regional pot, my boss was only too happy to oblige. He also paid to have a commercial hauler come haul off the "green" moose meat and store it until I could arrange for proper disposal (ultimately the local dump).

Having a little time now that much of the hunting traffic was tapering off, I spent some time getting to know the Customs officers. While we were talking, one Customs lad brought me a Declaration of Entry document he found amusing. It consisted of a shipment of very deadly snakes! I didn't say anything to him in order not to embarrass him in front of his peers because a load of such wildlife could not legally enter this Port of Entry without a nondesignated Port of Entry permit. In short, he had screwed up. If I remember correctly, the load of snakes consisted of six cobras, eight fer-de-lances, six Gabon vipers, and four taipans, or "two-step snakes," as they are called because that is allegedly all the steps one can take after being bitten! They had been imported by a professor at the University of Colorado in Boulder for research purposes, according to the declaration. What the hell he was doing way up here with a load of such snakes was beyond me, I thought. Then it hit me! Drugs ... I had recently read somewhere that serious drug dealers, instead of employing hired guns to defend their stashes, were now turning to deadly snakes and then letting the neighborhood know of the new "stash guards." Reports coming in from undercover drug officers had shown that as a result of these new "guards," thefts among drug dealers were way down! On a hunch, I called the special agent in charge for the Drug Enforcement Administration (DEA) in Denver, Colorado. I identified myself, told him the chap's name, and described the load of deadly snakes heading his way in the hope that the agent would recognize the name and be able to confirm or deny my theory. The DEA chap was very noncommittal about anything because he didn't know me from Adam, but he said he would take the problem under advisement. Realizing I may have appeared to be coming from left field, I tried the safety approach. I warned him that if the lad in Boulder was a serious dealer and any DEA officers ever had to serve a warrant on the premises, they might want to be *very* careful. I am sure he was thinking he had a crackpot on his hands as he hung up. Damn, I thought. I didn't do so well there with that chap. But he was a DEA agent; what could I expect?

I decided to telephone the Boulder Police Department next. I was transferred to a desk sergeant in Narcotics and once again related my importation discovery, emphasizing officer safety in case a search was made of the snake importer's house for any reason. There was a long pause on the line, and then the sergeant asked, "Who did you say you were?"

I told him again and then asked him to hold on for a moment. Gesturing for a Customs officer to come to the phone, I asked him to provide support for who I was and to give the sergeant a phone number in Denver to call to verify the name of the Customs officer talking to him. Through such a confirmation I could give the Boulder officer a little more assurance that I was who I said I was. The Customs fellow did as I asked, and I asked the sergeant to call me back once he had his confirmation so we could talk more about the shipment.

Five minutes later the sergeant called back and *really* wanted to talk. He had gotten his confirmation and wanted to hear more about my theory. My first question to him was whether he knew the name of the importer I had provided. Was he known to be dealing dope? The sergeant answered that he was one of the bigger drug dealers in the area! *Bingo!* I thought. I went on to explain that I had recently read that big drug dealers were now using deadly snakes to guard their stashes because of the reliability of the snakes and the lower costs associated with their "patrol" efforts compared to employing hired guns. All the sergeant could do was suck air. They apparently had a search warrant prepared for this lad once he returned from Canada, figuring he was coming down with a load of hard drugs. They had not figured on the snake factor, and now he was worried about how to handle that added danger. I told him to go to the Denver Zoo and recruit their snake handler or grab one of our wildlife inspectors who was snake certified. He thanked me for my time and said this was one raid he was not going on.

Turning from the phone, I was met by a sick stare from the Customs lad who had let the snake man from Boulder into the country without a proper permit or close inspection. "That's OK," I said. "Sometimes crap happens. If he hadn't come through your Port of Entry with the snakes, it would have been through someone else's." Then it hit me! "What kind of container was he using to carry the snakes?" I asked.

"A large metal box with airholes in it," he said as his voice trailed away. My look at him told him we were both thinking the same thing. The Customs lad was scared to death of snakes, so other than a quick peek, he had not examined the metal snake box very closely. We stared at each other, knowing that drugs had probably been carried in the box with the live snakes crawling all around it. I could only hope the lads in Boulder would be able to catch the fellow by using their warrant and that no one would be any worse for the wear. I later found out that no drugs were discovered at the snake importer's house under that warrant. The snakes were there, but no drugs were ever found. Either they had been sent somewhere else or the lads doing the searching, aware of the snake menace, were possibly not as good as they usually were. It was ironic that twenty-two years later I received a call from my son Richard, who at the time was a Service wildlife inspector in Los Angeles. He had just had a shipment of deadly snakes go through his Port of Entry, entered, as coincidence would have it, by *the same college professor in Boulder!* Only this time, as well as the species of snakes he had imported through Canada when I was there, he had added five of the deadly common brown snakes from Australia to his shipment. I again called my federal counterpart in the DEA (who now knew me because I was the special agent in charge in Denver for the Service) and the folks in Boulder as well. As far as I know, no officer of the law has been bitten by any deadly snakes, but the drug dealer–college professor, now retired, is still on the move.

By that time it was getting late, and I decided I would call it a day. Telling the Customs lads that I was going to get some rest, I started walking toward my patrol car.

"Hey, Terry, want to check this one before you leave?" yelled the inspector on duty.

Knowing it would not be good business to turn one down now that the Customs lads were hot to trot on wildlife violations, I said, "Sure, send him my way." Turning, I saw a Chevy Blazer coming toward me pulling a large dog trailer. Inside I could hear at least four dogs raising hell, wishing they were hunting or at least out doing what dogs do when they get to roam at will. There were four men in the vehicle, and they looked like typical hunters, dirty, unshaven, tired, and happy. As they stopped and tumbled out of their rig to stretch their legs, I greeted the lads and identified myself.

One of the passengers said, "Well, I am damn glad to see one of you boys out and about checking the hunters. We saw a lot of abuse in Canada this trip by our American cousins, and to be frank, the provincial conservation officers need to get off their dead hind ends and catch some of those guys."

Knowing there was little I could do about the violations in Canada, I just shook my head in sympathy and asked them how they had done. "We all got limits," two of them said in unison as they headed toward the back of the Blazer and opened the back door. Following them, I watched the two biggest fellows swing down a huge ice chest, and judging from all the grunting and groaning, it was full. They opened the ice chest's dual lids and stood back to let me examine the contents. Inside were duck and goose breasts clear to the top of the cooler, all with fully feathered wings attached in accordance with the law. All the birds had been skinned and butchered, so all the lads had was almost solid meat along with the required wings. Seeing that the coolers were going to be quite a load, I asked the lads to take them over to my table so I could count the birds there and check for compliance with species. They did so without any grumbling, and it was nice to check some decent fellows for a change, I thought. It would take a few minutes to check such a large number of birds and get a sex and species count, so I told the men where the bathroom was and where Customs would let them exercise their dogs, which by now I could tell wanted out to walk around a bit. The lads split, heading off for the bathroom and such, while I continued to count out over sixty wet, icy birds. I was glad to see the birds so well cared for even if it damn near froze my hands to check them.

Finishing the count and species identification, I found the hunters were within the bounds of the law. I took their big, now almost empty ice chest, dumped out the bloody ice and water, and repacked it with fresh ice and replaced the birds. After I closed the lids, two of the heavier-set lads came over to put the chest back into the truck, but before they did I checked their other ice chests. They were full of foodstuffs, beer, and a little ice, but that was about it. After I had checked all their hunting licenses and duck stamps, they loaded up into their rig and prepared to leave.

"Aren't you guys going to let the dogs out for a run and a chance to wet down some fire hydrants?" I asked.

"Naw, they are all right," said the driver as he started the engine.

That is damn funny, I thought. The dog trailer is just barely big enough for all those dogs, and the owners are not going to let the poor animals out for a run after a long, confining trip. "Wait a minute," I said. "I think I would like to take a quick look in that dog trailer, and that way the dogs can get out and stretch their legs as well." I really hadn't done a complete inspection as far as the dog trailer went, and if I had them remove the dogs so I could do so, it would give the animals a little relief. Little did I know that little bit of consideration for the dogs would lead to a "hoorah"! The driver just looked at me, and all the chatter inside the Blazer stopped. Uh-oh, Terry, you just struck a nerve, I thought.

"Look, officer, we have a long way to go and if you don't mind would like to be on our way," said the driver. With that, he put the Blazer into gear and just drove off!

"Hey," I yelled as I started to run to my patrol car. About that time a Customs patrol officer back from a border run drove up and, seeing me yelling at the fleeing Blazer, he spun his Ram Charger around and gave pursuit with red light and siren, waking up the world in the process. Minutes later my Blazer with the dog trailer returned, carrying a very contrite driver to meet one very pissed-off special agent.

I asked the four men to get out of the vehicle again, and the Customs officers and I searched the vehicle for any kind of contraband. Customs, finding two fifty-count boxes of Cuban cigars, seized those and took the driver inside for further questioning and introduction to the paperwork associated with smuggling. Finished with the Blazer, I turned my attention to the dog trailer. I had one of the hunters let the dogs out and, once the trailer was empty, took a look inside. In the front of the trailer were two ice chests! Pulling the first one out and opening it, I discovered another box of Cuban cigars, six "forties" (roughly quart-sized bottles) of Canadian rye whiskey, and seven slabs of Canadian bacon. Hauling this ice chest over to the Customs folks, I left it for their examination and further questions for the driver. Reaching in and removing the last ice chest, I opened the lid while it sat at the rear of the trailer. It was clear full of duck and goose breasts, just like the earlier ice chest they were carrying in the rear of the

Blazer. I carried it over to the table and dumped it out. Minutes later I had counted an additional sixty ducks and fourteen white-fronted geese. That put the lads over the limit in all the duck and goose categories. I got a Customs lad to assist me as I removed the first large ice chest from the rear of the Blazer for seizure as well.

By now it was pretty apparent that the lads who had been so happy before were now rather sick. They got even sicker looking when Customs announced the seizure of the vehicle and trailer (they were later returned through a plea-bargain arrangement). Once Customs was through with the driver, I gathered all the hunters around me and questioned them about the illegal ducks and geese. As they pocketed citations for over-limits of ducks, over-limits of geese, and over-limits of some restricted species of ducks and geese, you could have heard a pin drop between them, even over all the barking of the dogs.

I had no more room in the borrowed Customs freezer, so I put all the birds in plastic sacks and loaded them into the trunk of my car. Leaving the men with an evidence receipt for their seized property, I bade them and Customs farewell and headed for my motel. After a later personal visit by me with the federal magistrate in Devils Lake, the lads were informed by the court that an appearance was required, and several weeks later the four showed up in court. After hearing their individual pleas, the magistrate fined each chap $500 per offense, or $1,500 each. In addition, he sentenced each to six months in jail but suspended the jail time providing none of the lads was found guilty of any Fish and Game violations over the next three years. Man, you talk about a bunch of whipped pups when he finished.

I was standing in front of the court building, enjoying the clean, brisk North Dakota air, while my culprits were settling up with the clerk of the court inside. It was good to be alive, and I was very pleased with myself. I had discovered the importance of the border work, had made some good Customs friends who would be looking more closely at wildlife cargo in the future, and had made some damn nice cases to boot. Then I became aware that my lads were leaving the courthouse and coming my way. I stood waiting until I was confronted by the men whose wallets had just undergone such a severe flattening. The driver of the vehicle stuck out his hand and

said, "Mr. Grosz, I want to apologize for my actions back there at
the Port of Entry. I don't know why I left after you said you wanted
to check the dog trailer—just scared, I guess. But after that night and
today, you can bet I will *never* do that again! I have learned my
lesson, and then some. You were just doing your job, and did it very
professionally, I might add. Keep up the good work, and keep catching those sons of guns breaking the laws. What you are doing is for
the good of our children, and we all really do appreciate what you
are doing." With that, I shook hands all around, and the lads left.
Now my day was really complete!

As was usual, Cooper and I found ourselves at the Portal Customs
Port of Entry in the spring short-handed and looking at a steady
stream of fishermen coming down from Canada with loads of sport-
caught fish. We had a couple of refuge buddies to give us a hand. but
aside from our new evidence freezer in the Customs office, we still
had just one Winchester between us.

The first loads of fishermen through my part of the check station,
probably through the seventeenth car that morning, were clean as a
hound's tooth. Everyone seemed to have behaved themselves in
Canada and obeyed the law. Aside from being slimy with fish scales
and juice, it was good to be back in the saddle checking the lads along
the Canadian border in an effort to see what was going on in the
world of wildlife. Everyone coming through so far had full possession
limits of fish, and I knew it was just a matter of time before someone
would go "into the toilet." The next car, number eighteen for the day,
did so in fine style. In pulled an old Greyhound bus made over into
a homemade camper, belching diesel smoke from a bad set of rings.
I walked over to the driver's window, and before I could explain, he
asked, "What is going on?"

I identified myself and explained that we were conducting a fish
check for compliance with Canadian and U.S. laws and would like
to check any fish they were carrying.

"Yeah, I kind of figured so. We heard it on the radios miles up into
Canada. How long will this take?" he asked.

"Not long," I said as my gut instinct began to hum. It always seemed that when anyone asked how long this delay would take, they often had a *reason* for being in a hurry. Not in all instances, but in a majority of such situations we discovered something wrong.

The lad set the brake and bailed out of the bus with his buddies. "The fish we caught and didn't eat are in the back bedroom of the bus in two ice chests," he replied. With that, all of the lads headed, casually chattering among themselves, for the bathrooms in the Customs office. Bob, my refuge partner, and I headed into the back of the bus, retrieved the two ice chests, and took them over to our tables to count the fish and examine them for number of each species and scale patches in accordance with provincial regulations. There are specific limits for each species because some are more highly desired than others, and bag limits and seasons are set to avoid overfishing the better-eating species. With such limits, the biologists can manage the fisheries to avoid overfishing and destruction of a resource. However, when a fisherman fillets a fish and removes the skin, identification of the fillet becomes a bear and allows a game hog to bring home just the best-eating fish. So a one-inch patch of skin is required by law to be left on the side of the fillet, from which experienced officers may identify the species.

Readers might also wonder why special agents of the Service would be checking fish, and Canadian fish at that. The world is a small place, getting smaller all the time, and if we are to survive, nations must cooperate with one another. Canada is dependent upon the U.S. sportsmen's dollars, and American visitors enjoy the great freshwater fishing Canada has to offer. However, for those fisheries to remain healthy in light of the masses of fishing U.S. citizens, Canada must manage its resources well. As part of that management, Canadian officials have asked the United States to assist in the enforcement of wildlife laws along the international boundary. There are times in which the United States needs Canada's assistance as well, so what you have are two good neighbors working together for the benefit of all. In addition, there is a U.S. Law called the Lacey Act that prohibits any wildlife or plants taken or possessed in violation of state, federal, tribal, or international law to be transported across state, federal, tribal, or international lines. The bottom line is that if a fisherman takes too many fish in Canada and transports them across the international border, he is in the toilet as far as the Lacey Act is concerned (in those days it was the Black Bass Act, which has since been incorporated into the Lacey Act).

Laying out our lads' fish, we counted and checked for species, and they were right on the numbers in compliance with Canadian law. We reloaded the fish, covered them with fresh ice from our ice chests, and replaced the coolers in the back of the bus. I waited until the lads returned, asked for permission to search the rest of the bus, and was given permission to do so. "Don't go in the bathroom without a gas mask," advised the driver. "Dale here has the runs and has been stinking up the bus something fierce."

I laughed, saying, "OK," and then boarded the bus, thinking this situation with bathrooms on buses was beginning to be a common thing! Starting in the back of the bus, as I always did on a big vehicle, I searched forward. Passing the bathroom, I could tell Dale had a problem from the "perfume" coming out the open door of that compartment. Just as I was taking a quick look into the bathroom, the driver popped his head into the bus and said, "Careful around the toilet. It is plugged, and Dale had to use it regardless, so it is a mess and quite full." With the smell coming from the room, I didn't feel I needed to spend much time there, and a quick check in the shower showed only a dirty tub and a floor covered with dirty laundry. As I was moving out of the bathroom, I spotted a uniquely colored can sitting on the water closet of the toilet (yes, the lad had installed a regular toilet in the bus instead of a water-efficient one). Picking it up (I don't know why to this day), I discovered it was a can of "Farts"! Still curious, I squirted a little of the canned essence into the air to find that it was the same smell as that of the "full" toilet. Looking at the toilet with its lid down, I wondered whether it was worth a look after the driver's warning. It wasn't long after lunch, and because I had eaten liverwurst-and-onion sandwiches, I thought better of my instinct and turned away. But as I was leaving the bathroom, I berated myself for conducting a sloppy search and returned to the toilet. Then I noticed that the toilet bowl was sweating! Laying my hand on the bowl, I was surprised to find it cold. I lifted the toilet seat, expecting to see the worst, but was pleasantly surprised to discover a garbage bag inside! Opening the garbage bag, I was rewarded with a sackful of ice (which had caused the toilet bowl to sweat) and a large quantity of walleye fillets (excellent eating fish)!

Carefully lifting out the heavy bag so it wouldn't burst, I walked to the front of the bus and, as I passed the sick-looking driver, commented, "Dale is really having a problem with his bowels. He is apparently passing fish fillets and plastic bags, not to mention ice, without any evidence of digestive action taking place. Kind of like an elephant. Flowers in, flowers out—only this time fish in, fish out."

Walking over to our check table, I dumped out eighty-four walleye fillets. That put all the lads over the limit for walleye, and each man was again asked to produce his fishing license along with his driver's license. Four citations for possessing over-limits of walleye and seizure of the fish left my guys shaking their heads and grumbling. One of the lads, Dale, as it turned out, came over to me and said, "What gave us away, if I might ask?"

"I don't mind sharing what tripped you lads up," I said. "It was the can of 'Farts.'"

"*What?*" he said.

"Yeah, it was the can of 'Farts.' You had sprayed it all around in the bathroom, hoping I would smell that and not go near the toilet after being told it was full of 'you.' Then you screwed up and left it in plain view. Well, I sprayed it into the air, being curious, and discovered it smelled just like the bathroom. Then, looking at the toilet, I saw that it was 'sweating' like a container holding something cold will do in a hot room, and once I placed my hand on the bowl of the toilet, I figured there must be iced fish inside. I was right, and you guys were wrong." He just shook his head and then extended his hand for me to shake. Shaking his hand, I said, "Better luck next time."

He just grinned and said, "There won't be a next time. I learned my lesson here today, and I imagine once I have to pay this ticket, I will learn it once more. No, you don't have to worry about us anymore. This was our first time doing this, and we learned. Just so you know, we didn't catch those fish. We bought them off a bunch of

Indians who had just gill-netted them. Walleye are good to eat, and the deal they offered us was just too good to pass up."

"Good," I said, "because we do this all the time and know where every hiding place is on any vehicle. If there is contraband, we will more than likely find it because hundreds of you lads have tried us on for size before, and there are just so many places where things can be hidden. And by now we know them all."

"God, I never thought of it that way, but it makes sense. By doing this every day, you are bound to get good at it. No wonder you caught us. That just reinforces my desire never to do this again." There was another hand shake, and then hand shakes all around, and then the lads with the smelly bathroom were gone. But not before I had obtained the names of the Indian fishermen who had illegally sold gill-netted fish to white men. I later turned that information over to my provincial counterpart for prosecutorial consideration.

Bob just grinned as he watched the bus drive out of sight and then, turning to me, said, "From now on you are no longer called Tiny. Your new name on my refuge will be 'Crapper.'"

I just grinned—after all, what else can you do? I couldn't shake him like a rat because I needed the help, so ... "Crapper" it was. That was all right, though. It was a good case, and maybe the other side learned something about not being game hogs.

By now I had a line of cars stacked up in my lane, so I just waved the first six on through. Stacking them up like that could be dangerous because of our limited work area, not to mention the fact that the long wait caused a rise in the tempers of the fishermen. Stopping the next four, Bob and I hurried through them and found everything in order. They continued to pour in, and I noticed that Cooper was just as busy as we were. The next vehicle sent to us by the Customs lads contained two Asian men. They were well dressed, and there was no outward evidence in their car that they had been fishing. Realizing Customs had sent them to us for a reason, I asked if they had been fishing. They said they had but had eaten almost all the fish or given them away and were now returning home with only a limit apiece, which was in the ice chest in the back seat. I asked to check their fishing licenses, and they obliged. While I was doing that, the passenger got out the small ice chest in the back seat and opened it for me to examine their fish. They had just two limits of fish fillets in a Tupperware container. I asked if they would mind if I looked in the trunk of their car. There was just the slightest hesitation, and then the driver got out and opened the trunk. There was the usual collection of fishing poles (cased), tackle boxes, hip boots, and the like. Not seeing anything of interest such as an ice chest, I was starting to thank him and let them go on their way when I noticed that their hip boots were both folded the same way, with the tops underneath as they lay on the floor of the trunk, and that the leg portions were not riding flattened out as hip waders usually do. I reached in and grabbed one hip wader and discovered that it was heavy with something inside it. Opening the top and looking in, I was surprised to see plastic sacks full of frozen fish fillets. I grabbed the boot end and tipped the wader over, and out slid three packages of frozen fish fillets! I did the same with all the boots and was rewarded with twelve packages of fillets.

Giving the sacks of fillets to Bob, I asked him to go inside and thaw them out in the sink so we could get a count. In about twenty minutes he returned with the information that there were 150 fillets, all without any skin patch for identification. He believed they were all walleye because of the lack of 'Y' bones (typical in northern pike, another commonly imported fish). Returning to the lads, I asked them who the fish in the hip waders belonged to. They sadly admitted to catching the fish and bringing them in. They had apparently stopped just north of the border to get gasoline and had heard from the locals about the fish check at the border. Knowing they were over their limits, they had taken the extra fish from their ice chest and stashed them in their boots, figuring that when they got through the fish check, they would put the fillets back into their ice chest and proceed happily on down the road. Well, suffice it to say, no cigar, but they did receive a citation for a fairly large over-limit of fish along with another for importing fish without any means of species identification.

Letting Bob write those citations, I took the next vehicle in line, a camper unit, and once they stopped rolling into our area identified myself and told the folks what we were doing. They were pleasant enough and bailed out to stretch their legs and show us the fish they had in the back of the camper. One man jumped up into the camper, dragged out a large ice chest, and opened the lid, and there in front of God and everybody were four large blocks of frozen fish fillets! Damn, I thought, there had to be at least sixty fish in each block! Plus, the blocks of frozen fillets were going to have to be thawed so we could count the fish and get a species count as well. When I told them that, the lads came unglued, first because they had read the Canadian regulations incorrectly and had brought too many fish across the border as a result. Second, we were going to have to thaw the frozen blocks of fish to get a count, and they figured that would ruin the fish. Since the fillets couldn't be refrozen without destroying their quality, the men figured they would have to eat them all at once, and that would ruin their planned fish fry set for later in Iowa.

Getting out the regulations, I showed the lads where they had gone wrong on the limits. Then I showed them the part of the regulations that pertained to leaving a one-inch square of skin on the fillets for identification. Since I had four large blocks of iced fish, I had but one route to take, and it sure made my lads unhappy, to say the least. Bob had finished with the Asian lads and now began to thaw the four large blocks of fish in a sink of warm water in the Customs office. I had the now loudly grumbling lads park off to one side to wait for Bob to finish while I continued to check other fishermen as they rolled into my station in large numbers. Man, you talk about working your tail end off—for the next hour all I did was go like a house afire. Finally Bob got the blocks of fish thawed and discovered that the lads were exactly forty-six fish over the limit! Citations were issued all around, and then the Iowans wanted to know if they got to keep any of the fish. I told them they were going to lose all their fish because in a court of law there would be no way to determine which fish were from the legal limit and which ones were from the over-limit. That explanation produced a lot more grumbling, and then one lad said, "Now I suppose you game wardens will eat well on our fish."

I had heard that comment so many times before that I had just put a number on it. I called that smart remark Story Number 2B. "Mr. Jamison," I said, "we have been out here all day checking fish. We are tired, haven't eaten all day, and are covered with fish slime and scales.

Additionally, we have had dozens of you chaps who have broken the law grousing at us, and there is still more work where this came from. Do you honestly think that after this is all said and done, we would want to eat a fish for dinner? I think not. Personally, I am going for a large steak if we finish up in time before the restaurant closes."

He looked a little sheepish as he thought over what I had said, and then with a wave of the hand said, "Enjoy eating our fish anyway," got back into his vehicle, and left.

What a horse's bazoo! I thought. By now our evidence freezer was beginning to fill, and if we kept it up at this rate, we would soon need another sixteen-cubic-foot freezer! Just imagine how many fish fillets it takes to fill a freezer that size.

The rest of the afternoon continued like the morning, and we finally did fill our evidence freezer. Cooper had some damn meeting to go to, so he left, taking his refuge officer assistant with him. He also took a trunkload of evidence fish so we could have some more room in our freezer. I decided I would stay a while and see what came through after the supper-rush hour in Canada. My refuge lad had to go as well, so soon I was the only one there, watching the stream of humanity flowing back into the United States. By nine in the evening I had written about a dozen more citations for small over-limits or for fish coming in without any means of identification. Then one of the Customs guys came over and said, "Terry, you have to come over and see this."

"What is it?" I asked.

"Just come on over and see for yourself."

The Customs chaps had inspected a semitruck full of fruit and vegetables heading for the United States. In the back of the trailer sat a red ice chest surrounded by crates of oranges, cabbages, and the like. Sliding the ice chest to the edge of the trailer, I could hear scratching sounds coming from inside. Opening the lid, I found myself staring at about five hundred little turtles, all pawing at each other to get on top of the heap. What the hell! I thought. Taking another hard look at the turtles, I recognized them from my days as a port officer in San Francisco, when I had substituted for Ben Crabb while he was on vacation. They were yellow side-necked turtles. No big deal except that they were endangered and their importation was prohibited by the Endangered Species Act!

The driver was standing off to one side as I examined the little guys, and, turning, I said, "What are you bringing these little guys in for?"

"I don't even know what they are, Officer, except some kind of turtle that I was bringing in for a friend to sell in his restaurant."

"Who is this friend?" I asked.

He replied, "Jimmy Lee."

"Where does he live?"

"He runs the China Gardens in Bismarck," he replied. The driver really did not seem to understand what he had done, so I took down all the information on him, his truck, and Jimmy Lee and told him I would be in touch. Then five hundred little turtles were dumped into my ice chest and went into the back seat of my car as evidence. I told the driver I would be getting in touch with Lee and that he should expect a visit from me in a day or so. The driver, happy to be out from under a legal action, agreed to pass on the message, got into his truck, and left—but not before I had told him that if he was lying to me, he could expect me and a federal judge to be talking to him again in the near future. Damn, now I had seen everything. In the early 1970s that species of turtle had been a hot food item in the Bay area of San Francisco. What the hell were they doing out here in the middle of nowhere? I thought, shaking my head. It seemed that nothing was safe from harvest as long as humans were around.

Filling up my car early the next day with evidence fish fillets and other meat seized from previous details that had cleared the court docket, I headed east to the Turtle Mountain Indian Reservation and dropped off the load at the Community Center for distribution to needy Native Americans. Then, heading further east to Pembina, I took on another load just of fish fillets from cleared cases from our freezer at the Port of Entry and headed for Bismarck. Arriving late with my load of fish fillets and coolerful of live turtles, I met Mark Christianson from the Bismarck zoo and dropped off my load: the turtles for some kind of display Mark wanted to make, and the fillets to feed the injured eagles and other birds of prey Mark always took in and cared for when I brought them in. It was a good ending for a bad situation, I thought, but things didn't turn out so well for the turtles. A week later the heating light over them went out, and all the little guys succumbed to the cold. However, there was a bright spot there as well. Mark had a grizzly bear at the zoo that had to top the scales at 1,500 pounds if he weighed an ounce. It seemed that Old Ephrim made short work of my turtles, except a few that were retained for evidence, so they weren't entirely wasted.

As for Jimmy Lee, by the time I arrived he was a mess. The trucker had called and apprised Jimmy of the events at the Port of Entry, seizure and all. Jimmy, realizing he was in deep slop for initiating the illegal importation, had stewed himself into a mental mess by the time I arrived. All he wanted was to get his ticket and pay. He didn't even care how much it was; he just wanted to pay it off and be done with it. It was probably one of the easiest interviews I ever had to do—though my family and I never ate at the China Gardens again.

A WEEK OR SO after my spring visit to Portal, I visited all the other Ports of Entry across the northern edge of North Dakota, working my way over to Pembina. All the other smaller ports had similar problems with fishermen, and while visiting I made about a dozen over-limit fish cases as some of the more evil-thinking fishermen tried to run across those smaller ports, thinking they would have a better chance there to squeeze into the United States without detection. It was just good fortune that I was there, but I told every chap I cited that we were everywhere and that to continue bringing in their over-limits since I had taken over federal wildlife enforcement in the state would unfailingly get them pinched. It was mostly a lot of hot air, but when one has to call in for permission to buy every tank of gas, one uses every tool one has in the arsenal to stem the tide. ... You know, Christ was a fisherman, but he didn't have a season or bag limit. I wonder what these guys were thinking?

This time I drove an old Service Dodge pickup so that I could bring back a really big load of seized fish and other items for Mark and the always hungry zoo critters. That way I could keep our freezer at Customs empty and ready for use while returning a favor to Mark for all the crippled birds of prey he had cared for over the years. Many readers, especially those who have eaten walleye, are probably wondering why I would take such good food to the animals instead of giving it to needy humans. Most of the fish, waterfowl, grouse, cranes, deer, moose, and the like that came into the port in good shape and were seized were in fact given to the needy. But the meat I felt was subpar for whatever reason (for instance, thawed to get a count and then refrozen) went to the zoo animals.

Pausing in a town whose name I have now long forgotten, I gassed up the truck and purchased some items in a local grocery store to eat along the way so I could keep going and cover more ground. One of those items was a Sugar Daddy. I hadn't eaten one of those since I was a kid, and when I spied them, I had to buy one. Fifty miles down the road I was chewing the soft, gooey caramel like a damn camel until I bit down on something hard. Taking the candy out of my mouth, I discovered a filling firmly attached! Needless to say, the Sugar Daddy sailed out the window to a tune of swear words that would have made a sailor proud. Knowing I couldn't work wetland easement cases or border cases missing a filling as massive as the one I had just tossed out the window, I headed for the town of Bottineau. I located a dentist's office there and found that the dentist had a little time in his schedule to fix my tooth. He told me to go on in and sit down in the chair, then took a quick look and said he could fill the tooth in no time. He headed off to get a needle and some painkiller. Finding his piss-anty chair somewhat more narrow than my two-axe-handle-wide hind end, I got up and took my .45 pistol out of the holster. Sitting back down, I found that made all the difference in the world because the chair now fit. But what to do with my pistol? Looking around and not really thinking, I laid the gun on the little tray next to the chair, among all the dental tools. The dentist came back through the door with a needle upraised, squirting painkiller out the end to remove any air bubbles trapped in the syringe. As he started toward me to give me the shot—and remember, now, he didn't know me from an apple—he spotted the .45 lying on his dental tray! I never saw a man stop what he was doing so fast in my life. Looking at me with needle still in hand, he said in a high-pitched voice, "Honest, mister, this won't hurt a bit!"

Not realizing what had just happened, I smiled and said, "I hope not."

That was the only time I had a filling take almost two hours! He would drill a little and then ask if I was all right, then repeat the process. Damn, I just couldn't convince him it was all right to pick up the pace. Finally I realized that my .45 was causing him some gas and worry. Oh well—I got my tooth filled, and I think the dentist filled something else!

I spent the next two weeks meeting with the wetland management wing of the Service in the Devils Lake area and assisting them in trying to adjudicate drainage violations throughout the eastern portion of the state. I would work with those lads for several days and then, for a change in pace, head up to Pembina and work the wildlife importation traffic for a day or so. That way I could kill two birds with one stone and make it look like law enforcement was everywhere. It made it a little tough, working fourteen-hour days in the wetland arena and then sixteen-hour days at the port, but I was young in those days, so I figured the body would heal, and it didn't seem to matter. Man, let me tell you, burning the candle at both ends like that when one is young sure is hell when a person who has lived like that reaches sixty or more! That is, if he does …

On one of my Pembina trips during that two-week period, I decided to just pick and choose the vehicles to be inspected while Customs was doing its thing. Being a task force of only one, there was no way I could take on a string of returning sportsmen and do them justice not only in the search but in their time while they waited for me to finish with the people in front of them. So I took a short cut. I would look over the shoulder of the inspector as he examined the Declarations of Entry, Form 3-177 (everyone must fill out one of these upon entering the United States, listing everything purchased or acquired in the foreign country) to see what the traveler was importing. That document was for the listing of wildlife as well, including their parts and products. If something looked interesting, I would ask that person to move their vehicle over to my station, and then I would conduct my wildlife inspections.

On one of those days a huge custom-made motor home towing a trailer stopped the Customs checkpoint. There were four couples in the motor home, and they had been in the Northwest Territories and then fishing in Saskatchewan. Giving the Customs inspector the high sign that I wanted to check this big rig, I headed for my spot. Soon the big motor home pulled into my inspection site, and I walked over to the driver and introduced myself and briefly explained why they were being stopped. I could tell he was a little grumpy at being held up, but he consented to an inspection, and he and his party got out of the vehicle. They had their fish in the trailer they were towing, and within a short time I had inspected eight limits of fish taken in Saskatchewan. There were also limits of fish taken in the Northwest Territories, including some monster fish taken in the Great Slave Lake. The monster fish were being brought to the States to be mounted by a taxidermist for display in their homes. Checking my set of Northwest Territories fishing regulations, I found the folks to be exactly right regarding limits of species of fish. I asked if they had any other game or wildlife on board and was told no, but to go ahead and look for myself if it would speed up the process so they could get on their way. Remember my thoughts regarding full limits of everything and people in a hurry to get somewhere? Well, these folks were starting to get my interest up, and I made a very thorough search of their trailer and motor home. Nothing! Everyone just stood out on the asphalt and quietly watched me as if holding their breath. Damn, I knew something was wrong, but I just couldn't put my hands on it. Finally finishing up inside the motor home, I walked outside to meet the driver, a retired doctor.

"Satisfied, Officer Grosz?" he asked in a rather stinging tone laced with triumph.

"Yes, sir," I replied as I gave the motor coach a visual once-over. I had searched the trailer, all the compartments underneath the coach, everything inside, including the bathroom, and *nothing!* I stood there as all those good folks quietly loaded back into the coach, and then my eyes swept to the top of the vehicle. There on top were two air-conditioning units and a large storage compartment with a hinged top. *The storage compartment on top.* I had not searched that because of its lack of access for a person as heavy as I was! There was a little ladder on the rear of the motor home leading to the roof of the vehicle.

I knew that if I tried to go up that wimpy ladder, I would probably pull it right off the side of the motor home, and then the nasty letters to the government about the elephantine special agent would start to fly. Even if I didn't break the ladder, I would probably fall through the roof of the motor home, so I had just ignored that aspect of the search. But not today, I thought as I hailed the driver and asked him to wait just a moment. He growled something I did not hear as I took off for the Customs office to find a smaller officer than I. Returning with Don, a Customs officer who was considerably lighter, I had him scramble up the side of the motor home and across the roof to the storage compartment. He opened it, then slowly stood up, turned, and grinned down at me! He began to examine something inside the storage compartment while I did a silent jig inside.

Soon Don turned and said, "Terry, there is an ice chest up here full of fish fillets of some kind. There also appears to be parts of a deer or two and some other things you might want to look at as well."

Hot damn, I knew it! My instincts and those people's body language had told me something was wrong, but I had almost missed it.

Don got on his portable radio and called back to the Customs office, and soon two other officers came over to provide assistance. The ice chest was lifted down off the roof, and brother, it was clear full of lake trout and walleye fillets. Then the deer parts began to come down, and eight hindquarters of deer meat (the steak and roast portions), all nicely wrapped up in deer bags, were eventually lowered over the side. Then two shopping bags were let over the side, and a quick look showed boxes of gift items made from marine mammals! Talk about a treasure trove! This was a case of great expectations fulfilled! Within moments I had seized the ice chests of fish in the trailer owing to the fact that the fish fillets in the ice chest from the storage compartment put the folks way over their collective limits. I heard one of the women inside the coach say, "See, I told you to leave all those damn fish at the lake with the guides!" I just grinned as I checked the deer meat (closed season). There were eight hindquarters, representing at least four illegal deer. As it turned out, the driver of the rig had a farmer friend in Saskatchewan who had shot the deer for him and given him the hams. The farmer had used the rest of the deer for sausage for his own consumption. I later turned the provincial officer on to this farmer chap, and he was waxed in his own back yard as well.

Well, so far I had Black Bass Act violations and violations of the Lacey Act. A good day was in the offing, and now for the bags of gift items. One shopping bag yielded a dozen Native craft Eskimo dolls made from sealskin. In the other were fifty-three pieces of carved walrus ivory depicting Native scenes and wild arctic animals. Both the dolls and the carved ivory represented violations of the Marine Mammal Protection Act. Then the icing on the cake! Rolled up in a plastic bag was a three-foot-by-two-foot swatch of polar bear fur! Another violation of the Marine Mammal Protection Act, and a serious one at that! It seemed that the lad driving the motor home was a fly fisherman who tied his own flies. Polar bear fur had the makings for a great kind of fly, and apparently he had purchased it in the Northwest Territories.

With all the goodies unearthed, thanks to my smaller-sized Customs friends, I called the driver of the motor home over for a little come-to-Jesus meeting that was going to end up like a damn good woodshedding. The driver, who had a defiant attitude, sat down and said, "Before you say anything, I have just two things to say. First, I took everything myself and am the only person to blame. Second, none of the rest of my party will speak to you further without a lawyer present." With that, he sat back and would not say anything more.

Some come-to-Jesus meeting, I thought, and the only one who landed in the woodshed was me! Well, even though God loves game wardens, he sometimes has to discipline them for their runaway attitudes and big heads. Getting off my high horse, I took down the information I needed for legal adjudication and told the lad he was free to go. With a snort, he grabbed back his driver's license, and as he walked back to the motor coach, he turned and took a sweeping low bow toward the Customs lads and me, then boarded the motor home to cheers from those inside. The Customs guys looked at me like "now what" because their boss wasn't interested in seizing such an expensive vehicle for a few fish and ivory carvings. I just grinned. I had a *very* good magistrate and chief judge on this side of the North Dakota judicial district, and I couldn't wait to present this case to an also excellent U.S. attorney's office. When the smoke had cleared, my doctor friend (who I found out through records checks had been here before) paid $3,200 for the Black Bass Act violations, $10,000 for the Lacey Act violations, and $5,000 for the Marine Mammal Act violations, plus confiscation of all the items seized that day, which had to represent at least another few thousand dollars. All in all, it had been a very good day's work.

Several days later, back at the port, I again waited in the Customs checkpoint to observe vehicles returning from Canada. One, a carload of U.S. Native Americans returning from a powwow in Canada, caught my eye. Realizing I was a little biased, even though they looked like a good bet, I passed. About an hour later a new Dodge one-ton truck with a huge camper on it stopped. It was driven by a stereotypical Native American, braids and all, and this time the instinctive alarms went off. He had a Pine Ridge sticker on his windshield, and most Native Americans I had met from the Pine Ridge Reservation were poor as church mice. Even in those days they had at least a 50 percent unemployment rate on the reservation, and here was a chap obviously in the money from somewhere. Tapping the Customs lad on the shoulder and giving him a nod toward my station, I started to walk toward my inspection site. Soon the big camper unit pulled into my area, and I introduced myself to the driver. He said nothing as I explained what I was doing, asked him to step down from the cab, and requested permission to inspect his vehicle.

"And if I don't give you permission?" he smartly asked.

"Then I will have Customs inspect your vehicle," I flatly said (in a Customs zone, the right of inspection is the legal word of the day).

He sat there a moment, then jumped out and briskly walked back to the camper unit. Taking a set of keys out of his pocket, he located the one he wanted, opened the back door, and stepped back. Lord almighty! Scattered all over the floor, table, and side benches were Native American handicraft items made from eagle and other bird parts! I couldn't believe my eyes. The Indian stepped forward, blocking my view, and said, "Those are all mine and old family hand-downs."

Asking him to move aside, I beckoned a Customs inspector from the office, and soon the two of us were looking at this latest find. Stepping up into the camper, I was presented with another surprise. Every item had a price tag affixed to it! Turning to my Indian lad, I said, "If these are all family hand-downs, why do they all have price tags?"

He said nothing, just glowered at me. I began to gather up all the feathered items with price tags. It was obvious that he had just come from a big powwow in Canada and had been offering these items for sale, a violation of both U.S. and Canadian law. Seizing two boxes of items, plus one double-train and two single-train war bonnets, I got out of the camper. We walked over to an interview room, and my lad soon admitted that he had taken the birds in the United States but had brought them to Canada only for display. Yeah, I thought, and the Japanese would never bomb Pearl Harbor! Something was still wrong, and I transmitted those feelings to my Customs friend who was standing at my side. Soon the vehicle was being given a thorough search, and within moments I got the high sign from one of the inspectors searching the camper. Leaving my Indian friend in charge of another Customs officer, I walked over to the truck. Lying on the kitchen table was a freshly killed golden eagle that had been discovered under one of the bench seats!

Since nothing more had been discovered, I took the eagle over to the interview room. I laid it down on the floor by the door, quietly walked over to where my Indian chap was sitting, and sat down. "That a family hand-me down as well?" I asked.

"Those were given to me in exchange for a bunch of handicrafts I had put together," he answered dryly.

I explained that it was illegal for *anyone* to import or export eagles or their parts or products and that *no permits shall be issued for such activities.*

He just shrugged and said, "Do what you have to do; I have nothing more to say."

I could tell he meant it, and a few more questions on my part that met with no response confirmed my thoughts about his attitude. Taking down all the information I needed, and seizing all the feathered items as well as the fresh eagle, I let him go on down the road. Special rules applied to Native Americans as dictated through the Fish and Wildlife Service's long list of investigative policies and procedures.

It was OK to investigate such a case, but once that phase of the operation was completed, the officer had to submit the investigation to the Washington office and wait for clearance to proceed. Washington would run the investigation by Bureau of Indian Affairs (BIA) attorneys (the weakest link in a chain of democracy, as far as I am concerned), and they in turn would review what was allowed under the treaties applicable to the fellow under investigation (remember, the secretary of the Interior is in charge of the BIA as well as the Fish and Wildlife Service). If any treaty allowed certain acts that were normally prohibited under federal wildlife laws, then that part of the investigation would have to be dropped because the treaties superseded the federal laws. The officer could move forward with prosecution for whatever charges remained. For example, some treaties allow Native Americans the right to kill eagles! Therefore, if an officer caught a Native American from that tribe killing an eagle, he could not take that person before the courts for a violation of the Bald Eagle Protection Act because a violation had not occurred as far as U.S. laws were concerned.

In this particular matter, all the items containing migratory bird feathers (other than the eagle feathers) had to be returned under the advice of the BIA attorneys. Under treaty, the man was allowed to possess them even with the price tags on them. And since he was not in the act of selling the items when he pulled into the Customs area, all I had was simple possession with price tags attached. It still appeared to be an offer to sell, given the tags and all, but Washington disagreed, and the items were returned. The dead eagle and eagle feathers were seized and confiscated because of the illegal importation. But because of the sensitive nature of the investigation, with the man being Native American, Washington *suggested* that the matter be handled civilly without any other penalty than forfeiture of the feathers. Because I was somewhat boxed in, I did as they suggested. I discovered later that the chap purchased a large motor home after our little run-in and now uses that to go back and forth to Canada when he attends his gatherings and powwows. ... I never could understand how such a person could pour his culture down the drain and never bat an eye. Years later my officers caught this chap when the legal climate was a little less protective, shall we say. Many thousands of dollars later, he slowed his illegal trade but in the process became a whole lot more crafty and has since had to be apprehended again.

Three days later, feeling frisky after working the wetland easement wars, I told the Custom officers I would take every third car coming through with fish unless they saw that I was busy writing citations. If they saw me writing citations, they were to let all the cars through until I had finished and then start the process all over again. With that, I set up shop and was promptly greeted with about a million vehicles carrying returning U.S. sportsmen and their tons of fish. For about an hour they all behaved and proved to have brought back only what they rightly could. Then a rather clean-cut gentlemen came through driving a Cadillac. Introducing myself, I told him what I was doing and asked if he had been fishing. He said he had and that the fish were in his trunk. He got out of the car and opened the trunk, exposing an ice chest. Opening the ice chest, I was greeted with at least three possession limits of fish, all in the fillet stage. Counting out the fish, I found that the cooler in fact contained five possession limits of fish! Turning to my lad, I was faced with a handful of paper.

"What is all this?" I asked.

"Fishing licenses for all the limits of fish and a written affidavit from each fisherman. The others all had to fly home for a wedding, and I was picked to bring all our fish back."

This was another story I had heard so many time at wildlife inspection stations on the highways that I had given it a number— Number 4B. Being fair-minded, though, I took the papers and licenses and began to examine them. Each affidavit clearly stated that the men had been fishing together in Saskatchewan, had caught full limits, and had asked their friend Gary to transport all the fish back so they could fly home to attend a wedding. In good faith, they had attached their fishing licenses to their affidavits to speed this importation and transportation process.

Looking over the licenses one more time, I noticed that the handwriting of the signatures on the licenses did not match those on the affidavits. A grin began to form as I kept that observation to myself.

Taking the letters, I walked into the Customs office and had one of the secretaries call information and get me the telephone numbers of all the chaps on the affidavits. Armed with that information, I walked back to Gary and said, "I am going to call all these lads and see if their stories match yours. If they don't, then you and I will have to have a little talk. If what you say is true, then you have nothing to worry about, but if you are lying, then there will be trouble in town before nightfall." I looked long and hard at him, seeking any clue as to who did what.

"Go ahead," he said without a moment's hesitation.

OK, I thought, there is always an easy way and a hard way to do things. Out West we call that coming in riding in the saddle or across it. ... For the next half hour, I talked to everyone on that list except one. Each lad confirmed that he had been fishing in Saskatchewan, had caught a limit of fish, and had given Gary his license and affidavit so Gary could transport the fish across the border. Damn, these guys had it all together. In fact, *almost too all together*. ... Calling the last chap, I got his wife on the phone. He had gone out to get some cigars, she said. When I asked if he had just been in Canada fishing, she said, "What?" I repeated my question, and she said, "Yes, he was, but that was last year."

"He wasn't just in Canada fishing last week?" I asked.

"Oh, heavens, no. He was with me last week in the Florida Keys on a houseboat fishing trip."

My smile at that point ran from ear to ear! Then I heard a door slam and a voice saying, "Who is on the phone, honey?"

"Oh, it's some guy from the Fish and Wildlife Service. He has a bunch of Gary's fish and is asking questions."

"Give me that phone, quick!" he said, and the next thing I heard was a man's voice. "This is Burl; can I help you?"

"Yes, this is Terry Grosz, special agent for the Fish and Wildlife Service up in Pembina, North Dakota. I have a Gary Douglas stopped, and he is carrying not only his possession limit of fish from a fishing trip in Saskatchewan but those of four other fellows as well, and I am trying to confirm that you were one of the fishermen whose fish he is transporting."

I could plainly hear a sigh of relief that he had gotten to the phone in time. "Yes, yes, he should be carrying a possession limit of fish for me," Burl stated.

Now my grin was even wider. "Have you ever heard of conspiracy?" I asked right out of the blue.

"What?" came his surprised response.

"Yes, conspiracy. Where two or more people get together, plan a crime, and then do something overt to further that crime. Like, for example, agree to have someone bring more fish across the border than he is legally entitled to and then get some of his buddies to lie for him. Then when his buddies are called, they do in fact lie for him, thereby closing the ring on a conspiracy. And, for your information, being part of a conspiracy carries the same penalty as for the chap committing the crime."

"What are you talking about?" he asked sternly.

"Just what I said. Before you got home, I talked with your wife. She told me the two of you were in Florida last week, fishing. That should be easy enough to validate when I subpoena your credit card records and the like," I said.

There was complete silence on the other end of the line.

"Hello," I said, "are you still there?"

"Yes," came the meek reply.

"Well, then, why don't you tell me in your own words and not that of another what actually went on so I might get this matter all squared away."

As it turned out, all four of the lads whose affidavits Gary was carrying had in fact been elsewhere, not fishing in Canada. The bottom line was that Gary, fishing by himself, had done so well that he had paid four Canadian friends to buy the extra licenses in his friends' names. Then he had had several other fishermen at the motel where he had been staying forge the affidavits so Gary could bring down a mess of fish for five instead of just one.

Thanking Burl for his honesty (even though I had had to get lucky with the call to his wife), I told him he would be getting a notification from the court for his part in the little charade and to expect it in the mail within fourteen days. He said that would be fine because he had been stupid to get involved with Gary in such a matter in the first place. "You can bet it won't be me paying this fine!" he said.

I called back all the men I had called before, and after a bit of interviewing fun dropped the bomb on each and every one of them, using Burl's information as the pry bar. Boy, once they found out how much I knew, they all broke like eggs. In turn, I informed each man that he would be hearing from the court about the "fishing trip."

When I finished, I moved back to Gary, who was by now looking a bit uneasy. I had been on the phone a long time, and now he was worried. Sitting down with him, I dug out all the fishing licenses and affidavits. Asking him to look at the signatures on the fishing licenses, I then handed him the affidavits and asked him to compare the handwriting of the signatures on the fishing licenses to those on the affidavits. As he looked closely at the differences between the two, I could see the color drain from his head and his neck turn brilliant red from the increasing pressure of the moment.

He looked up at me and said, "They don't match very well, do they?"

"No, they don't, and neither do the stories of the lads those licenses represent."

"They all told you the truth?" he quietly asked.

"Yep, and every one of those lads will receive some legal attention from the court as well for this little conspiracy."

"*Conspiracy!*" he repeated, his voice trailing off.

"Yes, that's right. All of you conspired to break the law, and you did. In my book, that fits the elements of the crime conspiracy, and you and your buddies will now have to stand the heat for coming into that kitchen!"

He visibly sagged in his chair, and I thought for a moment he might pass out. Finally getting hold of his faculties, he asked, "What now?"

With the paperwork done and all his fish seized, Gary headed off down the road a wiser and, I am sure, sicker man. He still had a meeting with the judge ahead of him, and he was also going to have to meet all his buddies and fix it up with them. A plea arrangement was made several weeks later, and each lad forfeited $400 to the government plus probation. I am sure before all was said and done that Gary was looking at $2,000 dollars' worth of expenses above and beyond what he had planned for on this memorable fishing trip.

THE INTERNATIONAL BOUNDARY between Canada and the United States, when it came to the border wars, was always a zoo. However, it did not compare to the border war going on between Mexico and the United States, according to my southern counterparts. Somehow, I was glad that I was responsible only for the northern line of demarcation in North Dakota. ... It always struck me as sad that so much illegal activity was going on, yet the Service never provided the necessary law enforcement resources to even minimally do the job Congress mandated! Throughout my thirty-two-year career, I can *never* think of a time when those of us in the Division of Law Enforcement had enough funding or political backing to do the border justice and slow down the volume of illegal contraband flowing across the checkpoints. You can't blame Customs for this either. They are already enforcing numerous other laws and can't take on the extra burden of enforcing our laws as well. In addition, Customs officers are not trained, nor should they be, to enforce wildlife laws. As a result, smugglers of all kinds enjoy what is almost a free-fire zone in the killing and smuggling of wildlife, and now rare plants, across the border. This is one area in which the "thin green line" is breached regularly, with alarming results! As I said earlier, let us hope those doing such deeds find a fiery reward for their greed and ego. Extinction is continual and final—and so is the way of the Almighty. Someone needs to heed that clarion call before it is too late, and that goes for either camp, be it high government officials poorly funding a vital program or those bleeding it dry from the other side.

7

From Ashes to Ashland

BECAUSE OF THE UNIQUENESS of the people in the Dakotas, their agricultural industry roots, the immense richness of the state's flora and fauna, the presence of an international border, and the advent of an aggressive law enforcement program protecting federal interests, those of us in the Division of Law Enforcement were constantly involved in "first law" situations (that is, areas with no legal case precedents). These frequent problems gave the U.S. attorney's office, the Washington office for the Division of Law Enforcement, the U.S. solicitor's office, and yours truly headache after headache trying to figure out what legal plan of action to follow. In referring to first law activities, I mean Service legal actions involving wetland easement contract violations; the taking of eagles and the sale of their parts by Native Americans; major interstate check stations to inspect the wildlife taken by returning hunters; importation and exportation of eagle products by Native Americans; and the illegal taking of fur bearers from an aircraft. I often found myself on the phone with the chief of Law Enforcement in Washington for some guidance through the many legal minefields created by the latest in a string of such situations. But more often than not I could obtain little or no help because those in high positions had never been in these situations either. It is tough to lead in a case in which one has no experience! The bottom line was that many of the activities my officers were involved in had not previously been experienced by anyone in the Service; hence the lack of procedural guidance based on legal history.

After a while, being an impetuous young supervisor, I became less and less patient with the Washington office as I realized that the officers there had little or no information on how any of our first law activities should be handled. In fact, I often found myself talking to someone who was dumber than a post or just plain didn't care what we did in the field just as long as it didn't rock the boat! Because of my large mouth and Germanic thickheadedness, I often tangled with Washington over such matters, mostly because of my frustration as I quickly came to understand that the people there were neither the last word nor a fount of knowledge. Frankly, in those days the Washington office was a dry well on many first law issues. Yet many of the first law legal issues raised by my officers were of national importance. When moving in such an arena, one tries to involve the national office so that practices initiated in one area under a federal law will be equally applied elsewhere in the nation. I was trying to make sure that what was done in my area of the country could be done elsewhere and that everyone would be treated the same, with what I hoped would be the same courtroom outcome.

During one of those times when I was seeking assistance and finding none, I gave Deputy Chief of Administration Bert Falbaum a piece of my mind regarding the lack of support my central office was providing. Bert, in his usual reaction to such antics from someone he considered a lesser mortal, told me that if I thought I could do better, I should get my big, fat hind end to Washington and show the rest of the world how it should be done. In one of my many immature moments of frustration at being advised to put up or shut up, I boiled over! I told Bert that if the Service ever created a desk officer position at the GS-13 level (desk officer positions were GS-12s in those days, which meant less pay than a GS-13), I would compete and if successful would come in and show them how "the cow took a dump in the clover"! In retrospect, it was a classic case of letting one's alligator mouth overload one's hummingbird hind end. ... But my mom didn't raise a fool. Since there were no existing GS-13 desk officers in the Service, I figured no one would create such a position just for me, so I was safe in shooting off my big mouth.

Thirty days later I received a desk officer vacancy announcement in the mail listed at the GS-13 level with an accompanying note from Bert. "Your move," it read, and that was the extent of the message, at least on paper. Damn, I thought, here I had shot off my big mouth and someone had just stuck both of my feet in it! Mulling over the new, first-ever GS-13 position as a desk officer, I began to get itchy feet to try it on for size. I had only been in the Dakotas for two years and was just getting my wetland easement, cattle trespass, and international border programs up and running, but the lure to go to Washington and show those boneheads a thing or two was also strong (there went that "hummingbird" thing again).

Bringing the announcement home, I let my bride look it over, all the while watching her closely for any reaction. "You know I will go wherever you go, honey, so the decision is up to you," she said softly as she returned the announcement to me. "Just remember that when the kids hit high school, I want us to put down roots so they can have nice memories of their own, and that means your running days are done at that point in time!"

I looked into her deep blue eyes for any clue as to how she really felt about this instant promotional opportunity, but to no avail. She cleverly hid anything from me other than how pretty her eyes were when she smiled. For the next two weeks I looked at all the pluses and minuses and finally decided to throw my hat into the ring for the new position and see whether I was successful. I knew the agents I would be leaving behind would carry on the much-needed easement, border, and cattle trespass enforcement programs now that they were in place. I also knew that we had two of the very best assistant U.S. attorneys in the nation in Dave Peterson and Lynn Crooks, not to mention Hal Bullis, the U.S. Attorney for North Dakota, so the legal support would remain strong whether I was there or not. I had good state-level support from the chiefs of Law Enforcement in North and South Dakota, and the refuge folks in the field in both states strongly supported a good enforcement program, so that helped in my decision-making process as well. In fact, without the Division of Refuge's strong support during those turbulent years, I never could have gotten any of my enforcement programs off the ground because of my limited staffing and fiscal resources. I began to realize that with these hole cards I could go to Washington without any feeling of guilt because I had done what I had set out to do.

During the period between submitting my application for the new position until I could expect to be notified, my family and I took a long-overdue vacation to California to visit Donna's and my aging parents. We had just returned to our home in Bismarck, and I had just opened the car door in the driveway when I heard the telephone ringing inside the house. Donna ran to answer the phone and came back shortly to inform me that Jim Gritman, the area manager in North Dakota, was on the phone. Bounding up the steps into my house, I picked up the phone and said, "Hi, Jim, what's up?"

"Terry, we have to leave right away in order to meet with the director and brief him on the wetland easement program and the need for more money in order to carry out our enforcement program." At that time the director of the Service was Lynn Greenwalt.

"Jim," I said, "I just got back this minute from California and need some time to unload our things."

"There is no time if we are to meet with the director," he replied. "He is on a short schedule, and we have just seven hours to get to him in Rapid City and make our point, or he is on the road again."

Realizing how important the wetland easement program was and appreciative of the support Jim had given me, I told him it would take me twenty minutes to pack and suggested that he meet me at my house. Hours later Jim and I were en route to a meeting with the director of the Service, discussing strategy and presentation as we flew down the highways. Later that afternoon we met with Greenwalt, and Jim and I briefed him regarding the magnitude of the wetland easement problem and the serious plight of the law enforcement folks attempting to hold the line in their support of the Division of Refuge. It didn't take me long to realize that Greenwalt truly didn't understood the depth of the wetland easement problem, no matter what Jim and I said. In all fairness to him, how could he? He had never worked easements a day in his life because his career had never taken him there. It was also clear to me that when the Division of Law Enforcement came up, along with the historical subject of a need for funding, he automatically tuned us out. Here we had a national-in-scope problem involving millions of acres of resource-rich wetlands worth untold millions and a director, at least to my way of thinking, limited in his efficacy because he did not understand how to use law enforcement as a wildlife management tool.

Jim and I both sensed the unspoken lack of support for our efforts and on the way home resolved to do whatever it took to capture the moment and get the protection job done for the wetlands and associated wildlife. Jim was an ex-marine and a fighter, pure and simple. To tangle with him would get you nothing but a damn good asschewing and knots about your head. When Jim set his course of management action it was like Admiral Dewey in Manila Harbor many years earlier during the Spanish-American War. Jim was a resource man with many rough edges, but the critters sure appreciated him, and so did I for the worlds of support he had personally given to me during the two years that my special agents had battled in the Dakotas to save a sleeping nation's one-of-a-kind natural resource. Without him and that level of support, we never could have accomplished what we did, which was monumental! In the first year after our program got up and going we reduced the illegal drainage of the wetlands by the dirt farmers in North Dakota by no less than 75 percent and had a 100 percent conviction rate for those who decided to face off against the Service and illegally drain those wetlands under Service protection!

As I had been packing for the trip with Jim, Donna had been going through several weeks' worth of accumulated mail. In that mass of letters was one from Washington promoting me to the desk officer position! That letter gave me about one nanosecond to get moved and present myself for duty. In the old days, the Service was not what you would call a good caretaker of its people. It just told you when to be there, which usually was in short order; your next paycheck would be sent to your new position, and if you were not there to receive it, tough! So, as is often the case in government service, my wife had to sell the house and settle all our affairs by herself because her fellow was on the road and out of pocket! When I returned from the trip to Rapid City and my meeting with Greenwalt, Donna had already sold the house and had the moving company en route! That is the kind of woman who would sit next to her husband on the wagon seat on the journey West with a Winchester on her lap and be able to use it!

When I showed Donna my letter of promotion, I saw a tear start to roll down her cheek, then another, and then a flood. "Now what is the matter?" I asked.

"I am just so happy for the both of us and the kids," she said through her flood of tears.

"What do you mean?" I asked, still not sure.

"Now I will have a husband and father home once in a while and not gone all the time, as you are now."

Then it dawned on me: I had been gone just about every day of the month for the past two years trying to shore up the cracks in the dam that occurred with regularity in the Dakotas. My wife hadn't said a thing, just supported me as she had always done at the expense of any life she and the kids might have had. Gathering her up in my arms and holding her, I quietly hoped she would forgive me, knowing that if I did my job well, my career in the Service would only get more consuming … and it did.

A month later we had purchased a home in Fairfax, Virginia. After figuring out bus schedules and the like, I headed off to the Washington office for my first day on the job. Walking into my new supervisor's office, I was surprised to find him cleaning out his desk! Chris Visas, my new boss to be, was an ex-FBI agent and a damn good supervisor, according to all who worked for him. I had hoped to learn the tricks of the trade from an outstanding manager. In fact, that was one of the reasons I had submitted my application for the desk officer position. Working under Chris would be nothing but career enhancing, I had figured as I had sealed the envelope holding my application. But it was not to be.

"Chris, where the hell are you going?" I asked, not believing what I was seeing.

"Anywhere but here," he cryptically replied.

"What do you mean?" I asked in utter disbelief.

"Terry, you had better be on your toes if you plan on having any kind of career with the Service with these miserable bastards," he gruffly replied as he continued to shovel his personal belongings into a box. "I have tried to work with these back-stabbing sons of a bitches and got nothing but misery for my efforts. All they are doing is going around behind everyone's back and creating hell through jealousy, ambition, hate, and stupidity. I don't have to take that kind of crap and won't."

I was stunned, to say the least! Five minutes later, with a handshake and a "Good luck," he was gone. Let me tell you, that was one hell of a feeling, having just given up a great job in the field for what now appeared to be, according to a damn good and highly respected man, a nest of spiders. ...

"Hi, I'm Dan Searcy," came a voice from behind me along with a hand on my shoulder. "Boy, am I glad to see you."

I turned to meet Dan Searcy, a stocky lad with a bit of a Southern accent who was to become a great friend. "I'm Terry," I replied as I stuck out my hand and warmly shook his. Dan was the Migratory Bird desk officer and, during my position's vacancy, had been carrying the Endangered Species duties as well. The duties of a desk officer are pretty simple—in print, that is. In reality, it was a zoo in those hectic days. Desk officers at that time were divided into specific areas with duties associated with the Migratory Bird Treaty Act, the Endangered Species Act (ESA), the Lacey Act, and so forth. Each desk officer responded to all phone calls in his specific area; responded to congressional letters of inquiry; provided expertise to any agents calling for guidance within a specific law's framework; wrote regulations, policy, and procedures relative to his field of assignment; provided support on major national raids; testified before congressional committees; acted as an adviser in his area of expertise to the chief and director; and did everything else under the sun even remotely associated with that position. The closest thing I can compare it to was riding a bucking Brahma bull, with the bell rope wrapped around you instead of the bull!

As Danny and I sat there visiting while he explained how the Investigations Branch, of which I was now a member, operated, his phone rang. From his end of the conversation, I gathered that it was one of the highest-level supervisors asking whether I had arrived. Dan said I had and, after a few more exchanges, hung up. "Bert Falbaum, deputy chief of administration, wants to see you right now in the chief's office," he told me. He continued, "Terry, watch your back in any dealings with Bert or his pet Viper."

"Who the hell is the Viper?" I asked, amazed by how that morning was beginning to play out.

"The Viper is an ex–lieutenant colonel from the air force named Dick Gordon who works under Bert as the head of the training division," Dan answered.

Brother, what am I getting myself into? I thought. Anxious to meet some of these people so I could judge for myself, I got directions and headed upstairs to the chief's office. When I arrived at the door, I was met by Clark Bavin, a smallish, balding, dapper man who was the chief of the Division of Law Enforcement. Seated in the chief's office was Keith Parcher, deputy chief of Operations and an old friend from my days in California as a U.S. game management agent. To his left sat Bert Falbaum and Dick Gordon, a mousy individual who looked a bit like a rat terrier, the so-called Viper, who was chief of the Training Division.

After I had shaken hands all around and sat down, Bert asked without warning, "Who should replace you as the senior resident agent in the Dakotas?"

"Joel Scrafford," was my immediate reply, which was interrupted by Bert's upraised hand.

"Of every agent in the nation, who should replace you?" he asked.

"I don't know every agent in the nation," I replied.

He nodded as he realized that my response was the only possible answer to his goofy damn question. "OK, of those you know, who should replace you as the senior resident agent?"

"Joel Scrafford," I quickly replied once more.

"Why?" was his rapid-fire response.

"Because he is an excellent officer, has an outstanding knowledge of the laws of the land, gets along very well with the state and federal attorneys, is highly respected by the rank and file in North Dakota Game and Fish, is a great 'catch dog,' and gets along well with the people he meets in the field," I responded just as quickly. Bert was shaking his head all the while. "I don't know what else to add," I said in light of Bert's negatively shaking head.

Bert said, "Will he make a good supervisor?"

"I think so," I replied, "but we won't know that until he works in that position for a while, will we?"

Bert just smiled, but I felt that as far as mind games went, I had at least won the first round. (In the end, Joel did go on to be selected for the senior resident agent position in Bismarck and did a fine job.) Then Clark took over the conversation, welcomed me to my new job, and laid out what was expected of me as a desk officer and how he wanted me to operate. Then we broke up and Bert asked me to follow him into his office. Walking in and sitting down, he asked, "What is your law enforcement forte?"

"The Migratory Bird Treaty Act and the Eagle Act," I responded.

"Good," he replied. "You will be our new Endangered Species desk officer."

I was stunned, to say the least! I was best in the migratory bird arena, and in light of that he had just assigned me to one of the newest laws on the books. It was a very complex, controversial act without any case law precedent—and one about which I knew basically nothing!

"Bert," I replied, "I am at my best in the migratory bird arena and would like to work in that area if at all possible."

"No," was his direct reply. "By putting you into another area, one in which you are not familiar, we are dragging you out from some of your parochialism and starting you on the way toward becoming a better, more rounded agent."

Well, I wasn't happy with my new assignment and thought it might have something to do with all the times I had crossed verbal swords with Bert, but he was right. Being assigned to the desk officer position responsible for the Endangered Species Act, an area I had neglected in the field, would do nothing but broaden me as an officer, and that really was for my own damn good.

Walking slowly back down the steps to the Investigations Branch office on the fourth floor, I received another jolt. The desk I had been assigned had been clean of everything but a telephone when I first arrived. Now it was totally covered with at least sixty pounds of stacked paper! Walking over to the mess and taking a closer look, I could see at least thirty overdue congressional letters (to which a desk officer was required to respond within two weeks) and everything else under the sun dealing with my new position. As I sat there in shock behind that mountain of paper, my phone started to ring off the hook. I started to reach for it, then felt Danny's hand on my shoulder once more.

"Terry, when you arrive here, the very second you sit down, you are the desk officer *expert*. How are you on the ESA?"

"Not worth a tinker's damn," I said, starting to let my frustration leak out after just an hour or so on the job.

"Well, if that is the case, let the phone ring. In here we only get those questions that can't be answered anywhere else. So don't pick up that phone until you are at least conversant with the ESA. The division secretary will take a number and put it on your desk, so you are safe from the crazy phone calls for at least a day," he said. "In the meantime, grab the *Regulations, Statutes and Treaties Manual* and start learning the ESA because it is a bitch, and if you give out the wrong information, it will kill a lot of critters, not to mention start up a pile of lawsuits."

I was beginning to like Dan a lot because what he had said to me so far was pure gold in the fast-track commonsense department in the Washington office scene. In fact, over the next thirty days while my learning curve caught up with the whirl of the position, Dan kept me under his wing and out of trouble. As a result of his unselfishness in assisting me and doing his own mammoth job as well, we developed a kinship that is still strong to this day. If it hadn't been for Dan and his support, his role in acting as a sounding board for the complex issues, and his acting as my partner in crime against the upper echelon, I would have had a devil of a time. He was not only a great friend but a damn good professional, and not once did I ever see him do anything in those trying times but provide the best professional assistance possible to those requesting assistance. My guardian angels had once more provided a place for me to softly land on my feet, as opposed to a hard crash.

Unfortunately, I couldn't be as complimentary about the divisions' leaders. There was almost open warfare, with Bert and Dick pitted against Keith and Clark. It was a kind of intrigue based on free-wheeling office sex, booze, ambition, mean-spiritedness, varying management styles, and disrespect that I have yet to see elsewhere.

Off to one side of this nest of worms were the desk officers and Nando Mauldin, special agent in charge for Special Operations (our covert operations branch), trying to ignore these entanglements and get the work done as professionally as possible. In the end Bert was tumbled from power, and Dick was essentially neutralized. Keith Parcher moved into the field to a special agent in charge position, and Clark began reorganizing his office once again.

Over my first six months, even in light of these destructive distractions, I grew rapidly into my new position and began to learn my trade as a desk officer. Then another set of laws dropped into my lap, titled the Convention on International Trade in Endangered Species of Wild Fauna and Flora (CITES for short). It was sort of an international Endangered Species Act, if you will. Suffice it to say, I was one busy son of a gun with that kind of workload and often found myself getting off the bus a mile or so from my house just so I could walk home and let a mind flying around with twenty thoughts all at once have some time to settle down.

In time, as I got better, I started to really enjoy the new challenges and realized Bert had been right. This new job was one of the best things that could have happened to me, and at the end of my career I considered it one of the several best experiences I *ever* had during my professional life. I found myself meeting the movers and shakers in government as well as those in the essential and widespread nongovernmental organizations. I wrote proposed regulations under the laws for which I was responsible and began to work within the regulations in the all-important wildlife import-export arenas. But probably the most important thing I learned was the intricacies of the agency in which I worked. I learned the ins and outs, the personalities, how things *really* worked, inter- and intraoffice politics, and how to work within the system and get things done. That last part was a godsend that I used many times throughout the rest of my career to the benefit of my staffs and the critters. In time I was made the division's foreign liaison officer, on top of everything else, and had to carry the international burden of providing information to the various CITES countries and undertake business-related foreign travel as well. One of my important functions was to provide the latest information on what could legally be done under the ESA or CITES and how to interpret the regulations.

Another equally important task was that of providing, through outsourcing, positive identifications of the many hundreds of parts and products of wildlife items seized by officers in the field who suspected they were covered under the laws forbidding import, possession, or export. I spent many hundreds of hours going from scientific places of learning to natural history museums and the like, trying to identify these evidence items that had been submitted to me from the field. As with questions from the field, I received only those items that the field officers could not easily get identified elsewhere. Most of the time I could get the species identified, but when it came time for those scientists identifying the goods to write a report on their findings or to testify in a court of law, their eyes rolled back into their heads and they disappeared into the ionosphere, never to be seen again. I never saw such terror at the prospect of having to testify in federal court as an expert witness as I did among those scientists. Now that I look back on it, I wonder how many were really experts and how many were just charlatans. For the most part, they seemed to fit into the taxonomic category known as "standing invertebrates" (a species commonly found in Washington, D.C.!). Pretty soon it got so bad that once they knew I was in the building, I had to look under their desks to get them to come up for air to identify my unknown parts and products. That, plus the fact that they would not testify under any circumstances, just about drove me to drink. Here I would go to the so-called experts only to be turned away with the most mundane excuses. Soon almost all my sources dried up when it came to identifying wildlife parts and products.

For those who don't really understand my plight, it was like this. Any officer presenting a criminal case in federal court has to prove the accusation beyond a reasonable doubt in order to win the case. In the case of the ESA or CITES, if a species or subspecies is seized as an animal protected by that law, the agent filing charges against the wrongdoer *must prove beyond a reasonable doubt that the species or subspecies in question is a protected and listed species or subspecies under the those laws*. Now, that isn't too hard when one is comparing a live

African elephant to the endangered Asian elephant and the like. But in many cases, the suspected wildlife being imported, exported, or possessed in violation of a particular law was in the form of hard-to-identify parts or products. How do you identify black rhino parts in a liquid solution, or the sperm of an endangered species of bird, or the blood of a tiger, or the egg of a protected bird, or the species of a small tuft of tiger fur on a bracelet, or the meat of a turtle? Well, you don't unless you have a capable wildlife forensic scientist, skilled in state-of-the-art techniques, who will make a good witness in a court of law. At that time, with few exceptions, I had a bunch of scientific dingbats who were scared of the shadow their souls cast and preferred to be left alone in their quiet world of scientific study.

My level of frustration went over the top when I took a bunch of pieces of tanned leather to an expert in the Smithsonian Museum of Natural History for identification. The scientist identified the pieces in short order as coming from a protected species of crocodile. Man, I was one happy son of a gun. The lad importing the leather had tried to hide it in a large containerized cargo shipment and had gotten caught on the New York docks. It was a great knowing violation by an importer who had been apprehended and prosecuted by the Service several times before. However, my joy was short-lived when the scientist announced that his initial identification was as far as he would go and that he would not testify in court. No amount of begging would change his mind, so I left in a somewhat grouchy state. I had had enough of the bended knee, always having to beg to assist the lads in the field, and this was the last straw! It didn't help that an eleven-thousand-pound shipment of green sea-turtle meat had entered the port of New York earlier that same week. During that period, all species of green sea turtles were protected under the ESA and CITES, except, if I remember correctly, the population around Australia. Of course that shipment listed Australia as the country of origin, even though it came from a company in South America known for its illegal importation of wildlife. Without forensic support, there was no way we could tell the meat from that of the protected species in accordance with the proof required by federal court. So we had to let it enter the U.S. for resale. Do you realize how many green sea turtles had to be killed to produce eleven thousand pounds of meat? Don't even ask because the number is gross and the overall destruction to the green sea turtle population monumental!

Arriving back at the Division of Law Enforcement building with a full head of steam, I stormed into the chief's office, threw the leather pieces down on his desk, and said, "If we can't do this animal identification thing right, you can take that part of my job and shove it!" I think he was somewhat taken aback at my angry explosion—plus my weighing in at over three hundred pounds, standing glowering over his desk with the chief weighing in at about ten ounces, kind of got his attention. He was aware of the identification problem I was having; hell, all of us were having, for that matter. It was just that no one had come up with a satisfactory solution to the nationwide problem, and it was getting worse.

"What do you suggest, Terry?" he quietly asked. "That is one reason why we bring new blood into desk officer positions, to get new looks at age-old problems. Earn your keep. Now is your chance to speak."

I had some ideas, but they were so far-fetched in light of our historically nonexistent budget and the almost total lack of support for the law enforcement function by the agency higher-ups, which in part was because they feared, were suspicious of, or disliked Clark for his sometimes close-to-the-vest ways, that I had held my tongue in check. Well, not today! Enough was enough, and I just boiled over! "I want your permission to start working on a Service-administered wildlife forensic laboratory so our officers will have the right kind of program to see them successfully through this identification thing and through the federal court system into the twenty-first century. That means a facility big enough to hold at least one hundred forensic scientists and the needed administrative backup! That means state-of-the-art equipment, even if we have to go overseas for it and pay a fortune!" (In those days we always had to buy American even if it were a second-best choice.) Still puffed up like a whale in heat, I continued, "That means the fiscal backing needed to do the job as we in Law Enforcement see fit and that means your 100 percent backing for the overall project no matter how long the haul." Having run out of bile, I quit bellowing long enough for the chief to get a word in edgewise.

"I don't know, Terry; you are asking for an awful lot," he said.

"Clark, if we can't get this kind of capability, the division is not going to be able to run with the bad guys, and eventually we will be able to prosecute hardly anything under the ESA or CITES. When that happens, the division is out of business in the world of imports and exports, and that means you as well." Then I threw in my ace, knowing that the chief was a *huge* fan of the FBI. "Clark, if the FBI can have a forensic lab, then we should be allowed one as well because almost all of our stuff is small and hard to identify, and it is getting worse!"

Clark's eyes sort of glazed over as visions of "J. Edgar" Bavin, director, Division of Law Enforcement and Forensics, drifted through the recesses of his brain. Damn, I think I have him, I thought, if his body language says anything at all.

Continuing my charge, I said, "Just think, Clark; we will have the only lab like it in the *world*—how would that look? Plus, we will get good enough down the line so all we have to do is have our forensic experts show up in court and the bad guys will roll over knowing what kind of devastating science and technology they have arrayed against them!"

Clark's gaze shifted back to the basic blue in his eyes, and he said in an upbeat voice, "You got it! Work up the budget, slowly at first, mind you, so we don't get picked off by the department before we are able to fire our first shot, and then we will go for more later. Let's put together the position description for the director as a starter, and let's go for it! I have enough money hidden away to advertise for the director's position, so let's get this show on the road." Now he was sounding excited, and just to be fair, even with all the work he was lining out for me to do in the process, I was getting a little on the wild side as well!

"Yes, sir!" I exulted. Turning to leave before "J. Edgar" changed his mind, I turned back for a second to face him and said, "Don't you piss backward on me on this one, Clark."

He was leaning back in his big leather chair, and the glaze over his eyes was back. He said nothing to my word of caution, and with that, I knew we were off and running. Hell of a deal, I thought as I vaulted

down the staircase, three stairs at a time. In so doing, I ran straight
into three black men, all carrying new electric typewriters from the
offices off the fourth floor. Wait a minute, whoa, I thought, that doesn't
look right. "Hey, where are you guys going with those office machines?
Let's see some identification lads if you are repairmen here on business!" I barked. All three electric typewriters hit the floor at the same
time as my three would-be crooks made ready to fly down the stairs
at a high rate of speed. Two got away, but one found out how hard it
was to run dragging my body weight firmly clamped to his hind end!
After the D.C. police left with my bad guy in tow, I returned to my
forensic task.

For the next month, in addition to my regular duties as a desk officer, I filled out every piece of paper known to government bureau-
crats, and then some. I wrote a position description for the National
Forensic Laboratory director, as directed by Clark. Then came orga-
nizational charts with all the collateral position descriptions. I did that
much detail work because if I left, I didn't want the project to die just
because someone was too lazy to do the paperwork. Then I began
work on the budget for the first position and several working papers
on the next few stages of the lab. Clark, true to his word, set aside
$50,000 in the budget for the new lab director, and I was in seventh
heaven. Then came the day to start the process moving through the
Office of Personnel Management so we could advertise the position.
Those of you not familiar with personnel offices, especially in government at the Washington, D.C., level, should thank your lucky
stars. Those folks are from another planet, and many times it appears
to be their dedicated task to hold all progress at bay. It is almost as if
everything that moves forward comes directly out of their own pockets; therefore, they must keep all progress to a minimum. For whatever reason, they made me redo several of the documents several
times, but I could tell they were just piddling, trying to figure out
what to do in this unusual circumstance. I could take a small delay to
make them feel as if they were important in this project just so they
didn't get carried away, but not a big one. Finally their goofy delays
got to me, and I had to take several of them out to lunch to a top-
drawer eatery in Georgetown, but with that, amazingly, I got their

blessing to proceed almost the same day. My bride wasn't happy over a luncheon that cost me $78 in 1977 on her tight budget, but it was a small price to pay for a facility that, once up and running like Merlin the wizard, would be like adding another one hundred special agents to the officer corps to tackle our wildlife problems.

The last step just prior to advertising for a position required me to fill out another document for some office, the name of which I cannot even remember, showing that the Division of Law Enforcement had the full-time equivalent (FTE), or space for the body, for the position and the money to fill said position. I sent that form off and waited for the expected clearance. It didn't come! I finally received word that the Division of Law Enforcement had the FTE but that there was no money for the position! What the hell? I thought. I knew the money had to be there. I checked the latest budget document with John Cross (an agent in my office getting budget training), only to find that the $50,000 had disappeared! Though I didn't really need extra administrative work, I was too deep in my quest to stop now, so I began digging to see what had happened to "my" money. Sure as God made little green apples, someone in the Service had just helped themselves to our little pot of money for his division's administrative needs, and it was really gone. I was beside myself! Well, grab your ass, you damn horse thief, because here comes the sheriff and he has a head of steam up, I thought.

Another lunch with a certain budget person who made me swear to keep what she told me secret divulged that one Richard, a.k.a. Dick, Smith (probably related to Soapy Smith of Montana and Alaska fame), a high-up in a national lab, had just reached into the Division of Law Enforcement's little money pot and helped himself to all of the $50,000 without a single look backward! I guess he figured we were a little division without any support (he had that right) and that he could do as he pleased (he had that wrong). Well, he forgot about the three-hundred-pound gorilla hot on his trail. ... I met with the division's deputy chief of operations and told him my tale of woe. With hardly a blink, Keith Parcher picked up the phone and called the Service director's office. The director was not available—I don't remember if we even had one at the time—but an appointment was made for us to present our case in front of the acting director, and that was good enough for me.

When the day came, Keith Parcher and I found ourselves in front of the acting director, a man called Reid Goforth. Also in the room was a giant of a man with a scowl on his puss to match his size. It was the notorious Dick, a.k.a. "Soapy," Smith, the one who had lifted my hard-fought-for $50,000, and the look on his face didn't seem to be saying he was there to happily return the pilfered bucks! I got to go first and laid out my tale of work setting up the new lab and woe when the money disappeared. Reid listened carefully and quietly, then said, "Dick, it is your turn."

"Yeah, I took the money because the Division of Law Enforcement doesn't need it. They can come to us for any animal identification work they need doing, and knowing that, I took the money for our use." There was a pause and, then he added, "I took the money figuring it would be payment in advance for the work we would have to do for them." With that said, Soapy just leaned back in his chair and looked at Reid with his trademark scowl.

Damn, I thought, this lad has a lot of guts. Not so much in the way of brains when it came to finesse, but lots of guts! This fellow and General Patton would have had a lot in common, I thought.

Reid thought for a minute and then said, "Dick, return the money to Law Enforcement."

Dick just froze and then, quickly regaining his composure and bullying tactics, charged. "I already spent the money. I needed two research positions filled and have already spent the money and filled the positions."

Reid just looked at him for a second and then said firmly, "Fire the folks you just hired or find the money elsewhere to fund their positions! The money you took belongs to Law Enforcement and you need to see it is returned."

"I can't do that!" bellowed "Soapy."

"Get it done, Dick," Reid said in a stronger-toned voice. Then, turning to me and Keith, he said, "You will have your money by the end of the week." Over the years I have run across Reid in various capacities, and to this day I admire the man for his integrity and fairness. He was there as acting director and handled himself like an experienced sitting director. A week later we had our money, and the process for advertising the new, one-of-a-kind-in-the-nation forensic lab director position went forward. Damn, you talk about pleased. The division was finally on the road to the twenty-first century, with me pushing at the rear. God, it was a good feeling to be part of such a thing as the creation of a national laboratory, a first of its kind.

About forty-five days later, Clark got a list of hopeful candidates for the new lab director position from the Office of Personnel Management. He let me look over the list, and I could see that we had candidates ranging from lab directors at small facilities across the nation to lab-tech types to sitting foreign lab directors. Damn, I thought; we had a good cross-section to look over, and boy, was I excited. I still had the blue flame going out to about four feet in those days, and that particular day was no different! Taking the list at Clark's direction, I set up the interviews to be spaced out over the next week. I wanted to move quickly because I didn't want to lose our money at the end of the fiscal year and didn't want Clark getting cold feet for any reason and backing out of the deal. Plus the "Soapy Smith" fiasco was still fresh in my mind.

The interviews were set up, and I couldn't wait. Come interview day, Clark and I began the careful process of weeding out those neither of us wanted for the lab director position. Clark asked most of the questions, and I sat quietly off to one side, closely examining every candidate for any hint of emotion or body language that would tell me this was or wasn't the one. I had only one question for each candidate, and that was held for last. When it came my turn, I swung into action. I gave a little history of the division and how hard it was to get and keep funding. I also made sure they were aware that there was a lot of opposition to this new lab and friction between the various divisions scrapping for any kind of funding they could get. I let the candidate know that even within the agency there were those who would not be too unhappy if our quest for our own lab to meet the challenges of the twenty-first century fell flat on its face so they could tell us, "I told you so." I made sure they realized that the Service directorate was skeptical about the formation of another national laboratory and wasn't too sure where Congress stood on the issue, and that a new lab in their budget would have to be hard fought for. I also made sure every one of them realized that the Service directorate did not understand the basic law enforcement issues, nor did they understand how to use law enforcement as a management tool. After all that warmup, I pitched a curve ball. Leaning toward each candidate and lowering my voice for effect, I said, "Being that the division is under so much agency fire, if the agents brought in a specimen that had to be a certain thing that it wasn't, would you, as lab director, present to us what we needed in the way of specimen identification in order to win the case and subdue any Service effort to take away or belittle our facility?" In other words, I was asking every candidate to fudge the results or outright lie so we could win and beat the Service at its own very well-played game!

Every candidate through the first seven said they could accommodate the system to save the game. They didn't come right out and say they would lie, but they all commented on the fact that wildlife forensics was a new science and that there was a certain margin for error in favor of the government if necessary! For a forensic lab to be caught deliberately shading the truth on their evidence samples would ruin the lab forever in the eyes of the court! I thought. A lab director who supported such ideas was not something Clark or I wanted, period. There was too much at stake, plus, right was right, and upon that concept, for better or worse, the legal system of this country was built. We politely thanked all the candidates and prepared to interview the eighth and last one. I was really down in the dumps, figuring we would have to start the hiring process all over again. Plus I could sense that Clark was already trying to figure out a way to spend the $50,000 elsewhere and call it a good try.

The last candidate, a wimpy, professorial-looking guy, walked into the interview room, and Clark and I introduced ourselves. The man had thrown his hat into the ring at the last moment, and if I am not mistaken was a bench chemist forensic scientist from a police lab somewhere in the San Diego area. He may have been on the personnel office's best-qualified list, but in my eyes he was an also-ran. We went through the canned questions quite rapidly, and surprisingly the candidate responded to them in a highly satisfactory way. He was relaxed during the entire interview and seemed at ease, if selected, with the prospect of establishing a wildlife forensic laboratory even if that had not been his field of experience. I kind of liked the chap, but I had liked several of the other candidates as well until they had responded to my curve ball. When the time came for my curve ball, I let it fly. Until I made my pitch from the mound, this candidate had looked pretty good—not terribly up-to-snuff on the wildlife thing but showing a great work ethic and enthusiasm for the challenges associated with creating a one-and-only national wildlife forensic laboratory. My "lie-if-you-will" pitch flew across his plate, clearly a strike, without him even taking a swing at it.

"Do I need to repeat the question?" I asked, looking at this candidate as he looked at me like someone who had just had his manhood put into the jaws of an alligator.

He continued to give me a goofy look and then, abruptly, without one word to Clark or me, got up and walked out of the interview room, out the office door, and out of the building!

Clark looked at me like *what the hell,* and I said, "That is the man I want for our new lab director!"

Clark just looked at me as if I had stepped off the deep end as well.

"Clark, that is our man! He is like all the rest, smart and able to build the lab of our dreams, but more importantly, he is *honest!* Don't you see, he was pissed I asked him to lie for us no matter the kind of evidence he or his staff were examining."

Clark got a big grin and said, "By God, you are right. I will select him, and let's see if he is still so mad at you and your question that he turns us down. If he does, we will have to work on him in order to get him to come on board."

Suffice it to say that Ken Goddard, our rather surprised man, who thought he had blown the interview (in fact, that was what he had told his wife), accepted our job offer and became the very first lab director for the National Wildlife Forensic Laboratory for the Fish and Wildlife Service.

When Ken came on board a month or so later, he met briefly with Clark, and then I was given the chore of showing him around, introducing him to the Operations and administrative staffs, and taking him to his office space in the building. With that and just the barest instructions to get his proposed laboratory organization down on paper so the chief could look at it, I left him to his own devices. However, before I left this likable sort of chap, I told him I thought the lab should be at least one hundred folks in size and have a building commensurate with those numbers and the status of the operation. He agreed, and we parted company with neither of us really having half an idea about the size of the physical laboratory or where it should go (keep in mind that this concept was brand new). I went back to my duties as a desk officer, and Ken set to work to organize and initiate the operation of a new national lab. Brother, I don't think either of us realized what a minefield we had picked to run across ... and would continuing to negotiate for the *next ten years!*

For the next year or so, I continued my duties as the Endangered Species desk officer while Ken worked as the lab director. We grew close because of our shared interest in the world of wildlife forensics and our mutual desire to get the lab up and functioning. I did everything I could to sell the lab to the field officers and their supervisors on an almost daily basis. I also cultivated staffers on powerful congressional committees and began to introduce them to the world that could be with this wildlife forensics resource. Last but not least, I continued to educate everyone in the Service hierarchy about this new concept and its overall value to the protection of the nation's wildlife and plant resources. As our wildlife investigations across the land got more and more into the realms of meats (processed and unprocessed), feathers, bones, hides (tanned and untanned), and medicinal seizures, my prediction of the need for a forensic presence in the Service began to steadily come true. Under our burden of legal proof, more and more wildlife dealers were challenging us in court to prove our accusations against them, and we were losing the major challenges regarding identification of parts and products with regularity. We just couldn't prove our cases in a court of law.

In the meantime, the Division of Law Enforcement came upon some more hard fiscal times. We were so broke that we took to rolling the bums on the streets of Washington in order to have enough money just to keep the lights on in our building. Well, not really—but we were driven almost to that level as the rest of the agency continued to expand exponentially. In addition, it seemed that we had even fewer friends in the agency, all the way up to and through the director. In times like that, it didn't take a rocket or forensic scientist to realize that any hope for building a lab would have to be placed on hold or considerably slowed. Ken had managed to get a chap on board who was keen on photography, and a secretary, but that was about it. I also began to see that Clark was losing interest in going through with the project. That was alarming because he held the keys to the kingdom, and to lose his support would be the kiss of death. I spent every waking moment trying to curry his favor by exposing him to those investigations requiring detailed and accurate identification of the many parts and products of wildlife that were pouring into the country through our thin but hardworking ranks of wildlife inspectors. I also made sure he was aware of the defeats in court the field officers were suffering because we could not identify many of these parts and products moving illegally in commerce to the species level beyond a reasonable doubt.

Then, as if I didn't have enough problems, Ken and Clark had a falling out! I was never privy to the actual reasons, but knowing Ken as I did and understanding his high values and integrity, I had a feeling about why they crossed swords. Sometimes Clark tended to cut corners, and I got the distinct feeling that Ken would not tolerate any shaving of ethical lines. After that it became obvious that whenever Clark picked up any extra money, instead of being funneled into his new forensics startup program, it went for the old traditional saws in the division, namely, travel, gasoline, and vehicles. Even the Training Division found itself with money during those hard times, but the new lab didn't. Finally, one day Ken came down to my office and tiredly slumped into a chair in front of my desk.

"I am getting out," he stated in a voice drained of emotion. "I have had enough of that lying bastard Clark, and I am going to quit!"

Knowing what he had been going through, I couldn't really fault Ken for his decision. But goddamnit, we needed that lab, and I had given up a lot of skin off my knuckles and hind end in order to get it to that point, so I wasn't interested in the "roll me over" mood Ken was now exhibiting. I had had a really terrible morning, and my afternoon was shaping up to be even worse, and when I heard what Ken had to say, that absolutely tore it! Looking Ken right in the eyes, I said, "If you try to quit and walk away from our lab, *I will personally kill you with my bare hands!* Now, I am not good at killing someone with my hands, rather awkward, in fact. But if you dump it now, *plan on dying before you take three steps, and plan on it being ugly and messy!*"

Ken just stared, not believing what he was hearing from his old friend. Then he got that look of realization that I meant it! Quickly getting up and leaving my office, he tossed over his shoulder the words, "I think I will reconsider."

About two weeks later, Clark and I crossed swords over my being truthful to officers who called to ask what the work conditions were like in the Washington office. These were officers who were toying with the possibility of coming into the Washington office to fill some of the vacant desk officer positions. I had a reputation for being straight-arrow with the lads and spoke the truth about the high cost of housing, riding the damn buses (as long as it didn't snow or rain), working under Clark and the other infighting supervisors, the type of work, and the meager rewards of desk officer work. I also told them not to come into the Washington office as a desk officer unless they had at least five to seven years' experience in the field. I would follow up these comments with a genuine pitch that the desk officer job was becoming one of the best experiences I had *ever* had and for them to plan on it becoming one of theirs if they chose to come to Washington. I also advised them that all the other problems could be overcome if they had the right attitude and work ethic when they came to the central office. Nonetheless, upon hearing what I was telling the officers calling in about the vacancies, Clark went into orbit. Calling me into his office, he asked what the hell I was doing in a very pissed-off manner.

"Sure, there are problems, but those calling in don't need to know what they are," he told me. In short, Clark asked me to shade the truth and sugarcoat the situation, that is, lie, so that officers would transfer into the Washington office and fill some of the badly needed positions even though they weren't ready professionally. He just wanted heartbeats, and those officers' careers be damned.

I went back downstairs to my office, called Bob Hodgins, the special agent in charge in Minneapolis, and asked if his deputy position, recently advertised, was still open.

"It sure is, Terry; want to throw your hat in the ring?" he asked.

"Sure do, Bob; my application will be there by the end of the week."

"Had a gutful of Clark and the Washington office?" he softly asked.

"We can talk about it later," I told him, "but for now, hold open the advertisement so my application can make it in under the wire." I hung up and forty days later was the new assistant special agent in charge in Minneapolis, or Region 3.

Saying good-bye to the Washington office staff, I took a few special moments to bid farewell to my friend and lab director without a lab, Ken Goddard. I told him not to give up, that I had no intention of doing so myself, and that I would keep trying to help him from my new position.

"Thank you, Terry, for what you have done, and rest assured, I will not let Clark get the best of me or my lab."

That was what I wanted to hear, and I just smiled. You could go to the bank on Ken's word, and with that I knew that we would eventually get our lab. I didn't know when, but it was coming. With that, I closed that chapter of my professional life and transferred to my new assignment. Ken, in the meantime, continued in the midst of the chain gang.

I spent only two years in the position of assistant special agent in charge and in 1981 was promoted to special agent in charge and transferred to Denver, Colorado. As usual, the Division of Law Enforcement was in some of the hardest fiscal times I had ever seen. We in Law Enforcement were at least $1 million in the red (not our doing; we were never funded), and Director Robert Jantzen took some rather drastic action. He reduced the special agent in charge positions in the Service from thirteen to seven and the number of first-line supervisors, or senior resident agents, from forty-five to twenty-two! Not one other division stepped forward to help us out, nor did any of the Service leadership, and so, with the stroke of a pen, many officers' hardworking lives, and those of their families, were changed forever. When the dust had settled, although junior to everyone else in that rank, I remained as the Denver special agent in charge. My guardian angels had done it again.

Since I was one of the remaining seven special agents in charge, I pledged to make the most of my position, including removing that albatross hanging around my neck called the national forensics laboratory. I got my first chance several weeks later at a special agent in charge conference. Clark had called together what was left of his field leadership so we could talk about the ruined lives of the dumped supervisors (for example, some supervisors found themselves demoted to the number two position and their assistants promoted over them in the same office), what our priorities would be, how to get along better among ourselves, and what we were going to do with no funding prospect yet still having an enforcement responsibility to honor. That first gathering of the leadership was so outrageous and out of control, because the agents in charge were so angry over the state of the division, that Clark had to put a gallon of whiskey on the table during the evening meeting in order to tone things down. At the end of that meeting two hours later, the jug was dry. ...

One of the issues that came up was how to cut seemingly unnecessary corners so we would have some money to operate. All kinds of ideas came up, such as not replacing worn-out patrol vehicles, just driving them until they died or their operators did; canceling all training (real smart when an officer's training is what pulls him or her through dangerous situations); reducing travel to almost nothing; and *eliminating the forensic laboratory and putting its funding into the operations of the field units!* When it came time to discuss that last item, my six counterparts got the front end of a grizzly protecting its "offspring"! I was close friends with all of my counterparts. One had originally hired me from the state conservation officer ranks in 1970, and another had been my highly respected boss just before I was promoted to my current position. As it turned out, this was a situation in which the Queensberry Rules did not apply. I very frankly, between long drafts of good whiskey, challenged every man jack there to explain to me why the future of the division didn't require a forensic lab.

Man, talk about going round and round—it was the word of the day. I had been raised in logging and lumber camps as a kid, trying to earn enough money to go to college because I came from a single-parent family. In order to survive as a boy among men, I had learned how to fight and fought to win, no matter the process or odds. I put those skills to use that evening, and with a level of force that surprised even me. Not one of my counterparts could see the value of a forensic lab in a changing world and bitterly fought to transfer the funding from that operation to field officer use. As I expected, I got little or no support from Clark, the man who had let me set the whole concept in motion in 1977. Clark just didn't have a whole lot of guts for a fight when the odds appeared overwhelming. That was OK with me, though. It just allowed me a sanded deck to operate on and made it less slick when the bloodletting took place! Suffice it to say, at the end of that rough-and-tumble meeting, the forensic lab concept remained … but just barely!

Over the next several years, the lab was always an issue with my counterparts, but no one wished to return to the sanded decks to see who slid the least in their own blood … so that subject was handled pretty carefully, at least in front of me. Realizing that the agency was never going to fund the Division of Law Enforcement adequately, no matter what, I initiated a Plan B to save the concept of the forensic lab. Officers should have a Plan B for every occasion, and in the forensic lab matter, I was no exception. I started quietly meeting with powerful congressional staffers to try to sell the forensic lab concept. They in turn quietly set up meetings with congressional representatives, and I again laid out the forensic lab concept as a significant way to stop some of the ongoing wildlife destruction, and certainly that which would occur in the future. I made many friends and finally got some of them to put pressure on the Service directorate in their own ways for establishment of the lab. My greatest selling point was that without such a lab in the near future, the laws Congress had passed, and continued to pass, would not be enforceable if we couldn't identify beyond a reasonable doubt those species or *their parts and products* listed under the various federal wildlife laws. I also reiterated that to add a fully staffed lab would be like adding another one hundred officers in the field because the field officers would have a new forensic "sword" as one of their weapons. In addition, adding a lab would be a whole lot cheaper than adding one hundred new officers to do less of the same thing they were doing now!

One day my secretary told me that Chief Bavin was on the phone and wanted to speak with me. Picking up the phone I said, "Good morning, Chief."

"Good morning, Terry; got a moment?"

"Sure; what do you need?" I asked.

"I will be coming out to meet with you on a very sensitive matter and would like to know what your schedule looks like this coming Thursday."

Quickly looking at my schedule and seeing it clear, I told him my time was his that day.

"Good," he replied. "How about picking me up at the airport around ten in the morning. We can then meet at your office, get our work done, and I can catch a plane out around four in the afternoon."

"Fine with me, Chief; I will meet you out in front of the passenger pickup area and when we get back into town, I will treat you to lunch; how does that sound?"

"Great," he said, and we both hung up. I sat there and wondered what the hell would bring him clear out to Denver only to go back the same day. Quickly running through my mind all the covert operations we had going on in the region, I could find no holes to cause me concern. I ran through the sensitive points between us and the many congressional offices in the region but couldn't find any problems there either. I knew I was getting along great with my regional directorate, so no problems there. And on it went for the better part of twenty minutes while I researched my operation. Finding nothing out of the ordinary, I relaxed a bit and got back to my paperwork at hand as my secretary brought in another foot-high stack of paper for me to process.

I picked Clark up at the airport, and we went to the Briarwood Inn, a five-star eatery in Golden, for lunch. Clark always considered himself a bit of a patrician, so we dined accordingly. I picked up the tab, and the two of us drove to my office, still discussing routine business and the other odds and ends typical of two people who are cautiously circling one another.

Once in the office, Clark hit me with what he had in mind. "Terry," he said gravely, "I have no support among all your counterparts for continuance of the forensic lab." I started to object, having forgotten that possibility in my earlier run-through of probable subjects for Clark's visit and caught somewhat off guard. "Let me finish, please," he said, holding up his hand for me to wait. "Plain and simply, as I said, not one of your counterparts wants the lab funded one day further. They all got together and called in to complain about the lab and their lack of support for a pie-in-the-sky concept. They want me to cancel the program and split the money up among the districts based on a per agent funding basis. Now, to be frank with you, I feel that unless you can come up with some sort of a magic bullet, I am going to have to agree with the majority and kill the program. Now, I know I gave you the go-ahead some years ago, and at the time it sounded like a great idea. But that time has passed, and I really can't see the value of a forensic lab down the road. Plus, I have no support for such a lab from the other Service chiefs. They just don't see the value in creating another national lab and have made that point very clear to me every time we meet."

I sat there stunned, not believing what I was hearing from a man who was highly educated and dedicated to the Division of Law Enforcement. In the mid-1970s, Clark had been responsible for changing the division's officers from game management agents to special agents and getting us not only national recognition but annual training and standardization in many areas. He had almost single-handedly gotten all of us promoted to GS-11s in the process and headed the division down a road that would lead us into the twenty-first century. Now, listening to his thoughts about the value of the lab, I just couldn't believe it. "Clark," I said, "without that lab, we won't be able to enforce the Endangered Species Act, the Convention on International Trade in Endangered Species of Wild Fauna and Flora, parts of the Bald Eagle Protection Act with the upcoming Native American activities, and probably several others I am not thinking about at this moment. We will lose the ability to assist the states through the forensic function and bring those folks into the twenty-first century as well, not to mention bringing all the good will from them we can stand. There is no doubt in my mind that once operational, the forensic lab will be one of the crown jewels in our Service system. Additionally, it will be able to support other Service divisions and provide expertise and training not only to the state but to international law enforcement communities as well. Then there is what they can do for the division directly in our field investigations, especially the complex ones. The lads in the lab can come out and do the tricky crime scene work on complex investigations, all the while providing training to our agents in the process. They can also send their experts to our training sessions, teaching us the latest techniques and how we can reach further in our everyday investigations. There are going to be species introduction problems down the road, like with the wolves, and they can support those sections of the Service through their work, especially in the new arena of DNA. My God, Clark, there is a whole new world out there for the lab to explore and teach us how to do a better job. Once they do that, our guys with that new knowledge can reach out even further, and then think what kind of a force we would be in the law enforcement community."

Clark just sat impassively and picked at imaginary lint on his tie and the sleeve of his suit. I could see that his mind had been made up long before he got to Denver, and nothing I said was going to change that. "Terry," he said, "nothing you said will change my mind. When I go back, I am going to pencil the forensic lab out of my budget, *and that is that!* It was a nice thought way back when but is one without standing today."

Standing up, I said, "Clark, we must go or you will miss your plane." I don't think he heard the determination in my voice or saw the fire in my eyes to have one more go at it, and this time, if I crashed and burned, so be it! Dropping Clark off at the airport after giving him a perfunctory handshake, I couldn't wait to get back to my office and the telephone. Once there, I called my congressional staffer buddies and asked them for any kind of immediate support they could give in getting their bosses to micromanage the Service's Division of Law Enforcement budget without my hand being seen in the process, especially as it related to the creation and support of the forensic laboratory. They said they would do what they could, and two of them told me not to worry; they thought they might be able to stop "J. Edgar" Bavin in his tracks. They wouldn't comment on how much money they might raise for the cause but thought they could make a dent in Clark's attack on the concept of a new forensics lab and at least get it up and running.

Finished with that little bit of behind-the-scenes work, I sat back, patted myself on the back, and smiled. Working with those staffers for the past two years, in the process providing five quiet fishing trips; my great outdoor cooking on several of those trips; and one successful hunting trip with a staffer killing a seven-point bull on his first elk trip ever, arranged through me and my state buddies, certainly hadn't hurt in getting them on my side, I thought. Then it hit me! Terry, where is your Plan B? For a moment I bolted like a young colt. I didn't have one, and I always made it a point to have a Plan B. Damnit, Terry, Clark is a worthy opponent, and you'd better have a second barrel just in case he is not hit with a killing shot the first time!

Then I had it! Quickly dialing my phone, I impatiently waited as it rang and rang. Finally a young lady responded, and I asked for Amos.

"He is in a meeting right now," came the reply.

"Young lady," I said, "would you please tell him Terry needs to speak to him *right now,* and it is serious!"

"Just a minute, please," answered the polite voice. Amos Eno, a longtime friend who at that time was with the National Fish and Wildlife Foundation, had bailed me out in my grizzly bear program some years before. He was a man small in stature but monumental in ability to get things done. Plus he was a great friend of the nation's natural resources and had one of the keenest sets of eyes when it came to being able to look down the road on important issues. He had long been a supporter of the forensic lab, and I was counting on that dedication to the moment to prevail now. Moments later Amos's voice came on the line. I could tell from his tone that he wasn't happy at being removed from the meeting, but I also could tell he recognized that a battle was on and that I needed his cannons.

"What the hell did you do now?" he jokingly asked.

"Amos, I just spoke to Clark, and he is going to pencil the forensic lab project out of the budget."

Now, I had spoken previously to Amos about the lab and the value it would add to the law enforcement capabilities of the division in our fight against people illegally trafficking wildlife. He had been sold on the project from the get-go, and every time he landed in Denver, I filled his head with everything I had read in the world of forensics until he, like me, was excited by the prospect of our own forensic lab to fight wildlife crime through the twenty-first century. Amos's voice changed instantly to glacial blue ice and he said, "Listen to me and don't screw me around with any crap. Tell me in finite terms why we need this forensic lab, and don't leave out any details that I must have. Terry, this is a fight for life, so treat it that way!"

I repeated what I had told Clark in detail and added several other important items I had forgotten to discuss with Clark. Then I gave him a run-down on the size of the facility (at least forty thousand square feet) I thought would be sufficient to carry the state, federal, and international wildlife law enforcement communities as they got used to having this kind of tool at their fingertips, the number of people needed (at least one hundred forensic scientists, plus technical and administrative support), and figures on startup as well as maintenance costs. After I finished, the line was quiet. I knew Amos was taking notes, and I remained silent.

"Give just one great example why we need the lab, and make it short," he said in clipped tones.

"Amos, the Service let enter through the port of New York eleven thousand pounds of green sea-turtle meat in the late '70s. Informants had told us that the meat was from the protected populations in Central and South America, not from the Australian population, which was not protected at the time. However, the import permit listed the meat as having come from Australia, and we couldn't prove differently, so we had to let it in. That company continued to import between five thousand and seven thousand pounds of green sea-turtle meat annually until the Australian population of green sea turtles was finally listed, closing the doors to importation of the meat for commercial purposes. Because we couldn't run forensic DNA tests on that meat to determine what subspecies that meat represented, we had to let it go each and every time! Do you know how many green sea turtles that represented at about an eighty-pound weight for each entire animal, not just the meat?"

"All right," he said, "you were right. I needed to come out of my meeting for this one. Now, listen, are you prepared to go all the way with this one?" Before I could answer he said, "This one is going to get messy, and you may get burned."

"Let her rip," I said. "I have almost ten years of heartache in this project and know it is right for the Service, so bring on what you have. I have broad shoulders and can carry whatever you bring my way."

"It is not the shoulder region on your miserable carcass I am worried about," he said. "Wait by your phone, and whoever you talk to, give the most sensitive information possible in answer to their questions; don't hold anything back. You can trust who I send to talk to you." With that, he was gone. Opening my heart and soul to perfect strangers was not what I was all about. But this time the cause was just, and Amos and his word were gold, so I decided to do what was right and let the chips fall where they might.

Within minutes my phone was ringing, and as promised, I bared my heart and soul to the politically powerful information requesters. Each time I did, I could feel myself sliding further down into a black hole if Amos had been wrong about the integrity of the folks he was sending my way. Oh well, I thought; this is a fight to the finish, and if they want me, they had better bring a lunch because when all is said and done, I will be hungry. ...

Amos called and asked if I would call Ken and tell him what was going on and instruct him that he was to lay it on the line as well for anyone who called. As an afterthought he said, "Will he do it?"

"We will find out," I said. "Let me call him." Moments later I had Ken on the line. I told him what Clark had said about the pending death of the lab, that I had stirred up a hornets' nest to keep the lab, and that now some of the "hornets" wanted to talk to him. I told Ken I wanted him to speak to these folks who were soon to call him, and he had better lay it on the line regarding the value of the lab, now and in the future.

Ken was silent for a few moments and then said, "OK, Terry, if you say so, but here goes my career."

"Ken," I said, "Amos told me to speak very frankly to the folks who called and nothing would happen to me. I think the same goes for you, so speak your piece, but just be able to back it up."

He said, "OK, but I just know by tomorrow I will be looking for work because what I have to say is pretty hot."

"Let it rip, my friend; this man Eno may be the key to your and the division's lab."

With that, we hung up and I waited. In about twenty-five minutes Ken called. "Terry, what you said about protection I hope is valid because I just got through explaining what was going on behind the scenes on establishment of the lab, and also about the values of the lab right through the next century."

"Excellent," I said. "Now we wait."

We hung up, Ken's guts just churning and me with my mad coming down a little. I had just fired my two best shots, and if that didn't work, I had damn near ten years' worth of hard and sometime acrimonious work about to go down the drain. That would be especially galling because I knew full well that the Service *really* needed the lab in order for the Division of Law Enforcement and many fine federal laws to survive.

Thirty-three minutes after my initial phone call to Amos, he called me back. "You got your forensic lab," he said matter-of-factly. "Now keep your mouth shut until the shit hits the fan."

"How the hell did you do it, my friend?" I asked, stunned at the speed at which he worked.

"Remember our conversation years ago during the inception of your backcountry grizzly program when I asked if the grizzlies were still dying after you asked me that same question?"

"Yes," I slowly responded.

"Well, you are getting the same answer. You just take care of getting the lab up and going, and I will take care of my end of the bargain. Now, I have a meeting to go to." He hung up. I sat back in my chair, closed my eyes, and looked back into the annals of my mind. For the better part of ten years I had fought, many times bareknuckled, to get that lab on line, and in thirty-three minutes a man one-third the size of a small duck had finally gotten it done. No one, and I mean no one, but Amos could have pulled off such a thing, I mused. Well, I thought, I don't have the lab in my hands yet, but it sure sounds like it is coming. Little did I know, it was *really coming!*

About ten days later my secretary called me to say Chief Bavin was on the phone, and he sounded really upset! Picking up the phone I said as if all was well, "Good afternoon, Chief; what's up?"

"Grosz, you son of a bitch, did you have anything to do with the lab?"

"Well, yes, Chief. Working with you, we got it started years ago; you know that."

"You know goddamn good and well what I am talking about. Somehow that goddamn forensic laboratory is back in my budget after I penciled it out, and I see your handiwork all over it! You miserable bastard, how dare you go behind my back and have my decision to deep-six that lab overridden! If I am ever able to put my finger on you for doing that, I will have your ass drawn and quartered, not to mentioned fired from the Service!" he continued to shout.

"Fire me on what grounds, Chief?" I calmly asked, full well knowing he couldn't have me fired for speaking my piece just as long as I was right.

"Don't get smart with me, you son of a bitch. You hung it to me, and I know it!"

"Chief," I said, "I can't do much about it if someone in a position of power in Washington thinks the forensic lab is a concept to hang on to and puts it back into your budget. For years you supported me in those endeavors, and I am sure I must have talked to a thousand people about the lab. I am not surprised that some of that talk took."

Clark slammed his phone down, and it was some time before he spoke to me again. I never lied to him about my involvement; he just didn't ask the right questions. ...

Some time later, after the lab was a done deal, Frank Dunkle, a special assistant to my regional director who had high political connections, became the director of the Fish and Wildlife Service. Frank and I had developed a good friendship working together in the regional office, and he had come to respect me and my law enforcement program. Once Frank had been confirmed as the Service's new director, he came into my office one morning and sat down. He was always one to get right to the point and asked me if I would consider becoming a deputy regional director in Region 1, which he considered out of control. Basically, he wanted me to keep the regional director and several other senior-level supervisors in the endangered species program in line until he could get better control of the "leaking to the press" problems.

"No," I replied. "I am happy here, still have a lot of work to do in the region, and don't want to move, causing my wife to quit her job for the third time and lose all the retirement years she has worked to build up."

He just looked at me for a moment and said, "If you change your mind, let me know, will you? But do it quickly."

"Yes, sir," I replied.

"Now, what can I do for you personally once I get the reins in hand?" he asked.

"Well, you can get rid of the quarterly Administratively Uncontrollable Overtime Report nationwide and change it to an annual or biannual report," I said. "The way it is set up right now, it is a mess and makes meeting the time requirements during two quiet periods of the year very difficult for the agents. Additionally, many of the districts are short on funding, and that again makes it difficult to make the reporting requirements when one is on short fiscal rations, so to speak."

"Done," he replied. "What else?"

"You can see that the agents in the Service are upgraded to GS-12 journeymen grade levels, where they belong and have belonged for some time."

"Are they truly doing that level of work, Terry?" he asked.

"I wouldn't have brought it up if it were not true, Frank."

"Done," he replied, "but you will have to help shepherd that one through. Who else do you want on your part of the team from the Washington office?"

"Jerry Smith would be a good one," I said.

"Done; what else?"

"Nothing," I replied.

"Where do you want the forensic lab located?" he asked right out of the blue.

Man, I hadn't even thought of that, but now that he mentioned it, what a great opening. "Not anywhere near where Clark Bavin can get his hands on it or control it," I said.

"Why?" he asked.

"Because Clark, at this time in his life, does not support the concept, see its value, or want it. If he had his way, he would kill it in a heartbeat and pour the money into the field because we are so underfunded."

Frank looked long and hard at me for a moment and then said, "I don't like that little bastard. If I have my say, he won't see the light of day on that lab as far as supervision. In fact, one of the first things I have to do once I get to D.C. is meet with him on that very issue. As I understand it, he has a proposal for me to consider on locating the lab in the Patuxent Research Refuge under his control. I guess he figures if he can hit me cold turkey right out of the chute before I can get my feet on the ground, he will have his way. Well, I have a surprise for him," he coldly purred. "I will just string him along and then put it where I want to. Any problem with that?" he asked.

"No," I said. "You are the director. But I would suggest you make sure it is near commercial air and rail service so we can send and receive evidence. Other than that, anywhere is fine with me."

"Good, consider it done." Out the door he went without another word. Frank could be a tough old bastard and very hard on his people, especially if he didn't like you, you screwed him, or he *thought* you had screwed him. But he has my lasting gratitude for not only helping the lab to get up and going but also having the backbone to stand up to the states and their greed hidden under the guise of hunter opportunity to get rid of the point-system method of hunting waterfowl. By so doing, he saved thousands of ducks from the hunters and their inability to identify birds in the air, much less in hand on the ground. That system of hunting, in my opinion, allowed a higher-than-biologically-acceptable level of take of our nation's waterfowl. Many of the incorrectly identified ducks under that harvesting system were either sneaked into the freezers or just stomped into the mud to avoid a citation. It was a method based on flawed science and human behavior that did nothing but allow for the overharvest of North American waterfowl by legal means. Some species such as the pintail have yet to recover at the time of this writing, partly as a result of such massive legal overharvesting.

After much political maneuvering over where the money was coming from to fund the lab, the size of the facility, the size and composition of its staff, its mission, and the like, the National Wildlife Forensic Laboratory was created and safely positioned, out of Clark's immediate reach and control, in Ashland, Oregon, by Director Dunkle. Frank called me several days later, after some of the dust had settled, and asked what I thought. I told him that if he wasn't so damn ugly, I would gather him up in my arms and give him a kiss on the lips right on Main Street in front of God and everybody! There was silence on the phone for a moment, and then he said, "If you were to do that, you would be looking for work!" Good old Frank, always a man of few and hardly understandable words! "You owe me now," he gleefully said. "I still need you to go to Portland and get that nest of snakes cleaned out for me."

"Can't do it, Frank, and you know the reason why," I replied.

"Yes, but I was hoping you would be grateful for what I did for you on the lab and now help me."

"Don't give me that kind of crap, Frank," I said with a laugh.

"Well, you can't blame me for trying, can you?"

"No, and I forgive you for making a short run at me, you old scudder," I replied.

"I've got to go," he said and hung up. Incidentally, Frank was good on all the other promises he made me as well. … For an old man from Montana, you did well, Frank. … may you rest in peace.

Today, in a beautiful valley near the quaint town of Ashland, Oregon, sits the world's first and foremost National Wildlife Forensic Laboratory, all twenty-seven thousand square feet of it. Through the work of many people, the Service's newest crown jewel, almost ten years to the day after I started out on that quest, became a reality. It is not what I dreamed it would be in size and staffing level, but it is there and doing what I envisaged. Ken Goddard, that quiet behind-the-scenes little chap, has remained as the lab's director and assembled a staff of forensic scientists and support people that is second to none in the world! Those folks within the forensics community are really different sorts. Give them a forensics problem, and it will be solved in short order with some of the most state-of-the-art equipment or a slide ruler, an old sandwich, and a protractor. They and their work have been marvelous and of such a nature that the Service's Division of Law Enforcement has increased its enforcement efforts by more than a country mile. Using new forensic tools developed by the lab, agents of the Service are truly reaching for the stars and, in many instances, plucking them from the heavens and using them here on Earth to hold the Grim Reaper and his work in the world of wildlife at bay. Not all the time, mind you, but enough times out of ten to make life better for the resources of the world and hell for those determined to rape that which is being saved for those generations yet to come.

At the time this story was written, the National Wildlife Forensic Laboratory has worked over eight thousand investigations in addition to all its other duties, such as teaching, research, crime-scene work, and the like! This lowly lab, the one no one wanted or saw a need for, is now considered by the Service as a crown jewel within the national lab system. There are plans to expand the facility by another twenty-five thousand square feet and add another thirty or more positions just to meet the tremendous demand from all quarters for its legendary quality services. With that expansion and increased staffing, just think what it will be capable of. ... I am sure that thought has crossed the minds of those in the business of extinction as well.

Some time after the lab was made possible by the likes of the chief, Ken, Amos, their congressional counterparts, and other supporting citizens, Clark suffered a serious illness. This was shortly followed by what appeared to be a stroke, which proved to be his final "ride." I find it ironic, after all he did to kill the lab and its concept, that today the lab is named the Clark Bavin National Wildlife Forensic Laboratory. However, in fairness to the man, he did give the initial go-ahead to form the lab and supported the concept through some terrible times, and I am personally extremely grateful for that insight and consideration. Unknowingly, Clark brought the Division of Law

Enforcement into the twenty-first century and beyond with his initial support of this dream. The forensic laboratory may not have been one of his happier dreams at the end when money was tight and the pressure to dump it growing, but I would bet it is a dream he smiles about wherever he is today.

And, as Paul Harvey would say, now you know the rest of the story.

8

Asia, 1978

PICKING UP MY RINGING PHONE, I gave the customary greeting: "Good morning, U.S. Fish and Wildlife Service, may I help you?"

The familiar voice of Clark Bavin, chief of Law Enforcement for the U.S. Fish and Wildlife Service's Division of Law Enforcement, responded: "Good morning, Terry; I need to see you right away if possible."

"Yes, sir," I replied, only to be met with a *click* as he hung up without further discussion. Typical Clark, I thought; all business and no manners. Hanging up my receiver, I made my way quickly up to the chief's office on the fifth floor. Clark usually didn't call unless he had a very good reason, and he didn't like to be kept waiting. His FBI-style formality coupled with my respect for his position ensured that when the chief called, I got my carcass moving.

Entering his office, I said, "Good morning, Chief; what's up?"

Clark motioned for me to sit on the big leather couch in front of his desk, which I did. After looking critically at me for a few seconds, he began, "The trip request you submitted for Asian travel just came back from main Interior, and it has been approved."

Damn, I was floored! I had just been turned down by Secretary of State William Rogers after being approved by my agency for a similar trip to Africa. That is, my request was turned down after I was accused of being a Central Intelligence Agency (CIA) agent by the African government involved. I needed to go to both the African and the Asian continents because of the constant stream of wildlife import problems at our Ports of Entry from those countries, so I wrote another travel request for Asia and fired it off as any *good* CIA agent would do. Now here I was again, poised on the edge of a life adventure that would take me through a whole new facet of the world of wildlife. My heart raced at this unexpected turn of events and the prospect of foreign travel as a special agent for the Service. The very real possibility of another tremendous learning experience whirled through my mind as I made every effort to remain calmly unreadable to the "Old Man." He considered any kind of emotion a weakness, so I didn't give him any room for comment in that department.

"Think you can handle it?" he slowly asked, still looking at me closely with a critical eye.

"Yes, sir," I said calmly, though my heart was racing. "Otherwise I wouldn't have submitted my proposal to you in the first place. Additionally, Chief, if you didn't think I was ready for such responsibility, you wouldn't have signed off on the original proposal for the trip to Africa, much less the one to Asia." I hoped my challenging retort wouldn't be taken as insubordination. My eyes never left his, nor his mine.

Finally satisfied that I was the man for the job, he slowly handed me the authorization without rising from his chair. "The rest is up to you: the meetings, their times, topics to be covered, embassy contacts, procurement of airline tickets, and all. I am assuming you will build up our LAW-17 files on these countries' latest wildlife and plant laws in the English version as one of your agenda topics. Also, I would expect you to have those laws certified by the respective countries and in addition teach the different import-export leaders of those countries our laws so their shipments aren't always being seized when trading wildlife across this country's borders," he said.

"That will be central to my mission as well as sharing our raw intelligence files on some of their outlaw wildlife exporters with those countries I feel we can trust—unless you have a problem with that," I replied.

"Good," he responded. "Keep me in the loop." Clark then dismissed me, and I left his office with my head in the clouds owing to the endless possibilities of this adventure to the Asian continent.

It was 1978, and I was the Endangered Species and foreign liaison desk officer for the Fish and Wildlife Service in Washington, D.C. As

such, I was the point man on all Endangered Species Act (ESA) and
Convention on International Trade in Endangered Species of Wild
Fauna and Flora (CITES) laws and issues affecting the Service's Division of Law Enforcement. That meant everything from writing regulations to responding to phone calls from the field on the toughest
enforcement issues relating to those laws; responding to congressional
letters of inquiry; responding to questions from Congressmen in open
forum; procuring forensic work species identification for some of the
tougher-to-identify wildlife parts and products that were seized; contacting foreign governments through the State Department regarding
importation and endangered species issues; initiating investigations
through foreign governments for special agents nationwide; routine
State Department contact; and everything else hurled the way of a
desk officer responsible for interpreting those two sets of laws des-
tined to shake our country to its industrial, environmental, and de-
velopmental roots.

During the two years after my initiation as the Endangered
Species and foreign liaison desk officer, I came to see many things
that needed to be done, nationally and internationally, within those
arenas. Nationally, we had many problems in the Service's Division of
Law Enforcement. We had new laws hitting the books almost daily,
along with major smuggling and illegal wildlife commercialization
problems coming at us from every angle of the compass. To combat
those problems we had glaring understaffing problems in our core of
special agents (short at least 150 officers) and wildlife inspectors (short
at least 100 inspectors). Along with those staffing problems, the division was perennially underfunded to the point that enforcement officers often had to simply turn and walk away from wildlife crime
because of the fiscal inability to conduct investigations. Many other
serious legal problems had their roots in identifying wildlife parts and
products down to the taxonomic levels required by the ESA and
CITES. And if that wasn't a big enough load, internationally we had
another whole world of problems—no pun intended. Corruption;
false documents; smuggling; importers marking a species of wildlife
to look like a less-protected one, through the painting and cropping
of feathers on rare birds, for example; animal cruelty in shipments;

outdated foreign laws, or none at all; international politics twisting
the tail of our national politics and politicians; and on it went. Early
on I recognized the need to send someone from our office to many
foreign lands in order to acquire copies of other nations' wildlife laws
for our LAW-17 files and also to work with those nations to increase
training, share intelligence, construct cooperative enforcement efforts,
and even provide state-of-the-art equipment. That not-so-simple notion was actually quite meaningful because the United States imports
approximately 45 percent of all the world's production of live animals
and wildlife parts and products!

With that realization, and since I was also the foreign liaison officer, I had written a justification for going to Africa to work with a
passel of governments during an East African wildlife conference in
an attempt to straighten out some of the wildlife import-export problems that existed between our two continents. Africa was one of the
worse continents for us in the wildlife importation arena during that
period, followed by many countries on the Asian continent. Illegal
shipments of wildlife and wildlife parts and products were flowing
into the United States from Africa on a daily basis. Our small but
dedicated core of wildlife inspectors was hard pressed to hold the line
against this flood of importations, both legal and illegal. In light of
altered importation documents; outright forged or counterfeit documents; wildlife or wildlife parts or products just plain smuggled in
false floors of crates or within containerized cargo; live wildlife disguised with clipped feathers, painted and mixed in with hundreds of
species requiring less protection, or even strapped to the bodies of
passengers, especially women, it was obvious that the Service had
major problems. We had the laws to stop such practices but plain and
simply lacked the wherewithal and staying power to put the rubber
on the road.

Realizing a trip to Africa was sorely needed, I went to work. Going
through all the administrative motions of justification and certifica-
tion, I forwarded the request through proper channels. Well, that trip
got shot down owing to a pissing contest between some of the African
officials and Director Lynn Greenwalt of the Service because another
Service employee (playing politics with the foreign country in hopes

of taking a joy ride back to the country where he had done his research so he could visit old friends) had invited himself along just three days before I was to depart. Officials of the African country in which the conference was to be held, not being able to convince Director Greenwalt of that scientist's value on the trip, which truly was nil, requested that I not be allowed to come either, calling me a CIA operative. In this way, they hoped to force Director Greenwalt into allowing the scientist to go. Greenwalt, to his credit, wasn't "crowbarred" and refused to give in to this pressure. Everything came to a screeching halt when the big dogs got involved! Secretary of State Rogers stepped in, canceled my part of the trip, and sent a different scientist to placate the African country. As it turned out, that scientist did nothing but go on an African camera safari. As I said, there was never anything but politics and controversy under the ESA and CITES. I was mad as hell over the African turn of events and just sulked for a while and let the many preventive inoculations I had received in the hind end before my trip was canceled heal, along with my pride. I was beginning to learn about my agency and its inner workings, not to mention its brand of politics. All the lessons of point and counterpoint that I learned in Washington never left me and ended up serving me well throughout the rest of my career.

Shortly after the African fiasco, I submitted another outline, justification, and overseas travel request to include eight Asian countries. The purpose of that request, like the African one, was based in part on my frustration at my inability to get anyone from that part of the world to respond to investigative inquiries from my office. Their responses often would not arrive in less than six months, if at all. Then those responses were usually so vague or loaded with political overtones that they weren't of any evidentiary value to the case agent conducting the investigation in the United States. As a result, the Service many times had to let the subjects of investigations walk, taking their illegal contraband with them, because we couldn't prove such cases "beyond a reasonable doubt" in our courts!

In addition, my job included keeping an up-to-date file on all the wildlife laws of the countries of the world. These laws were kept in what we then called the LAW-17 files and were used almost daily in responding to questions from the field agents, wildlife inspectors, and U.S. attorneys regarding the import of wildlife from foreign soil. I had tried all of the local embassies in an attempt to get English copies of their wildlife laws, but almost to an embassy, they directed me back to their countries' import-export agencies. That alone almost made a personal trip necessary because past history showed those folks would not correspond with a "voice crying in wilderness." The bottom line was that if the Service was to continue to enforce foreign wildlife import laws, we needed the up-to-date information in our LAW-17 files.

With these issues in mind, I picked what in my opinion were the worst Asian wildlife "laundering" countries and proposed in my application for foreign travel that I meet with our counterpart agencies, educate those lads in our laws, have them do the same for me, get certified copies of their laws and export documents (in English, as required by the federal court system), and see if I could share our intelligence files on some of their better-known smugglers.

For two years I had sat frustrated at my desk and watched the movement of wildlife across the globe through the many Service intelligence documents. Millions, probably billions, of dollars' worth of wildlife in every form was moving in commerce, much of it from other countries to the United States. Intelligence from our field inspectors, U.S. Customs, the CIA, friendly wildlife importers, paid informants, and Service agents indicated that at least 40 to 50 percent of the wildlife products entering the United States was illegal in one aspect or another, not to mention that live wildlife was often transported in extremely cruel and inhumane conditions. One example of the latter problem is that many importers considered a 90 percent loss of their bird imports allowable as the cost of doing business!

After seeing so much criminality and animal cruelty in such a short period, all for the almighty dollar, I was bound and determined to get to Asia and show those lads where the line in the sand of their national heritage needed to be drawn. In short, I wanted to show them in black and white what needed to get done and *how they should do it*. That way they wouldn't get crosswise with the United States and at the same time would save their wildlife and plant resources for Asian generations yet to come. What arrogance and insensitivity to other peoples and their cultures on my part, as I was soon to discover! All I needed was a lance, a windmill, and a critter strong enough to bear up under the lead weight in my head and last part over the fence to carry me forward so I could tilt at the whirling blades! Boy, did I ultimately get a wake-up call—and, in the process, almost my "final call." As a result of those sixty-seven days of nonstop travel and interaction with my foreign counterparts, I grew tremendously not only as an officer but as a human being. Suffice it to say, that trip provided me an opportunity to mature in a unique way, and fortunately, I was able to take advantage of those lessons and apply them throughout the rest of my life and career.

In my excitement earlier in the day, I had forgotten to thoroughly read my travel approval document, and when I studied it at home that evening I found that I had not obtained approval for all the countries I had requested. I was to travel through Japan (one of the leaders in the world when it comes to exploiting the planet's resources without thought of the consequences), Hong Kong, Thailand, Malaysia, Indonesia, Singapore, and the Philippines. My disappointment at not being able to also visit New Zealand, Australia, and New Guinea was somewhat compensated by the allowance of sixty-seven days to accomplish my mission in the seven approved countries. Again, petty bickering and jealousy among other Service personnel had eliminated the other three countries—but my new learning experience was beginning! The "big picture," as Deputy Chief Bert Falbaum called it, was beginning to manifest itself, not only in the work arena but in that slippery one involving human personalities and their weaknesses. ...

As I examined my travel documents, I realized that the countries to which I was going were in my view some of the worst ones for illegal wildlife commerce. Birds, primates, live tropical fish, meats, hides, raw leathers, coral, sea turtles, ivory, and everything else under the sun with any value seemed to be moving from those few countries into the United States in overwhelming quantities, most of it carrying questionable import documents or none at all. There was no doubt about it: a shortened country list was looking better all the time because it allowed me more time to work extensively with my counterparts in those nations.

I already had most of my inoculations for overseas travel because of my planning for the African trip, so I needed to make only a few more trips to the State Department for the remaining shots and pills needed to travel safely in Asia (in those days doctors in the State Department provided these services for government travelers). My passport and appropriate visas, which I also picked up at the State Department, came through a few weeks ahead of schedule. Several days later I was packed and loaded for my latest peregrination into the Asian theater of operations, and boy, was I ready to go. I wasn't happy to leave my family, but I was excited at what I might be able to do for the world of wildlife with the power of the U.S. government backing me up. Boy, talk about arrogance and naïveté. ... I might not have been so ready to go if I had known what was in store for me and what events the trip would bring!

The first hop of my sixty-seven-day detail was a flight from San Francisco to Hawaii, with a layover on the big island for meetings with its wildlife inspectors and Senior Resident Agent Jim Bartee. The point of that meeting was to gather the Hawaiian agents' ideas regarding major Asian and Pacific Rim wildlife import problems that affected Hawaii's area of responsibility. Jim was, as usual, full of good ideas about what needed doing but was not optimistic about any project's chance of success in the international arena. He seemed to realize that I would be lucky to just tilt at a windmill, much less accomplish anything. I wish I had listened more carefully to what he *didn't say*. ... Then I was off to Japan, where I made a short stop to change planes, and then off on a night flight to Hong Kong for what was next in store.

Hong Kong, the Pearl of the Orient. As we approached, I could see it in the distance from the airplane window. The Boeing 747 drifted earthward as only those giants of the air can, descending between the skyscrapers of Hong Kong, in some places only several hundred yards from the buildings. In fact, in several instances I was able to look into the rooms of the skyscrapers and view the occupants as they went about their business, not knowing someone in the airplane had just observed them carrying on with their lives. This experience was made all the more memorable by the intensity of all the colors of this city, owing in part to the blackness of night in which I was traveling. It was midnight and darker than all get-out, but the city was all lit up as if it were Christmas in shades of red, soft blues, purples, and yellows in breathtaking profusion. Never in my life have I seen such beauty in a city as I saw that night flying into Hong Kong. It was such a magnificent sight that I will take that moment to my grave along with many others of like intensity.

My first real stop on the Asian trip, Hong Kong, enabled me to become familiar with the process, procedure, pace, and protocol of foreign travel required of an official representative of the U.S. government when dealing with an Asian government and the Asian way of doing business. Hong Kong is one of the world's leading trade centers for the movement of wildlife from all over Asia to the markets on the North American and European continents. It is also a trade center that reputedly bends the rules and regulations of wildlife trade. With that reputation documented through my desk in Washington, as well as on the desks of wildlife inspectors across the nation, it was easy to see why I was there to try to clean up the centuries-old way of doing business. As I said, I ultimately grew by leaps and bounds through all the life lessons this trip was to offer one rather large but dumber-than-a-post world traveler, and the Pearl of the Orient was as good a place to start as any!

The next day at seven A.M. I was briefed by a U.S. Embassy staff official regarding what I could do and say; given a history of the many cultures on the island; assigned my embassy escort, Customs Officer Tom Gray; and then sent off to numerous meetings with members of various government agencies associated with wildlife commerce. These meetings and activities went on from daylight to dark with few breaks. In Asia, almost everyone seems to work seven days a week, and I was no exception. There were a ton of people to meet, and the embassy had scheduled me rather tightly throughout my stay. It was exhilarating, but I was having trouble hitting those damned windmills as meeting after meeting clicked by! They were there in abundance, but for the moment I was unable to get lined up to take a good whack at one.

Right from the first meeting with Hong Kong Customs, I could tell there were problems in the wind. They received me politely and listened to me intently, but it was obvious that because wildlife and wildlife parts and products were in huge demand and briskly moving as a trade item my efforts were almost certainly doomed. In almost every instance I was met with knowing smiles and typical Asian politeness, but it quickly became apparent that wildlife market demands would rule, and damn this thing I called heritage, or even obeying the regulations of trade set by my country or any other. The laws were nothing more than minor impediments to be circumvented, and the quicker one could move around or through such impediments, the quicker one's goods could hit the marketplace at the preferred price. Those successful movements around regulatory impediments were pure money in the bank, and with that "oil" the wheels of trade continued unabated, regardless of the legality or rarity of the species being traded.

It also became very apparent that my efforts to advise, educate, or assist the Asians were going nowhere fast. I had the feeling that the Asians, polite as they were, had had their bellies full of Westerners during the colonial periods, and they were going to do as they desired when it came to wildlife commerce. That feeling went double for the arrogant Americans and the society we represented. There was money to be made—*big* money—and these folks, in some cases struggling for their very existence, meant to have it all, just as the Americans had done in their times of abundance.

The Hong Kong Customs officials showed me warehouse after warehouse filled with what would be wildlife contraband if imported into the United States, especially tons of Asian elephant tusks. I was informed by exporters and businessmen holding the stocks of ivory that if the United States would not allow the import of such items, they would be shipped to Asian and European countries that were not so idealistic. My mind ran to the international Convention on International Trade in Endangered Species of Wild Fauna and Flora (CITES), which Great Britain had signed for Hong Kong as a signatory member and which prohibited the import and export of such goods. Crossing over the threshold of Asian politeness, I asked in typically blunt American fashion about the presence of such goods in Hong Kong in direct violation of the convention. All I got was a

shrug of the Asian businessmen's shoulders and a lame explanation
that "country of origin was Hong Kong" (thereby getting around
some of the prohibitions of CITES).

"Hogwash," I said, raising many eyebrows. "Hong Kong hasn't had
Asian elephants as country of origin since the Punic Wars, if then."
My combative statement was met with polite smiles, and then the
Customs officers told me that the laws of Hong Kong were weak and
that they didn't have enough people to do the job. In fact, there were
only six Customs officers for the whole of Hong Kong. Pardon me,
is this the United States and the Fish and Wildlife Service? I thought.
Why is it that in every instance, except maybe the FBI, there was
always a staffing and money shortage when it came to the field of law
enforcement? In my extreme naïveté, I could not believe my ears!
Hong Kong is a world trade center, I thought, yet it did not have
enough people to control its trade! I was flabbergasted! A piece of
ground no larger than 391 square miles, and they couldn't control the
illegal wildlife trade. That detail alone told me I might not win this
battle I had set out to fight in Asia.

There was a long pause, and then the British Customs officer, seeing my look of disbelief, in typical British fashion said, "Well, Yank,
that is the way it is over here and the way these blighters want it, and
since they have been doing it their way for centuries, no amount of
what you or I want computes; sorry. Also, in a few more years this
will be the People's Republic of China, and they will do it their way,
which will be even worse than the way this ship is currently being
run. They are in it for the coin of the realm, Yank: a little thing called
fiscal survival." He was basically telling me it would be business as
usual, Asian style, and to move on or look the other way. Looking
hard at me, the British officer said, "First time in Asia, eh, Yank?" I
slowly nodded, and he smiled knowingly, showing two missing front
teeth. I had finally found a windmill to tilt at, only to find that my
lance was too short.

The point of massive wildlife losses from a country's heritage to
feed the marketplace was not lost on me. I quickly began to sense the
futility of my current efforts and mission of trying to get parts of the
Asian community into the conservation or common-sense (as I saw it)

mode of thinking and working in addition to improving the legality of trade practices. In Hong Kong, I was learning, life was cheap, and it was survival of the fittest. Aside from that, not much mattered. The acquisition of one's next meal was much more important than leaving something for those yet to come or obeying the regulations of one's own country. Humankind isn't interested in talking about conservation when the big guts are eating the little guts.

Tom Gray, sensing my frustration at a dinner in his home after several days of polite but essentially fruitless meetings with representatives of China and Hong Kong, told me with a sly smile, "Welcome to Asia. Get used to it, Terry. What you are seeing is a way of life over here, and you are not going to change it. And it is not just here but throughout Asia."

Maybe, I thought, but I wasn't a quitter. I would be taking those lessons learned in Hong Kong to my next country, Thailand, and you could bet your sweet tail end I would make good use of them when I dealt with *those* folks. I didn't have to roll over, I thought, like the regulatory folks I had met in Hong Kong, just because that was the status quo. I began to realize the scope of my detail and that to get anything of value accomplished, I would have to push the envelope. That I now swore to do as I shoveled something into my mouth that had to have been dead and lying in the sun for months! Tom, seeing my eyebrows go up at the unique flavor, laughed and said, "That particular item takes some getting used to."

Man, he had that right. I can't remember ever before eating something that was as hard on me as I was on it. ... It turned out that the "thousand-year-old" egg that took me on that evening was even worse the next day, with the people in the streets of Hong Kong paying the price as I walked out and about. ...

The next day I arose about five in the morning, donned my shorts and tennis shoes, and went for a walk through the numerous marketplaces near my hotel. I didn't have any meetings until eight-thirty that day and figured I would get a real, unescorted tour of the city and see for myself what life here was all about. A several-block walk found me in the heart of the market district, and boy, what a collection of sights and smells. It brought back the moment of the mystery egg I had eaten the previous evening at Tom's house. The vendors were jam-packed throughout the area, and in addition to the intense, and I do mean intense, smells, the air was full of the sounds of a thousand high-pitched, singsong voices hawking their wares. Water was running down the steep streets from the people washing their wares and cleaning their animal products or from melting ice. Every vegetable known to humankind was here as well as pork, chicken, duck, and seafood in every known form.

Stepping over and around the constant streams of sewage, I entered a medicinal store and was amazed at what lay before my eyes. Shelves ran clear to the ceiling and were filled with every kind of preserved wildlife and plant known to humankind that did something for the body or soul. As for the stink, man, did that place have a life of its own. I thought the open-air market was bad, but this was like nothing I had ever experienced before. As I walked up and down the aisles looking at many dried things that were looking right back, I had a fine olfactory sampling of the spices of the Orient. One minute the smell of rotten and the next pungent. Then many of the smells mixed, and I was unable to even start to identify what the hell had just assaulted my nostrils. In one glass display case I saw dozens of rhino horns. In another antlers, both hard and in the dried velvet stage, greeted my eyes. I saw animal hooves, blood and bone from tigers, dried eyes from animals I had never heard of, entire dried reptiles, hair, stems and leaves from unknown plants, beetles, seal penises, and many other items I have long forgotten. This experience was repeated in every medicinal store I entered, and I entered several dozen that morning. I began to wonder if there were any exotic wildlife or plants left in the Asian wild.

Realizing I was running short of time, I hurried back to the Hilton Hotel and sprinted up the steps, through the large entryway, and into a waiting elevator full of people. In moments I began to notice that they all were sniffing the air as if something was wrong. I did the same, but I couldn't smell anything, and when the elevator arrived at my floor, out I went and into my room. Quickly undressing, I showered, throwing the clothes I had worn in the marketplace into a corner of the bathroom, and went out to begin my day's schedule.

Returning to my room around eight P.M., I opened the door and was met with a horrific smell. What the hell? I thought. Something died in my room! Looking around, I finally discovered the culprit—it was the clothes I had worn that morning. They had absorbed the many strong odors and now smelled putrid! No wonder those folks in the ritzy hotel elevator had their noses working overtime. I had to laugh as I washed my clothes in the bathtub. Welcome to the Orient, Terry, I thought. My tennis shoes were another matter. I had to pack them in an airtight plastic bag to avoid their "eau de essence" from contaminating my suits and ties, though that would have given me an excuse to throw the polyester suits away. Then I could have worn jeans and at least been comfortable in that damn hot and humid climate.

Finishing my several-day stint in Hong Kong, I again headed for an airport. It seemed as if I was always traveling at night in Asia, and my journey to Bangkok wasn't any different. Flying into that city at night, I noticed that it wasn't as pretty as Hong Kong, and after a few days I found that it wasn't as clean either. I spent the better part of my first day at the embassy going over my schedule, the customs of the Thai people, what I could do and not do, whom I should report to in case of scheduling or other problems, where I should eat and not eat, which (clean) brothels to frequent and those to avoid at all costs, and the embassy contact in case I got into real trouble. Armed with that information, I was out and about by late afternoon in my polyester dress suit and tie with my embassy "support troop" to keep me from becoming an "Ugly American." In this first exposure to Thailand I met with several American and Asian businessmen located in Bangkok who were involved in the wildlife export trade. The meetings went on into the night with few breaks, but I was starting to get used to the Asian way of doing business.

The next morning found me at the embassy waiting for my ride and embassy official ride-along. It was already hot, and the humidity was causing the sweat to run down my body in places I had never known sweated. Off we went through the busy, dirty streets of downtown Bangkok, but at least the embassy limo was air conditioned, and I might live, I thought. My first meeting in this stifling heat and humidity was with one Koon Ha Gee, a government official who controlled wildlife imports and exports for Thailand. We were supposed to meet with this chap at nine A.M., but our limo got us there a few minutes early. We were politely ushered into a palatial office and served cold Coca-Cola, which I welcomed owing to the heat, and then we waited and waited ... and waited. Around eleven A.M. a nicely dressed man came into the office, rapidly passed us, saying, "Excuse me," and disappeared through a door into a back room. Following him were what appeared to be two manservants carrying fresh clothing and bath supplies. They also disappeared into the back room. In a few moments I could hear a shower running. I thought that strange, but not as strange as the pieces of brain and spots of blood on the left shoulder of his suit that I had noticed when he briskly passed by. I looked at my embassy aide, who was looking annoyed at our meeting starting so late and having to be there, only to realize he had not noticed the blood or brains. If he had, he chose not to say anything. That was not a good sign, I thought. I had hunted big-game animals all my life, not to mention butchered a lot of large domestic animals such as cattle and hogs, and I was well aware of what brain tissue and congealed blood looked like. I could only surmise what had happened to that fellow to get that kind of a mess on his $500 sharkskin suit and in all probability ruined it—*not to mention someone else's day.* Keeping my thoughts to myself (I was learning), I sat in my leather chair and let the sweat run down the center of my back and somewhat uncomfortably down into my shorts.

Shortly thereafter the man came out of the back room wearing clean clothes and a large, friendly smile, as he introduced himself as Mr. Gee. He apologized for his lateness, which he blamed on an "unfortunate incident." He sat down, and we got right down to business. I gradually realized that he was the first honestly resource-concerned Asian I had met during my short stay in that part of the world. He was bright, was very up-to-date on the wildlife import and export laws of Thailand, was aware of the wildlife smuggling problems associated with his country, and seemed to want to improve the country's international reputation in these areas. It became apparent that he believed cleaning up the illegal wildlife industry so prevalent throughout his homeland should be a priority. He was especially concerned with the counterfeit wildlife export documents being issued by the government of Laos for the export of rare primates illegally taken from Thailand. He, like the officials in Hong Kong, acknowledged a shortness of resources and the penchant of neighboring countries to counterfeit Thai wildlife import and export documents, seals, or signatures in order to move wildlife in commerce, especially through the Port of Bangkok. He told me that the biggest traders in illegal wildlife parts and products as well as live wildlife were Thai nationals and that their trading partners were the peoples of Europe, Japan, and the United States. There was no animosity in that remark; it was just a tired statement of fact. Then he grew quiet for a moment, looked at me, and commenced to roundly condemn the Japanese as if the war had just ended and the wounds and bitterness were still fresh. I was surprised at his rancor but remained silent to see what would follow. Over the next fifty days this theme would recur throughout my entire Asian trip. There was a real hatred for the Japanese because they did not play by the rules in wildlife trade but just took what they wanted, laws of the land or not. Then Mr. Gee targeted national zoos and zoological gardens in Japan, Europe, and the United States for the major illegal movement of live wildlife, especially those of breeding-aged rare or endangered primate species.

My scanty but valuable Hong Kong experience was beginning to kick in, and I got a lot done with this chap over the next six hours in the areas of false documents, names of the largest traders, trade routes commonly utilized for certain species of animals, prices of animal species in the countries of origin, and the like. The minute I had a question or requested a document, a clap of his hands brought staff members who shortly thereafter supplied what was needed. Things were going smashingly well, and I thought that I could trust this man enough on security issues to go one step further and impart some intelligence regarding illegal exporters from Thailand.

Before leaving the United States I had compiled intelligence data from our law enforcement files as well as shared CIA files on some of each country's worst wildlife smugglers and animal traffickers. I was prepared to share that intelligence with officials of the countries I was visiting if their representatives appeared to be honest and interested in doing something to stop illegal activities. I had cleared my information with my chief and with the appropriate officials in the CIA and Department of State and was now ready to see whether I could provide information that would cause some heartburn for the lads in Thailand breaking U.S. laws with their illegal shipments. I told Mr. Gee that I had some raw intelligence to share on some of his country's worst wildlife smugglers in the eyes of his counterparts in the United States. Mr. Gee showed great enthusiasm and, getting up from his chair, said, "Excuse me for a moment; I must get my deputy chief of law enforcement involved." Before I could say anything regarding security, he left the room. Now I am getting somewhere in this damn continent, I thought. A smug smile crossed my face as I recalled the cautionary words Tom Gray had spoken in Hong Kong. We will just see, I thought. These Asian lads are about to meet their match in this thick-headed German chap, especially if I meet more like Mr. Gee!

Gee soon returned with another chap, whom he introduced as his deputy chief of law enforcement. Once Gee's office door was closed, I distributed the intelligence information on Thailand's worst offenders in the form of a briefing such as I would have given a U.S. attorney. The information consisted of not only verbal information but numerous papers and copies of forged documents to illustrate my points. I don't remember all of the people or companies I talked about during the next hour or so, but I do recall one in particular, the Bangkok Wildlife Company. That company had a criminal record a mile long in the United States for just about every kind of illegal wildlife importation imaginable, especially relating to primates, and in particular those from Thailand and Laos. The two men listened closely as I shared dates, times, places of import, names of U.S. dealers, types of wildlife, and other inside information on these illegal operations. The deputy chief took copious notes but said very little. There was something about that lad that I just couldn't put my finger on. If I had been in my own country, I would have been more on the alert. I didn't know anything about the lad, but my gut instincts were just not at ease in his presence. However, Mr. Gee seemed to trust the chap and had vouched for him, and that was going to have to be good enough for me. Blaming my gut instinct on the acid from the four Cokes I had drunk trying to rehydrate myself, I settled back and continued doing business with my counterparts.

When we finished up about seven P.M., Mr. Gee thanked me for my time and effort and asked if I would like to go on a routine inspection with some of his people to examine a company dealing in crocodile hides and products near the small town of Kwai the following morning. Turning to my embassy escort, as I had been instructed to do in all such situations, I said, "I would like to go, but it is your call."

My less-than-enthusiastic embassy chap asked several halfhearted questions to make sure the detail was noninvestigative in nature (I had no authority to conduct investigations in a foreign country, and to do so would have been illegal), determined that it would not turn into a security or safety issue, and ascertained my arrival and departure times as well as what gear would be necessary and whom I would be with. Satisfied, he told Mr. Gee, "Mr. Grosz can go, and I will rearrange his schedule for tomorrow."

Hot damn, I thought; a trip to the outback that would let me see firsthand what was going on in the Thai grassroots crocodile industry. This excursion had my interest up in no small measure because of the importation problems we had with crocodiles and their parts, especially the saltwater crocodile and many of the Thai exporters.

As we left the office, Mr. Gee apologized again for his late arrival that morning and said he had experienced a small problem in coming to work but that everything was settled now. I didn't give it any more thought until we were on our way out of the compound in the embassy limo. As we drove by the back of the building in which we had just spent the day, I chanced to see a large official Thai sedan parked behind Gee's office with what appeared to be at least thirty bullet holes in it! If that was Gee's limo, it certainly answered the question of the origin of the blood and brains on his suit, I thought, especially in light of the number of bullet holes in the driver's-side door and window! Tom Gray's warning words rang again in the survival annals of my mind and were finally beginning to make sense. My bored embassy chap didn't even notice the vehicle and its telltale bullet holes, or if he did, he didn't let on. Damn, the acid from all the Cokes I had drunk that day was beginning to create havoc again. ...

When we reached the embassy, my escort saw to it that I was issued some good boots and military camouflage clothing from the embassy stores for the next day's adventure. It seemed that my polyester was not considered good jungle gear. Returning to my hotel, I was beginning to prepare for the trip into the Thai jungle the following morning when my phone rang. Picking it up, I discovered the deputy chief for law enforcement, the man I had met earlier in Gee's office, on the other end asking if I would like to come down to the hotel bar for a few cold Thai beers.

"Damn right," I said without hesitation. "I will be right down." I had been nothing but hot and dry since I had hit Asian shores, and a cold beer would hit the spot, I thought as I left my room. Man, was I in for a surprise. Arriving in the bar, I met the deputy chief and a friend of his whose name I have long since forgotten. I ordered three beers, and when they arrived the unknown lad was identified as the president of the Bangkok Wildlife Company! I was stunned! The deputy chief quietly continued unabashed with an offer of 200,000 baht (Thai currency), about $10,000 American in those days, if I would sign a letter absolving the Bangkok Wildlife Company of any wrongdoing! Goddamnit, I was furious! This weasel piece of dung who called himself the deputy chief of law enforcement had spilled his guts to the Bangkok Wildlife Company president just as soon as he had left the meeting. As if that weren't bad enough, he had the unmitigated gall to offer me a bribe to back off from any further efforts in that arena! His boss appeared to have almost been killed defending right from wrong, and here in his own camp was a turncoat piece of crap dragging those efforts down into the mud of the street. That was one of the three times in my professional career that I came close to killing a man with my bare hands! The sad thing is, in that instance I would have enjoyed it.

Instead of doing what needed to be done to that chap, I quietly got up, paid for all the beers, and stalked back to my room with Tom Gray's words ringing in my ears. I was now really beginning to realize the odds that were stacked against me as far as making any changes for the better in the Asian world of wildlife. It was beginning to seem that the only success I would realize on this trip was the lessons of life I was picking up as I went from country to country. In fact, my learning process was about to take a major turn, and damn shortly.

It is amazing what happens when one applies Occidental ways and mores to an Asian society. It really blinds one to the real world and any warning signs flowing by. I should have been more alert because the signs, such as the overall corruption and outright savagery when it came to trade in wildlife, were not what I would have called good. Yet I continued on my way, and hoping against hope that some of the lessons would take hold and make a difference when it came to trading with the United States and, in the process, somehow taking better care of their national heritage.

The next morning, before I left for Kwai on my cottage-industry crocodile trip, I met my contact in the embassy and reported the bribery attempt, as required by embassy policy. Expecting a sharp reaction, I was mildly surprised by my liaison's halfhearted response. "Don't worry, Terry; this goes on all the time," he said. "I will record the event and forward it up through channels, but that is the sum total of what we in the embassy will do."

Shaking my head in disbelief and still steaming over the previous night's events, I left the embassy to meet my escort group of what I assumed were Thai wildlife officers or the equivalent. I boarded a Land Rover in front of my hotel with three English-speaking Thai conservation officers, and we were soon joined by two other government Land Rovers, each holding four men, who I assumed were more conservation officers. However, I discovered that one of the Land Rovers was occupied by Thai soldiers, and it was followed by a Thai Army six-by-six truck filled with more soldiers. Damn, I thought; was this a routine inspection of people dealing in the crocodile market? Oh well; maybe that was the way things were done in Thailand. I settled back into the seat next to the driver, thankful to be right in front of the air conditioner. As the convey proceeded toward the small town of Kwai (and yes, there really *is* a bridge over the River Kwai), I had a great opportunity to discuss our two countries' import and export laws with my comrades, and the Thais got to practice their English on me. I was even able to introduce them to some slang words and a few logging-camp terms, which they relished as delightful and which, I am sure, enriched their English vocabulary.

Reaching Kwai, we all disembarked and ate lunch at a small restaurant right on the river, which my Thai wildlife officer said was a safe place for me to eat. I had to be careful about what I ate because my schedule didn't allow any time for me to get sick with the Asian form of the "two-step." We were joined there by another truckload of Thai conservation men, who I assumed were local officers who would be going along with us. I ordered a soup that everyone at my table recommended, especially to one who was visiting Asia for the first time and suffering from the heat and humidity. When it arrived, I looked at it. It was a bowl of light-green, clear broth with a few stems, leaves, white berries, and flowers of a plant that looked familiar floating in the liquid. Continuing to stare at the plant floating in the thin, watery gruel, I told the senior officer next to me that the plant looked like a member of the nightshade family, which was usually a deadly poison. The commander just laughed and in perfect English said, "It is from the nightshade family and is a deadly poison over here as well if not prepared correctly." I continued to look dubiously at the soup, and he laughed again and told me to go ahead and eat it; I would find it most refreshing. Slowly, I did sample the watery-looking soup and found it to be quite good. In fact, it was so good that I ordered another bowl and surprisingly found that it did seem to help me cope with the jungle heat and humidity. After lunch I found that the heat wasn't bothering me so much and that I was sweating less than before. Not bad, I thought, for a soup made from a poisonous plant. Then again, maybe the shutting down of my sweat glands was the first symptom of my dying. ...

As I waited for the rest of our party to finish lunch, I walked out of the bamboo building to the bank of the Kwai River and looked at the old bridge pilings that had represented so much misery for the Allies and Japanese during World War II. All that was left of the expenditure of so many lives were a few stone pilings working their way across the river as if they had nothing better to do. It was apparent that the Allied bombers had done their job well. I shook my head at the example of man's inhumanity to man represented by what was left of the stone pilings, put my camera away without taking a single picture, and slowly walked back to my party, deep in thought about the passage of times that shrouded the deaths of thousands.

After lunch we loaded up and started our journey to a little jungle town, whose name I have long forgotten and probably couldn't pronounce anyway. It soon became apparent that the military six-by-six was having engine trouble. After a hurried conversation between the Thai Army officer in charge, the senior wildlife officer, and the truck driver, the Thai military officer waved us on while he remained behind with his Land Rover to supervise his lads in the repair of the truck. The Land Rover filled with the officers who had joined us at Kwai led the way, followed by our vehicle and the remaining Land Rover filled with conservation officers. We followed a paved road for a short distance along the Kwai River, then turned off onto a well-traveled dirt road and after another short distance turned onto a smaller road, heading off into the true jungle. Damn, I was fascinated. It was gorgeous. Hot and humid, especially under the jungle canopy, but gorgeous just the same. Greens such as I have never seen, and thick growth like there was no tomorrow.

Soon our dirt road narrowed even more, taking us along a *klong* (canal) that was typically filled with raw sewage with maybe two inches of more-or-less clear water flowing over the top of the black sludge. Damn, I thought; I just don't know how people can live like this. I had yet to see any clear water since I had been in Thailand, except that which came out of a tap at the hotel or that which had been in my soup. Yet I would see the Thai people bathing, washing their vegetables, or cleaning their clothes in these *klong*s as if there was nothing wrong with the water. I did notice, however, that they were careful to dip into the clearest-water on top of the black sludge with little hand-held pans and then would use that water to wash themselves or their other items. Nonetheless, that water flowing over the top of the sludge had to be loaded with everything in the world that would make you deathly sick if you were an American and foolish enough to drink it. I just shook my head and was thankful for the relatively clean waters of the United States.

The green canopy over our road continued to narrow, with jungle foliage hemming us in as we proceeded, and the heat and humidity were now really making themselves felt. I was glad for my cool camouflage gear and the air conditioner in the Land Rover, let me tell you. In fact, it was so hot and humid that the cool air coming out of the air conditioner in front of me looked like smoke as it was damply blown out over my lap!

Then it happened! The Land Rover in front of our vehicle exploded bright red inside the passenger compartment with a spew like the way a watermelon reacts when shot with a high-powered rifle bullet! The vehicle slewed off to one side and hit a tree, slamming to an abrupt stop. I still remember the bright green leaves raining down on the vehicle. The officers in that vehicle boiled out of it as if a bomb had gone off and dove behind the trees and stands of bamboo alongside the road. Then the windshield of our vehicle exploded into a million diamondlike particles that stung my face, neck, and hands as our driver groaned and collapsed forward onto the steering wheel! I quickly grabbed the steering wheel and turned off the key so we wouldn't go into the *klong*. As the vehicle rolled to a stop, I became aware of the *thunking* noise of bullets hitting our vehicle and the panicked yelling of my compatriots. Looking quickly over at the driver, I could see blood gurgling from his face and head. *Christ,* I thought; *that is a bullet wound. He has been shot!* The lad in the vehicle before us had also been shot, probably in the head given the bright red explosion of blood, I realized as I quickly opened the Land Rover door for a damn fast exit into some sort of cover. The lads in the back seat of my vehicle were yelling even louder in Thai and, even though I didn't know a word of the language, I understood that they too wanted to get the hell out of the target we were sitting in!

The whole area around our convoy was pure primal confusion and hollering mixed with shooting from every quadrant of the compass, or so it seemed! More *thunk-thunk-thunk* noises followed by the unmistakable sound of machine guns going off in the jungle got my tail end into gear, and I do mean into gear! Grabbing my driver's M-16 and bandolier of ammunition, which were lying between the seats, I bailed out of the vehicle and jumped feet first into the sewage-filled *klong* for cover. Not knowing how deep it was, I grabbed an armful of the long grass growing on the bank as I sailed over the edge, landing neck deep in the black, evil-smelling slop. By now those not injured by the initial hail of bullets had bailed out of our vehicles and were returning fire with their M-16s and pistols at unseen targets in the thick jungle foliage. Straining my eyes for the people who were causing our problem (later identified as Burmese insurgents who had crossed over into Thailand and were killing and robbing people as they found them), I noticed a man running through the jungle, wearing blue jeans and a faded red shirt and carrying an AK-47. Knowing that our guys were all wearing uniforms, I figured he must be one of the chaps who had fired on us. Without another thought, I sent a full clip of .223 bullets from the M-16 his way. I was shooting behind him from my position almost neck deep in the *klong*, and as the bullets sped through the thick jungle I could see leaves and stems exploding and falling as the bullets missed my fleeing lad, striking just behind him. However, my swing was fast, and just as I ran out of bullets I saw the plants directly alongside my target explode and fall as he sprinted, stumbling and crashing behind a tree for protection.

I ducked down behind the bank, took a magazine from the bandolier, dumped the empty magazine from the rifle into the *klong*, and slammed another full one in. Sticking my feet hard into the mud along the bank for balance, I indexed another round into the M-16 and peeked over the bank to see what I could see. Bullets were flying everywhere and hitting the dickens out of our now stationary vehicles. There was a lot of shooting and yelling, and it was as close to hell as I could imagine, never before having been in the thick of military-style combat. However, I had been shot at before and had great respect for those "steel bees" that whizzed alarmingly close whenever I stuck my head up too high over the bank.

Ducking back down to get a better hold on the grass before I jumped up to shoot again, I happened to look down the *klong*, and lo and behold, here came a crocodile swimming my way! The V his head was making in the water told me he was coming at a fairly good clip, and more than likely with an empty gut and evil thoughts on his mind! Goddamn, as if I didn't have enough problems, here that son of a bitch came to add to my stinking misery! All I could picture was the Walt Disney movie with the crocodile going *tick-tock-tick-tock* as it pursued Captain Hook! Then the image flashed through my mind of the rolling action crocodiles perform with their prey as they kill it and tear it apart, and I knew right then and there that the *klong* was not big enough for the both of us! Swinging my rifle one-handed his way, I found that I was breathing too hard with the adrenaline rush to make an accurate head shot, and knowing that a shot with such a flat trajectory would probably miss and make him submerge, that was all it took. I boiled out of the *klong* into the world of copper-coated steel bees as I headed for shelter behind the engine block of one of the vehicles. Damn, it seemed as if I was running in slow motion. What a sickening feeling, not being able to move any faster! From the sound of the bullets flying by me as I ran, they certainly seemed to be moving a whole lot faster than I was. But when I look back on that moment, I think the bullets and I were moving about the same speed! Skidding head first into the dirt alongside the front tire of one of our vehicles, I was aware that bullets were hitting the front of the Land Rover searching for me. From the way they were tearing through the engine compartment and out my side, I began to think all the training I had had about hiding behind the engine block for protection might have been fine for pistol bullets, but these damn rifle bullets were sure making a mess of my choice of cover! As if that were not enough, I became aware of the roar of another oncoming engine behind us and more yelling and shooting from my left. Figuring these were more lads attacking us, I turned to defend myself, all the while thinking of the Lakota named Low Dog saying, "Today is a good day to die" as they went into battle with the U.S. cavalry. It was amazing how cool I was, almost a simple resignation to dying and that was that! Suffice it to say, I was relieved to see the arrival of our army six-by-six along with the military Land Rover and the men in it. In a few seconds after the arrival of the Thai cavalry, the shooting from the jungle slackened and then quit altogether. The hollering continued, and a few more shots sounded as our soldiers from the six-by-six pursued our attackers into the jungle and out of sight.

I stayed put and tried to get my wind, realizing that for the most part, our fighting was over. My heart was going a hundred miles an hour, and I had about all of this flying-bullet horsepucky I could take. I remember thinking that I didn't feel like dying in some forgotten piece of jungle in Thailand for no apparent reason. Sounds like what the soldiers in Vietnam must have thought, doesn't it? Moments later our soldiers came back and set up a defensive ring around the vehicles while those of us left alive rose up out of the dirt and began to pick up the pieces, which included helping those who had been wounded. Out of our group of twelve conservation officers, three didn't need any help except from the Old Man above. Three others were horribly wounded, and it was all we could do to get the bleeding stopped before help in the form of a military helicopter arrived. There was also a dead soldier, killed as he bravely pursued the insurgents into the jungle. This was my first experience in assessing the wounds caused by bullets fired from AK-47 rifles, and I was impressed by their destructive capabilities. Jesus, those lads were horribly mangled where the bullets had met the flesh and bone, almost as if someone had shot them at close range with a shotgun! The Thais were small men, and the damage was unreal. Turning one chap over carefully so I could stem the bleeding from his shoulder wound, which was leaking all over my legs as I held him, I found that the entire back of his shoulder was gone. The exit hole made by that bullet was big enough for me to put both my hands in it! That poor chap, if he lived, was going to have only one arm and shoulder to hold his wife and kids for the rest of his life. ...

Damn, the "angry" was beginning to well up in me to the point that I was looking for another go at the lads who had caused this carnage to a bunch of simple, innocent folks. Standing up so the medical folks from the chopper, which had landed down the road, could have a go at my man, I was aware of the stickiness in my lap where I had laid his head and shoulders as his life leaked out. Then, as a little breeze passed by, I became aware of the fluttering of my collar on the right side of my shirt. It was a fuzzy mess of cloth and threads. Sometime during the battle a round had caught the collar of my fatigue shirt and somewhat messed it up, to say the least. Oh well; they say close counts only in horseshoes and hand grenades. ... That sure said something positive about the efforts of my two alert guardian angels, though!

About that time there was a ruckus in the jungle off in the direction where I had shot at the fellow wearing the jeans and faded red shirt. Two Thai soldiers were dragging a wounded man out of the jungle who looked like the lad I had shot at. It was plain that he had been hit in both thighs and couldn't walk. Another soldier was dragging another insurgent out of the jungle feet first who was dead as a hammer. The Thai military commander approached the wounded man and began to question him in a loud, excited voice, kicking him in his wounded legs. His legs had been shattered by the explosive bullets, and I could see bone sticking out both legs. The pain had to be immense, as demonstrated by the screaming of the wounded man every time he was kicked. That interrogation tactic apparently didn't work, so the commander grabbed the lad by the hair and, lifting him off the ground, continued to holler at him. The wounded man didn't respond, and as I turned my head to check on the wounded Thai officer I had been tending, I heard a muffled *bang*. Looking back toward the prisoner with the bad legs, I saw the Thai commander calmly walking away from the now twitching body on the road as blood poured out of a fresh wound in the insurgent's head and spread across the ground in a bright red pool! The Thai soldier replaced his pistol in the holster and, turning toward me, stared hard into my eyes, justifying his actions without one word being exchanged.

The helicopter carried away our wounded and dead, and the rest of us rode quietly back to Bangkok in the remaining operable vehicles without having visited the crocodile farm. I was dropped off at my hotel as if nothing had happened and went to my room to get out of my rotten-smelling bloody and soiled clothing. Other hotel guests looked at me as I trudged across the lobby and into the elevator. I am sure they were wondering why the hotel let such a disgusting person into such a nice place. Getting into the elevator, I realized just how bad I smelled. Man, was I a mess, not to mention how mad I still was at the lads who had turned my day of happy adventure into a tragedy.

After a thirty-minute damn hot shower, I sat on the edge of my bed and ran the day's events through my mind. I was amazed at how calm I was. What had started out to be a beautiful day had turned deadly. Over wildlife? I will never know, but somehow I think that little bastard deputy chief or his friend had something to do with it! Was I the one who had crippled the lad in the blue jeans and red shirt? I didn't know, but I did know I had sure been trying to put him out of commission, and I harbored no regrets for what I had done. The way he had stumbled just as he went behind the tree and out of sight led me to believe I had been the one who had slowed him down until the Thai captain stopped him forever. As I was finding out, life was pretty cheap out there in the jungle. Another part of the "big picture," I guessed. ... It helped to have several quarts of Thai beer and no dinner before going to bed that night. I don't remember waking up all night—in fact, I slept like the dead.

I visited the U.S. Embassy the next morning to see if I needed to get any extra inoculations to prevent anything happening to me as a result of my swim in the *klong* and to report what had happened. When I walked up to my liaison, he motioned me off to one side of the room so we could have some privacy. As I started to explain the previous day's events, he stopped me and said, "Mr. Grosz, that is a dead issue. When the embassy gave you permission to go on that detail, we did not have any inkling it would turn out the way it did. The embassy did not have, nor would it have given you, the authority to get involved in such a deadly situation had we known. As far as I am concerned, the event never happened. Do you understand?" I just looked at the lad in disbelief. Several men had died and several had been badly wounded, and this event hadn't happened! My contact continued, "You are directed by me to forget this issue, and it is not to appear in your trip report when you get home; do you understand? In fact, if I see this anywhere on paper for the next twenty years, you will have problems with the State Department, my friend. Do we have an understanding?"

Since I didn't see any reason to pursue the issue myself and wasn't aware of any patent illegality in this request, I nodded, and we parted company shortly thereafter. I always had the feeling that this fellow had screwed up, and that for him the best way out of this unseemly event was to bury it. How legal that was I don't know, but I will tell you this: when he told me to forget it, his eyes telegraphed that same meaning and more. After all, this was Asia, and life was cheap.

Compared to that event, the rest of my trip was pretty tame. Flying into Malaysia, I was met by the usual embassy staff person and quickly escorted to the U.S. Embassy. Arriving at the embassy, I was greeted with another surprise far surpassing my ride in an armored sedan. The embassy was a building that was nothing less than a modernized bomb-proofed bunker. I had to show my ID at the front door to an armed marine standing behind a mountain of sandbags and, once inside, had to show it again to another armed marine who stood behind his own pile of sandbags and bulletproof glass—and this was *inside* the building! I began to wonder if I had left the frying pan in Thailand to jump into the fire in Malaysia. I guessed there were folks in this country who did not like Americans.

Once inside the building I met my escort for the duration of my stay, a pleasant young Malaysian woman, and received a cable from my boss, the special agent in charge in Washington, D.C. The cable instructed me to cease all work at once because Congress had not passed the Department of Interior's budget, so I was no longer authorized to work until such time as there was a budget. I sat there grinning and shaking my head. Here I was, a zillion miles from home in the middle of a foreign country, and I was being told to stop work and bury my head in the sand until our members of Congress got off their dead hind ends and earned their keep. It was at that moment that I truly began to realize that I was fighting on two fronts in my profession, a sure recipe for disaster in any army. I crumpled up the cable and tossed it into a handy trash bucket before I was escorted to another guarded room, where I was briefed on what to do and what not to do while in Malaysia.

For those who have never sat through an embassy briefing in a foreign country, I will give you a little taste of at least the cultural portion of the briefing. Because of the large Muslim population in Malaysia, I was instructed not to look very long at any of the women I met on the street, and especially to avoid making long eye contact. To do so was considered offensive. This was especially true if the women were bathing in a public place. It seemed that in the backcountry, the Muslim men, if they caught you staring at their naked women, would cut off your manhood, stuff said articles into your mouth, and sew your lips shut as a warning to others not to do the same. I was told that I should never shake hands or touch anything that needed to be touched by another with the left hand. The left hand in Muslim culture was considered to be the "unclean" hand. Not knowing why and too damn dumb to ask, I didn't find out why the left hand was unclean until I reached Indonesia. Not to keep you in suspense, the left hand is the one used to wipe one's last part over the fence once the business is done. Now, that doesn't sound so bad, especially if one was to wash one's hands after the event, except that most bathroom facilities had a toilet but no toilet paper. Alongside the toilet would be a perennial two-gallon can of water, which the users dipped their left hands into to wash their bottoms. I think you can now get the picture regarding the unclean hand, especially since the can of water was changed only once a day. ... I was also told never to cross my legs when sitting during a meeting, thereby showing the soles of my feet to my host. To cross one's legs showed not only that you were a "closed" person but demonstrated disrespect for your host by showing him the unclean portion of your feet. The "closed" image was also shown to a host if you were to cross your arms while talking. Last but not least, I was advised never to eat or drink all of what was offered during a meeting. To do so showed that your host had not provided enough refreshment for you, and that would be a major embarrassment.

Damn, I thought. Here I am, dying of thirst the whole time I've been in Asia, and I can't even drink what is set before me. I could see that it was going to be a long stay in any Muslim countries I had the fortune (or misfortune) to visit. However, throughout my stay in Malaysia, I had nothing but the best of luck. The Malay people were very friendly and willing to help even an obvious American. Professionally, we got along famously, and the work I wanted to get done on this trip got done in Malaya. I had great exchanges with government representatives the whole time I was there. I had learned from my visits to the previous countries and was reaping the benefits of being more culturally aware and realistic. We exchanged national laws; I obtained certified copies of their import and export laws; I instructed senior Malay Customs officials in the U.S. import-export inspection process; we set up contacts to use in future investigations; and we traded intelligence on each country's wildlife smugglers, very successfully, I might add. In fact, based on some of the information I was able to provide from our files, several exporters were rounded up and put out of business the next day—until the next time they decided to cross the line, anyway.

Aside from those successes, I experienced such an important event in my personal world of wildlife that I will carry it, like the lights of Hong Kong, to my grave. Traveling down an almost deserted highway in the embassy's armored limo, I chanced to see a tiger crossing the road not more than thirty yards in front of the vehicle, one of perhaps 750 to 1,000 that existed in Malaysia at that time. It appeared to be carrying a primate of some kind and stopped running right at the edge of the jungle to look back at us. Not wanting to miss this unique opportunity, I asked the driver to stop the car and held out my hand to my embassy escort and asked her to quickly hand me my camera, which was lying between us on the back seat. Keeping my eyes on the big cat, I waited for the camera to hit my hand. It didn't, so I quickly looked back, grabbed the camera, and then turned my eyes back to where the big cat had been standing. It was gone! In a couple of eye blinks it had melted into the jungle without a trace, just as Kipling had described the mystery of the tiger in many of his great works. God, I was disappointed beyond belief! I had the memory of this beautiful and very rare cat etched in my mind but not on film. Oh well; if God had wanted me to capture it on film, the cat would have held still for a moment longer. I looked at my escort and just smiled the smile of a person who has witnessed a great moment in nature that will never be repeated in his lifetime.

Because I was so damn happy over my successes with my Malaysian counterparts and seeing the tiger, I took my young escort out to dinner in a fancy restaurant in the next large town we came to. Before entering the restaurant, I cautioned my escort that the food had to be good and clean because I still had a lot of nonstop traveling ahead of me. She guaranteed the food to be not only the cleanest in the country but some of the best as well. Suffice it to say, I had one of the best Asian meals of my life. The waiters brought cart after cart of Malaysian delicacies, from quail eggs wrapped in delicate buns full of spicy sauces to fish, parrot, chicken, and monkey dishes cooked every way known to humankind. We must have eaten for over an hour. Keep in mind, these weren't full courses but just small portions of many exotic dishes. Damn, I remember that meal to this day, partly because of all the unique tastes I got to experience and partly because I was thinking in the back of my mind what that meal was going to cost one government employee on a less-than-adequate per diem. As it turned out, the meal cost me a total of $6.23 for the two of us in the coin of the realm! However, another "cost" was soon to manifest itself....

Leaving Malaya without the "hitch in my giddy-up" of not getting things done that I had experienced in previous countries, I looked forward to Indonesia. Arriving in Jakarta in daylight for a change, I was greeted with a slight case of upset stomach (probably from my recent restaurant experience) and 114 degree heat. I always loved stepping off an air-conditioned airplane into the heat and humidity of the tropics in a polyester suit and tie! As it turned out, the humidity was a savage 96 percent, and the air up to about forty feet above the ground looked as if it were the steam in a sauna, even though the sun was shining and the sky was a brilliant blue high above. I was met by my embassy liaison, a man named Monong Sitenjack, whose first case of business was to embarrass me as he ate the hind end off some poor damn Indonesian Customs inspector who was going through my luggage. Monong waved my red government traveler passport in front of the man's ever-widening eyes as he chastised the man very loudly for not recognizing an official government traveler who was supposedly exempt from routine inspections. Damn, I thought; I hope this isn't a taste of what is to come in this country. Excusing myself while Monong attended to my luggage, I headed for the bathroom to take care of a problem that was developing as a result of what now appeared to have been my indiscreet restaurant fling in Malaya. I was greeted with a row of toilets, not stalls, without seats and with the perennial can of brown, chunky-looking water alongside each toilet. Not seeing any toilet paper, I deferred relieving my growling gut and left for the embassy, hoping my Lomotil (a great medicine to control loose bowels) would start working shortly.

After the usual get-acquainted and "understand the culture" embassy meeting, I was driven to my hotel and let out for a rare afternoon of rest to prepare for an important meeting the next day with a highly important general in Bogor. I walked into my very typically British hotel and was shocked the second I walked through the doors. It was a cool and dry 68 degrees in the hotel lobby, and it was like walking into a wall after the 114 degree heat outside. It was refreshing, to say the least, but a damn surprise as my body functions tried to adjust to the radical temperature change. I checked in and took the elevator to my room on the eighth floor. What a palace it turned out to be: spacious, very clean, with fresh fruit and flowers everywhere, and in the bathroom were two "crappers"! One was the type I had been raised with, without the can of water alongside, and the other was a bidet. Never having seen, much less used, such a contraption, I immediately put it to use to rid myself of the trots picked up in Malaysia. Sitting way forward on the seat to read the information the embassy had given me about my schedule, and without thinking after finishing the "work" at hand, I reached down and turned on the water. Because I was sitting so far forward, up over my back and head came the stream of lukewarm water instead of hitting its intended target. Damn, I shot off that pot as if I had been shot out of a cannon, slipped on the now wet floor, and went flat on the deck with a *thump* surely heard three floors below! It took me a few seconds to regain my composure, and after I figured out what had gone wrong with the stream of water, I resorted to the regular toilet and never again used that damn water-squirting, back-shooting bidet.

Unfortunately, my day didn't end there. After finishing my bathroom chores, I walked to my hotel window and looked around. Below me on the hotel grounds lay a nine-hole golf course and a swimming pool large enough to hold the *Titanic*. Quickly unpacking my swimsuit, I split for the lower floor of the hotel and the exit to the pool. A waiter was sitting at a table near the door, serving cold lime drinks and handing out large towels. "Pardon me, sir, your first time in Indonesia?" he inquired.

"Yes," I told him.

"Please, sir, no more than fifteen minutes in the pool," he said politely.

Taking the proffered lime drink and towel, I thanked him, strolling out into the noonday sun, and walked down to the pool. Brother, I thought, telling me to stay only fifteen minutes in the pool! Fat chance, with me already a very dark brown. The nerve of the lad! I thought his caution probably had something to do with typical British training and reserve. With that kind of timidity, no wonder they lost the thirteen colonies in the War of Independence, I mused. Into the pool I went at a dead run, letting the warm, almost hot water close over my tired body. Boy, did my stint in the pool and in the lawn chairs at poolside feel good. I stayed out there swimming and sunbathing for at least an hour. When I started to get hungry, I returned to my room, dressed, and went down to a fine English buffet, which included monkey and crocodile as meal items. It was superb!

Waking the next morning, I could hardly move without intense pain throughout my entire body. It was not only on fire all over, but it felt as if my skin was stretched so tight that I didn't dare move for fear of splitting wide open! Then it dawned on me. The Equator! We were damned near the Equator, with the intensity of the sun at its fullest. No wonder that lad had told me no more than fifteen minutes at poolside. Damn, did I hurt all over. Rolling over in bed and wishing I hadn't just done that, I wished in the same breath, filled with swear words, that I had listened to that little Indonesian chap at the door. Getting up and looking in a mirror, I discovered that I was the brightest burned-red color I had ever seen. My great suntan had not been a barrier to the sun's rays at the Equator, and my body sure showed it. I had a schedule to keep, so into the shower I went, only to find that my trials had just begun. I discovered that I couldn't use any hot water on my inflamed body, only cold water, and so it went. For the next two weeks I could hardly bear any type of clothing because my skin was so severely burned. Try that wearing a suit and tie in Asia sometime. The skin on my belly, which is a considerable size, was so damn tender that five months later, back in the States, it was still sensitive to the weight of any kind of clothing or to sunlight! Damn, no wonder we Germans haven't won a war since the late 1800s!

Promptly at eight, sunburn and all, Monong, a marine guard, and an Indonesian driver picked me up in an embassy International Scout, and the four of us headed for Bogor. Monong briefed me on the general, who was Indonesia's main man when it came to issuing permits for anyone wanting to export wildlife from his country. Monong also explained that I more than likely would run into a pretty unhappy man because the U.S. government was seizing most of Indonesia's wildlife exports as they entered the United States. Because I was the contact import-export officer for the Washington office, I knew exactly why shipments were being seized. Indonesian law required that all wildlife being exported from Indonesia be accompanied with the appropriate permits. However, most shipments arriving in the United States did not possess the permits required by Indonesian laws and were consequently seized under the Lacey Act and forfeited to the government. It was a mystery to me why the Indonesian government would require a permit for export, yet no permits were arriving with the shipments. Well, I was soon going to meet the man who could answer that question and the many more I had, even if he was unhappy with the United States. I had met unhappy people before, including "wheels" in my line of work, I thought, and this one would be no different. Was I ever in for a memorable and pleasant surprise.

Now that Monong was through briefing me, I sat back in the left front seat (right-hand drive in Indonesia) and tried to forget the Malaysian rumblings in my stomach and my painful sunburn as I let my eyes sweep the countryside. The sight of the steamlike air coming from the air conditioner brought back unpleasant memories from the jungle firefight in Thailand, and I tried to push that thought from my mind. I studied the Indonesian labor force as we sped along, and the first thing I noticed was that every official, no matter what station in life he held, wore a military uniform, and they all looked like generals. I also noticed that every highway, from a two-lane to a four-lane, was eight lanes deep with hordes of humanity riding motor scooters, bicycles, mule carts, some automobiles, and many other forms of transportation. Humanity was the word of the day. At one point we came to a stop in the left lane of a four-lane road, and our driver signaled a left turn. The ever-present uniformed person was in the intersection directing traffic. While we waited for our turn to proceed, I saw a lad on a motor scooter with a crate of chickens lashed to the back drive up on the left side of our vehicle and stop. We were already occupying the left lane, but that made no difference to this chap; he just crowded right in alongside our vehicle and sat there inches away from my door. I assumed that our driver had seen this lad and thought nothing more of the matter. The officer in front of us beckoned our stream of traffic forward, and our driver turned left, as he had signaled. *Crash, crunch,* lurched our vehicle as we ran right over the top of the lad on his motor scooter! And I mean *right* over the top of him! Chickens and feathers went in every direction. It was obvious that we had driven right over something substantial, and all I could do was give our driver a shocked look. Without a word, he continued driving down the highway as if nothing had happened! Looking back, I could see the man wriggling on the ground, obviously dying, and a crowd starting to gather around him. Seeing that our driver was not going to stop, I turned to the embassy lad sitting in the back seat and said loudly, "Monong, we just ran over that man!"

Monong said nothing, nor did my marine guard as they sat there looking straight ahead.

"Monong," I said again, "we just ran over that man."

Monong, an Indonesian himself, looked out the back window of the Scout and coolly said, "He shouldn't have been there." I looked at Monong in utter disbelief as our driver continued in silence toward Bogor! Seeing the disbelief written all over my face Monong said, "The embassy has a formula where we make it right with the man's family."

By the tone of his voice, that was that. I was sure we had killed the man, and at that moment all I could think of was the book *The Ugly American* as our vehicle drove out of sight with its license plates reading, "U.S. Embassy." Shaking my head, I turned in my seat to try to enjoy the now not-so-interesting Indonesian countryside and prepare for my meeting with an angry army general ninety kilometers down the road.

When we arrived at the general's compound, we were ushered up to a large veranda outside his office. Since we had a few minutes to wait, I asked Monong where the bathroom was, and he pointed down the hall. Walking down the hall and around the corner, I found the men's bathroom and went in, figuring I would try to care for my still growling gut and the case of Malaysian trots it represented. I was greeted with the typical toilet without a seat, a pull-chain water closet, and the ever-present can of used brown water alongside of the crapper. Brother, I thought; I will just wait. Relying on the liberal doses of Lomotil I had taken, I walked back to Monong and got there just in time to be ushered into the general's office. Before I walked into the room, I saw and heard our driver in the courtyard below, beating out the dent in the door of the Scout that had been caused by the collision with the scooter driver and his chickens.

Entering the general's office, I found myself in a palatial setting. The spacious room was stocked with beautiful teak furniture, and pictures by many great painters adorned the walls. One caught my eye, a beautiful painting of the Grand Teton Mountains of Wyoming. Boy, was I glad to see a bit of the homeland about that time in my travels. The general, a dark man in his forties, got up from behind his desk and briskly walked toward me, warmly extending his hand for me to shake.

"Good morning, General; I am Special Agent Terry Grosz," I said, noticing that he ignored my embassy escort and made a beeline for me. He grabbed my hand, and I was not expecting the powerful grip in response to mine. Now, when I shake a man's hand, I always try to let him know there is a man attached to my hand. I had no trouble that day realizing that the general, from the power in his handshake, was my kind of man. He was about six foot two or three inches tall, strongly built, with a stocky frame representing about 260 pounds in muscular weight. He moved as lithely as a cat, and it was apparent that he represented, in his mind at least, the ideal man for the country of Indonesia, *period!* It was also apparent that he had a good eye for everything about him, as evidenced by his first remark to me.

"You liked my painting of the Tetons, Mr. Grosz. May I call you Terry?" he said.

Surprised at his observation and excellent command of English, I replied, "Yes to both questions, and the Tetons are a part of home as far as I am concerned."

"They are very beautiful," he replied. "I visited them one summer after I graduated from the University of California at Berkeley. Come sit down; we must talk." He gestured for me to sit at a large table near his desk. Only then did I become aware of three other Indonesian officers standing off to one side as the general motioned for them to join us at the teak table. We were introduced, but I do not remember their names because none of them spoke much English. The general asked Monong to interpret for the other officers as he and I spoke, and Monong agreed. With that, the general and I sat down across from each other, and he immediately launched into what was sticking in his craw. "Mr. Grosz—I am sorry; Terry—why do the Americans seize Indonesian wildlife shipments with the reckless abandon they do? We require our exporters to acquire export permits, and they do, yet your country still seizes our shipments almost without fail. Needless to say, our export industry has been financially damaged, and that industry's people are quite rightly angered over these incidents with your country. I hope I am speaking to a man who is prepared to respond to my concerns and has the authority to make the necessary changes so my country's exporters can get on with their business." With that said, and that was plenty, he settled back into his large leather chair, clasped his hands across his barrel-like chest, and looked straight at me with obvious unhappiness. His earlier smile was now exchanged for a red and somewhat clouded face. It was easy to see that he was pissed and anxious to get some answers.

Not to be intimidated, I settled back into my chair, aware that Monong's and the other officers' eyes were on me, crossed my arms over my chest as the general was doing, and said, "Well, General, there appears to be a slight misunderstanding between our two countries and their respective laws."

Before I could say more, the general leaped to his feet and, pounding the table loudly, said, "You're damn right there is a misunderstanding, as you are wont to call it, between our two countries! You damn Americans, who have it all, are trying to keep a developing country such as mine down, and I won't hear of it! We have every right in the world to our share of international commerce, and we won't be denied." He followed these remarks with another *whack* on the table with his sizable fist.

Surprised at his outbreak, as was Monong, who jumped like a bug on a hot rock when the general slammed the table, I remained outwardly calm. It was apparent to me that the general's fury was partly a show for the other officers, partly a demonstration to intimidate me, and partly an expression of a serious concern. I had already decided that I wasn't going to be berated by some damn hind end in a foreign uniform or let it get to me if I had to take a hind-end chewing, but I didn't get as big as I was by being last in line, so I softly but sternly replied, "General, you were educated in my country and while there had a chance to meet many of my country's people. Now, I wouldn't really call the people in the Berkeley area a representative cross-section of the people of my country, but I am sure you met others who would give you a good idea of what Americans are like. Right?"

He nodded and sat heavily back down in his great leather chair, realizing it was my turn.

"If that is the case," I said, "then you know it is uncommon for American people to jump up and slam their fist on the table to make a point. Hollering maybe, but the fist is saved as a tool of last resort. Now, you may think the fist was needed, but it isn't. As you found out while living in my country, big guys like you and me can usually get along, and there isn't a need for the two of us to stand in a pasture and bellow like a couple of bulls in rut." I noticed that Monong, in his attempts to translate what was being said, winced when I spoke about the bulls. Apparently, that wasn't in the embassy diplomatic code, I thought. Well, running over a man and leaving him to die on the highway wasn't my way of doing things either, so Monong and the embassy were just going to have to understand that they were saddled with a possible bull in their china shop. But that was their problem, not mine! I noticed a slight change in the general's face and body language, so I kept going. "General, I need to see a copy of your export laws, in English, please, before we go any further with our discussion."

He looked at me for a second and then said something in his own language to one of the other officers, who immediately left the room. The general just sat there looking at me, with his hands and arms still firmly clasped across his chest (remember, a closed person), and I sat there looking at him with my arms folded across my chest (obviously a very lovable person). I guess you could say two bulls, not in rut but definitely eyeballing and circling each other.

Within moments the other officer returned with an English-speaking chap who was an attorney for the Indonesian government. He was from the wildlife export regulatory section and produced a copy of Indonesian import-export laws. Watching the general out of the corner of my eye, I saw him assume a smug attitude, as if to say *I told you so,* and just sit there waiting for me to find what I was looking for. Feeling the pressure, I stood up, took off my damn polyester coat, and, looking the general right in the eyes, told him his country was one hell of a lot hotter then the Grand Tetons. Not letting him respond, I quickly let my eyes fall to the printed regulations in front of me and commenced to read. It took me all of about five minutes, during which not a word was uttered in the room, to find the problem. Indonesian law required every exporter of record to acquire an export permit and have it accompany any wildlife exported from Indonesia. So far, so good. However, the law further required the exporter of record to return the permit within *fifteen days of issuance.* Hell, there was the problem, I thought. Most exports were sent by ship and took many days, sometimes even months, to reach the United States. That meant that the shipper, in order to get his permit back to the Indonesian issuing authorities within the fifteen-day time frame, had to send his shipments without any of the documents required by Indonesian law. When the shipments arrived in the United States, since they didn't have an export permit, as required by Indonesian law, they were seized by our wildlife inspectors under the Lacey Act, which basically said that any violation of state or foreign law was a violation of the act that made a shipment subject to seizure and forfeiture. I was familiar with Indonesian law and didn't remember reading anything in the copy in our files back in Washington regarding the fifteen-day permit return period. As luck would have it, as I discovered after my return to America, the Indonesian embassy in Washington hadn't included that information when it provided an Indonesian-to-English copy for our use. So we had followed their laws to a T, figuring the embassy knew right from wrong.

Looking up at the General, I said, "I have found the problem, and it just requires a small fix before your folks can export wildlife parts and products to the United States to their hearts' content."

The general developed a huge grin of relief, unclasped his hands, leaned forward over the table, and said, "What is the problem?"

Showing him the offending section in his regulations, I said in the typical uncultured American way, "All you folks have to do is change *your* laws so the permit doesn't have to be returned in fifteen days. Just let the permit accompany the shipment, and the United States will accept your shipments without problem."

A frown replaced the smile on the general's face, and he bellowed, "That is impossible! Our laws are good and do not need to be changed."

"General," I said, "the law needs to be changed or your import seizure problem in my country will continue."

"The government of Indonesia is not going to make the change. You Americans will just have to make the change in your laws, and that is the way it will be!" he loudly roared. *Now* he was pissed.

I could see that Monong was struggling with our dialogue and that the other officers were supporting their general with some mumbling in Indonesian. Plus I had to once again "see a man about a horse," thanks to my great meal in Malaysia. On top of that, the general's office was not air conditioned, and I was sweating so badly, even without my jacket, that sweat was running down my legs. Polyester pants don't absorb moisture; it just runs into your socks and shoes, a not-so-nice feeling in 100 degree humid heat. In short, I certainly had felt better at other times of my life. Frustrated over the impasse, feeling unwell, unhappy in the heat and humidity, and still feeling the effects of being present when a man was run over by my country's representatives, I let it all hang out. "General," I said in a rather authoritarian voice, "do you know John Wayne?"

His eyes narrowed and he slowly said, "Yes, the great American cowboy." He rattled something off to his Indonesian colleagues, and

Monong grimaced. I figured I had better find out what the General had said later and continued, "Good. We will settle this regulations issue John Wayne style."

The general rose partway out of his chair and said incredulously, "With pistols?"

Monong, not thinking or not familiar with John Wayne, interpreted before he realized what he had just said, and all three of the other officers jumped up and began grumbling, I assumed about the supposed pistols proposition.

"No," I said. "We will settle it with our hands."

Again the general looked at me as if I was a madman and said, "With our fists?"

Grinning at the problems our lack of communication was causing, just like the clash of our two laws, I said, "We will arm wrestle. Whoever wins will be the one to dictate to the other what is done. In other words, if I win, you will change Indonesia's export laws. If you win, I will change America's laws." I said the latter with my heart in my throat because I didn't have the authority to blow my nose over here, much less change a regulation as if I owned the damn thing!

There was quiet in the room, and then the general stood all the way up, took off his military tunic, and started to roll up his right shirt sleeve as he rattled in Indonesian to the other officers about what was coming next. As if on cue, they all reached for their wallets and began to bet on the upcoming event. Meanwhile, Monong was going nuts. He was madly trying to get my attention with his embassy "don't do it" look and tell me not only no but *hell, no!* I guess my actions were again not in keeping with the embassy way of doing things, but at least I wasn't going to kill anybody on his way to market with a load of chickens. ... What I didn't realize was what Monong was trying to tell me: you don't beat a general in such a contest without the possibility of really embarrassing him in front of his friends, not to mention his government. Oh well, too late for that—the die had been cast, and it was now or never. However I had to admit, this seemed to be the closest thing to a windmill I had seen in some time! I was hoping my bout with the bad food in Malaysia hadn't weakened me too much once I saw the size of the general's arms as he rolled up his sleeve. They were as big as mine, and now I realized that I was in for a tussle.

Like a couple of damn-fool kids we got into the standard arm-wrestling position on that magnificent teak table, and I told Monong to say "Go" once we both said we were ready. As I adjusted my arm, I could tell from the general's hand strength that I might have a problem. He felt as strong as I was, and I began to wonder whether I could get out of this one, diplomatically, of course. As I was thinking, and not really set, Monong said, "Go." The general damn near pinned me right then and there with his great arm strength and speed. Surprised and pissed because he damn near had me, I put the weight of my 320 pounds below and behind my right shoulder (a little trick I had learned over many years of arm wrestling), powered my arm back up, and flattened the general in short order. There was disbelief in the room, not only from my general but among the other officers as well. You could have heard a small bug take a dump in the stunned silence! It became obvious that the general was pissed and embarrassed because I had beaten him so easily (in his eyes maybe, but not really). Glowering at me, he settled back into his chair, put his arm back down on the table, and through clenched teeth said, "Best two out of three."

Looking him squarely in the eyes, I said, "No; John Wayne would have done it only once, and I the same."

He sat there for a second and then quietly said, "You are right; you won fair and square." With that he got up and, turning to his legal fellow, who was still looking amazed at what had just happened to his powerful general, said, "Work with this man and change our export laws so our people can get on with making a living." The general turned back to me and said, "No one has ever beaten me before."

I said, "No one has ever beaten me either, General." (That held true until several years later, when Neill Hartman, who later became my deputy, beat me in fine style.) This remark allowed the general to save face, a very important Asian trait (see, I was learning). Sensing the general's continuing discomfort about the pending Indonesian regulatory change, I said, "General, I have an idea. Instead of changing your laws, how about this. You issue two permits, one being the original and the other a copy. Only you issue the copy with original

signatures and seals as well. That way your government can get the
original permits back in the fifteen-day period, and the United States
will honor the copy with the original signatures and seals for all legal
Indonesian exports." Man, he lit up like a Christmas tree, as did
Monong. For that I was happy. However, all I wanted at that moment
in time was to go somewhere and get rid of the growling in my guts
that was now taking on a life of its own.

The general, sensing I was not in the best of shape internally, asked
if I had gotten some bad food along the way. I admitted that I had,
and he said, "I never got over how great the toilets in America were
and had one installed in my office. Would you care to use it?"

Man, the glow on my face said it all, and with that the general, a
madman earlier, tended to another senior officer in his time of need.
Suffice it to say, that moment was the best part of the day. Shortly
thereafter, the Lomotil kicked in and I was able to survive the rigors
of the rest of Indonesia. In fact, the country proved to be a snap, especially after the general put in a good advance word for me to every
other agency I visited. Everything I asked for was provided in short
order. What had been our worst country regarding import and export
violations soon changed to a damn good legal trading partner.
Months later it was apparent that the general had kept his part of the
bargain and was keeping the wildlife export lawlessness at a workable
level. In addition, any inquiries sent via diplomatic cable after my
return to the United States were answered not in the old six-months-
later style but in a matter of days—sometimes even hours!

Before I left Indonesia, I asked Monong what the general had said
before we got into the arm-wrestling contest. Monong said the General had said, "This guy thinks he is the great John Wayne, and a cowboy to boot." I smiled, and Monong said, "After you beat him arm
wrestling, he told his generals that you were 'Pop Eye,' whatever that
meant." Again, I just smiled. Sometimes there is something to be said
for not being up on a culture.

From Jakarta, I headed for Manila via Singapore. However, my
adventures in Indonesia had not ended. Sitting in a Garuda Airways
DC-10, with the air conditioner on full, I settled back into my seat
to await the flight to Singapore. In due time the plane taxied out to

the runway and began to increase power until the engines groaned. Then the pilots really sent the power to the engines and the plane sat on the runway shaking violently all over. Damn, I thought, I have flown hundreds of hours in a DC-10 but *never* in one that had the engines run up like this. Then more power was sent to the engines, and I began to get a bit concerned because I could tell the engines were really objecting! The whole damn plane was shaking like hell and beginning to override its brakes. At that point the pilots released the brakes, and the plane fairly shot down the runway as they piled even more power into the engines. Dang, there aren't any mountains at the end of the runway, so what the hell? I thought. In short order the plane was airborne, but this unique flight wasn't over. The plane was jerked up into such a steep climb that it would have been all but impossible to get up out of the seat and walk down the aisles. We climbed like that for about five minutes, bodies pressed into the seats, and then the plane did a soft loop downward, which left everyone weightless for about fifteen seconds! We just hung there, held in the seats only by our seatbelts, and the air was full of floating pens, loose cigarettes, and a pillow or two. Presently the plane lined out, and we were normal again. *Never* having had such a ride in a commercial jet, and figuring the pilots must be ex–British fighter pilots, I asked a flight attendant, "What was that all about?"

She calmly replied, "Insurgents."

"Insurgents?" I repeated.

"Yes," she replied. "They wait at the end of the runway and shoot at the planes as they take off, so we must depart rather radically."

I just grinned. Man, people in America just don't know how good they have it, I thought as I leaned back in my seat and let the air conditioner take over, along with some badly needed sleep.

Arriving in Manila just before noon, I was picked up by the customary embassy official and whisked to the embassy for meetings with my contact, who in that case was the agricultural attaché. After a short briefing, he informed me that I had the rest of the afternoon off. Damn, after many straight days of working, I was to get some time off—hot dog! My liaison said the embassy was sending someone over to the island of Corregidor and asked if I wanted to go along. Being a bit of a historian, especially in the arena of military history, I could hardly suppress my eagerness. "There is only one problem," he warned. "We have a typhoon coming, and it will be here in about six hours, so you will be regulated to just a short stay."

"That is better than none," I said. "I will change and be right back. Where do you want me to meet you?"

He said the embassy limo would pick me up and take me to the marina near the embassy, and we would depart from there. Since my hotel was right on Manila Bay and not far from the U.S. Embassy, I hustled out of the building and into a waiting limo. As we drove through the embassy grounds, I became acutely aware of all the bullet holes in the embassy walls and surrounding structures. It was apparent that the U.S. government had left everything much as it was after retaking Manila, for history's sake. Quickly checking in to my hotel, I dressed for the occasion and met my limo out front. Minutes later I was on a hovercraft along with an Australian who had served on Corregidor and later became a prisoner of war. It seemed that the embassy was doing him and the Australian Embassy a favor, and my marine guard and I just happened to be included.

Off we went for my first trip in a hovercraft, into a dead calm and ghostly-yellow-colored Manila Bay. I could sure tell a weather change was in the offing. I usually get deathly seasick, but the way the hovercraft literally flew across Manila Bay, plus my excitement at being able to walk in some historical footprints, kept me in fine fettle. The hovercraft soon pulled up to the same concrete causeway leading from the island on which General MacArthur had escaped on one of Commander Buckley's PT boats. That was all the navy we had in the area at the time, the rest having been sent to the bottom or pulled out of the theater of war for later use when they had a fighting chance. As we walked over the island, which is only about two square miles, it became obvious that the Philippines government was keeping the area as it had been on the fateful last day of occupation. The Aussie and I walked all over the area, drinking in the history. In one area there were some fourteen-inch mortar pits. The huge mortars had spilled off their gun carriages, having been destroyed by the invaders' artillery and literally covered with nicks in the barrel metal from flying bullets. A set of steps led up from the road to a spot above the mortar pits. Walking up those steps, I could see that they led to a high, flat area with only some concrete foundations left. Looking over at the mortar pit, I could see that I needed to get higher in order to get a photograph of all that lay below, so I turned to climb the last steps to the high place with the old foundations. As I turned so I could navigate the last of the steps, I found myself looking a cobra right in the eye. It took all of fourteen microseconds to turn and achieve a speed of 170 miles per hour going down those steps, taking twenty-two of them per step. As I passed my Aussie friend, I heard him yelling, "Run zigzag, Yank; run zigzag." Run zigzag, hell, I was running at top end on the straightaway, and only an F-4 Phantom could catch me now. Why slow down when there was a sixty-foot snake waiting for me? Suffice it to say, the snake and I parted company, and I was a little more careful after that ... well, almost.

Shortly after that, my Aussie friend wanted to go through the Malitna Tunnel, which passed through a small mountain in which many except those lads on the front lines, especially nurses and the wounded, were housed during air attacks. In it were ammo dumps, hospitals, sleeping quarters, kitchens, and living quarters for the high command and President Queson. The whole setup was encased in concrete, as were the floors. We started into the tunnel without the benefit of flashlights, but the Aussie assured me that the floors were cemented over and that we would be walking on a smooth, flat surface. So with those assurances, and without my marine guard, in we went so we could get to the other side and he could show me where he had been wounded. The tunnel was darker than all get-out and smelled of age and history. Even in the darkness I could make out old signs pointing the way to a hospital, ammo dumps, or MacArthur's headquarters. Damn, I thought; I am walking in the footsteps of those brave souls who, by hanging on to this chunk of real estate, foiled the Japanese timetable and ultimately halted Japan's push to Australia. When we finally reached the other end of the tunnel, the Aussie had me take his picture to show where he had been standing when he was hit by shrapnel from a mortar shell.

About that time I could hear my marine guard yelling through the tunnel for me to come out. Remembering our embassy orders, my

Aussie friend and I hurried toward his voice. When we reached the other side, boy, did I get a tail-end chewing. My marine guard made it abundantly clear that I was not to get out of his sight for the remainder of the trip. Being the "big boy" that I was, I asked why the "hoorah."

"Snakes" was his response.

"Snakes?" I asked.

"Yes," he replied. "In the tunnel. When a typhoon is coming, the snakes out here move into the tunnel for protection. The tunnel is full of them!"

"Ahhh," I replied in disbelief.

He disgustedly said, "Come on." We went a short way back into the tunnel, into the real darkness, and he turned on his flashlight. All I could see were eyes glowing like rubies when the light hit them.

Damn, I thought, my Aussie buddy and I just walked many yards through the darkened tunnel through all of those! What little hair I had began to creep upward, and I realized that I might be a "big boy" in the United States, but out here I was nothing but a living target, and I had better wake up and fly right! After that I did what I was told, and nothing more. ... Our trip back was a real thrill. Manila Bay was by now an ugly gray patch of colored water with six-foot whitecaps and growing. The skipper of the boat was not happy about our late arrival, and we exited the island posthaste. The hovercraft would hit the tops of three waves and then plunge nose first into the fourth. Water would boil into the area where all of us sat, and pretty soon we were sitting in six inches of seawater as the hovercraft struggled along. It was exciting as we sped along and then shuddered to a stop on every fourth wave! Needless to say, by the time we arrived in the marina, we looked like drowned rats. Bidding my Aussie buddy good-bye, I walked to my hotel amid the rising winds of the typhoon. I could see that all the oceangoing ships anchored in Manila Bay were riding with double anchors at bows and sterns. Damn, I thought; this typhoon thing is some sort of serious. Heavy rains, tremendous winds, and coconuts flying through the air like cannon shot sent me staggering the last hundred yards to the safety of my hotel.

When I arrived, I found that the hotel was without power, so I would have to walk up the three flights of stairs to my room, which faced the bay. As I started for the stairway, the man at the desk told to watch out for the snakes. He said I should just leave them alone and they would leave me alone. What the hell? I thought. This is an expensive hotel; how the hell did snakes get into it so easily? Nonetheless, one trip up the stairs to my room confirmed what the lad at the desk had said. In every corner of the stairway was a ball of snakes of every kind and size. The emergency lights illuminated many colored sets of eyes, all intently watching as I walked by to see what my intentions were. The man at the desk was right; all they wanted was to be out of the fury of the typhoon, and I was more than glad to honor the truce.

Arriving in my room, I stood fascinated for hours watching the typhoon strike the city of Manila with a fury such as I had never seen. Everything seemed to be flying through the air, and I could barely see the ships riding at anchor in the bay because of the heavy sheets of rain that continued to pour forth from the heavens. Finally I crawled into a bed that was damp owing to the increased humidity accompanying the typhoon and the lack of air conditioning and drifted off to sleep wondering what the morrow would bring.

The next morning found the typhoon in full tilt with about a foot of water in all the streets. I could see the small "Jeepneys" (a gaily decorated Jeep form of transportation) moving around as well as taxis, so I made a quick call to the embassy to see what was scheduled for the day. The embassy said all my meetings were a go but that I could wear casual clothing owing to the difficult transport conditions. That was fine with me—after all, I did think I would look like a damn fool standing in a foot or so of water with a dress suit on. Around nine in the morning the wind had abated some, dropping to eighty-five to one hundred miles per hour, and I met the embassy limo in front of the hotel. The water in the street was such that I took my shoes off, rolled up my pant legs, and stood on the back seat of the car to avoid getting any wetter. I had never seen anything like this before. There was at least six inches of water inside the car, and the driver went along to my meeting, plowing through a foot of water like nobody's business. Along the way I saw several small taxis that had dropped into unseen openings where the force of the water underneath had lifted off manhole covers and the taxis had driven headlong into them, not seeing the danger ahead because of the water on the road. My driver turned and said, "Don't worry; this old boat is too large to drop anything more than a wheel into one of those openings." That sure made me feel better. …

Arriving at my meeting place and putting my shoes back on, I was greeted by two high government officials who whisked me off to a second-floor meeting room so they could prep me for the meeting to follow. It seemed that the meeting hall on the first floor of the building contained about three hundred angry Philippine exporters who were mad at the U.S. government for seizing many of their goods when they arrived in the United States. What is with all these angry countries? I thought. They pass the laws; we enforce them, which indirectly protects the country's interests; then they are mad at us for doing so. I just shook my head in frustration. I found out that day that some sort of corruption in the cost of the export permit was the root of the problem in that country (welcome to Asia). In order for the Philippine exporters to export their goods, they had to buy a very expensive permit from the government. As I soon learned in my hardball questioning of the government officials, part of the money went for the permit, and the rest appeared to be lining someone's pockets. It didn't come out that way, but it was abundantly clear to me that someone was benefiting from the overcharging going on. As a result, many of the Philippine people were bypassing the graft-ridden permit department and attempting to export their goods to the United States without the required permit. Unfortunately, Philippine laws mandated the export permit, so without it we in the United States were seizing goods under the Lacey Act. Ultimately, the importer of record was losing his financial shirt as well as his imported goods before the legal work in the States was even done. My two government officials were betting on me, through the hard-line enforcement approach of the U.S. government, to get the exporters to go back to the Philippine government and start purchasing the export permits again, thereby bringing more money into their coffers. It was apparent that they would be terribly disappointed if I was not successful in this endeavor. If I was successful, the exporters would be terribly disappointed. Damn, nothing like being thrown into a lion's den.

I was not happy at being placed in that position, but I was deep into the mess, being here to address such issues as getting the Philippine exporters to stop the illegal entry of their goods into the United States, so I carried on. I said, "Let's go, gentlemen, and see what can be done." With that, I headed down to the "lion's den" of three hundred unhappy Philippine exporters. All the way down to the meeting room, I was given advice from my embassy staffer and the Philippine government representatives on how to handle myself, what I could say and not say, and the like. I thought, That is fine and good, coming from two government officials, one of whom is directly responsible for the screw-up to begin with and the other of whom backs him up in the States with a seizure. As I got closer to the meeting room, aware of the historical Philippine penchant for temper and the use of butterfly knives, I began to wonder if this trip was necessary. I was nothing but a lowly government employee who just happened to be the U.S. expert on imports and exports. The next thing I knew, I was being thrown into a political hotbed between the Philippine government and a very angry and frustrated group of wildlife exporters. I didn't realize just how mad they were until I opened the door to the meeting room and was greeted by a rush of hot, humid, and fetid air, representative of three hundred angry exporters' sweating bodies, all waiting to talk to me about their problems, all at once, as soon as they got the chance.

My embassy lad stood just behind me as I was introduced to the throng. The exporters listened politely as I explained who I was and what I was doing there and gave a quick course in U.S. wildlife import-export laws. Sensing that they wanted to talk more than listen, I cut short my presentation and opened it up for questions. I was immediately blasted with three hundred questions madly flung my way on "wrongs" the U.S. had committed regarding previous wildlife shipments. An early-nineteenth-century madhouse in London was about as close to the scene as I could picture. People were yelling and shaking their fists at me by the dozens. Some stood on the tables to make themselves better heard. Others advanced toward me, shaking their fists and making gestures that would have led to a knot on their heads if I had been in my own country. Everyone seemed mad except one very heavy-set woman sitting in the middle of the room in a bright red dress, calmly watching me. At first, because I didn't have brain one, I tried to answer each and every question madly hurled my way. I tried that approach for about ten minutes until, realizing that I was going nowhere and the throng was just getting madder and madder, I changed strategies. Holding up my hand for silence, I just stood there until you could have heard a pin drop. I said, "Ladies and gentlemen, we are going nowhere doing what we just did. I am here to discuss the U.S. laws and import-export policies, not your individual problems that occurred at one hundred Customs Ports of Entry across America. In short, it is impossible for me to address what happened to all of your shipments without returning to the United States and looking into each and every one of them. So I will answer general questions on how our laws work and what is to be expected in order to assist you in your businesses, but no more specific questions about what happened to particular shipments. That information will be provided by the U.S. government officials seizing the shipments. But for now, since I have only three hours with you folks before I have to go to another meeting, I want to confine the questions to general import and export issues or the Endangered Species Act in particular and CITES in general."

With that, I threw the forum open to questions and was again hit with three hundred questions. Noticing that one of my Philippine officials and the embassy lad had slipped out the door and that the remaining Philippine official wished he could, I figured it was soon to get down and dirty. I wasn't far off. About a dozen exporters, whipped up to a froth, got up in unison and angrily headed for the front of the room and yours truly. I just stood my ground with some foolish thought they would be afraid of a man my size, but they were stopped dead in their tracks by a soft comment in Spanish by the lady in red. I noticed that she had only raised her hand, and, as if on cue, everyone went silent in a hurry. Even the lads advancing on my carcass returned to their seats. "Mr. Grosz," she said, "as you can tell, we exporters are not a happy people. We have to pay a very high price for our export permits and then have to pay even more at every turn in order to get our goods out of our country and into yours. Then, because we have at least two agencies competing to issue permits and many different people signing them, we find that your country still confiscates about half of our shipments. We are trying to do it right, but at this point, as you can see, are very frustrated.'"

I was aware that one Philippine agency signed permits for fishery products, and another signed permits for landed flora and fauna. I was also aware that the exporters would often get permits for fishery products and then incorrectly export wildlife on that fisheries permit, or procure a wildlife permit and use it to export coral. As a result, the U.S. wildlife inspectors would rightfully seize the shipments being imported under the invalid permits. Still trying to figure out who this very articulate and obviously very powerful woman was, I started to address the confusing Philippine two-agency permit issuance system. But before I could continue, the Philippine government official, standing behind me for protection, tugged on my arm. When I turned, he whispered that the two agencies were in the process of consolidating, and that soon only one permit would be needed to export any fish, wildlife, or plants from the Philippines.

Turning back to my lady in red, I advised her of this state of affairs, and I could see a ripple of relief go through this once hostile crowd. I also informed her that it was very difficult for the U.S. officers to figure out what the Philippine laws really meant and which signature from which agency was valid, since those authorized to sign such documents changed office so frequently. I said that the consolidation of the two agencies would save a lot of confusion for us in the United States regarding what was legally being imported and that we would welcome such a change. I asked the Philippine official how long before this actually happened, and he said the president of the Philippines was going to sign the law within the next thirty days. I passed this information on to the woman and told her that as a gesture of goodwill, I would notify my government and ascertain whether in the interim the United States would accept any Philippine permit for goods already exported, no matter which agency had signed the permit (which was done).

With that statement, I could see a lot of the fight go out of the exporters, and a lot of happy jabbering flew back and forth in the language of the land. Feeling better about myself and the direction the meeting was now going, I turned to my Philippine official and asked, "Who is the lady in red?"

He whispered, "Very powerful lady, head of the trade union and very powerful."

Turning, I could see that the woman had more questions for me. "Yes?" I said.

"What do you think of the Philippines' people?" was her next question.

Taken aback by this question, I paused and then said, "I think they are great. They always have a ready smile, are quick to help a stranger in their land, are a very proud people, and *great* cooks." I rubbed my obviously large potbelly and grinned. The whole assemblage broke out into loud laughter.

Her next question wasn't quite so easy. "Mr. Grosz, why does the United States, a very rich and powerful country whose citizens are all millionaires, wish to stop the Philippines' people from trying to make a living through the exports of our wildlife?"

About that time, not hearing a mad crowd anymore, my embassy lad and the other Philippine official reentered the room and stood behind me. "Well," I said, "the United States, for years, has taken many countries' natural resources and left very little behind for the citizens of those countries."

"Be careful," hissed my embassy counterpart in such a way that the crowd before me did not hear him!

I continued, mindful of the cautionary hissing to my rear, "The United States consumes about 45 percent of the world's total production of wildlife parts and products. As such, my government has unilaterally decided, through the Endangered Species Act and the Convention on International Trade in Endangered Species of Wild Fauna and Flora, along with other federal laws, to no longer consume other countries' resources as we have done in the past."

"Careful" was the word again, coming from behind me in clear "embassy English," while the mood of the crowd before me had softened considerably. It was clear that the folks in the room were listening very closely to what I was saying.

"So," I went on, "if the Philippine people want to exterminate their wildlife species for their own consumption, so be it. For example, if the Philippine women want to wear Philippine crocodile purses, thereby exterminating the species, that is your call. However, the American people no longer want to be part of that extinction process and through our laws will now prohibit all imports of animal, fish, or plant species we consider, through the best science, to be rare or endangered. As far as we are now concerned, those items are to be preserved or exterminated by the countries in question, and we no longer wish to be part of that activity. So, in conclusion, we are not prohibiting you from importing such species because we wish to oppress your industry but just because we don't want to be a part of the extermination of a species in your country. Those are your resources to do with as you please, not ours, and as it now stands, American women will not be carrying purses made from rare crocodiles from the Philippines."

There wasn't a sound in the room. It was just hot and humid, with the sound of the wind whipping around the eaves and rattling the windows as if the dying typhoon were listening as well. Then the lady in red said, "I like you. You don't try to lie to us like the rest of the Americans do."

"Boy, did you fall into that one and come out smelling like roses," said the embassy voice behind me.

She continued, "My trade union will return to our government agencies and get the appropriate permits to export our goods. Additionally, we will meet en masse as we have done here with our government officials and see if we can't make our lot in life a little easier with the permits we have to procure."

I could hear sighs of relief from the two Philippine officials behind me. With that, the meeting changed to an orderly question-and-answer period that ran for the next two hours. At the end of the meeting the lady in red stood up to thank me, and the people dissolved into the still roaring typhoon outside as if it were an everyday occurrence. Realizing that I was sweating up a storm, I turned to meet two obviously happy and jabbering Philippine officials. The one who had waited outside while the meeting was at its hottest was, I now discovered, a very high-ranking official, probably equal to our secretary of the Interior. He was excited, to say the least.

"Mr. Grosz," he said, "you have done something here today we have been trying to get the trade union to do for months. They are now going to come back to us and get the required permits and not fight us as they have done so in the past. Do you know what you have done? You are going to *save* the Philippine government *millions* in lost revenue, not to mention elimination of all the trouble that came from seized goods in your country." By now he was pumping my hand like a pump handle would have been worked by a dirt farmer in Oklahoma on a July day in the '30s.

"Look," I said, "the arrival of the good news on your agency consolidation swung the day, and all I did was give them someone to bellow at."

"No, what you did here today was a miracle," he said.

By now I was getting a little embarrassed at the fellow's antics, but he just wouldn't quit. Turning to my embassy staffer, he requested that both of us follow him over to a warehouse next door. The embassy staffer agreed, and since I still had a few minutes before I met a group of conservationists, I went along for the walk. On the way over I asked my staffer what was in the warehouse, and he responded, "Examples of everything commercially produced or manufactured by hand by the people here in the Philippines."

"What am I supposed to do when I get there?" I asked.

"Just watch," he replied.

In a few moments, after ducking across a street full of water and howling wind, we entered the warehouse. Man, what a place! It was probably a city block square and full, in display fashion, of everything imaginable handmade or commercially produced by the people of the Philippines. The Philippine lad who had been so excited said something to his partner, who left and shortly returned with the floor manager and several assistants. "Mr. Grosz, for what you did for my government today, anything in this store is yours." With that, he formed a large grin and, with a flourishing sweep of his hand followed by an exaggerated bow, beckoned for me to begin shopping. Mindful of the restrictions placed on U.S. government employees when it came to gift acceptance, a $25 limitation in those days, I smiled and declined. Man, did the stuffin' come out of Grandma's turkey at that response! My Philippine official said, "Oh no, you are to be rewarded for what you did for us this day. Take anything, it is yours!"

Again I declined, telling him it was my duty to assist him in any way possible, and my reward was just having the great opportunity to work with him. That should have stopped anyone in their tracks, but not this guy. He really got insistent, and I could tell he was offended that I was not responding to his generosity. It was as if he felt that everything made by his countrymen that lay before me in the warehouse was not good enough for this American. I turned to my embassy liaison for assistance, and he said, "Terry, let's just look around, OK?"

With that, having been given the green light, so to speak, I started to look around. At every juncture the Philippine chap tried to give me something his countrymen and -women had put together for display. The place was full of everything from carvings, ivory, teak, and brass to copper workings and knives—you name it and it was there. I later found out this warehouse housed every kind of craft known to the Philippine people, and it was customary for merchants to come from afar, select the goods they wanted and in what quantities, and order the same. Then the order would be filled and shipment made to the buyer for sale in other countries. Finally, after much prodding from the Philippine lad, I selected a five-pound sack of dried papaya. It was scooped up by one of the floor manager's assistants, and the Philippine lad said, "What else?"

"That is plenty," I said.

"No," he responded, "you must look some more."

Catching the look that it was OK to continue from my embassy staffer, I continued to look for something else under the $25 dollar limit imposed on me by my government. As we passed by a furniture section, I was struck by the beauty of one hand-carved table. It was about six feet long by four feet wide and maybe two feet from the floor to the table top. The table itself was about six inches thick, solid teak, and beautifully carved in relief to a depth of about four inches. The scene so beautifully carved in the table was a Philippine pastoral scene with a Neta hut, a man plowing a rice field with water buffalo, and the like. On top of the beautiful carving was a one-piece beveled glass table top about an inch thick, countersunk into the table. It was stunning, and damn me, instead of being in control of my big mouth, gasped, "This is outstanding!"

"It is yours!" came the quick reply.

Holy crap, I thought; what have you done, Terry? My eyes quickly went to the price tag, and it was $3,250 American—*in their country!* I could just imagine what the thing sold for in the United States. My eyes about fell out onto the floor. I became aware that the Philippine official was giving instructions to the floor manager to "wrap it up."

"No," I said, "I can't accept something like that."

The Philippine lad really got uppity, and I could tell I had struck a national nerve by turning him down. Before I could say anything, my embassy staffer stepped forward and said, "Mr. Grosz would love this table. If you would, have your folks package it for shipment by sea and send it to the American Embassy. We will see that it is shipped to Mr. Grosz's home in the United States."

I just looked at my embassy staffer in disbelief. He knew damn well there was no legal way for me to could accept such a gift! Seeing the "wait until later" look, I kept my mouth shut and just let the act play itself out for a change. Thanking the Philippine lad profusely for the most beautiful gift I had ever seen, we dismissed ourselves so I could make my next meeting and left the showroom floor. Once out of earshot, I said, "You know damn well I can't have that! Now what?"

Without missing a step, my embassy staffer said, "That's right, you can't have it, but *the ambassador can.*"

I just looked at his impassive face and shook my head. A god-damned little nobody like me couldn't have such a gift but the "big wheels" could. No wonder the statue of Justice wears a blindfold! I thought. On we went to many more such meetings over that day and several others, none of which carried the impact of the first one, which was nice for a change.

Finally the time came for me to leave the Philippines, and I was driven to the Manila International Airport for my trip to Guam, Hawaii, and home. We were still in the tail end of the typhoon, and

I remember sitting in my seat on the 747, air conditioner and all, waiting for takeoff. We waited for quite a while, and the pilot finally came on the intercom and informed us that he had to wait for the wind to die down below one hundred miles per hour before he could take off, so we should please be patient. After a few more moments, rocked by still very strong winds, the pilot began his run down the runway, and I would bet it wasn't fifty yards heading into the high winds before we were airborne! Other than the excitement of losing an engine between Guam and Hawaii, I just sat back, ate good old American food (yes, even airline food was great), and reveled in the air conditioning. ... At the end of my sixty-seven-day peregrination, I was glad to get home. It had been hot and humid the entire trip. For someone who weighs as much as I did and was required to wear a polyester suit and tie, that was a struggle in and of itself. In addition, I had eaten everything from spider in Indonesia (a great dip) to monkey in Singapore, Thailand, and Indonesia (great flavor but stringy) and crocodile in Malaysia. I was really looking forward to a simple American meal, prepared by Donna, of fried chicken, mashed potatoes, gravy from scratch, and fresh peas. Knowing her, there would also be a fresh homemade pie for me to enjoy, with a crust that would knock your eyes out at thirty feet!

I had been shot at in Thailand, procured a beautiful hand-carved teak table for an ambassador in the Philippines, and ridden out a mild typhoon. I had observed cities such as Manila that still showed extensive battle damage from a war that had occurred thirty-three years earlier and had suffered the frustration of the "Asian way" in Hong Kong. But most importantly, I had learned a lot about other cultures, other peoples, and myself. I had learned to really compromise, had learned to deal at a level of diplomacy I had never before thought possible, was more observant than I ever had been, had been educated about life in the real sense for two and a half billion Asians, and had learned what I was really capable of when the chips were down and the air was full of bees of a worse variety than the African killer bees (although the result could ultimately be the same).

Probably more than any other professional event in my life, this experience set the course for how I approached life over the next twenty years. The Orient, not unlike Alaska, has a way of reaching into the inner sanctums of one's soul and making changes. I still remember standing high on one of the mountains overlooking Hong Kong, looking one way into the People's Republic of China and the other way into the gold-colored South China Sea under a sunset of unparalleled color and magnificence. At that moment I actually felt an inner change that has guided me ever since.

It is no small wonder that greater men than I fought so hard to conquer, hold, live, understand, and die in this part of the earth. Its immediate life experience and form of kinship absorbed by my soul was truly unique, as was the gift of knowledge and human understanding granted to me.

I know I will never return to the Far East, and I will never have to. However, its essence will be with me until I move into that final life challenge yet to come.

9

Three Days in Missouri

Picking up my ringing telephone in the Minneapolis office about six A.M. one Tuesday, I said, "Good morning, Fish and Wildlife Service; may I help you?"

The booming voice of Ed Nichols, my senior resident agent in Jefferson City, Missouri, said, "What are you doing this weekend?" Just like Ed—no greeting, just down to business. Even at that time in the morning I just had to smile. Ed was a damn good officer and criminal investigator, not to mention human being. He was older than all but one of my other senior resident agents and had served in the navy during World War II. He had been assigned to the battle-ship *Missouri* as a kid of seventeen when it was hit by a kamikaze pilot and was a strong officer with those wartime experiences under his belt. In fact, his work ethic, compassion for his fellow humans, and excellent common sense made him one of the best in the business.

"Well, I haven't planned it out yet, but you can bet it won't be any-where near my home because of the likes of you," I chided. I was the assistant special agent in charge in the Minneapolis office and because of all the illegal wildlife activity in the region, I seldom had a week-end to myself or with my family because of our hardworking agents' constant enforcement efforts.

"That's good because I could use some help down here working the dove hunters. I have been getting a lot of reports on the use of bait and over-limits being taken and thought since you didn't have anything else to do, you might want to get off your dead hind end and earn a paycheck for a change."

"Damn your scrawny hide," I roared back to my large friend. "If you were close enough for me to get my hands on you, I would shake you like a rat! You know damn good and well I hardly have a moment to even go to the bathroom, much less fool around."

He just laughed heartily and then in a serious tone said, "Boss, I really could use some help, especially from someone who has worked baited dove fields before and knows how to handle hot-tempered people if the need arises without getting himself or others killed."

"When and where?" came my tired reply as I realized that my bride and three kids were going to be disappointed over another lost weekend.

"Get your tired hind end into Jefferson City, and we can work the dove-hunting areas anywhere 360 degrees to the compass from there if you want," he said.

"All right, I will have Barb make the airline reservations so I arrive Thursday evening, and that way we will have a good three days in the saddle before I have to return."

"Sounds good to me, but travel light. You know how Missouri can be this time of the year. Hotter than all get-out with a fair degree of humidity thrown in just to make you more than miserable."

"Yeah," I said, tongue in cheek, "just the kind of climate I am looking forward to working in."

He laughed again, and then our conversation slipped into a discussion of an investigation into the illegal taking of hellbenders (a type of salamander) and how badly a Region 6 agent had mishandled the case. Neither of us could figure out how that agent had left so many loose ends and asked so many wrong questions to screw the case up so thoroughly. Now, as a result of his handling of the investigation, parts of it would have to be redone. With a lilt of disgust in his voice that came from knowing he would have to pick up the pieces and finish the investigation himself, Ed signed off, and I began to make plans for another always interesting detail in Missouri.

I had worked dove hunters in Missouri several times in the past, the first time in 1977 when I was a senior resident agent like Ed, only located in Bismarck, North Dakota. That trip had been to enforce the Migratory Bird Treaty Act as it pertained to the dove hunters in what is called the "boot heel" of Missouri around the Malden area. It had been some experience for me, working with Southerners for the first time. I don't know why, but it seemed as if just about everybody we had run across on that trip hunting dove was in violation of the Fish and Game laws. Many of those folks had been raised living off the land and, laws or not, would continue to live off the land and do as their "great-granddaddy had done." Despite the heat and humidity, it had made for a grand time as we caught lots of chaps doing what they should not have been doing in the world of wildlife. I expected more of the same on this trip. Ed was not prone to asking for assistance unless he really needed it. I suspected he must have had many troublesome areas where dove hunting was occurring and just needed someone to give him a hand checking things out. On my previous trip it had seemed to me that the state had more places to hunt dove and hide in the outback than anywhere I had ever worked. Little wheat or grain fields of some sort were tucked away everywhere, and there seemed to always be a gang of hunters taking the little elusive dove as it hammered through the air en route to those places dove like to go. Many of those Missouri ridge runners were damn good shots, and it didn't take them long to amass a pile of dove, many times in excess of the daily bag limit. As I said, the local culture made dove hunting a traditional pursuit heralding the joy of the beginning of all the fall hunting seasons. This was true not just in Missouri but in the entire South, as I came to discover in my later working years.

Thursday evening Ed and I left the airport, Ed in his patrol car and I in a rental car because Ed figured it would be best that each of us have an unmarked car to work from. Ed had also arranged for a state Fish and Game warden to work with each of us and had ensured that they would be excellent officer-guides with a thorough knowledge of the area and local landowners. He cautioned me that Missouri could be a very political state and not to expect these officers to go into places that would get them into any kind of trouble politically. Ed felt that if those kinds of occasions arose, we feds would handle the tough stuff and protect our state counterparts by leaving them out of it. I had no problem with that strategy, having suffered the same situations in California when I was a state officer there.

Back at our motel, I met the two officers we would be working with. Ed had drawn a younger officer and, it appeared, was going to provide some training for that lad in working dove hunters. My officer, whose name I have forgotten, was an older fellow and a captain, if I am not mistaken. He seemed nice enough during this first meeting, but I instantly felt something amiss about him. I couldn't quite put my finger on it, but if I had had to guess, I would have said that I felt as if the lad wouldn't have any staying power if the going got tough. But I put those thoughts aside, and the four of us had a wonderful peeled shrimp and catfish dinner—and let me tell you, the beanery lost its shirt on its all-you-can-eat price with the four of us that evening!

At three the next morning, the four of us had a typical Southern breakfast of grits, chicken-fried steak, and the like as we set our plans. Ed had a list of areas about which he had received complaints regarding over-limits and baiting. He took half, and I took the rest. Ed and his partner would be working to the south, and I and my partner would be working to the north and west in the Boonville area. After breakfast we headed for the parking lot, and since I did not have a state radio in my rental car, my partner insisted on taking his marked patrol car along as well so we could have state radio contact. His thinking was that if we spotted an interesting area in which suspicious hunting was going on, he could quickly leave his car and join me in my rental so we could work in closer with that vehicle. It sounded a little bulky, but it was his state and he was sharing his time with me, so I agreed. With hearty "good lucks" all around, off we went into the dark of the morning with visions of lots of dove hunters doing the wrong things.

Not far from Arrow Rock the two of us pulled our vehicles onto an abandoned farm road, got out, and listened for the telltale heavy shooting of a many-person dove hunt. It wasn't long in coming. Just to the north I heard three quick shots, as did my partner, who pointed in the direction from which they had come. For the next ten minutes or so we just listened to the shooting going on around us while we decided which group of gunners we would work based on the frequency of shooting. There seemed to be at least six gunners to the north who were doing a lot of shooting, and that was finally the direction we headed. I led in the unmarked car, and my partner followed some distance behind me so as not to give us away if we inadvertently drove right up on our hunters in front of God and everybody. Driving and stopping every mile or so, we finally echo-located the shooting in a small field surrounded by trees behind a clump of dilapidated farm buildings that had seen better days. Parked in and around the old abandoned farmhouse were four pickup trucks, which I assumed belonged to our dove hunters.

My partner parked his car out of sight along the gravel road leading in to the farm buildings and got in my car with me. We drove to within one hundred yards of the parked pickups, stopped, and got out to proceed the rest of the way by "shank's mare." Slipping into the parking area, we looked inside the pickup cabs and saw empty shotgun-shell boxes, leather gun cases, and the like, all indicating shooters in the field. Recording their license plates and vehicle makes in case they ran from us and got back to their trucks before we did, we moved on. Sneaking around an old, partially collapsed barn, the old mail-order kind one could get from Sears around 1918, I crawled into a pile of abandoned rusting farm machinery. My partner, fearing snakes, stayed back by the barn, where he could see the ground better. By agreement, I took the three shooters on the east side of the field and my partner took the three on the west. That way it would be easier to count the number of birds the lads were killing, and the two of us were close enough together that each of us could clearly hear a hushed voice from the other.

Our lads were shooting dove over a watermelon field and seemed to be doing quite well. That is, a lot of dove were falling to their better-than-average shooting, but none of them had dogs, so finding the dead dove in the heavy growth of the melon field was proving problematic. Getting out my notebook and laying it on a cast-iron tractor seat, I began to take notes on the number of shots fired and number of dove killed by each shooter. Resting my elbows on the rear tractor tire, I could plainly observe the lads through my binoculars, and it was a piece of cake seeing and recording the morning's events. The dove were pouring into the field as if it was baited, but I was unfamiliar with watermelons and what they might have to offer to the dove, so I let the question sit on the back burner of my mind. More and more birds fell until I had at least five over the limit for each of my shooters. Because they had been shooting for at least thirty minutes before we arrived, they probably had even more. Turning to my partner, I asked in a hushed voice if his lads had exceeded the limit yet. He had not been keeping notes, just watching—but he said he felt his three shooters had killed plenty of birds as well. Damn, I thought. He should be keeping notes in case he has to testify later in court. Oh well, when in Rome. ...

Since his lads were closer, I suggested that he move to my pile of farm machinery and wait for them to return to their pickups in case they had the inclination to run once they figured out who I was. In the meantime, I would take my ever-present shotgun and walk out to my lads as if I belonged there and was going hunting myself. Once I had grabbed my chaps, the plan was for him to show himself and move to his shooters in a perfect pincher move. He nodded in agreement as he moved to the farm machinery, still on the lookout for snakes, and I quietly crawled to a grove of trees from which I could emerge like one of the boys and head for the east end of the field. Walking casually out of the brush and trees, I headed down the farm road around the melon patch as if I owned the place. It was a few moments before the lads took any notice of me through their killing veil, and since I was carrying a shotgun and looked like one of them, they gave me only a passing glance. Only when I turned the corner on the farm road toward my shooters did they stop shooting and begin talking with each other as if asking who this new shooter might be. I continued toward them, kneeling occasionally when a dove came within shotgun range as if I were going to shoot. My three fellows quit shooting altogether and just watched my advance. Finally one of them broke and ran off into the brush and timber, leaving his two partners to nervously watch me coming toward them. By now the lads on the west side of the field had quit shooting as well and were staring at me as I approached their buddies. Finally reaching the two remaining shooters, I took out my badge and credentials and identified myself. With that, the three lads to the west picked up their dove and hurried to their vehicles, only to run right into my game warden friend. With the exception of my single runner, a perfect plan, I thought.

"How you boys doing?" I asked.

"All right," came the rather weak reply.

They had that right, I thought, looking at the rather large pile of dead dove at their feet, which were already attracting the inevitable ants. "How many you got?" I asked.

"Don't rightly know," replied the tall, thin one.

"Well, why don't we find out?" I replied. Thirty-two and thirty-six dove later, respectively, they were both over the limit of fifteen. "Why don't you boys dig out your hunting licenses and driver's licenses while I check your shotguns for plugs," I said. Without a word both men took out their wallets while I checked their shotguns, only to find both of them lawfully plugged (a plug is a device that limits the magazine capacity to two). Their licenses showed that both men were from the small town of Napton, and both professed to be farmers. "Who was the lad who ran off into the woods just before I arrived?" I asked. Silence greeted my ears. Repeating the question, I threw in the possibility of both lads going to jail instead of being issued a citation for their over-limits, and it was amazing how quickly their memories improved.

"Dale Peterson," the short one blurted out. The tall one looked at his partner as if he were the worst thing that crawled on the earth for giving away his runaway buddy. The short one defended himself by saying, "Look, I am on probation for beating the hell out of my wife. I can't afford to get into any more trouble of any kind, so to hell with Dale."

The tall one shrugged, and I said, "Why don't one of you go into the timber and bring him back for me before I make it any tougher for him."

My two chaps looked at one another, and then the short one turned and walked off into the typical tangled Missouri woods. I still held his shotgun and his licenses, so I knew he wouldn't run. I began to count the dove that had been shot by the man who had run off. It was easy to see why he had run. He had forty-four dove in two piles next to his shooting stand. Writing up the information on Bell, the tall fellow, I was somewhat surprised to see John, the short hunter, coming back through the brush and trees with the lad who had taken off. Usually when you have a runner, he ends up at the county line before stopping for a breather! Soon they joined us at the edge of the melon patch, and I went through the song and dance of identification, checking Dale's shotgun for a plug, and requesting licenses. I found that my runner didn't have a hunting license and that he had been using an unplugged shotgun. Writing up my other lads up for the over-limits, I suggested we comb the fields for any more dove that might be injured or dead among the watermelon vines.

The three lads just looked at me, and then Dale said, "I am not going out in that field. It is full of rattlesnakes this time of the year, and screw you, I am not going out into that."

"We aren't either," came the collective reply from John and Bell. Still hanging on to their licenses, I walked over to a nearby bush at the edge of the farm road and broke off a long stick. Telling the lads to sit down on the road, I slowly walked out into the melon field with my "snake stick" poking along ahead of me, looking for dead or dying dove. Man, did I get a surprise. The watermelon field was full of wheat seed! The damn area was baited just as tight as a tick. No wonder the lads had tried to scare me off with that snake story. Not saying anything after getting over my initial amazement, I continued to poke around and in about thirty minutes discovered another thirteen dead dove. Satisfied that I had found most of their losses, I quietly walked back to my hunters and, referring to my notes on who had shot or killed what, added the thirteen dove to the totals for the respective shooters and hence adding to their over-limits.

Gathering up all the dove, ants and all, I loaded them into the game bag on my hunting jacket, and the four of us walked back to the farmhouse where the pickups were parked. Back at the vehicles I met my partner happily counting out his three shooters for over-limits as well. Not bad for the first contact of the day, I thought—six lads, and all six good for over-limit cases. I waited until my partner was finished and then asked all the hunters to sit on the tailgates of two pickups. They, along with my partner, gave me strange looks but did as I requested.

"Now, gentlemen, while combing that melon field for any dove that had been killed and missed, I discovered the ground to be covered with wheat seed."

Not a soul moved, nor did their eyes, including those of my partner.

"Who put the seed out?" I asked.

Silence once more.

"Well, here is where we are, gentlemen. I want to know who put the wheat out into the field, making it a baited field. If it was one of you, I want to know. If it was all of you, I want to know that as well. Well, I am waiting," I said as I quietly looked each man in the eyes.

There was silence for the longest time; in fact, I was getting ready to make another run at them, figuring no one was going to talk, when Bell said, "I put it out, Officer. This is my uncle's land, and I knew he wouldn't mind, so I put it out so we all could have a hunt of a lifetime."

"Well, before this is said and done, you all will get a hunt of a lifetime," I said as I dug out my notebook and quietly recorded what had just been said. After recording our exchange, I asked, "Now, gentlemen, how many of you knew the field was baited and shot over it knowing that?"

Again, there was silence for a few moments, and then all of them admitted to knowing about the bait before they had shot over the field.

"OK," I said, "I appreciate all of you being so truthful and acting like men in taking your medicine. As a result of the bait and all of you shooting over it, all of you will receive an additional citation for shooting over a baited area." No one even blinked. I must say, for being so deep into the slop, they took it quite well. "One last thing, boys," I continued. "The area is a baited area and cannot be shot again until ten days after all the grain or lure and attractant is gone. I would say, for that field anyway, that to hunt dove over it anytime during the rest of the season would again place you in legal jeopardy, so I would suggest abstinence. Do we understand each other?"

They all nodded. We finished with our lads, let them go, and then walked back to our vehicles and brought them into the farmyard. We bagged up all our evidence dove and placed them in an ice chest so they wouldn't spoil. It was then that I was able to see how my partner had fared. His three lads had all shot over-limits, and every one of them lacked a valid hunting license to boot! Suffice it to say, we had had a very fine morning for the relatively small amount of time we had put into our scouting effort so far. The two of us went out into the melon field to view and record the bait. It was scattered in patches throughout the small melon field but in substantial quantities. We gathered fresh wheat from several places in the field and documented it with the camera and drawings in my notebook. All the while that we were moving around the field, the dove continued to pour in as if there was no tomorrow. For the coolerful of dead dove in our vehicles, there wasn't! For the life of me, I never understood why someone would want to shoot over a baited field. It was so unfair and unsportsmanlike, and to stoop so low really showed humankind's true predatory colors. To have all the advantage over the little dove and then add the bait as an extra killing measure certainly showed what humans are made of—and many times its smell can be detected downwind for miles. ...

For the rest of the day my partner and I wandered throughout the Boonville area, catching the usual road hunter and occasional hunter without a license, but all in all it was pretty tame. That evening, as we prepared to work dove hunters shooting after sunset (taking of migratory game birds must end at sunset), we came down a long, narrow, one-way dirt road leading to another old, deserted farm. I stopped by the gate, which was chained shut with a large lock. For the last half-mile or so I had noticed fresh "No Hunting" signs posted about every hundred feet. Every time I saw "No Hunting" signs at such close intervals, I became suspicious. It was a sign that whatever "they" were doing behind their locked gates and signs was of such a nature that they had to be extra-exclusionary in order to get it done! Also, each sign had been signed off with the name, "Sheriffs' Gun Club." I figured that language was meant to scare even the most stronghearted away from poaching the area, or maybe even from looking in on the chaps in a neighborly sort of way.

I could not see any farm buildings, but I surmised they would be at the end of the road past the locked gate. My partner and I parked our cars at the gate; we could see from the tire tracks on the dusty road that a lot of traffic had recently passed through the gate.

Because it was very hot, we got out a couple of soft drinks and just stood there enjoying them while we listened. It was about time for the dove hunters to come back out into the fields for the evening shoot, so we just held tight, hoping to echo-locate another bunch of hunters.

Around four in the afternoon, shooting began in the timber behind the locked gate, perhaps half a mile or three-quarters of a mile away. At first it was occasional, but then it grew into a barrage that could only mean someone was having one hell of a good time at the expense of the dove. I quickly drained my second soda and threw the empty can into my vehicle. Walking up to the lock, I turned it over to get the lock and key identification numbers to see if any of the keys I carried from my California days would fit. To my surprise, the entire identification system had been filed off! This was another clue that whoever was behind this locked gate wanted no one there but their own heartbeats. Well, we will see about that, I thought as I strode to the trunk of my vehicle and opened it. There in a military duffel bag lay my "master key"—in this case was a forty-inch set of hardened steel bolt cutters.

You may be wondering how the hell I could go behind a locked gate on property that was posted against trespass. Simple! The Migratory Bird Treaty Act was intended by Congress to be a conservation law. An officer cannot conserve wildlife if he has to get permission to go in and check a shooting affair when he has good reason to suspect that hunting of migratory birds is going on. If he did, the damage would be over and hidden by the time he got there. That would not help conserve these species! So congressional intent, later backed up with a blizzard of case law, allows a federal officer to legally go behind locked gates or onto fenced lands if he suspects that the hunting or killing of migratory birds is taking place—even if state law prohibits that kind of trespass. In the legal scheme of things, federal law, based on the Constitution, supersedes state law, which supersedes local or county laws. In our particular case, dove season was on; this area was commonly hunted for dove; my partner knew that the lads behind the locked gate were peace officers who often hunted dove, turkey, and deer on their club; there were shotguns going off in large numbers;

and we had seen a lot of dove flying to and fro in the area. That was plenty of reason for me to go and check, and so, with my "master key" in hand, I headed briskly for the locked gate

"Whoa, where the hell are you going?" asked my obviously worried partner.

"I am going to cut a link of chain holding the lock and go in and check those lads having one hell of a shoot at the end of the road," I said without breaking stride.

"You can't do that," he barked.

"Yes, I can," I retorted, fastening the bolt cutters to the link of chain nearest to the lock. The government would be liable civilly for any damage caused by my actions, so I knew to limit the damage to just one broken link of chain.

By now my partner was having a fit! He ran to the gate and said, "There is no way this can legally be done, and I won't stand for it!"

Another barrage of about fifteen shots told me there was plenty of reason to go look, and I was not to be deterred. "What is the problem?" I asked.

"I will get my tail end fired if I go in there with you after you cut the chain!"

"Well, that is not a problem. Ed said to protect you folks from local politics, and I can do that. Why don't you work those other shooters we can hear back in the direction we just came from, and I will tend to this. We can meet at that little country grocery store at the crossroads we just passed when we're both finished."

He just looked at me as if he had seen a ghost and backed away from the gate. "If you continue to do what I think you are going to do, I can't work with you," he said.

Now I felt that this chap was validating my feelings from our first meeting. He was apparently selective in his law enforcement practices, and peace officers were among those he didn't want to bother. "Is there some reason besides the politics that you can't go into this hunting club and check the members?" I asked.

"You bet there is. These are the guys who might have to back me up someday, and I don't ever want to queer that. Even if they take a few too many, it ain't worth going in there and stirring them up! Those are federal birds, and I ain't going to queer my local law enforcement relations because I pinched them for a few lousy birds over the limit."

By now the shooting at the end of the road was hot and heavy, heavier than we had heard all day, and by damn, there was no reason I wasn't going in there for a look. Partner or no partner, I felt that what was going on behind that locked gate was wrong, dead wrong, and I needed to get in there and square it away. "Do what you have to do," I said as the jaws of the bolt cutter severed the link of chain. Before I had put away my bolt cutters, he was gone in a cloud of dust, and I didn't see him again the rest of the time I was in Missouri—and neither did Ed Nichols.

Swinging open the gate, I drove through and then shut the gate behind me. Driving slowly with my windows down and the air conditioner off, I listened to the sounds of the shooting as I cruised down the road. Getting to within about a quarter of a mile of the still going-strong shooting, I parked the car off the road, grabbed my gear, and headed for the source of my concern. Within several hundred yards I came to an old farmhouse that had been fixed up into a hunting camp. There were eight vehicles parked around the building, and the shooting appeared to be coming from an open area maybe another hundred yards from the clubhouse. As I slowly walked by the clubhouse, I looked into the kitchen and saw that in the sink, guts, feathers, hide, and all, were at least one hundred dove waiting to be cleaned! Holy catfish, I couldn't believe my eyes! Raising my binoculars, I confirmed what I had just seen and shook my head. If these lads had had a shoot like that in the morning and were now doing it again, there would be more than enough over-limits to go around, I thought. Now I wished my partner had not flown the coop! Moving slowly past the clubhouse and staying hidden in a row of trees along the road leading to the field, I continued moving toward the guns. Soon, in the failing light, I could see eight hunters having one hell of a dove shoot. They had surrounded a small weed field, and as the dove poured into it for their night's feeding, many fell to the guns. And there were some damn fine shooters in the group! Realizing there was no way to accurately count drops now that these fellows had been going at it for some time, I retreated to the clubhouse, hid myself, and just waited for the lads to arrive with their afternoon's birds.

Soon the shooting slackened as the twilight turned to darkness. One by one, the shooters came walking back to the clubhouse, and one by one, I was able to ambush them, so to speak, without alerting any of the others. In about thirty minutes I had contacted eight hunters, and every last one of them had a legal limit. That made it very interesting, especially in light of the pile of dove still in the kitchen sink. Also, when I gathered up their hunting and driver's licenses, every one of them turned out to be a deputy sheriff or some other form of peace officer! Once I had all the somewhat surprised men gathered in one place, the nine of us walked back to the club-house. Once we were all inside, I asked how long the lads had been hunting. They said they had arrived the night before, and that day had been their first day of hunting. I asked that question because in those days, a hunter could have a bag limit and a possession limit in their possession, and the possession limit on the second day of hunt-ing was usually double the daily bag limit. So, with a fifteen-bird daily bag limit, one could possess twice that many birds if one had hunted at least two days and had shot the limit both days.

After I settled that point, I pointed to the dove in the sink and said, "Are those this morning's birds, then?"

No one said anything for a moment; they just looked at each other as if to say, "Oh, crap." Finally a gray-headed gentleman said, "Well, I guess those are ours as well."

"Do you have a bucket or something like that so I can count them?" I asked. Reaching under the sink, he took out a garbage bucket, and I began to count the dove into it. There were exactly 120 dove in the sink, or a legal limit for each man, all taken in the morning shoot. The 120 dove from the sink plus the evening's shoot of another 120 put the lads slightly over! I explained that I was going to have to seize their birds and that they would all be issued citations for federal court. *Not a man blinked an eye!* They were all gentlemen, and not one asked for any "professional consideration," as is often the case when one officer arrests another. But something was wrong! These fellows were just too calm and acted as if they were not trying to provoke me any further than the current situation. It was as if they were hiding something, but I'd be damned if I could put my finger on it.

When I finished all the information gathering and handing out evidence receipts, I asked if I could look in their ice chests, refrigerator, oven, and the like. I was given the green light and went ahead but found nothing other than the usual food and drink. Borrowing a garbage bag (I offered to pay for it, but they refused), I loaded up my evidence birds and headed down the darkened road with a cloud of questions hanging over my head. These lads had been just too nice and not nearly pissed enough at having been caught by another officer. Not one of them had even asked what this would do to their records or jobs. In short, they had been as quiet as a bunch of mice pissin' on a ball of cotton! I couldn't figure it out as I put the dove in another ice chest and iced them down. Heading home, I stopped at the old grocery store at the crossroads to look for my partner. He was nowhere to be seen, and I wasn't surprised. I went inside and bought some more ice for my evidence, along with several plugs of Brown's Mule chewing tobacco. I always made it a point when traveling in different parts of the country to sample the home cooking and the local brands of chewing tobacco. Man, that policy was a mistake that evening. I was hot and dehydrated, not to mention damn hungry since I hadn't eaten for many a long hour. Chewing that damn Brown's Mule, I about died. Now, I can chew with the best of them, and even better than most. But I guess I should have known that tobacco as black as a lump of asphalt would have a kick just like a mule. Before long I spat it out the window as I headed for the motel and had not only double vision but a rolling gut to match! I somehow made it back to my motel room and, after icing down the dove one more time, skipped dinner and wobbled off to bed.

After I had lain in bed for a while waiting for the room to quit pitching around like a canoe in a Type 8 gale, the answer to my questions hit me! With shooting like that, those peace officers must have had some help. Bait! Doggone it, they had to have been shooting over a baited field! That would explain the huge number of birds killed and the shooters' laid-back attitudes. They had been quiet in the hope that I would not go back to the field and find the bait. Flying out of bed and damn near hitting the wall as the load of nicotine in my blood hit me again, I climbed back into my dirty clothes and headed out to the car. Backtracking along the backcountry roads, I parked my car out of the way on an old logging road and walked to the gate at the head of the road. It was locked once again and this time with a lock and chain that could have been used to anchor the battleship *Missouri!* That was OK, I thought. The chain was not big enough to stop the bolt cutters if needed. I crawled over the gate and began the long walk into the shooting club.

By the time I reached the clubhouse, all the lights were out and my lads were asleep. Thank God they didn't have any dogs or it would have been hard for me to get by into the field. Once there and after checking in the direction of the clubhouse, I turned on my flashlight and, with diffused light pouring through my fingers, began to look for bait. I didn't have to look long. The center portion of the weed field had been bush hogged, or chopped into fine duff. By keeping the bush hogging to the center, they had basically kept it out of sight of the casual investigator. That arrangement in and of itself would have been enough for a baiting case, but they had had to further sweeten the pot. Scattered around on the ground, in some places just as it had been dumped out of a bucket, were strings and piles of wheat! Walking the entire field, I guessed about one thousand pounds of wheat had been dumped to make their dove hunt memorable. Well, they would soon get their wish, I quietly said to myself through a tight set of lips.

After gathering about a dozen samples of wheat and weed seeds from around the field, I photographed the worst piles and then headed back. Sneaking back by the clubhouse, I almost had a seizure when, just as I walked by the back porch, I noticed a man standing there not twenty feet away! I froze and stood there waiting to be discovered or shot at, or both. Finally I could hear a sound that brought gladness to my heart and slowed its beating down a bit. The lad was urinating over the back porch rail. Thank God my dad had taught me to walk like an Indian, especially when it counted. It certainly counted in this case as my heart rate returned to normal and the man returned to his bed. Man, that was too close for creature comfort, I thought as I picked up the pace and got the hell out of there with my bait samples and secret.

About two in the morning I was sitting in a brush pile at the club-house end of the baited field. That position allowed me to watch every shooter from a clear field and record all of their shootings. One has only to take or attempt to take (one does not have to kill) one migratory bird over a baited area for the law to be broken. I was going to try to stick to that as closely as I could in order to keep the killing down, make my case, and get the hell out of there. This time I would bet a plug of that old Brown's Mule there would be hot cops on the town tonight.

Right at daylight I heard my lads walking down the road talking about their rotten luck at having been pinched the night before, the hunt today, and how they would make up for the birds they had lost to that damn game warden! The shooting got started right on time, one-half hour before sunrise, and by sunrise I had recorded every hunter killing at least one bird, and most more. The dove, like any game bird that has been baited, came in like bees. They cared little about the danger: even if someone was shooting at them, they were coming in to feed, and the devil be damned! If they got shot at by one lad who missed, they just headed for a different part of the field and got killed by another. Having what I needed for a court of law, I crawled out of my brush pile and came face to face with a pissed-off rattlesnake not three feet away. Freezing, I now wished for a damn good mouthful of that Brown's Mule! Then I could see just see how tough this snake really was with a load of juice right on top of his head. ... Instead we considered each other for the longest time before the snake sidled off and I realized how hot the day was going to be, based on the wall of sweat rolling off my forehead.

Standing up, I walked to the nearest lad, who didn't see me coming. When he turned in response to my good-morning, he damn near froze his heart. Asking him to unload his shotgun, I yelled at the rest to get their attention and then beckoned them to come to me. Man, you talk about a come-to-Jesus meeting! I had all the lads walk out into the field with me as I showed them the bait. There wasn't a chirp out of any of them, just a bunch of tight jaws. Then, standing in the middle of the field with hundreds of dove whistling in all around us, I explained the federal laws as they pertained to baiting and hunting migratory game birds over a baited area. I said, "Well, lads, who put the bait out?"

The gray-haired guy, after kicking the duff for a while, finally said, "Look, we all put the wheat seeds out. We have only had marginal hunts in this area in the past and finally decided we would do like everyone else and put some food out to see what kind of a shoot we would have. We never dreamed it would lead us to taking over-limits or the passel of trouble we are in today." About that time several of the lads began to pop their lips like a grizzly in a day bed and ask for some kind of consideration, officer to officer. Two of them even went so far as to tell me how they had helped game wardens in the past and that they should get some kind of consideration now, especially in light of the over-limit tickets they had received the night before.

"Gentlemen," I said, "did everyone help in placing out the wheat?" Heads nodded all around in the affirmative. "Then, since every one of you hunted over the baited area yesterday and today, I will give you some consideration and write you only for today's errors." That seemed to make them happy until I told them of the restriction on their further hunting in this area, which was prohibited until all the lure and attractant existing in the field was gone, plus a ten-day waiting period after that. Man, you should have heard the howls! With a wave of my hand I said, "That is the law of the land, gentlemen. I don't make them, and anyone caught hunting over this field for migratory game birds until that situation has been met will visit the federal magistrate again. Now, since I have all the information on all of you, I won't need to go through that drill once more. However, all of you will again lose all your birds because they were taken unlawfully."

The grumbling had stopped, so I gathered all the birds, putting them into my game bag, and walked with the lads back to the club-house. There I issued evidence seizure tags for the dove I had taken minutes before and responded to a few more questions about the baited area. Sensing they had had enough of me and having no further business with them, I collected my things and left. As I walked back to my car with thoughts of a huge breakfast somewhere, since I hadn't eaten anything from the morning before, there was a smile on my tired face. They had been given some consideration, or at least they had thought so. But the real reason I hadn't cited them for the day before was that I hadn't taken the time that day to record and observe each and every one of them shooting or killing the dove over the baited area. That type of evidence is what it takes to make a baiting case, to my way of thinking, and since I hadn't known then that the field was baited, I hadn't taken the time to collect the needed data. Nonetheless, my apparent generosity in overlooking the previous day had made the club members happy. I suppose some attorney probably could have stretched the case to include that first day of shooting because of the dove in their possession, but in my opinion it would have been a thin pinch. I like the bird in the hand before I go after the one in the bush, if you get my meaning. Driving away from the club, I found a typical Southern mom-and-pop restaurant that was serving up fried chicken, mashed potatoes, homemade gravy, fresh peas, and pie. Talk about putting a dent in those grits—I put such a dent in that lunch that I paid the old folks double just to make things even. Then, because it was now the heat of the day and dove hunting had slowed, I headed back to the motel for some much-needed sleep.

That afternoon I worked to the south and west in the Windsor area checking little groups of dove hunters. I was unsuccessful in finding any big groups of hunters or any areas where a lot of shooting was going on, so I continued to work the back farm lots and the like for lone hunters or small groups. The heat and humidity continued as expected, and soon I was soaked with sweat after walking sometimes many hundreds of yards to check the hunters in the outback. There sure was something to be said for having a local game warden along as a guide. About four P.M. I located some pretty steady shooting by what I determined to be two shotguns and started working that way. After running down several roads that turned out to be wrong, I located the right one, which was near a little backwater slough and spotted two lads shooting the dove out of the trees as they came to the water for their evening drinks. Moving as close as I could, I hid in a row of trees and began counting the number of birds each man killed. Soon each man had killed fifteen by my count. That told me that the lads probably had over limits because they had been shooting before my arrival. Working closer on my hands and knees, I finally located their vehicle and, since I was still able to watch them, set up shop there. That way, if they waited until after dark to stop, I would be able to intercept them as they headed for their transportation home.

Soon daylight left the sky. The shooting had ceased, and as near as I could tell, my lads were cleaning their dove alongside the small slough. It was quiet for a while, and then I heard a loud, long *boooom, boooom!* I took a look with my binoculars in the dimming light, but I could see nothing—no movement, nothing. But when a shotgun makes a long sound like the one I had just heard, I knew someone was shooting over water. *Boooom, boooom, boooom, boooom ... boooom!* That time both shooters were firing, and I glimpsed a wood duck as it flared, climbed up from the slough, and headed out through a copse of trees as fast as its broad, paddlelike wings would take it. *Damn,* I thought, they are shooting ducks! There was no duck season open. I scrambled for a better view by standing alongside their pickup and looking through the windows. From my vantage point I could now see both hunters as they crouched by some brush alongside the slough. Then both rose in the binoculars, and I could see flame shoot out the ends of the shotgun barrels as four more wood ducks shot skyward to avoid the shooters below them. *Booooom, boooom, boooom, boooom* went their shotguns as two ducks froze in midflight and then pitched to the ground to fly no more. One of the lads ran out into the field, picked up two birds, the last two killed, I thought, and then sprinted back into cover as his partner rose and fired two more shots at six ducks coming into the slough.

As it got darker I could see less and less of my shooters, but I could still see the flame shooting out the ends of their shotgun barrels as they rose to shoot at what must have been more incoming ducks. Soon it got too dark to shoot, and all was quiet along the waters of the slough. One hour passed, and then another. Still no one showed up at the pickup, and I began to wonder if I had the right truck. Then I heard the unmistakable sound of two muffled voices coming my way. Soon I could hear footsteps, and I prepared my flashlight and made sure my pistol had not fallen out of its holster when I crawled to the pickup. I was ready. Then the footsteps and talking stopped, and I heard nothing for about twenty minutes. Probably standing off at a distance and watching their truck to make sure no one is waiting there for them, I thought. When they were satisfied that all was clear, I again heard the low talking and footsteps as the two approached the truck. When they arrived, they tossed a bunch of gear into the bed of the truck and then unloaded their shotguns. Opening the truck doors, they put their shotguns into gun cases and slid them in behind the seat. As the driver started to get in, I stepped out of the brush and in two quick steps was at his side.

"Holy jumping Jesus, who are you?" came a surprised yell when he saw me at his side.

"Federal agent. Hand me your keys, please," I replied as my flashlight beam struck him dead in the eyes, wrecking any night vision he had previously had. Putting his hands up to shield his eyes, he handed me his truck keys as his buddy just stood on the other side of the pickup in shock, not knowing what to do. Switching my beam of light to his eyes for a quick moment, I instructed that lad to sit down in the pickup, which he promptly did. Good, I thought; things are pretty much under control. Getting out my credentials, I identified myself and asked how the hunting had been.

"It was good," replied the driver, who was later identified as Randel Cummings from Calhoun, Missouri.

"What does 'good' mean?" I asked.

"We got our limits," Randel replied.

"May I see the birds?"

Randel got out of the truck, as did his partner, an older man named Rufus James, who was from Bowen, if I remember correctly. They walked back to the bed of the pickup, lifted out their hunting coats, and removed two plastic sacks from their game bags of totally picked and cleaned dove. Laying the carcasses out on the tailgate, I counted fifteen in each sack, or a legal limit.

"Where are the rest of the birds, boys?" I asked.

"What birds? Those are all we have," replied Randel. I quietly looked first at Randel and then at Rufus without saying a word. Rufus looked away, but Randel stared hard at me as if to assert, "I am innocent."

Taking a different tack, I said, "May I see your hunting and driving licenses, please?" The licenses were quickly produced and, sticking them in my shirt pocket, said, "Now, what is going to happen when we backtrack your footprints in the soft dirt of this plowed field?"

For just a second there was a fleeting look of alarm in Rufus's eyes, and then he got busy examining something very important on his shoes. Randel said, "If you find anything, it ain't ours."

That statement told me what I wanted to know, and I said, "Let's go, boys."

"Where?" asked Randel in a worried voice.

"We are going to backtrack your footprints clear back to the slough if we have to because I saw the both of you not only shoot an over-limit each of dove but kill some ducks as well!"

That statement hit the lads like a thunderclap! "We didn't do any such thing," came Randel's not-so-truthful-sounding denial.

"Let's not sit here and argue," I said. "Let's just backtrack you lads and see for ourselves. Let's go." With my flashlight beam pointing the way I wanted to go, I let my two lads lead the way. We hadn't gone twenty yards when we came to several plastic sacks lying in the dust. Two sacks were like the ones back at the truck with the picked and cleaned dove. One held eleven picked and cleaned dove and the other eight. There were also two plastic bread bags, each containing the dark-colored breast meat of five and six ducks, respectively. "What do we have here, boys?" I asked. "Before you respond, take a look around. There are only two sets of tracks leading from here to the truck, and if you lads look at the soles of your shoes, you will see by the footprints that they are yours. So let's not lie. I need the both of you to lead me back to the gut and feather piles so I can identify what was killed. If you choose not to, that is all right because I am going to do it anyway. Either way, I will discover what you the two of you did, and the federal court will be informed accordingly." With that, I just looked at my two lads in the light of the flashlight and waited. They looked at one another, and Rufus started walking back into the field toward where they had been hunting. After a moment's hesitation Randel followed, and I brought up the rear, using my flashlight beam to illuminate the way for all of us.

Twenty or so minutes later we arrived at the slough. There at the edge of the water where I had last seen my chaps shooting lay several piles of shotgun shells and a large pile of dove guts and feathers. There were no duck feathers or carcasses to be seen. I flashed my light around the brush pile, still without finding any duck feathers. Having taught waterfowl identification for years in the National Academy and worked for years before that in a waterfowl district, I knew breasted-out duck meat when I saw it, so I knew the remains had to be in the area somewhere. Then, out of the corner of my eye, I saw movement in the slough. Shining my flashlight into the water, I saw a turtle of some kind tugging on a floating wood duck carcass. Flashing the beam farther around the waters of the slough, I counted eleven floating wood duck carcasses. I looked over at my two lads, but all they did was look at their feet.

"Fish them out, boys," I said.

"What?" came a dual reply.

"Take your shoes off, and pants as well, and fish those duck carcasses out of the water."

The two lads just looked at me, and Rufus said, "Ain't no way I am going in there!" With that he took several steps back, and if I had insisted on him going for a night swim in those black waters, he would have run all the way home. I couldn't blame him because I wasn't too keen on going in there myself. But a rustling beside me told me Randel was taking off his shoes and pants, and in a few moments he was wading in the pond up to his waist and picking up the duck carcasses.

"Thank you," I said, as he put his clothes back on after laying the duck carcasses at my feet. I gathered them up, and the three of us walked back to the car. At that point the two lads began to lighten up and laugh a little about their situation. The only thing that still bothered them was the worry that their wives might find out about their little error in judgment. So after I took down the information I needed to issue the citations, I made sure the mailing addresses where the citations would be sent were their places of work instead of home. That seemed to satisfy them, and after letting each know that they would receive citations for the over-limits and for taking ducks during the closed season, I issued the usual evidence receipts for the dove and ducks and let them go on their way.

After watching them leave, I gathered up my load of dove and duck carcasses and headed back to my still hidden car. Once at the car, I sat recording the day's events in my notebook in case I ended up in court to testify against my two chaps. When I was finished I got out of the car, opened the trunk, placed the dove and duck breasts in a cooler along with their evidence tags, and iced them down. Then I sacked up the duck carcasses, tagged them, and put them in a separate cooler.

Ka-boom echoed the sound of a very close-by rifle shot! Slamming the trunk and dropping to the ground, I grabbed my pistol from the holster and tried to echo-locate the direction of the shooting. *Ka-boom* went the heavy sound again, and it seemed to be coming from the field I had just come from. Jumping up as I realized I was not the one being shot at, I grabbed my binoculars just in time to see the lights of a vehicle go out not far from where I had caught my two dove and duck shooters. I had been so busy recording in my note-book and tagging my evidence that I had not seen or heard a vehicle enter the field. Apparently whoever was there had just discharged what sounded like a heavy rifle. Whatever that person was shooting at, there certainly wasn't an open season—unless it was for raccoons, and they were usually taken with a light rifle or pistol!

Using my binoculars to scan a spot some thirty to forty yards away where I guessed the shot had come from, I saw nothing. Straining my ears, I was at first rewarded with silence. Then I could hear what sounded like two men grunting as if they were lifting something heavy and then a loud *ka-plunk* as that heavy load hit what sounded like the bed of a pickup. I thought, I bet those lads have just spot-lighted, killed, and loaded a deer! Then I heard two doors slam and a vehicle start up. It drove out of the field without using any head-lights. Running down the road on which my car was parked toward the road leading into the shooters' field, I cussed the fact that I was not a credentialed state Fish and Game officer in Missouri! This was obviously a state matter and not one covered under my federal au-thority. Oh well, I thought; I will just have to make a citizen's arrest and hope it sticks.

About that time the darkened form of a pickup using its parking lights turned down the road on which I was running and came my way! Diving off to one side of the road and hoping I wouldn't land on one of Missouri's many rattlesnakes, I knelt and watched it. The pickup passed me, moving slowly, and I could make out the forms of two lads inside the cab by the lights of their cigarettes. A moment later they realized my car was in the road on which they were traveling, and on came their taillights, followed moments later by their headlights. Their stunned silence was broken when a large form that had been jogging down the road after them stepped up on the running board on the driver's side and announced through an open window who their "passenger" was. As I did that, I took a quick look in the back of the truck and was rewarded with the sight of the still twitching form of a large, ungutted white-tailed buck deer. In that same microsecond the driver threw the truck into reverse and gunned the pickup backward, throwing me off into the dirt. Rolling and coming up at a run, I took off after the two lads as they screamed down the dirt road in reverse, leaving great clouds of dust in the process. *Crunch!* The sound of metal objecting as it hit an immovable object reached my ears, as did the instant changing of gears and the screaming of spinning tires going nowhere. Running as fast as I could, I hit the driver in the face with the light from my five-cell flashlight, temporarily blinding him, jerked open the door in the same instant, and hurled his hind end out into the dust-filled air and onto the road with a *whump!*

The passenger, seeing his friend disappear right before his eyes, started yelling, "Don't shoot, don't shoot!"

Seeing he was frozen with fear, I quickly turned my attention to the stunned man on the road and grabbed his flailing carcass before he decided to split. "Federal agent; you are under arrest!" I yelled.

My fellow in the dirt went limp and said, "I surrender; please don't hurt me; I surrender."

Lifting him up off the ground with the strength that comes from the heat of the moment, I marched him back to the pickup and, still holding on with one hand, reached in with the other, turned off the still running engine, and removed the keys. My passenger was still frozen to the seat and in fact had wet his pants, he was so scared. I spread-eagled my man on the front of the truck, quickly searched him, and handcuffed him. Holding on to him with one hand, I beckoned for his partner to exit the truck, which he hastily did. I searched him (other then the urine-soaked areas), handcuffed him with my second set of handcuffs, and sat him down in the dirt in front of the truck.

Now that the emotion of the moment was over, I took a look at the situation. The pickup in the hurry to escape backward down the road had run over a small tree and high-centered on an old stump. My two lads both appeared to be in their early twenties and were desperately in need of baths, haircuts, and several damn good meals! Their dress was hardly that of someone making it, and their pickup was a beat-up 1950s Chevy that had seen better days. Inside the pickup was an old handheld spotlight that had been hot-wired to some wires under the dash. Lying on the floor was a pre-1964 Winchester bolt-action rifle, caliber .308, and several spent cartridges. And, as I said earlier, there was a large, ungutted white-tailed buck, eight point (eastern count), weighing in at about 240 pounds, in the back of the truck.

Not having my state game warden buddy to assist, I loaded my two lads into the front and back seats of the rental car (one as a passenger, one sitting behind the passenger) and then loaded the buck, hide, horns, howl, and all in the back seat directly behind me. That had to make some picture, hot-footing it down the road with three humans in a car with a large white tail riding in the back seat with its head resting on the back of the front seat! Their rifle and spotlight went into my already crowded trunk, and down the road we went. I came to a combination gas station and small mom-and-pop grocery store and stopped. Asking the owner to call the local deputy sheriff to transport some prisoners caught poaching a deer, I went back outside and waited with my lads for his arrival. About thirty minutes later the deputy arrived, and as he stepped out of the car, I recognized him. He was one of the peace officers I had cited that morning and the day before for shooting an over-limit of dove and shooting over a baited area! Man, talk about a small world. ...

Walking over to me, he stuck out his hand and said, "This is getting to be a habit."

"Sure is," I replied. "Want a couple of poachers?"

"Sure, what did they do?" he asked. Walking out of earshot of my lads, I filled the deputy in on what had happened. He listened closely and then said, "Well, let's get them loaded up into the patrol car and off to the bucket. I will need you to follow me in and file a complaint, but that will just be a formality. Both of these guys are on probation for a breaking-and-entering conviction, and I am sure it will be a while before they get to eat deer meat again."

That work with the deputy done, I headed for the motel for some much-needed sleep and a little air conditioning. When I arrived at the motel I found that Ed had changed locations and was now working in the Hermann area to the east. Since I was leaving Monday, and he didn't figure we could hook up before I left, he suggested that I take my evidence with me on the plane in case there were any trials and said he would get together with me on filing the citations in federal court. With that, dead tired as I was from the heat, humidity, and long hours, I went to bed. I didn't wake up until nine the following morning and did not get started working until after ten due to a great leisurely Southern breakfast. Man, I am here to tell you, long hours along with the climate had sure done a number on me. It seemed that I was running on "tired" all the time; hence my late entry into the field on my third day in Missouri.

Wanting a change, I followed some of Ed's intelligence reports and went north, above Columbia. However, I ran into very few hunters even though there was some pretty good dove hunting in the area. I had not run into the big crowds I had been led to expect from the Southern hunting community, but I wrote that off to being too far north from Old Dixie. I checked not more than a dozen dove hunters in about five hours and was getting a little tired of the lack of activity, blaming it on the supposition that everyone was in church. I stopped at another little grocery store in the outback to buy some sliced ham, sweet pickles, bread, mustard, and soda for a late lunch. Finding a little side road overlooking a vast, rolling, hilly area covered with beautiful trees, I stopped and set up my picnic on the hood of the car. I had just started on my first sandwich when, miles to the south, I heard the faint sounds of heavy shooting. Deciding I was going to have a peaceful lunch, I ignored the shooting as long as I could. But the shooting continued, and my lunch became becoming less and less peaceful. Finally I jammed the last of the sandwich into my mouth, gathered my things, took one more look in the direction of the shooting and at my map for bearings, and set out, heading south.

It took me about forty-five minutes to locate the area where the shooting was going on, and I finally found it in some fenced grounds. I circled in search of a quiet entry point but soon discovered there was no way in other than driving in past a well-kept farm house. If I was to go in unobtrusively, it would have to be on foot over some distance. The shooting had not stopped or slackened, and I estimated that there were possibly thirty guns in the area. Parking my car alongside a main road, I raised the hood and put a note under the windshield wiper saying I had broken down and had gone for help. Hoping that would suffice as a cover, I sprinted across the highway, vaulted the fence (yeah, it surprised me too), and disappeared into the brush and timber.

After about thirty-five minutes of sneaking, I came to a forty-acre wheat field that had been burned off after being harvested. There was a mess of hunters scattered all around the edges on shooting stools and the like, having one hell of a dove hunt. I couldn't find any vehicles parked in the area so surmised, correctly, I might add, that they had been ferried into the hunting area to avoid the clutter of personal vehicles. Working in as close as I could, I began to see that there was no way I could watch all the hunters or catch them at a constriction point as they left the field. The shooting was hot and heavy with a lot of birds in the area, but the hunters, a mix of young and old men, didn't seem to be much in the way of really good shooters. Finally I singled out four men who were fairly close to me and set up on them. They all had good sized piles of dove either at their feet or in wire-screened boxes (like milk delivery boxes), and when I felt they each had a limit, if not more, I made my move. I figured I would appear less suspicious if I just walked right up to the lads as if I belonged, so that is what I did. I walked up to two of the lads, identified myself, and, seeing that they had over-limits, asked them to gather up their dove and walk with me to the other two fellows.

They looked at me as if I was a ghost, and then the older of the two asked, "How the hell did you get in here?"

"I just walked to the sound of the guns and figured I would check some of you chaps since I was in the neighborhood," I replied with a sweaty grin.

The old lad shook his head in disbelief as he walked with me toward his friends. When we reached the other two, I identified myself and began to notice that the sound of shooting around the field was declining. Looking around, I could see that the gunners were all departing through the trees like a bunch of quail. Soon there were only my four shooters and one federal agent! Damn, something is wrong here, Terry, I thought, but I had my hands full of four hunters who were getting more and more pissed off. They were mad that I had walked in on them and ruined their shoot and couldn't wait for the landowner to find out and raise some hell with me. Well, after greetings and salutations all around, I commenced to check their hunting licenses and shotgun plugs and to count the dove they had killed. Every lad had an over-limit! Not big ones, mind you, because they couldn't hit a bull in the tail end with a two-by-four, but they were over.

I was in the process of counting the last fellow's birds, which I had dumped out on the ground, when I noticed that the birds' crops were filled to the gills with seeds. No big thing, but a little out of the ordinary. I noticed that dove were continuing to land everywhere and were feeding like little gray pigs in the black duff of the burned wheat field. Again, it was no big thing because dove loved any kind of seed field that had been burned, making it easier to feed with their little stubby legs and soft bills. Then, as I counted the birds by moving them from the ground back into the wire box, I noticed not only that the shooter was six birds over the limit but that under the broken bodies of the dove on the ground were a few safflower grains! Safflower is a member of the thistle family and a very expensive crop in many parts of the country. But one didn't have safflower and wheat growing in the same field!

Standing up and walking across the field, I began to see safflower seed scattered throughout the area. Turning to my four lads, I noticed that they had grown very silent as they watched me. "Gentlemen,"

I said, "there appears to be one hell of a lot of safflower scattered around in this here wheat field. That would make it a baited area, a violation of federal law, and also make all you fellows in violation of that set of laws."

No one moved, but I could tell from their body language that they had all known it was a baited area and that to shoot over such an area was a violation of the law. I asked for and received their driver's licenses, which I added to my handful of hunting licenses. This is why everyone drifted off into the timber when they saw me starting to check these fellows, I thought. Having seen this bunch shoot over the baited area, I began to write up the information on a field informa- tion report and ended up charging each lad for taking an over-limit and for shooting migratory game birds over a baited area. I had just finished with the last chap when here came a cloud of dust with a pickup on the front end of it. The landowner, I thought—and he was *mad!* The fellow, who I later found was named Arthur Ringo, boiled out of the still-sliding pickup and in a loud voice, mostly for show, I thought, yelled, "Who the hell are you? What the hell are you doing on my land without permission? I need some answers, mister, and I do mean now!"

"Well, if you will let me get a word in edgewise," I said, only to be interrupted.

"Don't smart off to me, boy, or I will have you arrested and hauled off my lands."

"Let me try again," I said, hoping the heat and humidity would not get a hold of my better sense and make me overload my hum- mingbird hind end with my alligator mouth. "I am a federal agent with the Fish and Wildlife Service and, hearing all this shooting, decided to investigate. In the process I found these four fellows with an over-limit of dove and shooting over a baited area."

"That is horse crap, mister! This is only a burned-off wheat field and nothing more."

"If you would, sir," I said, "follow me for a moment."

With that, the two of us walked out into the field, and I showed Ringo all the glistening white safflower grains, which showed clearly against the black, burned duff of the wheat field. When we got out in the middle of the field and out of earshot of the four hunters, Ringo gently grabbed me by the arm and said, "I put all this seed out, Officer. These folks are my friends, bankers, associates, and the like, and I just wanted to show them a good time. If there are any citations to be paid, I will pay them. Please don't embarrass them any more than necessary. Give me the tickets."

"Mr. Ringo," I said, "that admission means you are also going to receive a citation for aiding and abetting because you assisted them in shooting over a baited area by putting the bait out in the first place."

"I don't care. I just don't want my guests to be embarrassed any more than they are."

"What about all your other guests who fled when I made the scene?" I asked. "They are just as guilty."

"I can't do that. You will just have to find out yourself who they were, and by now most of them are long gone, fearing what these fellows are getting. Most of those folks are important people, and just please understand, I can't tell you who they are. In fact, if I wanted to, I don't know who all of them are because I sent out so many invitations and didn't check who came in today. That is usually done when we all have lunch after the shoot."

"All right, Mr. Ringo, I will go along with that. But remember, sir, hunting on this field or taking any birds going to or from this field will be a violation of federal law. Those hunting restrictions will remain in effect until ten days after all the lure and attractant is gone."

"OK, that is a fair exchange for not going after the rest of my people. The hunting is done, and I won't be so foolish as to ever do this again. I don't need to anyway with the wheat feed that is still here after harvest."

"Did anyone else help you put the safflower out, Mr. Ringo?" I asked.

"Well, yes, my two sons." His voice trailed off as he realized what he had just uttered.

"I will need to see those two lads because they are guilty of aiding and abetting as well."

He just looked at me for a second and then walked back to his pickup. Getting on the radio, he called his farm office and had his

two sons come out to meet with me. Eleven citations later for violation of the Migratory Bird Treaty Act and 18 USC 2 (aiding and abetting), I walked off the field and back to my car. Loading those birds
into the last remaining space in my ice chests, I headed for the motel,
tired but happy.

Everyone apprehended for shooting over a baited area received
fines of $150 each. For chaps over the limit, depending on the size of
the over-limit, the fines ranged from $350 to $500 per offense. The
landowners putting out the bait were fined $500 each. Those hunt-
ing without hunting licenses or taking dove with the use and aid of a
motor vehicle were fined $25 per offense. That might not sound like
much, but in those days of the early 1980s the larger fines were a fair
amount out of anyone's pocket. Also bear in mind that in those days,
fines for petty offenses such as these were limited to a maximum of
$500 and/or six months in jail. No one went to jail except my two
deer poachers, and they did a year's time each for their probation violations. The charges for the deer were dropped in that matter because
the men were sent back to the bucket to serve out their time. At least
they got some decent clothing and three squares a day!

My three days in Missouri didn't end there. For some reason I was
routed back to Minneapolis through O'Hare Airport in Chicago.
I hated that airport because of its hustle and bustle and masses of
humanity, not to mention always (at least it seemed that way) delayed
flights. Arriving late (what else is new) and finding my plane already
in the air en route to Minneapolis, I had to book another flight.
While waiting in the crowded terminal, I heard a woman one row of
seats ahead of me scream and then say, "Help me; someone please
help me!" A man about her age was trying to rip a baby out of her
arms, and she was fighting back.

Everyone just sat in stunned silence, including me for a second.
Then, leaping to my feet, I jumped over the row of seats and grabbed
the man by the shoulder as he almost ripped the baby from the lady's
arms. "Federal agent," I yelled. "Hold it right there!"

Turning without warning, the man swung and hit me square in the
mouth. Suffice it to say, he didn't hit the floor until he had cleared
one row of chairs! After hitting the floor, before I could get to him

once more, he was swarmed by Chicago's finest and airport security. I later found out that he had lost custody of the child in a divorce action because of child abuse and was under a restraining order to never see his kid or wife again. Somehow he had sneaked into the airport and had almost succeeded in getting hold of his child. I was asked if I wanted to press charges, but I declined in light of what was awaiting him once he returned to the judge who had issued the original restraining order. He was immediately hauled off to the bucket.

Nursing a sore mouth, I was glad to be out of the heat and humidity of Missouri, not to mention O'Hare Airport, once I was able to board my plane. Then a grin through those sore lips began to spread across my mouth. I had issued over fifty citations in just a three-day period to folks who really needed catching and had given the little dove some extra breathing room. In fact, catching that many chaps in such a short period of time was just like being back in the Sacramento Valley in my earlier days. True, I had checked maybe 150 dove hunters in that three-day period, but I had been blessed by being able to get into several bunches of them who really needed some attention. Even better had been looking into the eyes of that chap who had just shot the deer and had no realization I was even in the country. When I hit the running board and door on his side of the pickup and looked in on him from just inches away, I was amazed at how much white there was around his eyes. … That really must have given him a start. I know it startled his partner, who was so surprised that he wet his pants. I imagine it was a good week before either of them had a decent bowel movement as a result of being ambushed by the thing from the dark. …

Sinking back into my seat and enjoying the air conditioning, I continued to grin as the plane droned along on its way toward home and my family. Just another day at the "office," I thought.

10

Saint Lawrence Island

THE WALRUS, a larger-than-life three-thousand-plus-pound marine mammal, has been a resident of arctic waters and ice fields for thousands of years. Existing in historical harmony with the walrus during those times were the Native Americans and Native Siberians. These people's very existence was dependent upon the wise use of what Nature had to offer in their hostile environment. When taken, the walrus provided everything from food to raw materials for clothing; heavy skins for boat covers; and ivory, which was used for everything from utensils and religious articles to carvings used in trade. In short, the walrus was to the Natives in the northern reaches of the North American and the far eastern European continents what the bison was to the Plains Indians. This natural balance existed for thousands of years until the arrival of modern-day Europeans, with their technology and their insatiable desire for marine mammals' furs and ivory. As European culture and technology invaded and corrupted the Natives' historical way of life, the Native people began to kill just as wastefully as white people. The walrus along with other pelagic mammals, most notably the whales, fur seals, and sea otter, began to suffer. The uncontrolled harvesting of the walrus for its ivory tusks in particular went on for several hundred years until the passage and enforcement of state and federal conservation laws in North America limited the killing basically to subsistence, display, and scientific purposes.

It has long been understood by the U.S. government that Native Americans occupy a unique place in this country's fabric of history and politics. Their cultural need for walrus and other pelagic mammals in order to survive has also been understood, though perhaps not thoroughly. Early territorial and state laws attempted to deal with the cultural subsistence issue, but it wasn't until the passage of the Marine Mammal Protection Act of 1972 that the issue of marine mammal harvest was formally addressed in some detail. Under that protection the Native Americans were provided allowances for subsistence hunting of many marine mammals, including the walrus. Unlimited commercialization of marine mammals and their products was controlled, but the Natives had more or less free rein in killing most marine mammal species for subsistence, cultural, and religious purposes.

Then along came another of the wonderful "trade items" that have so deeply affected humankind's current history: drugs. Illicit drugs swept through the North American Native communities just as they did through the rest of contemporary society. Lacking many of the usual ways of making money to purchase goods and services, the Natives resorted to the resources available to them. Of particular value were raw walrus ivory tusks and teeth as well as finished carvings. The walrus's two prominent tusks and lesser-known jaw teeth were very high-quality ivory and made excellent carving materials. Those carvings commanded very high prices in any market, especially in the United States and Asia. It wasn't long before some Native Americans were in the same sewer occupied by many other forms of unscrupulous humankind exploiting the natural resources of the land through such well-known techniques as mass slaughter and commercialization.

In the late 1980s and early 1990s, bloated, headless walrus by the score began washing up on the beaches of eastern Russia and northwestern Alaska. It was evident that another grim chapter of commercial-market hunting was going on. The walrus discovered on the beaches or floating in the waters had had not only their heads removed but also their ossified penises (called *oosic*), which were used in carvings and curios. They also had many deep cuts in their bodies, an old market hunter's trick to allow the carcasses to lose their gases and sink out of sight and minds. Plain and simply, these headless examples were nothing more than the ugly results of mass killing by another generation of humankind hell-bent on self-destruction. It was plain to the practiced eye that the killings had been done by Native hunters and that almost all the walrus taken in such a manner were killed for the illegal ivory and *oosic* trade. Through this senseless killing and sinking of the bodies, many thousands of pounds of meat normally consumed by the Natives was allowed to rot.

Finally these killings got so bad that even the Russian communities, known for their own out-and-out destruction of their lands and natural resources, began to complain to U.S. authorities. Those increasing international complaints, along with the walrus market hunting intelligence gathered by special agents in Alaska, finally caused the Service leaders to take note. The Special Operations Branch of the Service in Washington, D.C., detailed several officers to initiate a covert investigation into the walrus killing and illegal sale of walrus parts and products. The officers selected were new to the business of the illegal commercialization of walrus but were experienced hunters of men, and it didn't take them long to understand the problem and formulate a plan of attack. In just a short period, two of the covert officers, George Morrison and Bob Standish, were able to break into some of the rings of illegal walrus killers by establishing relationships of trust and confidence with some Native Alaskans. This trust was so great that the officers were allowed in on many of the market hunters' field operations and subsequent business deals. They were even being allowed to videotape some of the actual slaughtering activities on the ice floes. These videotapes showed the killers butchering the animals for their prized ivory teeth and *oosics* and then sinking the carcasses alongside the icebergs to hide the evidence of their wasteful and thoughtless actions. The scene was repeated many times and was not lost on the courts during later legal proceedings. Shortly after these two officers had gathered enough information on the various illegal rings that the field investigation began to wind down, and the next phase of the investigation—rounding up and arresting the culprits—was in order.

In late February 1992 special agents from all over the nation began to quietly assemble in Anchorage to begin the second phase of the covert operation. The guidelines for security specified that the agents were to arrive not as a large group, which might arouse suspicion, but in harder-to-spot ones and twos. So I arrived alone in the Anchorage airport but soon happened to notice a fellow agent, Tom "Butch"

Riley, struggling along with three large duffel bags full of obviously heavy equipment. Butch was a well-known character in the Service. He was not a huge lad, maybe a tad over six feet, but hell for stout, with a body that was almost bull-like. This magnificent carcass was the result of years of weight training and taking excellent care of himself. The resulting product included biceps larger than most men's thighs and everything else in like proportion! Butch had come to the Service via the Baltimore Colts football team. It seemed he had been a linebacker but had tired of awaiting his turn to play first string, so he had come to us to start a new life. As I said, he was a pretty stout lad and absolutely fearless, but for once he had his hands full with the three duffel bags he was struggling with. Now, Butch was the kind of guy who, when he went into a firefight, any kind of firefight, would come out in first place. To do that, in addition to his own common sense and prowess, he sported a high-tech arsenal and detailed knowledge of its use. I should have realized that there was a good reason he was grunting under the load, but without thinking, I gave him a hand. As I walked by I reached out without fanfare to avoid any undue public notice and latched on to one of his duffel bags. Once he recognized who it was, he let it drop into my hand. *Goddamn!* The weight of the bag damn near carried me through the floor to the lower level of the building! Now, in those days I was not the wimp that I am today. I was pretty damn strong in my own right, but whatever was in Butch's duffel bag had to be nothing short of at least two main battle tanks!

Butch gave me a sheepish grin as the two of us staggered out to a waiting taxi, carrying his implements for this latest war. We loaded the gear into the trunk, which raised the taxi's front wheels off the ground (well, almost). Then the two of us *filled* the back seat, putting the taxi down on the axles. Looking over at Butch, I said, "Damn you, hauling that kind of weight around like it was nothing and then letting someone give you a hand without any warning as to what he was letting himself into. That would have killed a lesser man."

The man, who considered any fight longer than fifteen seconds a long fight, just grinned his boyish grin, hiding a real man behind it, and said he'd buy me a beer in return for my somewhat strained assistance. I agreed, and we went on our way to the hotel. When we arrived we unloaded our gear and headed for the meeting room where all the actors for Operation Whiteout, as this law enforcement operation was called, were to assemble. Once there our agents teamed up with state and federal officers from many other agencies and started going through a several-day survival school put on by the National Guard. Because there would be arrest and search teams all over the state of Alaska when the takedown went down, survival training was included in the extensive briefings so that if any of the teams crashed or were isolated, forced down, or marooned, they would be better able to survive.

During the training period team assignments were made, and many of us spent our limited spare time going over the case reports, getting acquainted with our team members, and meeting with the covert operatives to become even more familiar with our individual defendants and our assignments, whether they were arrest, search, or interview. I was on a team of sixteen that was going to the town of Gambell on Saint Lawrence Island to arrest eight poachers and conduct numerous interviews. Saint Lawrence Island is situated in the Bering Sea due west of Norton Sound, just a few miles from Russian air space and the International Date Line. In other words, we would be so far in the outback, the chickens would be wearing snowshoes and have square faces! My personal assignment was to arrest a giant of a man known for his mean temper and proven ability to hurt people. He was a drug dealer and ivory merchant who lived in Gambell and would trade drugs, primarily marijuana, for walrus ivory. In Anchorage in 1992, a kilo of high-grade marijuana sold for about $3,800. When that same kilo got out to Saint Lawrence Island, it was worth approximately $38,000! In other words, a handful of marijuana cigarettes was all that was needed to purchase an entire walrus head with all its ivory. When that head was taken to Anchorage, a profit of $1,500 for that skull and ivory could be realized. Now it is easy to see, with the Natives almost crazy with drug hunger, why the great slaughter of the walrus, a ready cash cow, if you will, was such a problem. Thousands of dollars could be made in short order by anyone in the illicit ivory business, and in fact even the Service made money in its undercover operation with operatives posing as illegal merchants. That situation was unique, almost funny, in fact, because we tried to lose money in our covert business operations, if at all possible, to avoid all the nasty paperwork involved in documenting any profit.

The success of the second phase of the law enforcement operation, out of necessity, was dependent on the weather across the state of Alaska. The entire operation with its many officers was set to begin at seven in the morning the day the agency decided to pull the trigger. That way there would be total surprise as everyone was rounded up at the same time. So for total success, safety, and security, all of us would have to reach our targets at the same time, and in Alaska in the dead of winter, that achievement was somewhat problematic, depending on the weather. The sixteen of us going to Saint Lawrence Island were to be transported by the Alaska Air National Guard in a C-130 Hercules aircraft. Though a covert wildlife operation may not seem to fit into the Air National Guard's mission statement, there are now legal allowances between various branches of the military and other federal agencies allowing the military to assist when drugs are involved. Because drugs played such a major role in this operation, the military could offer assistance, and did.

The plan called for the plane to drop off our snowmobiles and officers; leave; and then, weather permitting, return that evening to haul all of us, including the prisoners and any evidence, back to Anchorage. It was quite a tall order when you think about it. We would be sixteen against the village of Gambell when the crap hit the fan. If the weather closed in on us, we had a problem. We were carrying only three days' worth of survival supplies, including water and sleeping bags. In the event of being marooned owing to bad weather, we were to sleep on the floor in a quonset hut operated by a National Guard Native Scout contingent from Gambell. We could not expect the townspeople to provide food or drink for us in the event of our being stranded there, especially if they were pissed at our flying in unannounced to arrest their kin.

By way of personal preparation, I was carrying a heavy-duty sleeping bag good to a zillion below zero. My coat and pants were insulated and good to minus 100, as were my boots. I carried a heavy-duty pair of wool half gloves (which left the ends of my fingers exposed so I could work a handgun if necessary) and heavy-duty insulated snowmobile mittens that could be pulled over my coat sleeves to my elbows. I carried a Sig Sauer .45 ACP pistol in a shoulder holster with four additional magazines, and a grin for good luck. My clothing would be layered, with wool shirt and pants and a pair of insulated coveralls. Over that would go my shoulder holster, and over all that went all the other gear. When I was completely dressed, I was bigger than a polar bear and discovered I could move only as fast as a five-toed sloth! I hoped the anticipated minus 62 temperature on the day of our outing would lighten up a bit, say to minus 30, so I could wear only my insulated coveralls and be a whole lot more mobile. Then if my lad wanted to get nasty and "dance," I would still be able to do the tango and put a nice set of bracelets around his wrists when the number was over!

Come the day of the raid, we had bad weather over parts of Alaska in which some of our lads were to operate, which meant postponing the operation. It was imperative that we strike all at once so none of the bad guys would be the wiser and end up destroying their evidence or tipping off their confederates. However, when you get that many officers in one town, the longer you have to hold off on pulling the trigger, the better the chance of the word getting out. This was especially true in our hotel, which was lodging over one hundred officers from all over the United States. It was just a matter of time before someone slipped and said something he shouldn't, and then the race would be on. In the case of our Saint Lawrence Island team, the prospect of losing the element of surprise was even worse. It is a very small and tightly knit Native community, and if the people there suspected anything, we would be totally unsuccessful in our arrest endeavors. Where we were going, like many of the raid teams, was plain and simply the bush. That meant no roads, no highway signs, no street signs, people who are generally suspicious of your presence, and people who by their nature are very closed mouthed even if they know the answer to your question. On Saint Lawrence Island we would be using snowmobiles to root out our suspects. That should tell the reader something of the ordeal facing us in locating our targets and then getting the lads and ourselves back to the temporary lockup on the same mechanical horse we rode in on!

In addition, when an enforcement officer is ready to go, it takes a certain edge off his readiness to have to put everything on hold as we were doing now. The tension just mounted as we all ran our parts of the operation again and again through our minds. Most of us would rather have been in the thick of a real "hoorah" than sitting on our hands waiting for the weather to clear. Keep in mind that most of us prima donnas had come from the lower forty-eight states and were not used to letting the weather get to us because on the mainland we had a town just over every horizon. But you learn to adapt to each other's problems in law enforcement operations, or you fall by the wayside.

Finally, the military weather people said the next day was a marginal go, and the Service leaders made the decision to go even if we had to push the envelope of weather danger just a bit for some of the teams (including mine). Everyone, relieved and impatient for activity, roared into action closing last-minute loopholes and making last-minute preparations for being dropped into the remoteness of the Alaskan bush. The next morning at three A.M. I was standing in line on the Air National Guard tarmac with my loads of gear, awaiting my turn to board a C-130, a four-engine turboprop transport known for its ruggedness under all conditions. It was minus 30 degrees, and for top cover I wore only a wool shirt to avoid breaking out in a sweat under all my layered cold-weather gear. Boarding the transport, I saw that our snowmobiles were already neatly loaded and secured in the cavernous bay of the plane. For seats all we had were nylon slings attached to the aircraft walls, with the sides of the aircraft as back support. They were comfortable enough however, and after sitting down I stowed the rest of my gear around my feet. After we strapped ourselves into the nylon slings, the crew chief went around securing any remaining gear. Once that was done, he passed out earplugs and outside hearing protection. Those of you who have never ridden in the back of a C-130 Hercules aircraft are in for a noisy treat if you ever do. The four engines are so noisy that you will be unable to carry on a conservation without shouting to be heard. Settling back into my seat, I looked around the space that would be my home for the next three and a half hours. It was a typical military transport, with just the bare necessities for survival. It was so cold that there was ice on the inside of the plane, and more accumulating all the time from the condensation of our sixteen breaths. When the loading was finished, the door was shut and the engines were started and allowed to warm up. We put on our hearing protection as the sounds of the whirling propellers on the engines just a few feet from the side of the plane began to roar and vibrate around inside our cylindrical tube called a fuselage. Soon we taxied out onto the runway in preparation for leaving, and the engines began to roar even more loudly as we hammered down the airstrip to Saint Lawrence Island and the adventures it would bring. The powerful aircraft lifted easily into the frigid, wintry dark morning, turned west, and began climbing to altitude. We were off into the unknown! I couldn't help but notice the increase in my heartbeat and the grins on all our faces. ... To kill walrus for subsistence was OK. To do otherwise to Mother Nature would sometimes get you a knot on the head, and the appropriate knots were now en route.

Once the aircraft hit its cruising altitude, the pilot reduced our speed and we began a noisy drone to our destination, now some three hours away. Not being able to hear a damn thing, most of us opened our briefcases, removed our case reports, and reread them for the hundredth time in the dim interior light of our airborne home. The rest of the flight was uneventful as the capable hands of the Air National Guard crew did what they do best. Around six-thirty A.M., as the plane began its descent into Gambell, we put away our loose gear and rechecked our weapons and other vital equipment. Then we added our extra layers of clothing, sat back, and quietly awaited our surprise emergence from the airplane and the race to reach the targets of our investigation before they realized the purpose of this early-morning flight to their polar-ice-locked island. Looking over my shoulder out the tiny porthole window of the plane, I could barely see the island below. All I could see was snow, and lots of it! In and around the snow fields below, I could see the faint winking lights of snowmobiles being operated by the inhabitants as they raced to and fro in the frozen vastness. The *clump-clump* sound of the wheels of the plane as they were dropped and locked into place brought me back to the moment at hand and the landing just minutes away. The tone and speed of the engines changed as the pilot began to make his final descent toward a runway of some sort below, unseen by those of us in the interior of the plane. Lower and lower we dropped as the pilot made final adjustments to land and disgorge his surprise crew of law enforcement officers on the island.

All of a sudden the pilot jammed the throttles forward as he "fire-walled" the aircraft's engines to gain speed and altitude! *Clump-clump* came the familiar sound as the wheels were retracted to lessen the drag and we began to climb quickly away from the island. What the hell, I thought as I, like my compatriots, was jammed back into the bottom of my seat by the pull of gravity! The look on the face of the crew chief, who had been in the bay of the aircraft undoing the tiedowns on the eight snowmobiles, was concerned. He quickly got on his radio, but because of the increased howling of the engines I couldn't hear what he was saying. The plane strained and groaned as it made an obvious emergency climb back into the heavens, leaving the snow fields of Gambell and the winking lights far below. Soon we were again high above the clouds as we all just looked at each other with questioning eyes. Finally the aircraft commander came on the radio system loudspeaker to tell of us he had hit a whiteout just before he was about to land and had had to climb out of it to avoid crash-landing. However, he continued, he had seen a break in the clouds to the northwest and was heading for that spot so he could drop down through it and try approaching from another direction.

Meanwhile, the plane continued to hammer along at about 300 to 350 knots, which I found strange. I had flown a bit as a kid and a lot as a young agent with the Service. I was also a student of military history, weapons, and aircraft. I could plainly feel that our aircraft, ever since pulling away from Saint Lawrence Island, had not had the throttles reduced one whit! Something wasn't right. You just don't hammer these transports at full throttle, even the very tough C-130, unless you have a serious situation on hand! But the pilot did not back off one inch on those throttles, and the plane fairly shook in objection to the pounding its engines were taking. Looking toward the internal radio speakers, I hoped for some information from the cockpit regarding what the hell was going on. Almost as if ordered, we got it. ... *"Hang on,"* came captain's voice as the lumbering four-engine aircraft did an abrupt steep left-wing-over through the clouds and dropped like a rock toward the Bering Sea at a speed in excess of 300 knots! Damn, this guy must be a frustrated fighter pilot, I thought as I looked at my fellow officers on the other side of the aircraft hanging out in space in their seats while my side's occupants were jammed against the wall. Down, down, down we went, and the pilot did not reduce speed once! Finally the pilot winged the plane over into level flight as our asses mashed themselves down hard into the seat bottoms again. Then the plane climbed radically and dove down, lunging from side to side in fast, erratic flight! What the hell? I thought again as I looked out my window. *Whooosh* went a huge iceberg not thirty yards from our left wing as we continued this engine-straining flight just feet over the polar ice as the aircraft dodged around and up and over the various icebergs on its way back toward Gambell! Damn, I thought, this is not a fighter plane! This is a four-engine transport zipping over the ice and around the icebergs as if it has a kid at the helm! *Whooosh* went an-other iceberg just off the left wing, and this time we weren't more than ten yards from its icy blue, towering form!

At that moment the pilot backed off the engines just a little, and I heard the hard *clump-clump* as our wheels came down once again in preparation for a landing. *Whump,* just that fast, we hit the runway with a perfect three-point landing and then began to skid slightly! We slid first one way, then another as the pilot professionally used the thrust of his engines and brakes to keep the plane on the runway—what there was of it. As he jockeyed the plane down the runway at a damn good clip, the crew chief finished untying the eight snow-mobiles and started their engines so they would be warm and ready to go the minute we stopped moving and the pilot dropped the exit ramp in the tail of the airplane. We did a sliding left turn on the icy runway and stopped just as the ramp finished dropping. Down the ramp went the crew chief with the first of the snowmobiles as we offi-cers scrambled to grab our gear, load it onto our respective snow-mobiles, and head for the National Guard quonset hut. The crew chief warned each of us before we left the plane not to look into the

engine prop wash; it had a wind-chill factor over 100 below zero in
the blasting air from the still hot running engines and would have
frozen our faces in a second. If that happened, the victim would have
to be airlifted immediately back to an Anchorage hospital for treatment of a severe case of frostbite on all exposed flesh.

Even with the C-130's engines running full tilt in preparation for
a quick takeoff, the Natives were speeding toward the runway on their
snowmobiles to see what was up. As they pulled up to see the enforcement teams tumbling out of the plane and firing up our snowmobiles, they started asking who we were and what we were doing on
the island. The officers who were asked first just pointed back to the
officers starting to load up at the back of the plane as if they were in
charge, and so on, until there wasn't anyone left to contact. By the
time they had figured that ruse out, we were gone, and they couldn't
contact the pilot because he was rapidly disappearing down the runway. We raced down the snowmobile trail to the quonset hut,
dropped off our gear, and quickly headed out to try to find the homes
of our assigned targets. As it turned out, we had hit Gambell just
right. A whale had been sighted earlier, and half the town was out
among the pack ice and open leads in their walrus-skin boats trying
to harpoon it. That made for fewer people to get in our way and also
made it easy if any of our targets happened to be out in a boat. Just
as fast as they came back to shore, we could shake down each boat
until we got our man if that is where he happened to be.

Dropping off my gear, I hooked up with my partner, a National
Park Service lad weighing in at about two hundred (remember the
mean temper of the chap we needed to arrest), and out we went to
see if we could find a house matching the picture we had been given
by one of the undercover officers. There was nothing but snowmobile
trails, more snow, and little houses half buried by the snow sprinkled
all around. That was it! No street signs here. ... I hadn't driven a
snowmobile since I had been a game warden in California in 1967,
but we half zipped and half controlled-crashed our way to where I
thought my lad lived, according to our undercover agent's description
of the area. Finally arriving between several twenty-foot-high drifts of
snow, I was confronted by two houses that looked identical and both

matched the picture of the *one* home where I was to execute my arrest warrant. Damn, which one? I thought, knowing if we hit the wrong one it might spook our culprit if he was home and not on the whale hunt. Turning to my Park Service lad and handing him the picture, I said, "Which one?"

"Don't know," came his reply. "They look identical to me."

Standing out like sore thumbs in the middle of the trails around the homes were the two of us, towering at over six foot four each in a town of people all a foot shorter, I made a choice. Turning off the snowmobile, I headed for the first house while my partner took a position where he could watch the second one. If we happened to see our guy walking along outdoors, it would be a cinch. He was six foot seven or eight, so we knew we would recognize him in a heartbeat! Walking into the porch of the first house, I was greeted with the sour smell of rancid seal oil and black lumps of seal and polar bear meat hanging from the rafters and heaped up in a dirty pile on the floor. Walking carefully so I would not slip on the many years' accumulation of grease on the floor, I knocked on the door. A very short older woman, dressed like the typical *National Geographic* Eskimo woman in seal fur, opened the door and said, "Can I help you?"

"Yes," I said. "I am looking for Richard Stone; do you know where he is?"

"No," she replied politely.

"Does he live in this home?" I asked.

"No," came the polite reply as the strange smell of cooking mystery foods flooded out from her tiny kitchen.

Hoping not to be asked in for any of the food, I continued, "Do you know where Richard lives?"

"No," she said just as politely as before. "Why do you want him?"

"I owe him fifteen hundred dollars and would like to see that he gets it," I replied. Using money as an enticement will often inspire people to help you find someone.

"Oh, then why don't you call him?" she said.

"How do I call him, young lady?" I asked, not believing it was really possible out here in the middle of nowhere and all.

"You can use my phone if you would like," she responded.

Damn, I couldn't believe it! Here we were out in the middle of nowhere, and they had a phone service. Sure as God made little green apples, there hung a phone on her wall. "Do you know his phone number?" I asked, hoping against hope.

"Sure," she said. "It is right here," and she handed me her phone book.

Man, I couldn't believe my luck. Picking up the phone, I dialed the number, and after one ring a man's husky voice answered, "Hello."

"Is this Richard?" I said.

"Yeah, what do you want?" he replied curtly.

"Richard, this is Terry and I have fifteen hundred in cash and another twenty-five hundred in a certified check that says you and I need to do some business together."

"Terry who?" came the reply, now tinged with interest.

I remembered a name from the case report of a man who was Richard's friend on the mainland and said, "Dowd told me to look you up so we could do some business."

"Dowd said that?"

"Yep," I replied, "but I would rather talk to you personally instead of over the phone from this lady's house."

"I agree; where are you?" he asked.

Looking over to the lady who was letting me use her phone, I asked her name, and she gave it to me. I repeated it to Richard, and he said he would meet me in front of her house in a minute or so. He also said the woman was his mom! Brother, I thought. Here she acts as if she hardly knows Richard and doesn't even know where he lives on the island. As it turned out, Richard lived in the house just behind hers, the second of the two we couldn't tell apart. Thanking the lady for the use of the phone, I beat it outside, careful not to fall on the slick porch floor, and informed my partner that our lad was on his way out to meet me. My partner slipped off to one side and out of sight by the lady's house as I waited in the middle of the empty trail by our snowmobile.

Soon from the other house came this mountain of a man. He walked right up to me and said, "Are you Terry?"

"Yep, that I am; are you Richard?" I knew who he was from his police mug shot in my case report but wanted to confirm the identification.

"That's me," he replied.

"Richard," I said as my partner started to quietly move in behind him, "I am a federal agent for the Fish and Wildlife Service." I showed him my badge and credentials. He never moved or said a word. I continued, "I have an arrest warrant for you for the illegal commercialization of marine mammal parts in violation of the Marine Mammal Protection Act." At the words *arrest,* his eyes narrowed, and I could tell he was sizing me up for lunch. "I have a copy of the arrest warrant if you would like to see it." He didn't move or speak, just glowered at me like a now raging bull. Taking a stance calculated to turn him with a right cross if he decided to get froggy on me and jump, I said, "Richard, even if you are found innocent of the charges currently lodged against you, grab me and it is an automatic five years in the federal penitentiary."

He continued to glare at me. He was a big man, taller and heavier than I. But I had several aces up my sleeve. First, I was wearing a sap glove on the hand of my strong right arm. A sap glove is a soft leather glove with three-quarters of a pound of lead sewn into the leather padding across the knuckles, designed to amplify the force when the wearer hits someone. In occasional fights in which I was outnumbered five or six to one, the sap glove with my three hundred pounds behind it was able to knock out the first three people who got within range of my right hand every time. Even a man the size of the one now confronting me, when struck in the face with a strong right cross supported by a sap glove, had only one way to go, and that was down. The other ace was my partner. He was a stout lad and a good one who did not appear to be afraid of anyone or anything and who had now taken a position right behind Richard.

"Richard," I said, "in order to help you make up your mind, you need to look behind you."

Richard, without taking his eyes off me for a moment, said, "There is someone behind me, isn't there?"

"Yes," I replied, "and he isn't much smaller than the fellow you are now looking at. Now, you can go the easy way or the hard way. That means in the saddle or across it—it is your choice. But I mean to leave this island with you in my custody or across the saddle, if you get my drift."

He continued to look hard at me, but I detected a softening look. "All right," he finally said, "I will go peacefully."

I said, "That brings up the second question. You can go handcuffed in front if you behave or behind your back if you choose to be nasty about it; your choice."

"I will behave," he said as he held out his arms for me to handcuff. In order to be ready for bear if necessary, I had my partner handcuff him while I continued my stance and stare in case Richard changed his mind. Richard was such a large man that the handcuffs only went *one* click of the locking ratchet on his wrists! I have seen that happen only two other times in my thirty-two-year career. That done, Richard was loaded onto the waiting snowmobile and taken to the quonset hut for interrogation and holding until our plane returned, weather permitting.

After getting Richard safely settled in the hut, my partner and I informed him of his rights and began to question him. I reviewed what the government already knew about his illegal activities and, armed with that, began to seriously press him. His eyes filled up with tears, and he started to bawl. Damn, I thought. Here we have a man mountain with a killer reputation, and he turns out to be as tough as a wet noodle. Richard's next words were, "I want an attorney." We were somewhat limited in that department there in the quonset hut on Saint Lawrence Island, and besides, once those words are uttered by a defendant, the interview must stop, so it did.

Once he quit bawling, he was hungry. He asked if I would contact his mom and have her bring him some breakfast. I said that would be all right, and what menu items did he want me to request? Richard said he wanted some seal oil, reindeer stew, and *muktuk.* When the breakfast arrived I took a look at it to make sure everything was all right and then let him begin eating. Observing something black and white that I had never seen before, I asked him what it was. *"Muktuk,"* he proudly proclaimed. "Want some?"

"Sure," I said since I was always willing to try new things. Taking a small piece, I got my first taste of whale. It wasn't bad.

Leaving Richard handcuffed, eating his breakfast and in charge of an agent who was watching all the prisoners, my partner and I took off again on the snowmobile to try to find the four people we still had to interview. It was amazing. Now that the Natives had found out who we were and what our purpose was, we could get no further information regarding where anyone lived. They all wanted the drug dealers cleaned out of their community, but no one would offer the slightest assistance when it came to rooting out the bad guys. Such is the song of the North ... actually, the song of just about anywhere.

I noticed a large crowd gathering on the beach and a ton of small boats with outboards towing in a dead whale like a bunch of Lilliputians from *Gulliver's Travels*. Figuring it might be a good place to find some of those not yet interviewed, we headed that way. Walking down to the frozen beach with icebergs grounded just yards away, I noticed a man kneeling in a docked boat surrounded by several dozen eager children. Looking into the boat at object of the man's attention, I spotted a large slab of hide and blubber that had probably just been taken off the whale being hauled in to the beach. I had heard that the man who got the first harpoon into the whale got to cut the first slab of blubber and give it to his friends and family, so I asked, "Who is the great hunter who got the first harpoon into the whale?"

"I am," he said. Then, realizing my voice was unfamiliar, he looked up. He held this look at me for a long moment, then returned to cutting the slab of whale blubber, and with the first cut from his *ulu* (a very sharp curved knife), he stuck a big piece on the end of the knife and handed it to me. Instantly all the little kids who had been clamoring for a piece of the blubber looked up at me as well and, observing this offer of blubber to the white man, grew silent as the dead whale being towed to the beach. Realizing that to refuse might not be a smart move on my part, I took the piece of blubber. The man just looked at me without a word, as did all the little kids. I thanked him, popped the entire piece into my mouth, and began chewing. A big grin broke out on both our faces as all the little kids cheered. Then the man went back to cutting slices for all the children while I was left with my mouth full of raw whale blubber. My partner turned green when I looked at him and said, "No thanks!" Still chewing, I marveled at the excellent flavor of the blubber. I thought it had the flavor of almonds. As for the tar-black skin the blubber was attached to, it was like eating a piece of shoe leather! I picked black strands out of my teeth for the next four days! The blubber was fine, but they could have the hide all to themselves, I thought.

In the end we, along with most of the other teams, were not totally successful in the general informational interviews. It didn't hurt the case, which was already made because of the excellent work of Morrison and Standish. But that extra information would have been nice.

My partner and I returned to the quonset hut after making a short snowmobile tour of the frozen wasteland surrounding the town of Gambell. When I entered the quonset hut, I was met by a National Guard Scout who asked if I was a supervisor. I said I was but that I wasn't in charge of the operation. I told him the fellow in charge was the special agent in charge in Anchorage and gave him that man's name. But he ignored what I had just said and said, "I want you to meet my wife, who is the mayor of Gambell."

"Fine," I said, figuring I would have to give her some explanation of what we were doing since I was the senior supervisor in the area. Around the corner came a tiny Native woman who, without warning, walked right into my arms and gave me a great big hug! Needless to say, I was more than surprised. ...

Backing away, she said, "I am so thankful you officers are here. This place is full of drug dealers, and what they are doing is hurting our culture as well as our little children. Your coming into our town and arresting these bad people has helped all of us who have little children because now we can show them what will happen if they break the law. Thank you for coming when you did and for doing what you did."

Surprised at this show of appreciation, I thanked her for her kind words and told her that what we had done today was only part of the story. I told her we still needed people like her to teach the children that their culture was in danger if everything was killed and sold for drugs and that those doing the bad things needed to be reported to the authorities. She agreed and with a big smile and wave of the hand left to talk to the rest of the village. I noticed a big grin on the face of my partner and said, "What?"

"Man," he said, "you should have seen how she disappeared into your arms, all five foot of her." We laughed and began to prepare our gear and prisoner for the trip home. The plane returned for all of us later that night, and we loaded our gear and seven of the eight prisoners we had come for. One team had missed their man, but it was because he was in jail in Palmer on the mainland, so he wasn't going anywhere anytime soon. Our ride home was uneventful, and we arrived in Anchorage about midnight. Our prisoner was booked, and my partner and I finally got some sleep after twenty-three straight hours in the saddle. At eight the next morning we took our prisoners before the federal magistrate and had them arraigned. Except for the report writing to follow, we were done with our share of the assignment.

Finishing my reports about four in the afternoon, I went down to the hotel bar for a cold beer before meeting a crew of happy agents to go out to dinner. While I was there the Air National Guard crew that had flown us to Saint Lawrence Island came into the bar. Waving them over to my table, I bought them a round of drinks for doing such a good job. As we sat there drinking and talking all at once, I brought up the rather radical wing-over maneuver the pilot had put the C-130 through the morning of our arrival at Gambell. The pilot just grinned and said, "Terry, I didn't have any choice. You see, that break in the clouds I saw just before we hit the whiteout over the landing strip was right at the edge of Russian air space. I figured I could hit it before we aroused the Russians, so I headed for it knowing I could drop through that opening and return to Gambell from a safer direction. We were doing fine until we apparently crossed over into Russian air space, and they locked in on us with their ground-based radars. Still having a distance to go, I just ignored their warnings and kept going, hoping to beat any threat they pushed our way. Then they scrambled two MiG-29 fighters from the sector they were already patrolling several miles away, and when we picked them up on our radar, that is when I dropped down through the clouds and flew along the ice, knowing they couldn't follow us there. So you were in Russia yesterday, had two MiG-29s locked onto us, and were part of the evasion as we flew above the polar ice and around the icebergs.

That was why I never backed off the throttles and flew so low over the pack ice. If I had backed off, you might have been a Russian 'visitor' tonight, or polar bear food splashed all over the ice!"

I just sat there dumbfounded! Damn, here we were, an unarmed four-engine transport in Russian air space flirting with a pair of the hottest MiGs around! I just shook my head, thinking of the time the Russians had shot down a Korean airliner some years earlier. The next thought that crossed my mind was that I was getting too damn old for this kind of horsepucky!

After hearing that tale, I never made it to dinner with my group of agents that evening but spent the entire night celebrating with our flight crew the success of the overall operation and our brush with a pair of Russian MiG-29s, who could have cared less what was happening to the walrus. I find it ironic that now that Russia has collapsed, the walrus is considered a very valuable animal to the economy in the new Russian way of thinking.

I have recently heard through my friends in Alaska that many headless walrus are again washing up on the beaches of northwestern Alaska. It seems that the lessons of history have been lost on the Alaska Natives, just like their counterparts across the Bering Sea. I wonder when Richard and his band of cutthroats will feel the sting of Mother Nature and her "assistants" once again?

About the Author

Terry Grosz earned his bachelor's degree in 1964 and his master's in wildlife management in 1966 from Humboldt State College in California. He was a California State Fish and Game Warden, based first in Eureka and then Colusa, from 1966 to 1970. He then joined the U.S. Fish & Wildlife Service, and served in California as a U.S. Game Management Agent and Special Agent until 1974. After that, he was promoted to Senior Resident Agent and placed in charge of North and South Dakota for two years, followed by three years as Senior Special Agent in Washington, D.C., with the Endangered Species Program, Division of Law Enforcement. While in Washington, he also served as a foreign liaison officer. In 1979 he became Assistant Special Agent in Charge in Minneapolis, and then was promoted to Special Agent in Charge, and transferred to Denver in 1981, where he remained until retirement in June 1998 (although his title changed to Assistant Regional Director for Law Enforcement).

He has earned many awards and honors during his career, including, from the U.S. Fish & Wildlife Service, the Meritorious Service Award in 1996, and Top Ten Awards in 1987 as one of the top ten employees (in an agency of some 9,000). The Fish & Wildlife Foundation presented him with the Guy Bradley Award in 1989, and in 1995 he received the Conservation Achievement Award for Law Enforcement from the National Wildlife Federation. His first book, *Wildlife Wars*, was published in 1999 and won the National Outdoor Book Award for nature and the environment. His next book, *For Love of Wildness*, was published a year later.